A guide to London's churches

Mervyn Blatch

Constable London

First published in Great Britain 1978
by Constable and Company Ltd
10 Orange Street London WC2H 7EG
Copyright © 1978 Mervyn Blatch
ISBN 0 09 462220 5
Filmset in Monophoto Times New Roman
and printed in Great Britain by
BAS Printers Limited, Over Wallop,
Hampshire

Author's Note

The dedication section is omitted in the cases of the better-known saints. To avoid cross-reference, in other cases it is shown separately for each church.

*Asterisks indicate features of special interest.

Contents

Acknowledgments

I am grateful to the National Monuments Record for permission to reproduce the illustrations on pages xxviii and 155, and to Miss D. M. Niblett of St Ursula's Hostel for the illustration on page 281.

Thanks are also due to Mr Francois Prins, archivist of All Souls', Langham Place for the photographs on pages 195, 196 and for the Nash cartoon (page 194) as well as for the drawing of St Peter's, Vere Street (page 255).

A special word of appreciation must go to Mrs Holsman of the Winston Churchill Memorial and Library, Fulton, Missouri for sending me the guide and photograph of St Mary the Virgin, Aldermanbury (page 185), and to Mrs Arlene Cusuman of Christ Church, Philadelphia for the photograph of the font in which William Penn was baptised (page 7).

All the other photographs are by the author.

Acknowledgement is gratefully made to the Vicar of St Martin in-the-Fields for permission to photograph the map which appears on the title page.

The drawings in the glossary came from the delightful engravings in Parker's 'A Concise Glossary of Architecture' published in 1846.

Preface

Two questions arose when I came to write this book: 'Which parts of London?', and 'Which churches?' The Greater London Council area today extends from Kingston-upon-Thames in the south to Barnet in the north, and is altogether too diffuse and varied a region to construct a coherent picture of Metropolitan places of worship. The 19th century saw an enormous growth of churches to meet the needs of an increasing and largely church-going population; many of these buildings are of little or no interest to the lover of churches.

It seemed to me that a proper compass would be the City of London, the City of Westminster and the eleven enlarged inner boroughs formed in 1965 and roughly corresponding with the boundaries of the pre-1965 London County Council area, and that I should restrict myself to pre-19th century buildings plus those later churches of special architectural, historical or social interest. I have only exceeded these geographical limits in the case of St John the Evangelist, Upper Norwood, a notable Victorian building in the Borough of Croydon; and two churches once in the City but transferred elsewhere: All Hallows, North Twickenham, and St Mary Aldermanbury, now at Fulton, Missouri, USA.

Non-Anglicans will deplore the omission of churches ranging from the Italianate Baroque splendours of Brompton Oratory to the quiet seclusion of St Mary's, Holly Place, Hampstead, the great Free Church centres such as Wesley's chapel and the City Temple; others may regret the lack of any reference to the grandeur of the Catholic Apostolic Church in Gordon Square and the architectural richness of royal or institutional places of worship like the Queen's Chapel or Wren's Royal Hospital Chapel. I can only plead that to go beyond what I have covered would have made the book unmanageable and excessively weighty to carry around. The same considerations apply in the cases of St Paul's and Southwark Cathedrals, and Westminster Abbey.

I have been indebted to many incumbents for giving up time to show me round their churches and correct my descriptions. Many work in difficult conditions and yet have achieved remarkable successes. And it is to the incumbents of London churches that I dedicate this book.

The guide-books, sometimes written by them and often by local historians, have been an unfailing source of information, some, like those of All Hallows by the Tower, St Bride's, St Clement Danes, St James's, Piccadilly, St Mary-le-Bow, St Margaret's, Westminster and the Tower of London Chapels are beautiful productions.

Of more comprehensive studies, I must single out the two
Buildings of England volumes on London by Sir Nikolaus Pevsner,
Parish Churches of London by Canon Basil Clarke, *Old London
Churches* by Elizabeth and Wayland Young, *The Old Churches of
London* by Gerald Cobb and *A London Steeplechase* by R. G. Ellen.
The debt which lovers of the English architectural heritage owe to
Pevsner is incalculable; he guides us with unrivalled architectural
scholarship and experience through the well-known buildings, leads
us to lesser-known places and draws our attention to others we
never knew existed. The comprehensive and informed accuracy of
Basil Clarke and the imaginative approach of the Youngs have
illumined my path, whilst Gerald Cobb is without equal on City
churches. R. G. Ellen has provided most helpful historical data in
his clear lucid style.

Except where I have quoted from other writers the opinions are
my own, based upon visits made to each church.

To my publishers I am appreciative of the free hand I have been
given to write as I feel would be most helpful to 'visitors' and in a
form which I hope will enable them to pick out quickly what they
may want to know. I have aimed at encouraging the church-lover to
wander off the beaten track, even if this means making special
arrangements to see interiors.

But, above all, my thanks go to my wife, for her support and
encouragement. I am deeply grateful to her.

'London' is probably derived from a Celtic word 'londo' meaning 'wild, bold', and we have every reason to believe that before the Romans came there were no permanent settlements and only a few huts where London now stands. But with their unerring eye for a good site the Romans saw the possibilities of the two hills above the high-water mark of the Thames (later to become known as Ludgate Hill and Cornhill) and they noted the natural harbours on the Fleet and Walbrook which made it easy for them to bring in supplies by river from their main port at Rutupiae (Richborough, Kent). For good measure, they saw that there was suitable building material to hand and that the soil around was well adapted to cultivation. So, within a few years of the Roman occupation of Britain, Londinium displaced Camulodunum (Colchester) as the focal point of Roman administration.

There is in consequence—as Roger Wilson points out in his guide to Roman Britain—much to see in London dating from Roman times but, although it is known that Restitutus, Bishop of London, attended the Council of Arles in AD 314, one will not find the remains of any Christian place of worship. It was no Christian church but a pagan temple that hit the headlines in September 1954 and caused a stir, when the lower courses of the Temple of Mithras were discovered near Walbrook during the digging of the foundations for a modern office block. These can still be seen, uprooted, beside the main entrance of Bucklersbury House in Queen Victoria Street.

Throughout the country Christian churches from Roman times are rare, despite the fact that Christianity was well established many years before the end of Roman rule. The little chapels at Lullingstone in Kent and Silchester in Hampshire are all that we have to tell us what the buildings looked like. The Lullingstone church formed part of a villa which at one time celebrated and continued to celebrate a pagan cult; the Silchester church measured only 42 by 33 feet over all, with an apse containing the altar at the western end of the nave, and aisles, transepts and narthex. The altar seems to have been of wood and the priest celebrated facing west with his back to the congregation.

As with other sides of life in this country, a curtain descends upon our knowledge of what happened after the departure of the legions and it may well be that for a time London, as other great cities in Britain, was abandoned altogether—some like Calleva Atrabatum (Silchester) and Verulamium never to rise again. The Anglo-Saxon

Chronicle records that Britons of Kent fled to London from the invaders, but it is not until 604 that history picks up the story. In that year St Paul's Cathedral—at the request of King Ethelbert—was founded by Mellitus, Bishop of London.

The Saxons were tillers of the soil and grouped themselves round the log hall of the lord. We do not know how soon London became a great city again but Bede, early in the 8th century, calls it the capital of the East Saxons with much trading activity. We know that, after the Danes sacked the city in the middle of the 9th century, Alfred the Great restored the walls, and London fulfilled his hopes as a bastion against attack when the Danes were on the warpath again a hundred years later. Despite being sacked for a second time in 982 it became a centre of power, wealth and independence—a position which it has never lost, and although Winchester was the *de jure* capital, London became the *de facto* capital. There was a great Saxon market in East Cheap which J. Sydney Taylor called 'this mart where Commerce had raised her throne', and the Saxon kings had a palace in the City until Edward the Confessor moved to Westminster (the palace was taken over by the Ealdormen—hence Aldermanbury).

The reflection of these developments in churches is hard to follow. We must assume that places of worship multiplied in later Saxon times even if many may have been made of wood. There is practically nothing to see in London from that epoch today: only the arch of a Saxon church at All Hallows, Barking, founded about 675, parts of crosses in the same church, a Danish gravestone found in St Paul's Churchyard (now at the Museum of London), and a fine rood at St Dunstan's, Stepney. All Hallows would appear to have been an aisleless church in which Roman bricks were used to a large extent.

It seems that William the Conqueror did not trust Londoners for he set up his palace (the Tower of London) to the east of the City, where he could both guard it from river attack and at the same time secure himself against uprisings from within the City itself by 'the vaste and fierce populace'.

There was no Domesday Survey of London so that we start the mediaeval period at a disadvantage. From the Norman period there remain the Chapel of St John in the Tower, the crypts of St Mary-le-Bow and St John's Clerkenwell, and parts of what is left of St Bartholomew-the-Great; and we can trace the transition to Gothic styles in the Temple Church, but the picture is far from clear in the early Middle Ages. Too much was swept away by subsequent re-building or destroyed by fire. William Stephen, writing in 1183 in the reign of Henry II, records that there were about 126 churches in London, of which it is unlikely that more than a dozen lay outside the walls. This at least shows that London, in developing as a city of merchants, had already become a city of churches. About 1192, the city was granted the status of having its own Mayor and Aldermen.

As the time gap narrows, the mist clears and we have 17th century engravings by W. Hollar, C. J. Visscher, and a more conjectural series of drawings by H. W. Brewer published in 1921 to show us what the City looked like in early Tudor times. It was a mass of small congested streets with revealing names like Blow Bladder Street (now Newgate Street) and Stinking Lane. A forest of steeples with more spires than today was dominated by the soaring 500-foot lead-sheathed spire of Old St Paul's. (The engravings do not include the spire because it was destroyed by fire in 1561.)

Around the edges of the City were many monastic establishments—the Augustinian Priory of St Mary Overie (now Southwark Cathedral), the Cluniac Abbey of St Saviour, Bermondsey, the Cistercian Abbey of St Mary Graces, Spitalfields, and Carthusian Charterhouse, not to mention the great Benedictine royal foundation of Westminster, together with many lesser establishments. Within the City were the Priory of Augustinian Canons of Holy Trinity Aldgate, Augustinian St Bartholomew's and the Benedictine nunnery of St Helen's. The Friars, too, built their houses in towns. They favoured long naves for public sermons and these were over 200 feet at the Franciscan house north of Newgate Street (Greyfriars) and the Dominican house at Blackfriars, compared with a maximum of 120 to 130 feet in the churches. There were also the Austin Friars, the nave and aisles of whose church were made over to Dutch and French refugees in 1550 with the aim of encouraging Protestant worship in London. These were all suppressed at the Dissolution, although the churches of Westminster Abbey, part of St Bartholomew-the-Great, the nuns' church at St Helen's, and the part of Austin Friars mentioned above were saved.

There can have been few such concentrations of ecclesiastical buildings in such a small space anywhere in the country and they had to be fitted in where space could be found. Apart from the monastic establishments and St Paul's Cathedral there were no stately places of worship such as St Mary Redcliffe in Bristol or St Peter Mancroft in Norwich, but relatively small and architecturally modest buildings, as can be seen by the few that survived the Great Fire of 1666. London in mediaeval times consisted of the City, Southwark and the Royal precinct of Westminster. The population in the one square mile of the City grew slowly and only increased from about 35,000 (Poll tax return) in 1377 to 50,000 in 1530 just before the Reformation. It is unlikely, therefore, that all these churches were required for parish purposes and even when they were, the parishes were sometimes very small; St Helen's comprised only a few houses. As T. D. Atkinson points out, many churches were very tiny affairs built in all sorts of odds and ends of places, over gateways and the like, and some were semi-private chapels.

The survivors of the Great Fire, mainly in the north and east of the City, are basically 15th and early 16th century and, therefore, late mediaeval. St Helen's, Bishopsgate, which was associated with the Benedictine nunnery of St Helen's, is the most considerable. But by and large, interesting as they are for what they tell us of mediaeval church-building in London, they are not especially notable and not greatly dissimilar from many in the south of England. Their furnishings, however, were probably a great deal more elaborate than the simpler and more decorous ones designed for Protestant worship that took their place later. No doubt there was a certain rivalry between neighbouring churches, and wealthy parishioners would make fine gifts and vie with one another in an effort to outdo their neighbour. Screens, above which was the crowning rood, the focal point of mediaeval worship, stained glass and statues would have made the interiors richer and more colourful than the inside of a post-Reformation place of worship.

All this was swept away by the zealous Reformers and with the dismantling of the monasteries London must have presented a sorry sight in the middle of the 16th century—crumbling monasteries, churches being stripped of their treasures and in some cases, like St Mary-le-Strand, actually being removed to make way for secular buildings—in this case, a nobleman's palace.

Between 1530 and the end of Queen Elizabeth's reign (1603), the population rose from 50,000 to over 200,000, but much of this increase was outside the City despite repeated attempts to stop the influx of poorly-off citizens from the country to the outskirts. Nevertheless, and although attendance at church was compulsory, no more ecclesiastical buildings were founded in London during this period. We have an admirable picture of what the City looked like in John Stow's *Survey of London*.

This lull continued with few exceptions (Queen's Chapel, St Katherine Cree, St Paul's Covent Garden, St Luke's Charlton) during James I's and Charles I's reigns. Growing dissensions between king and people leading to Civil War did not encourage church-building. And the Puritans certainly did not favour the erection of Anglican places of worship (St Matthias' Chapel, Poplar, dating from 1654 and All Hallows tower [1659] are rare examples).

But, at 2.00 a.m. on Sunday 2nd September 1666, a fire broke out in the shop of John Farynor, the king's baker, in Pudding Lane towards the east of the City. Samuel Pepys, who lived in Seething Lane further east, saw nothing to alarm him when he looked out of the window during the night and even the next morning, but this was the beginning of one of the greatest conflagrations this country has ever known. A strong wind blew from the south-east, an unusual quarter, and fanned the flames across and through the City like a great swath, destroying all in its path and continuing throughout three days. By the end of this time, approximately four-fifths of the City lay waste, including 88 churches and a badly damaged St Paul's Cathedral.

Fortunately, with the Restoration of the Monarchy in 1660, a wealth of talent had been released and a galaxy of great men appeared in the worlds of philosophy, science and the arts, including the son of a Wiltshire parson, not trained as such but becoming one of the most skilled and productive architects ever to have worked in England. Sir Christopher Wren was responsible for a new St Paul's

Holy Trinity the Less. Site

and for rebuilding 51 of the City churches, each with differing needs and on every shape of site.

Wren's churches were, with the exception of St James's, Piccadilly, outside the City, rebuildings, as even by 1700 the total population of London (including the outer areas) which had been decimated by the Plague, responsible for 100,000 deaths, was only about 600,000. But, by the beginning of the 18th century, London began to expand mainly around the Strand and towards the East. To cater for the eastward growth, Nicholas Hawksmoor built his monumental churches of Christ Church at Spitalfields, St Anne's at Limehouse and St George-in-the-East. These were erected under the Fifty Churches Act of 1711 after the Marlborough Wars 'for the building of Fifty New Churches in the Cities of London and Westminster or the suburbs thereof'. The target of fifty was never approached but although the quantity was meagre, the quality was excellent. Some of London's finest churches, which had to be of stone and have steeples, were built under this Act, such as the Hawksmoor churches mentioned above, St George's Hanover Square and St Mary Woolnoth (both Hawksmoor buildings), St Mary-le-Strand (James Gibbs) and St Paul's, Deptford (Thomas Archer).

This was followed by a further lull in church building and only twelve went up between 1750 and 1800.

By 1800, however, the population had mounted to nearly a million and, with the building of the docks, it shot up to two million by 1840, mainly in the poorest areas of the east end. The authorities were anxious that these areas should be protected from the moral dangers of their environment by an adequate supply of places of worship and, as a hundred years earlier, victory in battle was followed by a resurgence of church construction. Under the Church Building Act of 1818, one million pounds, later increased to one and a half millions, was set aside by Parliament—ostensibly as thanksgiving for victory at Waterloo—for this purpose, in which London's needs figured high. Many of the so-called 'Waterloo' churches were erected on the cheap but others like Holy Trinity Marylebone and St Peter's Walworth were buildings of quality, and the Commissioners were conscientious Churchmen anxious to do their best. In the next ten years 38 new churches were consecrated in the Diocese of London so that, if the quality was often not high, the quantity was much greater than under the 1711 Act.

Other efforts were made by the Church itself. Bishop Blomfield, and after him Bishop Tait, raised money through separate special Funds for church construction, and although the sums raised fell short of their expectations they were able to build or help to build 78 additional churches under Bishop Blomfield and another 41 under Bishop Tait.

But by this time the City was being affected by the building of railways. A process of moving out, first to the inner suburbs and then further afield, presented the Church authorities with a problem which has continued ever since—that of catering for a shifting population. Generally speaking, the City reached a peak in its number of residents during the middle of the 18th century, the inner ring (e.g. Battersea and Lambeth) in 1901 and the outer ring (e.g. Camberwell, Deptford, Fulham and Hackney) in 1921, since which dates there has been a decline, especially marked in the City (from 112,000 in 1861 to 5,000 in 1951), except in one or two favoured areas such as Hampstead and Kensington. In the City, a process of demolition began involving 20 churches between 1841 and 1908, as can be seen from the Corporation of the City of London's blue plaques placed on the sites, some like St Antholin's, Watling Street,

Plaque indicating site of demolished church

being of architectural merit. Money realised from the sale of sites was diverted to new churches elsewhere (e.g. St Michael's, Camden Town). The Luftwaffe in the 1939–45 War did much, although indiscriminately (St Alban's, Wood Street and St Mildred's, Bread Street were grievous losses) to correct the imbalance of churches, and the situation in the City has since been adjusted by rebuilding some only and turning others over to Guild activities.

Many churches that survived Victorian demolition were subjected to the attentions of Victorian architects, insensitive to work of earlier ages and determined to introduce changes suited to the ritual prescribed by the Oxford Movement. In particular, the introduction of choirs, also new organs and stained glass which Wren did not favour, seriously affected the atmosphere of his churches.

The War and bombing hastened the exodus from London, and today commuters live far away from the metropolis so that the inner suburbs have suffered from the same decline of population as occurred earlier in the central areas. They, too, suffer from reduced congregations and difficulties in making ends meet.

It is to be presumed, however, that the Church will gradually adapt its resources to these changing needs, although the process will inevitably lead to buildings of architectural merit being under threat (e.g. Hawksmoor's Christ Church at Spitalfields and St Anne's at Limehouse). Gordon Barnes in his book on Stepney churches describes how the original St Dunstan's serving the whole of this vast area was gradually broken up into fifty or so smaller parishes and how, with a drop in population from its peak of almost 300,000 at the beginning of this century to under 100,000 by 1951, these are now down to twelve. This is a process which has gone on elsewhere in London and will continue unless, perhaps, the high cost of present rail fares causes a reverse in the trend.

We must remember, however, that many churches have had to be built in the new residential areas so that the picture is far more encouraging than the above story indicates. There is, in my view, far too much pessimism about the number of churchgoers. Traditional forms of worship may have lost their appeal but many young people are deeply concerned with spiritual values and are searching for a faith to answer their needs. Where this is forthcoming, the response is surprising and the calibre of those who go when it is no longer a social convention may be much higher. And, even in London and nearby boroughs, there are places of worship such as All Souls', Langham Place, St Helen's in the City and St Paul's, Deptford, where the life of the ministry is more vigorous than ever it was.

St Mildred's, Bread Street

I am much indebted to the Introduction of Pevsner's *London — except the Cities of London and Westminster* in the 'Buildings of England' series for information contained in the above, and especially for the population tables towards the end of it.

City of London

1 All Hallows by the Tower with St Dunstan in the East

Dedication

'All Hallows by the Tower' is now the usual title of this church, although until recently, and because of the link with the Abbey of Barking, it was often known by the more high-sounding name of 'All Hallows Berkyngechirche by the Tower.' St Dunstan in the East, severely damaged in the bombing, was not rebuilt but turned into a garden and the parish joined to All Hallows. (See separate description)

History

The existence of a Saxon church in London is often largely surmise but here we are on firm ground. It is known that sometime before 675 AD, Erkenwald (Eorconwald), Bishop of London, founded a Christian community at Berkynge (Barking), seven miles down river, and made his sister Ethelburga first Abbess. The Abbey had a large estate near All Hallows and the church was probably used by its tenants and representatives.

The 1940 bombing revealed a substantial Saxon arch with Roman bricks incorporated, probably the entrance to a church which may have been as wide as the central part of the present church. The bombing also exposed the remains of a Saxon shaft inscribed with the name 'Werhenworrth'; later in 1951 half the circular wheel-head of a cross, also inscribed in Anglo-Saxon, was found under the floor. These remains, except for the rood at St. Dunstan's, Stepney, and a Danish gravestone in the Museum of London, are the only works of pre-Conquest ecclesiastical art in the capital to come down to us.

The Norman church which succeeded the Saxon building was constructed some ten years after the Tower of London next-door. This later place of worship, now represented by one isolated pillar embedded in the wall of the vestry and fragments in the crypt, had aisles. In the 14th century the chancel was renewed and a vicars' private burial vault (now a columbarium) built below the sanctuary.

Earlier, in the middle of the 13th century, a chapel dedicated to the Virgin Mary was built on the other side of the road to the north. Attached to this chapel was a Guild or Fraternity which was raised to the status of a Royal Chantry by Edward IV in 1465. The foundation disappeared at the Reformation.

The tower was shaken by an explosion in 1650 and was rebuilt in 1659, a rare example of church building in London in the Cromwellian period.

Seven years later, All Hallows narrowly escaped destruction in the

All Hallows by the Tower

1666 Fire and was only saved by Admiral Penn (father of William Penn) having houses in the area destroyed to halt the fire.

All Hallows was repaired in 1813–5 by D. A. Alexander and restored extensively by J. L. Pearson in the 1890s when the two-storey porch was built.

In December 1940 two air-raids left the church in a state of ruin from which it was restored by Lord Mottistone and Paul Paget. Reconsecration took place in 1957.

Exterior

Unlike many City churches, All Hallows is not hemmed in by buildings and stands freely on a commanding island site forming a striking group from the west with the Tower of London. The red brick tower survived the bombing and, set at a picturesque angle to the church, makes an attractive focal point, now enhanced by a Scandinavian-type spire of Columbian pine sheathed in copper.

Interior

Although much of the walling remained and the style of the present building is basically Perpendicular, the restoration has not attempted to reconstruct the old church. Instead, the ceiling is of reinforced open concrete. The new piers are made of Painswick (Gloucestershire) limestone, a more attractive material, reinforced by Pittsburg steel on the north and Texan steel on the south side. A gallery with theatre-box projections runs along the top of the arches. The plain rectangular east window has five cusped lights, and there is no division between chancel and nave. Lord Mottistone has succeeded in making the rebuilt church 'larger inside than outside'.

In the south aisle is the Mariners' Chapel with a crucifix made of wood from the famous tea clipper 'Cutty Sark' and a 15th century Spanish figure of Christ in ivory.

A 15th century figure of St James of Compostela and a slightly later one of about 1510 of St Roche are placed beside the nave columns, third from the east end. There is also a figure of St Anthony of Egypt at present in a wall alcove where stairs went to the rood loft; this is a 16th century figure with a high headdress.

The undercroft below the nave now houses a Roman tessera pavement and a museum full of fascinating finds—a showcase of Roman artefacts, Roman tombstone to Demetrius, plus the Saxon shaft and wheel-head (see History).

Furnishings

The furnishings, other than the exquisite Grinling Gibbons font cover (which was removed to safety during the 1939-45 War), sword rests, parts of the lectern and some of the altar-rails, all disappeared in the bombing. There are now:

Font In the south-west baptistry, a new font made of Gibraltar limestone by a Sicilian prisoner-of-war with the Grinling Gibbons cover (for which Gibbons was paid £12). It has cherubs, dove minus olive branch, leaves, flowers, wheat-ears, fir-cones etc. During restoration, it was found to have been made from more than 100 separately carved pieces, fixed in place by steel pins and glue. It dates from 1682.

Organ This is a new instrument built by Harrison & Harrison Ltd. in 1957 at an approximate cost of £20,000 to replace the much-altered organ originally made by Renatus Harris in the late 17th century. A second instrument (Mirfield Organ) in the south aisle was installed as a temporary organ for use in the Porch Room after the bombing.

Royal Arms The Royal Arms in front of the organ-loft are those of Charles II.

Stained glass The modern glass in the south aisle is by Reginald Bell. The well-designed windows in the baptistery are by Keith New.

Pulpit This is a Wren furnishing from St Swithun's, London Stone, with thick garlands and segmental pediments. It is supported on a slender stem and has a staircase with delicately-turned balusters

Lectern The rails, which survive from the original lectern, date from 1613 and are made of Sussex iron; they were most skilfully restored after the war damage.

Altar-table and rails The table is a replica of the old Jacobean table; the brass rails which surround it on three sides incorporate some of the original 18th century work which survived.

Mural The modern mural behind the altar-table depicting the Last Supper is by Brian Thomas.

Tate altarpiece The four panels used as an altarpiece in the north aisle are a precious survival from the chapel built by Sir Robert Tate (alderman) on the north side of the chantry chapel (see History). The four panels are all that remain of a winged altarpiece dating from the end of the 15th century.

Monuments

Alderman John Croke A tomb-chest monument with canopy to Sir John Croke, who died in 1477, has been restored by Cecil Thomas, who carved the bronze memorial next to it.

Hieronimus Benalius Further west in the north aisle is an attractive wall monument to Hieronimus Benalius (d. 1584) showing this Italian parishioner kneeling in a square frame with coat-of-arms above.

Brasses All Hallows has the largest set of brasses in the City. There are 17 in all, ranging from the most ancient (William Tonge, 1389) to the finest (Andrew Evyngar, a salter, with wife and children, 1530, Flemish). These are mostly in the sanctuary area.

Associations

All Hallows has rich associations.

Toc H The church, which is their Guild church, will long be remembered for its association with the Toc H movement founded by the Rev. Tubby Clayton, who became vicar in 1922. The tomb of John Croke (see Monuments) houses a casket containing the Lamp of Maintenance given by the Prince of Wales in 1922 as patron in memory of friends lost in the War and the north aisle in which the tomb lies is known as the Toc H Chapel. At the east end of the undercroft is an altar table built of stones from a Crusaders' castle at Athlit below Mount Carmel in Palestine; this contains the columbarium. Alongside is the Oratory of St Clare which became the oratory of Toc H Women's Association with the Association's 'Lamp of the Magnificat' behind a grille.

Victims of Execution The headless bodies of the saintly Bishop Fisher, the poet Thomas Howard, Earl of Surrey, Lord Thomas Grey (Lady Jane's father) and Archbishop Laud were all brought to the church after execution before being buried elsewhere.

William Penn William Penn was given his elementary education in the parish school room which stood somewhere near the Porch Room and he was also baptised in All Hallows (plate p. 7).

John Quincy Adams John Quincy Adams, sixth President of the USA, was married in the church in 1797. His father was the second President.

Knollys Rose A charming ceremony takes place each year under the auspices of the Watermen and Lighterman's Company when payment of a rose is made as quit-rent levied in 1381 for permission granted to Sir Robert Knollys and his wife to build a bridge ('haut-pas') across Seething Lane. The red rose is plucked from a garden owned by the Corporation of London near the site of Sir Robert's garden.

General

Although there is not much left of the mediaeval atmosphere, the associations and the recent discoveries make All Hallows a place of very great interest.

Font in which William Penn was baptised at All Hallows by the Tower (now at Christ Church, Philadelphia, U.S.A.)

2 All Hallows', London Wall

Dedication
The dedication of All Hallows' (All Saints'), London Wall reminds
us that it once stood on the old boundary of London. Moorfields,
open waste land where archery was practised, lay just beyond.

History
The shape of City churches was frequently dictated by the form of
the plot on which they were built. The All Hallows' site was a fringe
of land next to London Wall and the buildings erected on it had to
be long and narrow. The semi-circular vestry actually rests on a
bastion of the old Roman wall.

Evidence shows that the earliest of three churches constructed
here goes back at least to Henry I's reign (1100–35) for it is referred
to as having been linked by his Queen, Matilda, to Holy Trinity
Priory, Aldgate. The second known place of worship on this site,
dating from the 13th century and consisting of nave and aisle, was
raised well above street level behind a retaining wall. It had
Perpendicular windows and a weather-boarded tower surmounted
by a bell-turret. There was an anchorite's cell in the church, known
locally as the 'Anker Hole'.

All Hallows' survived the Great Fire but, by the 18th century, the
parish had become one of the most densely populated parts of the
country and, as the church had fallen into decay, it was decided to
build a new place of worship.

The successful applicant for the job of architect was George
Dance the Younger, son of the designer of the Mansion House and
St Botolph's, Aldgate. He was only 24 years old at the time and this
was his first major commission.

He produced between 1765–7, at a cost of £3,000, a building of
great charm which, although nearly put under the axe in Victorian
times because the style was out of fashion, has been saved by its
quality despite severe damage during the air-raids. The interior was
restored by Sir Arthur Blomfield in 1891.

Few parishioners remained after the war but, after lying derelict
for over 20 years, a new use was found for All Hallows' under the
Guild Churches Act of 1952 and it was sensitively restored by David
Nye, being eventually reconsecrated on 9th July 1962. The building
is now the headquarters of the Council for Places of Worship, which
advises on all matters concerning the preservation, repair, and
furnishing of churches all over the country. Religious services are
still held in the chancel and the Carpenters' Company continue, as

All Hallows', London Wall

they have done for over 600 years, to hold their annual Election
Day Service in the church. The parish has been united with that of
St Botolph's, Bishopsgate.

Exterior
The bare, plain brick walls give no hint of the beauty within. Semicircular lunettes high up are the sole concession to window space
and the only noteworthy features are the rounded apse at the east
end, the circular cupola in stone and the Tuscan west doorway with
frieze and pediment which looks out into the wider section of
London Wall. The tower projects from the main body of the church.

Interior
One is immediately captivated by the beauty and grace of the
interior, Despite the western half being given over to the library and
offices of the Council for Places of Worship, the redecoration is
fresh and gay, and faithfully follows the old pattern where it could
be traced. George Dance, the architect, was reacting against the
rather heavy Hanoverian style prevailing before he built All Hallows'
and introduced delicate but vigorous plaster motifs to the tunnel
vault of the nave and a delightful pattern of lozenges and rosettes
over the apse. The absence of projecting transverse arches further
increases the effect of lightness. Fluted attached Ionic three-quarter
columns carry the vault.

The west gallery still remains and the effect of a settlement of the
south wall during the period before the restoration can be detected
in the slope of the west gallery and the lintel of the door below.

Furnishings
Royal Arms The Royal Arms on the west gallery are those of
George III, who had just come to the throne at the time All Hallows'
was built. They date, however, from later in his reign (between 1801
and 1816).

Font This came from St Paul's Cathedral.

Organ This is a small 19th century chamber instrument which
had been found to accord perfectly with the needs of the building. It
was originally built about 1880 for a private house (Highbury Barn)
in Islington and came to All Hallows' from Islington Parish Hall in
1960.

Chandelier Originally one of a pair given by a parishioner who
shortly afterwards went bankrupt. It is inscribed with the date 1766
and the names of the incumbents and churchwardens.

Pulpit Once a three-decker until Victorianised, the remaining top stage is placed midway along the north wall. It is unusual in that it can only be reached by going out of the church and through the vestry.

Painting The painting in the apse is a copy of an early 17th century Italian painting by Pietro Berretini di Cortona showing St Paul receiving his sight. The copy was made by the architect's brother.

Monuments
Joseph Patience He was an architect who died in 1797. The memorial is in the form of a bust on a plinth with circular relief, standing on a sarcophagus.

William Beloe A tablet on the wall above the steps leading down to the crypt commemorates William Beloe, died 1817, who translated Herodotus.

Incumbents
In addition to William Beloe, who was rector, it is of interest to note that S. J. Stone, who composed the hymn 'The Church's one Foundation', was vicar here and that, at his own expense in 1891, he renewed the interior.

General
All Hallows' holds its secret until on entering one is reminded once again of the wealth of splendid 18th century ecclesiastical architecture which London possesses.

3 St Andrew's, Holborn

Dedication
According to tradition, the apostle Andrew—the patron saint of Scotland—suffered martyrdom on a diagonal or X-shaped cross, which became his emblem.

History
There is mention of a St Andrew's church in a charter of King Edgar dated 951 AD concerned with the boundaries of Westminster. Whatever Saxon church existed was succeeded by a stone Norman building which, in turn, grew into the later mediaeval church of which the tower was erected about 1446. It had many chapels for the Inns of Chancery in the neighbourhood, who contributed generously to the church's maintenance.

St Andrew's escaped the Great Fire but, by that time, was so
decayed that, like those destroyed, it had to be rebuilt under Wren
(in 1684–7). He kept the base of the tower and the west end, of
which the Gothic arches and window remain, and in 1704
refaced the tower in Portland stone and heightened it. Serving a very
large parish, the new place of worship was built on the lines of St
James's, Piccadilly, to enable as many people as possible to see and
hear the preacher, and was in fact the largest of Wren's churches
after St Paul's Cathedral.

Altered in 1818, the drastic treatment St Andrew's received later
in 1871–2, at the hands of the Victorian architect, S. S. Teulon, is
now obliterated by the destruction wreaked by the War and the
subsequent rebuilding by Seely and Paget in 1960–1. Teulon had
shown his usual insensitivity by interfering with the organ gallery
and case, altering the sanctuary, mounting the pulpit on what
Elizabeth and Wayland Young describe as 'a kind of Byzantine
wedding-cake', removing the christening pew from near the font,
covering the walls, columns and roof with polychrome decoration
and installing dark glass. The only gain was that, by tampering with
the organ gallery, he exposed the old Gothic arches.

The bombing in 1941 destroyed the church and all its contents,
leaving only the tower and walls standing, but the rebuilding is a
happy achievement which gives the visitor much to enjoy. The
reconsecration was on 25th October 1961.

Exterior
At one time St Andrew's stood at the top of what was Holborn Hill
but the building of Holborn Viaduct between 1867 and 1869 left it
below the level of the pavement. The approach (now down instead
of up) is from the south through imposing iron gates decorated with
a figure of St Andrew bearing his cross emblem.

On the north wall is a Resurrection carving (cf St Giles-in-the-
Fields and St Mary at Hill) which used to stand over the entrance to
the burial ground (now built over; more than 3,000 of the
parishioners died in the Plague).

The sides, terminating in balconies, have two tiers of windows,
large round-headed above and smaller segmental-headed below. At
the slightly projecting east end are two vestries with domes. At the
west end, opened up in 1968 by demolition of buildings and now
with a little garden in front are two figures of charity children (see
later). The tower is flanked by flat-topped constructions built to
contain the staircases to the galleries.

The dominating feature is the west tower, which has elaborate

belfry windows. The pronounced cornice above the balcony and
clumsy pinnacles looking like Roman altars with pineapples on top
but unfortunately no longer with vanes, give the steeple a top-heavy
appearance.

Interior
Despite Teulon, the pre-war interior was much admired and the
restorers have reproduced it as faithfully as possible, making it fresh
and bright in the process. The attractive elliptical ceiling is
decorated with green plaster panels in gilt frames; the wide aisles
have groined ceilings.

Side galleries are supported on panelled Doric piers which turn to
Corinthian columns at gallery level. There is also an organ gallery at
the west end.

Built into the 15th century vestibule at the west end is a charming
small chapel.

The lack of monuments and the width give a spacious interior,
undimmed by excess of stained glass and brightened by all the new
woodwork.

Furnishings
St Andrew's has succeeded in obtaining many excellent furnishings
to replace those lost in the bombing.

Organ From the old Chapel of the Foundling Hospital. A
Renatus Harris instrument altered and enlarged in a case of great
beauty, grey-brown, lavishly gilded and having flat tops with
cornices. Handel helped in its design and gave recitals on this
instrument. Boards with the Creed, Lord's Prayer and Ten
Commandments from an old reredos are fixed to the gallery walls
on either side.

Font A chaste furnishing of white marble, also from the old
Chapel.

Chapel Statue The statue of the Virgin Mary at the entrance was
specially bought for the church.

Chapel Reredos An English Baroque furnishing with pedimented
and coffered lintel, all lavishly gilded and with delicately wrought
iron Communion rails. This furnishing came from the ruined church
of St Luke's, Old Street.

Chapel stained glass The panel of the Holy Dove giving a *trompe-
l'oeil* effect is by Brian Thomas, who also designed the windows at
the east end.

Pulpit Another furnishing from the old Chapel. Hexagonal on
massive stem decorated with demi-Corinthian fluted columns on the

angles and Roman arches with keystone. Use is also made of a bead ornament.

Lectern The charming gilt lectern is of wrought-iron.

Reredos The segmental-headed altar-piece has a cherub in the head and garlands at the sides. In the front are free-standing Doric columns. The pre-war church had a 17th century altar of porphyry.

A statue of St Augustine of Canterbury is placed near the high altar.

The fine ornaments on the left of the sanctuary were given in memory of Comar Wilson of the Anglo-American Corporation.

Candlestick The large and beautiful veined marble paschal candlestick beside the font came from St Mary's Abbey, West Malling, Kent.

Stained glass A grievous loss from the bombing was the fine glass from 1718 by Joshua Price in the two-tier east Venetian window. The subject of the three lower lights was the Last Supper and of the upper three, the Ascension. There was also—on the north side—a window with the Royal Arms of Queen Anne and—on the south—those of Thavies Inn (John Thavies was a great benefactor). These were some of the only surviving glass from the Wren period. All have been reproduced by Brian Thomas.

At the west end is some old glass in a floral pattern.

Embroidery The banner of the Crucifixion, with the light of Easter beyond, is the work of Molly Arnold.

Monuments

Thomas Coram The tomb to Thomas Coram, founder of the famous 18th century Foundling Hospital for abandoned children in Bloomsbury, has been placed in a recess at the west end. This also came from the Hospital Chapel. The weeping child came from the monument to Thomas Manningham, rector and later Bishop of Chichester who died in 1722, as also did the charming cherubs placed on the wall above the tomb. The incised tablet from the Manningham memorial can be seen on the wall above the low door leading to the stairs of the tower. On the wall within the chapel is another delightful monument which survived the bombing.

Associations

The associations of St Andrew's are many and varied.

Charity children The two figures of a boy and girl outside the west front used to be on the wall of the parochial school in Hatton Garden, now turned into business premises but where two more can be seen. There are others in St Bride's, Fleet Street, and on the wall of the old parish school—now the parish hall—behind St Botolph's, Bishopsgate. Yet another pair are to be seen opposite St Mary's, Rotherhithe.

Henry Sacheverell This controversial character was put on trial for preaching what was considered a seditious sermon in St Paul's Cathedral against the 1688 Revolution which brought William III to the throne. With the help of Dean Swift he became rector of St Andrew's from 1714 until his death in 1724, when he was buried under the high altar. An oval tablet of cherry wood, by John Skelton, inscribed with fine white lettering, commemorates him. He did much to beautify the sanctuary, including the installation of the Price glass.

Henry Wriothesley, Earl of Southampton (father of the patron of William Shakespeare) was baptised here in 1545 with Henry VIII as godfather.

William Marsden, a local doctor, founded the Royal Free Hospital as a result of finding a young woman dying on the steps of St Andrew's one winter's night in 1827. A memorial tablet, designed by John Skelton, and erected by the Cordwainers' Company, can be seen on the wall opposite Coram's tomb.

Samuel Wesley, father of John and Charles Wesley, was ordained priest in the church by Bishop Compton of London, in 1689.

Marc Brunel, engineer of the first tunnel under the Thames and father of the more famous engineer, Isambard Kingdom Brunel, was married here in 1799.

William Hazlitt, the essayist, was married here in 1808 with Charles Lamb present and with his sister, Mary Lamb, acting as bridesmaid.

Benjamin Disraeli, the famous Victorian Prime Minister, was christened here at the age of 12 on 31st July 1817. His father, Isaac, was incensed at being fined for refusing the office of warden at Bevis Marks Synagogue in the City and came to St Andrew's to have the child christened in protest.

Henry Addington, Prime Minister unfavourably compared with Pitt in 'Pitt is to Addington, As London is to Paddington' was baptised here (date unobtainable).

General
This is a fine church, better inside than out, and most fortunate in the furnishings found for it and in the work of the post-war restorers and craftsmen.

No longer a parish church—the parish has been divided between St Alban's, Holborn and St Bride's, Fleet Street— St Andrew's is now a Guild church housing the diocesan offices for post-ordination training, youth work and moral welfare.

4 St Andrew Undershaft

Dedication
According to tradition St Andrew, one of the apostles, suffered martyrdom on a diagonal or X-shaped cross, which became his emblem.

'Undershaft' almost certainly refers to a shaft or maypole which, on May Days, rose above the steeple in front of the south door but which, after a riot directed against aliens by apprentices on 1st May 1517 in which many were killed, was hung up on hooks in Shaft Alley. There it remained until an impassioned sermon in 1550 at St Paul's Cross against pagan practices led the residents in the Alley who had wined and dined well to cut it up and burn it.

History
First mentioned in the 12th century, the church was referred to in 1268 as 'St Andrew juxta Alegate'. It was rebuilt in the early part of the 14th century and again, apart from the lower parts of the tower, in 1520–32. The second rebuilding was at the expense of the Lord Mayor and parishioners, some of whose arms are to be seen in the aisle windows.

There was a restoration in 1634 and repairs in 1723–5, when it was elaborately decorated with monochrome painting. A more thoroughgoing restoration by Sir Arthur Blomfield and Ewan Christian took place in 1875–6, when glass from the east window was transferred to a new west window, most of the 1723 paintings removed, the position of the organ changed and the Tijou altar rails consigned to the boiler room. (The fine Wren-period reredos was demolished about 1820.) Further restoration took place in 1930.

St Andrew's is one of only four places of worship in the City to have escaped serious damage both in the Great Fire and in the 1939–45 War but, in 1976, a serious fire in the heating system at the west end caused considerable damage. This has been happily made good at a cost of £42,000, and the church is exercising a most valuable ministry amongst under-30s working in the City, with talks, 'question and answer' discussions, theatre presentations, music, etc.

Exterior
Apart from the 19th century top of the south-west tower with its

stair-turret, the plain exterior is mostly Tudor. Situated at the corner of Leadenhall Street and St Mary Axe, entrance to the church is either from the south-west through iron gates, or the north-west doorway, the former having a fine 15th century door and interesting sanctuary knocker. The aisle windows have four, and the clerestory windows three, lights all without tracery. At the east end, the chancel projects.

Interior
A typical late Perpendicular design with nave of six bays, aisles and clerestory. The arcades have slender four-shaft-four-hollow columns with capitals on the shafts only, and depressed arches, in the spandrels of which the remaining part of the 1723 painting showing scenes from Christ's life on earth is being restored. There is no division between nave and chancel.

The almost flat panelled roof was rebuilt in 1949-50 and the 125 carved and gilt oak bosses put back. The slightly cambered beams rest upon corbels, on one of which the date 1532 can be discerned. The aisle roofs are original.

The large west and east windows of five lights with transoms have been restored.

This interior is lofty and light, well suited to its present uses, for which the pews have been removed.

Furnishings
Font Plain, marble, octagonal font with baluster stem by Nicholas Stone, master-mason to James I and Charles I, dating from 1631. The cover is later.

Pulpit A notable Wren-period furnishing.

Organ A particularly good instrument, being from the workshop of Renatus Harris and enclosed in a fine case of 1696 with two seated figures on top.

Communion Rails Although by Tijou (dating from 1704), these rails were thrown out by Blomfield and are now very properly reinstated.

*Stained glass The brightly coloured, mainly golden, glass in the west window was formerly in the east, but perhaps was considered unsuited to be above the altar. It suffered damage in the 1976 fire but has been ably restored. The figures of Edward VI, Elizabeth I, James I and Charles I were given by Sir Christopher Clitheroe, Lord Mayor in 1637; the fifth king added later may at one time have been Charles II but at the end of the century it was presumably deemed

expedient to substitute William III, who had just achieved his 'Glorious Revolution'. There is much 19th century work in the window, particularly in the heraldry.

The east window by Heaton, Butler & Bayne depicts the Crucifixion and Ascension of Christ.

Monuments
There is much to see, due to the number of parishioners who were men of note, some becoming Lord Mayors.

Sir Thomas Offley, died 1582, and wife, died 1578. They are shown with three sons as kneeling figures facing one another across a prie-dieu.

John Stow, died 1605. St Andrew's was the church of this painstaking and detailed chronicler of Elizabethan London, to whose *Survey of London* we owe so much, and to whom reference is made so often in this book. He lived to the age of about 80, but died in poverty.

*The monument of Derbyshire marble and alabaster in the north-east corner shows him, bald-headed, writing in a book at a table, flanked by square pillars richly decorated with ribbonwork, lions' heads, books and crosses.

Each year, near the anniversary of his death on 5th April, the Lord Mayor, attended by Sheriffs, renews his quill pen and presents a copy of Stow's book to the writer of the best essay on London received that year.

The monument was restored by the Merchant Taylors' Company in 1905.

Alice Byng, died 1616. She had three husbands, all stationers, and is commemorated by a small pedimented monument high up on the north wall wearing a ruff; she is kneeling at a prie-dieu under an arch flanked by richly-decorated square piers.

Sir Hugh Hammersley, died 1636. He was Lord Mayor in 1627. A large wall monument about ten feet high with kneeling figures under curtains. He is shown in armour with his wife behind him and there are two mourning soldiers outside the flanking columns.

Peter Vansittart, died 1705. This tablet placed high on the south wall is decorated with skulls and cherubs' heads.

Sir Christopher Clitheroe, died 1642, who gave some of the west window glass. He was Lord Mayor in 1635 and Governor of the East India Company. There is a simple tablet to him.

Brasses Amongst the brasses are to be noted one to *Nicholas Lewson*, died 1539, his wife, eight sons and ten daughters, shown as kneeling figures facing one another, and another to *Simon Burton*, who died in 1593 at the age of 85, with his two wives, one son and three daughters.

Associations
Hans Holbein, the painter, is believed to have resided in the parish and is commemorated by a brass tablet on the south wall.

General
Stow's 'fair and beautiful church of St Andrew the Apostle' is an important survival of a larger City mediaeval church. Subsequent alterations have not obscured its Tudor character and it is now entering upon a new period of active ministry amongst the younger workers in the City.

5 St Andrew by the Wardrobe with St Ann's, Blackfriars

Dedication
According to tradition, St Andrew—the patron saint of Scotland—suffered martyrdom on a diagonal or X-shaped cross which became his emblem. 'Wardrobe' refers to the department of the royal household in which the kings' stores, including arms and ceremonial clothing, were kept. It was moved from the Tower of London to Wardrobe Place, north of the church, about 1361 and remained there for more than 300 years until the building was destroyed in the Great Fire of 1666.

St Ann's, Blackfriars, was the church for those living within the precincts of the Blackfriars Dominican monastery, but it was not rebuilt after the Fire and the parish was united with that of St Andrew's. In a corner of one of St Ann's two churchyards is to be seen the only fragment of the great priory to survive above ground.

History
As with many churches, it is not known when worship first began on this site; it may have been that St Andrew's was founded at the time when the Fitzwalters took possession of the mediaeval mansion of Baynard Castle nearby, The church was sometimes referred to as St Andrew-juxta-Baynard Castle. First written mention is in a St Paul's Cathedral manuscript dated 1244.

Victim itself of the Great Fire, St Andrew's was rebuilt by Sir Christopher Wren during the years 1685 to 1693 and some of the furnishings date from that time, although not originally made for St Andrew's.

A west gallery was added in 1774 and many alterations were made early in the 19th century by the Victorians. They did not, however, follow their usual practice of substituting open benches for the existing box-pews, although these were altered in the 1889 restoration. The church was burnt out again in December 1940— this time by fire-bombs—and, during the subsequent sensitive restoration by Marshall Sisson between 1959 and 1961, he removed some of the fussy Victorian embellishments, including the balustraded parapet on the south wall and the vanes on the corners of the tower. He also partitioned off the north aisle to provide offices for the British and Foreign Bible Society and, for the sake of symmetry, the south aisle was similarly treated.

St Andrew's now has an enlarged parish which includes the pre-Fire parishes of St Nicholas Cole Abbey, St Nicholas Olave, St Mary Somerset, St Mary Mounthaw, St Benet's Paul's Wharf and St Peter's Paul's Wharf as well as portions of other parishes.

The tower houses the office of the Redundant Churches Fund.

Exterior

Despite its unassuming exterior, the completion of Queen Victoria Street in 1871 gave St Andrew's, perched up on its slope, a commanding position. The tower, which projects to the south-west, and the south wall with once more a plain brick parapet, survived the bombing and, stripped of their Victorian accretions, look much as Wren left them. The other walls also survived. What remained of the churchyard after the construction of the street was landscaped as a garden, and memorial gates were added in 1902 in memory of Banister Fletcher. The south portal dates from the same year. The crucifix by Walter Tapper was dedicated in 1937.

The weather-vane on the tower came from St Michael's, Bassishaw (demolished in 1900), after spending some time in the then Lord Mayor's garden at Sydenham.

Interior

Although the enclosure of the aisles has reduced ground-floor space and the old box pews have been replaced by benches in light-toned oak, the interior, with the aid of furnishings which have found their way here by circuitous routes, retains its Wren character.

The galleries on three sides are supported by Doric piers.

Emblems on the tunnel vault of Wren's ceiling have been reproduced as far as possible, the rest, including the groined vaults of the aisles, being white except for the gilded caps of the pillars.

Furnishings

Pulpit This was originally the pulpit of St Matthew's, Friday Street, a church built by Wren at the same time as St Andrew's but demolished in 1884. It came via St Peter's, Fulham. The sounding-board and back piece have gone, and the base, stem and stairs have had to be replaced.

Font The marble font and attractive font cover with cherub's head decoration also came from St Matthew's, but via St Clement's, Fulham. St Andrew's has another font cover which was once on the font of All Hallows, Bread Street (demolished 1876) whence it travelled to All Hallows, East India Dock Road and, when that was bombed, to All Saints, Poplar.

Organ The organ in the west gallery was orginally built in 1769 for Lord Hatherton of Teddesley Hall, Stafford. It was loaned to St Bartholomew-the-Great in 1953 by Noel Mander, from whom it was purchased for St Andrew-by-the-Wardrobe in 1961.

Royal Arms The Stuart Royal Arms at the west end of the south gallery were originally in St Olave Jewry (demolished except for tower in 1888). After a spell in the rectory of St Margaret's, Lothbury, they were presented to St Andrew's.

Reredos Boards from the former reredos were preserved. The present altar-piece was designed by Marshall Sisson with carving by A. J. Eyres.

Chandeliers The chandeliers are of early 18th century date and although similar, are not a matching pair. They are made of latten (a compound of zinc, lead and tin) and have 12 lights in two tiers.

Figure of St Andrew The figure of St Andrew with his diagonal cross in the sanctuary dates from about 1600.

Sanctuary chairs The sanctuary chairs date from 1687 and 1690.

Stained glass The panel of glass depicting the conversion of St Paul at the west end is 18th century. The four modern windows on the south side are by Carl Edwards.

General

St Andrew's is still a parish church holding regular services, running an advanced Sunday School including lectures by eminent churchmen on Sunday afternoons in the winter, as well as being the headquarters of the Redundant Churches Fund.

6 St Anne's and St Agnes'

Dedication

The double dedication, first mentioned in 1467, is unique in the
City. The church was once known as St Anne-in-the-Willows
although, even in Elizabethan times, there were no signs of willows.

St Anne was the mother of the Virgin Mary; St Agnes shares with
St Pancras the honour of being amongst the Church's youngest
martyrs, for she was only thirteen when she died for her faith in
Rome about 350 AD (possibly earlier).

History

Dates vary from about 1200 to 1291 for first mention of the church.
The old church had a Norman tower, repaired in 1629–30; before
this, the whole structure had been badly damaged by fire in 1548,
although soon repaired. Despite being further away from the seat of
the Great Fire than some churches, St Anne's and St Agnes' was,
except for part of the tower, completely consumed and Wren rebuilt
it between 1676 and 1687, his eleventh reconstruction. The church
next door, St John Zachary (Zachary was St John's father), was not,
however, restored and the parish was joined to St Anne's and St
Agnes' in 1670.

Internal alterations were made by W. M. Brooks in 1838–9 and
by Ewan Christian in 1888–9. Badly damaged by bombs in
December 1940, the church went through a period of neglect until
Braddock and Martin-Smith took restoration in hand between
1963 and 1968. They had to take down and rebuild much of the
walls and the rest was a careful reproduction of what the church had
been before the outside was stuccoed in 1820–1.

Exterior

The exterior has gained greatly both structurally and in its setting
from post-war work. The removal of the stucco has exposed the
pleasant red brick of the walls on the north, south and east sides,
which are symmetrical, each with a large round-headed window
under a pediment and flanked by two smaller ones, all with
rusticated surrounds. Both the churchyards of St Anne's and St
Agnes', and of neighbouring St John Zachary have been turned into
gardens affording an unimpeded view from the south-east.

The small, simple 14th century west tower is capped with a pretty,
slightly leaning bell turret, terminating in a gilded weather-vane with
a capital letter 'A' on top. (plate p. 23).

St Anne's and St Agnes'. Bell turret with weather vane

Interior

Only 53 feet square, structurally the interior is nevertheless one of Wren's most interesting designs, similar to that of St Mary at Hill and of St Martin-within-Ludgate. All three were clearly based on the plan of the Nieuwe Kerk at Haarlem, Netherlands, a plan which goes back to very early Christian days. It is a cross in a square with the four arms of the cross having high tunnel vaults and meeting to form a groin-vaulted centre section. The corner spaces between the arms of the cross have low, flat ceilings, whilst the lines of the cross are emphasised by an entablature which goes right round it. The central area of St Anne's and St Agnes' is marked by four fine columns on high pedestals with gilded Corinthian capitals.

The ceilings have restrained and beautiful plaster decoration, the corner ones having circles enclosing flowers and fruit with attractive cornices and egg and dart decoration, whilst the arches opening out into the centre have gilded and coffered rosettes, and panels. The groined vault is coloured blue.

There is no stained glass and there are no galleries, giving a light and spacious effect to this small interior. In accordance with Lutheran tradition (St Anne's and St Agnes' is now a Lutheran church) the building is so centrally planned that the space which goes right round the pews is plain to the point of bareness. The walls are panelled up to a height of over eight feet and the colour of the high, modern pews matches that of the walls.

Furnishings

The reredos and west doorcase belonged to St Anne's and St Agnes', but most of the furnishings came from other churches.

Doorcases A fine south-west doorcase with broken pediment supported on attached Corinthian columns and crowned by a gilded angel gives access to the interior. There is another doorcase at the west end, plainer but carrying a figure of Father Time, complete with gilded wings, sickle and hour-glass, given by Benjamin Williams in 1682–3.

Royal Arms A fine Charles II Royal Arms came from St Mary's, Whitechapel (war casualty).

Organ A moveable Noel Mander instrument, made in 1962 as a temporary organ for Coventry Cathedral, it came from there to this church.

Font The tall, circular font of white veined marble standing on an elegant pedestal was made after the War to replace one which came from St Mildred's, Bread Street and is a copy of it, except for the decoration. The cover is carved in high relief with leaves and

St Anne's and St Agnes'. West end with Charles II Royal Arms rosettes, and has a gold and red crown.

Pulpit The hexagonal pulpit, without tester, contains three inlaid panels from St Augustine's, Watling Street (burnt 1940). It is further decorated with foliage and winged heads of cherubs, one of whom looks very startled. The gilded lion nearby and the unicorn by the lectern were also in St Mildred's, Bread Street.

Lectern In the form of a brass angel supporting the reading shelf and standing under a dormered dome. It came from St Mary's, Rotherhithe.

Reredos The notable reredos (unfortunately stained black) contains paintings of Moses and Aaron in carved frames and came from St Michael's, Wood Street via St George's, Southwark. The open scrolled pediment carries a lamp with a flame on top and gilded cherubs. There are also carved swags and Corinthian pilasters.

Sanctuary Chairs Well carved sanctuary chairs are decorated with affronted birds having long wide sharp beaks, and intricate foliage, whilst the arms terminate in lions' heads.

Other items On the sill of a south window are two elevated busts, one of which may represent Sir Christopher Wren; in the middle of the north wall is a crown above two mitres, symbolic of the monarch being Head of the Church.

General

St Anne's and St Agnes' has been leased to the Lutheran Church for twenty-one years and was dedicated for this use on 23rd April 1966 in the presence of the Bishops of London and Lübeck. Services are held in Esthonian, Latvian and English, bringing together the various Lutheran churches in London under the name of St John's Evangelical Lutheran Church of London. These churches go back to the time when German workmen came to this country after the Great Fire to help in the rebuilding of the City.

N.B.: Special arrangements have to be made to see the church.

7 St Bartholomew-the-Great, Smithfield

Dedication

Bartholomew was one of the Apostles. He is said to have preached the Gospel in India and there to have been flayed alive by those opposed to his teaching. His emblem is a flaying knife.

'Smithfield' comes from Smoothfield, a largely marshy area in mediaeval times.

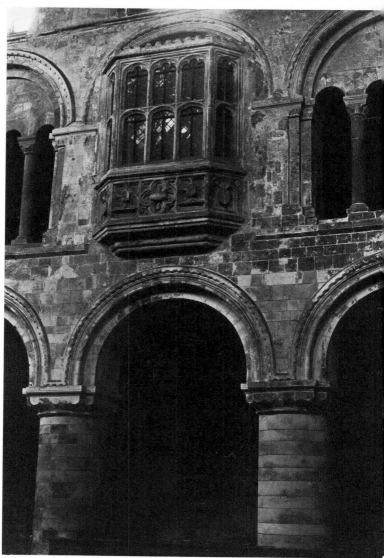

St Bartholomew-the-Great. Prior Bolton's oriel window

History

Rahere forsook the easy life of an obsequious courtier to become a pious monk in the reign of Henry I as a result of a pilgrimage to Rome and after being struck down by malaria. As thanksgiving for his recovery, and on the strength of a vision when St Bartholomew came to his rescue, he obtained a grant of land in Smithfield from the King and there founded simultaneously his hospital (affectionately known today as 'Barts') and a priory. Work on both probably started about 1103. The more usual date of 1123 associated with the foundation is more likely to be nearer the year of consecration of the eastern parts of the priory.

These were completed in his lifetime and his successor added the transepts and eastern part of the nave, the latter of ten bays being completed in the 13th century. The chancel originally ended in an apse, but about 1330 this was made square and a Lady Chapel added, which increased the over-all length of the church to 349 feet, longer than some of the smaller cathedrals like Bristol, Chester and Rochester.

Prior Bolton, prior from 1500 to 1532, installed the charming oriel window on the south side of the chancel to enable him to participate in masses without leaving his lodgings. He was succeeded by Prior Fuller, who compliantly handed over the Priory at the Dissolution on 25th October 1539 and was granted a pension.

After the Dissolution, the chancel was retained as the parish church but the nave was pulled down and only the old gateway to the south aisle left, plus the first nave bay largely concealed by the organ. The large central tower had already disappeared before the Dissolution but in 1622–8, the present red brick south-west tower with its pretty lantern was built and the chancel repaired.

Thereafter, this impressive place of worship was allowed to fall into a deplorable state, and despite restorations in 1789 by George Dance and in 1791 by Thomas Hardwick, the parts of the church not wanted were let off for various secular uses; a blacksmith's shop was installed in the north transept, a school in the triforium, stables in the cloisters, whilst in the Lady Chapel there were first tenements, then a printing shop and later a fringe factory. In addition, a fire in 1830 destroyed the chapter house and south transept. It was not until the 19th century that a start was made in clearing these encroachments, terminating in the careful restorations of Sir Aston Webb at the end of the 19th century. He finally got rid of the troublesome fringe factory and rebuilt the Lady Chapel. Later, eight bays of the east walk of the cloister were restored and opened in 1928.

The interests of the Prior and the Corporation did not always coincide in the Middle Ages and the Priory's ownership of Bartholomew Fair was a particular source of friction. On the other hand the sub-Prior appears to have been disgracefully treated in 1250, when the Queen's uncle, who had not even been ordained, made a visitation in armour as Archbishop of Canterbury and all but crushed the protesting sub-Prior to death.

There were rights of sanctuary from early times at the Priory.

Exterior
St Bartholomew's is still surrounded by small streets as it was in the Middle Ages, and hides itself behind the entrance gate from Smithfield, above which is a restored mediaeval timber house. This gate was the original 13th century south entrance to the nave.

Beyond is a path through the churchyard, to the right of which is part of the former outer south aisle wall. Beyond—also on the right—is the east walk of the cloister.

The porches are all 19th century; the northern one has a statue of St Bartholomew outside, whilst the main entrance has a statue of Rahere. The exterior is harshly refaced in flint and Portland stone.

Interior
One enters by the south side of the crossing and is presented with a magnificent example of rugged early Norman architecture, vigorous and uncompromising. Massive drum columns support the unmoulded round arches, which are compressed at the apse, restored by Sir Aston Webb at the end of the 19th century. Above runs a triforium with four bays and blank tympanum under an encircling arch to each bay of the chancel; in the apse there are two-light blind arches. There is a minimum of decoration—scalloped capitals and an outer ring of billet moulding. The clerestory windows are late 14th century.

It is possible to study the transition from Norman to Gothic in the crossing, which has round arches on the east and west sides and pointed ones (perhaps the earliest in London) on the north and south sides.

The transepts are a sadly truncated version of those originally built and are crammed up against the crossing, only the arches to the chancel aisles and the south nave aisle being mediaeval. On the south side, entry is gained to the east walk of the cloister, rebuilt in the 15th century, of which the old vault springers and two doors to the former chapter house remain but of which most is 20th century rebuilding. The cloister originally had 36 bays and the eight bays now restored are used as a museum.

*Prior Bolton's oriel window with canted sides is over the south ambulatory of the chancel and is a delightful feature. In the centre panels below the glass is his rebus—an arrow (bolt) piercing a wine tun.

Beyond in the south-east corner is the Chapel of Knights Bachelor.

Behind the apse, the rebuilt Lady Chapel extends eastwards up a slope. The south side is largely Aston Webb's restoration of 1897, but the character of this 14th century addition has been retained, with its three large lancet windows under an arch at the east end and two separate single lancets at the sides.

Furnishings
Of minor interest, except for monuments. The church is unique, however, in having five pre-Reformation bells.

Font A plain stone 15th century octagonal font, one of only two pre-Reformation examples left in London. The cover, shaped like a pyramid, has eight carved ribs which terminate with heads of tonsured monks.

Organ Purchased in 1886 from St Stephen's, Walbrook for which it was made in 1765 by George England. The instrument was restored in 1931.

Screen to Lady Chapel The work of a fine Victorian craftsman, J. Starkie Gardner, dating from 1897. Of wrought-iron, it consists of five bays with gates in the central bay, on either side of which are two candle brackets, whilst the uprights of the screen are carried slightly above the hammered iron frieze as single candlesticks.

Monuments
Rahere On the north side of the chancel and dating from the 15th century, 300 years after his death. He is shown recumbent in the black habit of the Augustinian Canons on a tomb chest under a canopy, his tonsured head resting upon a tasselled cushion. At his feet are two kneeling bedesmen and a larger angel holding a shield. The back wall is pierced, enabling pilgrims to make offerings from the ambulatory.

Percival Smallpiece, died 1558 and wife, died 1588. On the south side of the sanctuary in brown marble. Two frontal busts separated by a mullion and between side pilasters.

Sir Walter Mildmay, died 1589 and wife. He was Chancellor of the Exchequer and founder of Emmanuel College, Cambridge. On the north wall of the choir. Large wall-monument in Italian marbles with pediment and columns, but no effigy.

Sir Robert Chamberlane, died 1615. On north wall of chancel. A small memorial with kneeling figure and two standing angels holding open two curtains.

Elizabeth Freshwater, died 1617. On the east wall of the south transept. Another small monument with kneeling figure. She is shown under an arch.

James Rivers, died 1641. *Edward Cooke*, died 1652. On the south wall of the ambulatory. Both are frontal busts and each figure holds a book.

Brass On the south side of the south ambulatory floor is a brass to John Deane, first rector (1539–44).

Associations
Benjamin Franklin worked in the printing shop in the Lady Chapel in 1724.

William Hogarth, the painter, was baptised here in 1697.

City of London Squadron, RAF, whose Battle Honours standard is there, have their War Memorial in the Lady Chapel and hold a special commemorative service in the Chapel each May.

City of London Yeomanry ('Roughriders') memorial is in north transept. They hold their annual service in October.

John Wesley preached here in 1747.

Butchers' Company hold their annual service here.

General
Although only a shadow of its former self, St Bartholomew's is the most considerable Norman church in London. It is dark but compelling and one must be grateful for the sensitive and loving work, though not agreeing with some of it, which was put into the restoration by the Victorians.

8 **St Bartholomew-the-Less**

Dedication
Bartholomew was one of the 12 Apostles. He is said to have carried the Gospel to India, and there to have converted a king to Christianity by healing his mad daughter. The hostility aroused by his teaching amongst priests who served the local idols led to his being flayed alive. The emblem of his martyrdom is a flaying knife.

St Bartholomew-the-Less. Tower

History

Henry I's courtier Rahere founded St Bartholomew's Hospital in 1123 at the same time as the Priory next door and there was a chapel attached to the hospital from the very beginning, although on a different site. It was moved to where it now stands in 1184 but, despite the substantial Norman remains at St Bartholomew-the-Great, the earliest construction within the hospital area is the 15th century tower of the chapel. At the Dissolution, when it was known as the Chapel of the Holy Cross, it became the parish church for the hospital and has remained so ever since.

By the end of the 18th century the walls were in a crumbling state and the architect George Dance the Younger removed the interior and substituted a wooden octagon which extended above the roof and beyond the east wall, one of the few major church constructions in the 60 years between 1760 and 1820.

The wooden octagon decayed and in 1823–5 Thomas Hardwick replaced it with the nave of stone and iron we see today, said to resemble closely its predecessor. At the same time, he rebuilt the walls in brick. Forty years later in 1865, the architect's grandson, P. C. Hardwick, remodelled the sanctuary and added tracery to the upper part of the windows.

Badly damaged during the 1939–45 War, St Bartholomew-the-Less was restored by Seely (Lord Mottistone) and Paget, being reopened in 1951.

Exterior

The church is tucked away on the left after entering the hospital precincts. It is a strange mixture with the lantern of its 19th century octagon sticking up above the surrounding walls and unbuttressed 15th century west tower; the latter is stark and bare but has an unusual south-west stair turret on top with pretty ogee cap. The parapet is of brick.

Interior

Entrance is through the tower and on the left the vestry retains its original floor with two brasses (see *Monuments*); the arches are 15th century. The interior of the tower has recesses and is embellished with banded columns.

The vestibule opens out into the octagon of the nave with star-shaped plaster rib vault and a roof made of iron. Triangular chapels fill the spaces between the sides of the octagon and the rectangle of the walls.

Geometrical tracery in the clerestory lunette windows and post-war glass by Hugh Easton do not help the interior but otherwise the Gothic style of the octagon, now painted grey and white, is pleasantly original and bright.

The walls are lined with memorials to surgeons and others connected with the hospital.

Furnishings
The pews and fittings are mostly Victorian and there are some interesting monuments. The right window of the apse has representations of St Bartholomew and the hospital founder, Rahere.

Monuments
John Freke and wife On the west wall of the tower is a 16th century altar-tomb with canopy and inscribed slab to John Freke, surgeon, who died in 1756, and his wife Elizabeth, who died in 1741.

Lady Elizabeth Bodley On the north wall of the nave is a monument to the wife of Sir Thomas Bodley, founder of the famous library at Oxford.

John and Mary Darken Tablets by John Bingley to John Darken, died 1784 and Mary, his wife, died 1773 are to be seen on the west wall, left of the organ loft. The tablet to John has putti by an urn.

Brasses Two nicely incised brasses in the vestry are of William Markby, who died in 1485, and his wife. They are shown in civil dress.

Associations
Wat Tyler Although not specifically linked with the church, it is of interest to record that Wat Tyler, leader of the Peasants' Revolt in 1381, was carried into the hospital after being mortally wounded by Sir William Walworth, Lord Mayor of London, and it is said that Tyler was later dragged out of the building and beheaded.

Inigo Jones The great architect of the early Stuart period was baptised here in 1573.

General
There are other hospital chapels in London such as the attractive one at Guy's, built by Richard Jupp in 1780, with its outstanding monument to Thomas Guy by John Bacon (see plate p. 35). But St Bartholomew-the-Less is different in that it is a parish church. It is an architectural oddity, but with much of interest, and its special function is evidenced by the new doorway opened in 1969 at the south end of the east wall for invalid chairs.

Guy's Hospital. Monument to Thomas Guy by John Bacon, 1779

9 St Benet's, Paul's Wharf (now the Metropolitan Welsh Church)

Dedication

'Benet' is a shortened form of Benedict the Italian monk who, after living in a cave as a hermit, realised that monks sharing in a community could serve God more fully than as solitary individuals. He thus became the founder of the western form of monastic institution. He was born in 480 AD and died in 543. The full name of Benedict was often used for the church until the early part of the 19th century.

'Paul's Wharf' was owned by the Dean and Chapter of St Paul's Cathedral; stone for the rebuilding of the Cathedral after the Fire was unloaded there.

History

The church was first mentioned in 1111 as 'Sancti Benedicti super Tamisiam'. Stow, in Elizabeth's time, called it St Benet Hithe.

Destroyed in the Great Fire, St Benet's was rebuilt by Wren between 1677 and 1685; its neighbour St Peter's, Paul's Wharf—also destroyed—was not rebuilt and its parish joined to St Benet's. Since that time, St Benet's has survived, singularly free of later alteration. Beautified and repaired in 1836, it escaped bomb damage in the 1939–45 War, although a post-war restoration was carried out by Godfrey Allen in 1946; its luck slightly ran out in 1971 when a fire badly damaged the galleries and organ.

The church was in danger of being scrapped in 1854, but in 1879, when the parish was united with that of St Nicholas Cole Abbey, it was taken over by the Welsh Episcopalian Church and is still the Metropolitan Welsh Church within the Church of England London diocese, beautifully cared for by them. The services are conducted in the Welsh language.

Exterior

A delightful harmony in dark red and blue brick with Portland stone dressings, very Dutch in feeling. Roadworks have left St Benet's in a conspicuous position, but somewhat isolated from the main thoroughfare of Queen Victoria Street. The roof of the north side facing the street is hipped. In contrast to the homely red and blue chequerwork, there are stone festoons over all the round-headed windows and, over the middle bay of the east wall, a fine cherub's head.

The charming north-west tower projects slightly from the north aisle and has the same decorative treatment of architrave and modillion cornice, together with alternate courses of brick and stone

St Benet's, Paul's Wharf

at the angles, as the rest of the church. Faced with stone at the base, the mainly brick tower is crowned with a lead-sheathed curved dome lit with eight oval lucarnes, on top of which is a small lantern and a short lead spire. The contrasting curves of the dome and spire are captivating, described by Gerald Cobb as 'a little work of art—quite perfect'.

Interior

The interior is just as appealing. The dimensions are only $41\frac{1}{4}$ by $51\frac{1}{4}$ feet, the extra width from south to north being occupied by the north aisle. This is separated from the main body of the church by Corinthian columns with panelled bases supporting a gallery; there is no division between nave and chancel.

The gallery was repaired and, where necessary, renewed after the 1971 fire and carries on the front the arms of the Archbishop of Canterbury, the Royal Arms and the Fouled Anchor of the Court of Admiralty. It is decorated with carvings of fruit. This gallery was occupied, until their institution was dissolved in 1867, by the ecclesiastical lawyers of Doctors' Commons, who practised in the Court of Arches, and also by other courts. It is still reserved for the heralds of the College of Arms across the road.

The gallery at the west end—also repaired after the fire—is divided by the organ. Beneath this, a panelled screen shuts off the southern half of the nave from the rest, thus forming a vestibule.

The walls are panelled and the ceiling is flat. The church retains its old stone floors with many ledger slate monuments.

Curious features are the substitutes on the north wall, consisting of palm-branches, shells and cherub-heads, for the Corinthian capitals of pillars and pilasters round the rest of the walls.

Furnishings

Poor-box There is a poor-box in the vestibule with moulded top and base on a stand made up of four twisted balusters.

Doorcase and Royal Arms Opening out from the tower lobby is a splendid doorcase with a finely carved and painted Royal Arms of Charles II above. Cherubs' heads, which abound in the church, are carved in the spandrels.

Organ Originally a 'Bishop' instrument, dating from 1837 and much damaged in 1971.

Stalls and pews The pews have been lowered but are made of wood from the old box pews. Old wood was also used for the stalls, which have carved frieze-panels and capping on their backs.

Pulpit Richly carved of hexagonal form. Stairs, stem and base are all modern but the date 1685 can be faintly seen on one of the panels. The sounding-board has been removed and is now used as a ceiling at the base of the tower, and the panelled standard is in front of the lectern, which is attached to the stalls. The latter is modern and of wood.

Reredos The altar-piece of wood with pierced and inlaid segmental pediment and urns on top has the usual gilding and panels with Ten Commandments, Lord's Prayer and Creed.

Communion rails The rails have scrolled twisted balusters.

*Altar-table A sumptuous piece with top upheld by angels as legs and a fine figure of Charity sitting on the stretcher. The top is of inlaid woods. Cherubs' heads at the corners and a text at the edge with a modillion cornice encircle the top.

Sanctuary chairs The two sanctuary chairs are late 17th century.

Monuments

Of the many attractive monuments, including several from the 18th century, a number commemorate members of Doctors' Commons and the College of Arms.

Inigo Jones This great architect, whose paternal grandfather was Welsh and can therefore be said to have initiated the long Welsh connection of St Benet's, and who gave many furnishings to the church, was buried beneath the chancel of the old St Benet's and the memorial there depicted some of his buildings. A small tablet on the east wall of the present church records the original inscription and was put up in 1878.

Mark and Alice Cottle A curious large monument in the south-east corner commemorates these two. Mark died in 1681 and Alice in 1698. It consists of a shield of arms beneath a draped canopy and below a sphere, all made of black and white marble.

Sir Robert Wyseman, Dean of the Court of Arches, who died in 1684 and was buried in the chancel. It is in the form of a portrait medallion (good) in a foliated frame with a looped curtain. This large monument is of white marble.

John Charles Brook A tablet north of the reredos commemorates in glowing terms this member of the College of Heralds, who was killed in 1797 when a ceiling at the Haymarket Theatre collapsed. The Royal Family was present when this happened.

Associations

Twelfth Night St Benet's is referred to in a scene from *Twelfth Night*, no doubt performed at the adjacent Black Friars Theatre. 'The bells of St Bennet, sir, may put you in mind' says the Clown.

Private marriages Owing to the facility of Doctors' Commons to get over marriage impediments against payment of a fee, St Benet's, like St Marylebone old church, became a favoured place for quick marriages. 13,423 were celebrated between 1708 and 1731.

Henry Fielding Henry Fielding, the novelist, married his first wife's former maid here in 1747.

General

This is the most homely and lovable of all Wren's churches and one of the least altered. There are few which can better be appreciated in their entirety both outside and in.

N.B.: Not normally open except during services.

10 St Botolph's, Aldersgate

Dedication

One of three churches still standing in London dedicated to this 7th century Saxon abbot who became the patron saint of travellers.

History

In 1068 AD, William the Conqueror confirmed the patronage of St Botolph's on the Dean of the Priory of St Martin's-le-Grand. First referred to as 'St Botulph without Aldredesgate', there were probably two churches before the present one, the first lasting from about 1050 until 1350, and the second, with nave and aisles plus three east windows, until the middle of the 18th century.

Two, and possibly three, brotherhoods were instituted in mediaeval times: the brotherhood of the Trinity in 1374 and another dedicated to St Fabian and St Sebastian in 1377; but these two may have been the same, merely changing the name at the later date. Another to St Katherine was existing in 1389, although no date of foundation is known.

Much of the steeple was rebuilt in 1627. The whole church escaped the worst of the Great Fire, being protected by London Wall from the fate of nearby St Anne's and St Agnes'. Apart from St Botolph's, Billingsgate, the 'gate' churches survived the conflagration but, like St Botolph's, Aldgate and St Botolph's, Bishopsgate, it fell into disrepair.

Many petitions for money were made. Partial repairs were carried out in 1754 but a complete rebuilding, except for the east wall, took place between 1789 and 1791, the latter being under the direction of

St Botolph's Aldersgate, from Postman's Park

Nathaniel Wright, District Surveyor for this part of the City.

In 1829 the east end was set back eight feet for the purpose of improving the approach to the new General Post Office in St Martins-le-Grand. Since that time, various internal alterations have been made, especially in 1874 when the present pews, replacing the old box-pews, were installed.

St Botolph's ceased to be a parish church in 1954, the parish being divided between that of St Giles, Cripplegate and St Bartholomew-the-Great, Smithfield. Instead, it became a Guild Church, and was until recently the Servicing Centre of the Industrial Chaplaincy of the Diocese of London.

Exterior

The brown brick exterior (grey stucco at the east end) is formidably plain, only relieved by an engaging wooden cupola at the west end and a Venetian window between coupled Ionic columns, and a pediment with clock, at the east end. However the view from the south-west is greatly helped by the charming little Postman's Park (see Plate No. 12), where there is a Memorial Cloister recording the names of those concerned with little-known acts of heroism. The park is largely made up of the churchyards of St Botolph's, Christ Church, Newgate, and St Leonard's, Foster Lane.

Interior

After the dull exterior, going inside is an exciting surprise, for the interior is a well-preserved structure of the late 18th century, with coffered apses constructed inside the walls at each end and a charming organ gallery curving forward in elegant manner. The yellowish-brown of the marbling in the sanctuary and of the nave piers/columns is offset by the delightful Wedgwood blue of the beautiful plaster ceiling.

High lunette clerestory windows are cut into the barrel-vaulted nave in the same manner as at All Hallows', London Wall. Square piers support galleries on the north and south sides, below which are delicate plaster friezes. At gallery level, the piers change to columns, with gilded capitals supporting entablatures, above which rises the ceiling with its decoration of large plaster rosettes resembling flattened Prince of Wales feathers.

The half-domed east end apse is coloured blue and gold whilst, below the fine window (see *Stained glass*), are sanctuary panels of the four Evangelists.

Extra seating round the side walls is fitted with cast-iron screens below.

A vestry in the south-east corner has been converted into a small chapel.

Furnishings

Organ The organ in a case standing on Ionic pillars was made by Samuel Green in 1778. It was rebuilt and added to in the 19th century.

Pulpit This is a fine hexagonal late 18th century example of simple design in inlaid mahogany supported on a pedestal in the form of a palm tree. The former sounding board was given by a previous vicar to St Paul's Cathedral.

Stained glass The east end window is a unique work of 1788 in the form of a transparency by James Pierson after a picture by Nathaniel Clarkson, representing the Agony in the Garden, with the rare feature of moulded plaster curtains coloured purple enfolding it.

Many of the other windows, including two smaller works of Pierson, were destroyed by 1939–45 bombing. The post-war glass on the south side, by M. C. Farrar-Bell, depicts various events in the history of the church and surrounding district, including the original confirmation of patronage on the Dean of the Priory of St Martin's-le-Grand (see *History*).

Altar-rails and tables The rails are Victorian, but the table in the chancel decorated with Jacobean arches underneath dates from 1639. The Chippendale table in the sanctuary was used in its place between 1787 and 1872.

Monuments

Many survive from the old church.

Lady Anne Packington A recessed table-tomb in the south-east corner with panelled coving commemorates this noted benefactress of her day. At the back are brass figures of herself, husband and child. The inscription, incised and painted black, red and gold, records that her husband, Sir Joseph, was 'Chirographer' (nearest modern equivalent might be 'conveyancer') of the Court of the Common Pleas. The monument dates from 1563.

Anne Branch, died 1611. By the side of the Junior Warden's pew under the organ gallery there is a brass to Anne Branch.

Elizabeth Smith, who died in 1750 at the age of 15. The monument by L. F. Roubiliac is a cameo bust and has a simple epitaph.

Zachariah Foxall Near the entrance door is a monument to Zachariah Foxall who died in 1758. Putti hold a medallion and behind is an obelisk.

Catherine Mary Meade, who died at the age of 21 in 1791, the daughter of George Meade of Philadelphia. According to the inscription, she was 'transferred from Pennsylvania's friendly coast' to die on 'Albion's sea-girt shore'.

Associations
John and Charles Wesley On the gateway of the churchyard is a tablet commemorating the conversion of John and Charles Wesley in Aldersgate Street in 1738 when John felt his heart 'strangely warmed'—an event which led to the great Wesleyan Revival Movement.

Ironmongers' Company and *Plaisterers' (Plasterers) Company* St Botolph's is the Guild Church of these two Livery Companies.

Post Office Rifles The Roll of Honour of the 8th Battalion, City of London Regiment (the Post Office Rifles) is kept in a case with a glass top, affixed to the end of the choir-stalls, and a memorial tablet is placed against the column nearest the font on the north side of the chancel.

General
There can be few contrasts more striking in City churches than that between the stark, barrack-like dullness of the exterior and the delightful late 18th century atmosphere of the interior.

11 St Botolph's, Aldgate

Dedication
Very little is known about this Saxon abbot who died in 655 AD. His name has come to be associated with travel of which he became the patron saint.

In order that those on a journey could pray on arrival at and departure from London, no less than four churches situated near gates to the City have been dedicated to this English 'St Christopher'. One at Billingsgate has disappeared, but the other three (Bishopsgate, Aldersgate and Aldgate) remain.

History
The earliest reference to a church here is 1125. This first building, of which the foundation goes back to Saxon times, was enlarged in 1418 but completely replaced in Tudor times. Brewer's drawing of Aldgate as it was in Henry VIII's reign shows a building with a handsome tower crowned by flying arches supporting a small

St Botolph's, Aldgate

lantern and spirelet like the pre-Fire St Mary-le-Bow; it also had three gables of equal height as seen today in Kent and Cornwall. The drawing shows what an animated scene the area round the church must have presented. It lay just outside Ald (old) Gate, inside which stretched the great Holy Trinity Priory of Augustinian Canons, the most important monastic building in London after Westminster Abbey and to which St Botolph's church belonged. The road traversed the east courtyard of the priory and there was a constant traffic of travellers in and out of London. A Canon from Holy Trinity conducted the services of the church until the former was dissolved in 1531.

Although St Botolph's escaped the Great Fire, it later fell into decay and the church that we see today was erected in its place by the architect of the Mansion House, George Dance the elder, and consecrated in 1744.

Considerable alterations were made by the Westminster Cathedral architect, J. F. Bentley, in 1889. Despite receiving a severe shaking in the 1914–18 War and having a bomb which did not explode through the roof in the 1939-45 War, the church survived, only to be badly damaged by a fire in 1966. This has been made good by Rodney Tatchell, and the interior greatly improved and enriched.

The parish of St Botolph includes the former parish of Holy Trinity Minories, the two being united after Holy Trinity was closed in 1899. Originally the latter was the place of worship of the 'Poor Clares' or 'Sorories Minores', who gave their name to the Minories.

Exterior

The church is one of three in London which are aligned south to north instead of west to east. It is of red brick with stone dressings and on three sides there are Venetian windows. The tower rises on the south or entrance side and is completed with a pierced obelisk type of spire; there are domed entrances on each side. The façade of the fabric proper has a pediment, thus separating it from the tower. The building lies in a small churchyard.

Interior

To reach the nave one passes through the octagonal baptistery. This is an attractive addition after the 1966 fire; with glass doors at each end it now contains the font and some of the more interesting monuments.

The nave has aisles on each side which are under low sloping galleries supported by square pillars. One enters under another gallery at the south end. All have high balustrades. The interior space is comfortably and attractively furnished but the 19th century figured ceiling in a mauve colour by Bentley does not mix well with the 18th century architecture of Dance and one may perhaps wish that the plaster standing angels with their shields in the coving and the bands of square boss-like leaves were not so obtrusive.

The chancel is attractively furnished although the east window is highly coloured.

A reading area has been fitted out in the eastern part of the north (ritual) aisle.

Furnishings

St Botolph's is fortunate in its decorous furnishings and contains an organ and a piece of wood-carving of exceptional interest in the east aisle.

Font Now in the new baptistery. Dating from the 18th century, it is circular and has an attractive octagonal domed cover.

Organ The original Renatus Harris instrument, given by Thomas Whiting to 'the hole Parrish' in 1676, and therefore particularly notable.

*Wooden Carving Probably the outstanding feature of this church is the 'sumptuous' carving on the east wall, brought here from the destroyed St Mary Matfelon, Whitechapel. It shows King David, surrounded by musical instruments. It is in high relief and in the Grinling Gibbons tradition.

Pews A nice feature with their scrolled arms.

Pulpit The oak pulpit dating from about 1745 is plain but has interesting inlaid panels with various symbolic designs.

Altar-rails The fine gilt wrought-iron altar-rails are decorated with a winged angel on the gate. Others of this material are at St Magnus the Martyr, St Mary Woolnoth and Holy Sepulchre.

St Botolph's, Aldgate. King David wood-carving

Reredos By Bentley, and handsomely adorned with pilasters and Corinthian columns. There is more gilt decoration.

Stained glass The theme of the highly-coloured east window is Rubens' 'Descent from the Cross'.

Monuments
Thomas Lord Darcy and Sir Nicholas Carew On the north-east side of the baptistery is the monument to the two Catholics executed by Henry VIII for rebellion—Thomas Lord Darcy and Sir Nicholas Carew—together with members of their families. The memorial is in the form of a recumbent, emaciated figure between Corinthian columns, and dates from 1560–70.

Robert Dowe In the south-east corner is the Robert Dowe monument which has been re-coloured. It shows his bust with 'Geneva' cap in a niche and dates from 1612 (repaired 1675).

Sir John Cass In the opposite corner, there is the bust of Alderman Sir John Cass (1661–1718) whose schools and Foundation still work closely with the church.

William Symington Inside the church, under the south gallery, is a tablet to William Symington, who constructed the *Charlotte Dundas*, the first steamboat that could be put to practical use. But the invention was not taken up and he died in poverty.

Benjamin Pratt Another tablet commemorates Benjamin Pratt who 'affected to end his days in celibacy' and died 3rd May 1715.

Incumbents
Amongst the incumbents were:
Thomas Bray, who founded the Society for Promotion of Christian Knowledge (SPCK) and the Society for Propagation of the Gospel (SPG).

George Appleton, who became Archbishop of Jerusalem.

Associations
Chaucer lived in the parish in 1374.

Edmund Spenser was born there about 1552.

Daniel Defoe was married in St Botolph's and has left a harrowing description of the Great Plague of 1665, when over 5,000 victims were buried in two pits dug in the churchyard.

Duke of Suffolk After execution, the head of the Duke of Suffolk (Lady Jane Grey's father) was brought to Holy Trinity, Minories, and, when this church was united to St Botolph's, the head was removed to the churchyard and can no longer be seen.

General

St Botolph's still lies on a frontier between Inner and Outer London, between the bowler-hats of the City and the small shops of the East End. Many of its parishioners today are Jewish and St Botolph's is the headquarters of the Diocesan Council for Christian/Jewish understanding. It conducts in one half of the crypt a mission for homeless men, who are given food, hot baths, haircuts and discarded clothing when available. The other half is a club for local Asian boys.

St Botolph's is a place of worship cared for and caring, and the feeling that it gives on entering is one of warmth and welcome.

12 St Botolph's without Bishopsgate

Dedication

St Botolph's is one of three London churches, all outside the old City gates, which are dedicated to this Saxon abbot who became the patron saint of travellers. The church was beyond Bishopsgate, hence the name given of St Botolph's Without. A fourth St Botolph's (Billingsgate) was destroyed during the Great Fire.

History

During the building of the present place of worship, the foundations of the original church, which may have been erected by the Saxon bishop Erkenwald, were uncovered but the earliest mention of a church on this site was in 1212 when it was called 'Sci Botulfi exa Bissopeg'.

In 1247 land north of St Botolph's was given to found the Priory of St Mary of Bethlehem; this was converted after the Suppression into the Bethlehem Hospital for Lunatics (Bedlam).

At one time, an anchoress (female hermit) was attached to the church; she received 40s a year from the Sheriffs of the City.

In Elizabeth's reign the building adjoined the town ditch but, the historian Stow adds, was 'inclosed with a comely wall of brick'.

Although surviving the Great Fire, the building later became ruinous and was demolished in 1724. A new church was erected at a cost of £10,400 by James Gold and consecrated in 1728.

No less than seven restorations have been carried out since but St Botolph's, except for the destruction of the west windows, survived the air-raids of the 1939–45 War. During the Victorian period, the numbers of parishioners increased so much that a daughter church—All Saints, Skinner Street, (demolished in the 1860s)—had

St Botolph's, Bishopsgate. Steeple from south-east

to be built and towards the end of the 19th century the living was considered to be one of the richest in London if not of the whole country.

The parish hall to the west of St Botolph's was built in 1861, in the same style as the church. It is sometimes used by the Fan Makers' Company. The charming charity children in Coade stone came from an earlier building.

Exterior

St Botolph's is exceptional in having a tower at the east end. Being the principal façade towards Bishopsgate, this has been given a handsome stone face, decorated with coupled Doric pilasters, frieze and pediment. The sides are more modestly built of brick and have two tiers of windows. The square tower with gallery is crowned with a circular cupola, ogee cap and urn.

Interior

The interior, surrounded by galleries on three sides, has a coved ceiling and tall plastered Corinthian columns on oak plinths which stand above the Victorian pews. The frequent restorations have altered the original character but the insertion of a dome with lantern in 1828 has helped to lighten an interior which would otherwise be dark. Aisles and galleries are in classic style.

The 1878 restoration led to the remodelling of the chancel, which has marble panels on the walls. The east window dates from 1869. The south-east chapel is the memorial chapel of the Honourable Artillery Company (HAC).

The aisle vaults are nicely tricked out with crowns and mitres whilst, at the base of the galleries, the names of every incumbent back to 1323 are inscribed in gold lettering—an interesting variant to the usual list on a board. A quotation from Hebrews VII 23–24 underlines our temporary state and the permanence of Christ: 'And they truly were many priests, because they were not suffered to continue by reason of death: But this man, because he continueth ever, hath an unchangeable priesthood'.

The chancel arch is decorated with medallions of roses.

Furnishings

Pulpit and Lectern St Botolph's retains its original pulpit and lectern. The pulpit has a staircase with nicely turned balusters. The lectern has console feet and is embellished with cherubs and plaques.

Organ The organ was first erected in 1764 but was rebuilt in 1912.

Monument
Sir Paul Pindar A plain tablet above the staircase leading to the
north gallery commemorates Sir Paul Pindar, one of the church's
most famous parishioners, who was British Ambassador to Turkey
in 1611 and was buried here in 1650. The façade of his house in
Bishopsgate was moved to the Victoria and Albert Museum in
South Kensington.

Associations
Edward Alleyn, founder of Dulwich College, was baptised in the
church in 1566.
    John Keats, the poet, was baptised in the church in 1795.
    John Cornwell A memorial cross honours John Cornwell, of HMS
Chester, whose heroic conduct at the Battle of Jutland in 1916
earned him a posthumous VC.
    London Rifle Brigade This famous brigade is remembered by a
tablet in the south aisle and a Book of Remembrance below.

General
Although built only 20 years earlier than its companion at the other
end of Houndsditch, St Botolph's without Bishopsgate is not at all
the same architecturally. The Bishopsgate place of worship is
stately, the Aldgate church more homely, but both provide warmth
of welcome and are part of the rich repertoire that London has to
offer the lover of churches.

13 St Bride's, Fleet Street

Dedication
Until the beginning of the 19th century St Bride's was referred to as
St Bridget's. This is the only church in London dedicated to her.
    She was born about 453 AD and is second in fame amongst Irish
saints only to St Patrick with whom she was almost contemporary.
She founded the first Irish nunnery at Kildare. Amongst miraculous
powers, she is credited with changing well water into beer.

History
Nowhere else in London can one follow more closely the
development of a church from its earliest beginnings. It is possible
that this was the first place in the capital where Christ was
worshipped. This building lasted until the 10th century, when it was
replaced by another, possibly because the earlier church had been

destroyed by the Danes. Fire in 1135 may have swept this later building away, for it was followed by yet another building, which had an impressive tower from which rang one of London's four curfew bells. In this church the Curia Regis, principal court of the realm, was held in 1205 and, in 1210, King John granted a charter there.

Church number four was erected in the 15th century and it was here that St Bride's long association with printing and the press began. Many prelates had settled outside the walls between the City and Westminster because land there was cheaper and they trusted that their spiritual station would protect them from the risks of violence run by rich merchants. The clergy at that time had almost a monopoly of literacy and, therefore, they were the printers' best customers. William Caxton lived, died and was buried in Westminster but his Alsatian apprentice, Wynkyn de Worde, who acquired the press, brought it to a place alongside St Bride's and made a commercial proposition of it. Wynkyn was buried in St Bride's.

The 15th century place of worship lasted until the Great Fire. St Bride's was in the thick of it and virtually nothing was saved. As so often in the City, Wren came on the scene and between the years 1670 and 1675 designed the building we see today, one of the earliest to be rebuilt by him. The famous tower and wedding-cake spire followed in 1701–3. Victorian attentions were confined to the decoration of the sanctuary by Basil Champneys and the installation of new glass in the east window. The church was gutted by incendiaries in December 1940 but structurally was restored to its previous state and rededicated in 1957. Considerable changes, however, were made to the furnishings, principally with the substitution of open collegiate-type seating for the old box-pews and the removal of the galleries.

All this is most imaginatively displayed in an exhibition housed in the crypt, which alone makes a visit worthwhile. Survivals of tesselated pavement and walls from Roman times can be seen and the many and varied links with newspapermen and notable residents are also shown.

Exterior
St Bride's is hemmed in on all sides and the celebrated steeple can only be enjoyed from a distance. The main entrance is approached along a little alley from Fleet Street. The well from which Bridewell took its name was in the south-east corner of the crypt, but is now dried up.

*Although perhaps not reaching the architectural heights of St

Mary-le-Bow's steeple, the one at St Bride's, despite being struck three times by lightning, which in one case led to eight feet being taken off it, exceeds it in actual height measurement (226 feet). Without the variety of forms which at St Mary-le-Bow carries one easily from stage to stage, nevertheless the series of diminishing octagons with open arches and pilasters, whilst repetitive, is full of subtleties. The top stage, for instance, has square and not round-headed openings. As Sir John Summerson points out, although the arches and pilasters get smaller as one mounts, the pedestals get taller, and musical and bell-pealing analogies have been drawn from the various proportions, so that it is not without reason that William Henley described it as 'a madrigal in stone'. The belfry stage, moreover, is skilfully and beautifully designed.

Interior
Here, the post-war changes are strikingly evident and, although some may regret the loss of the Wren furnishings, there is a freshness and brightness which give an air of vitality. Structurally, the restorations by Godfrey Allen have been faithful to the old and we can see again the Tuscan columns (coupled sideways rather than lengthwise) and the tunnel vault with penetrations for the clerestory windows as they were, newly decorated with gilded rosettes in panels along the transverse arches of the ceiling and the nave arcades. Furthermore the view westwards is no longer impeded by the organ and we can now see 'Wren' vistas which have been hidden for nearly 300 years, including the old minstrels' gallery. A splendid free-standing oak reredos dominates the view looking eastwards with a *trompe-l'oeil* mural above making the flat wall resemble an apse; all by Glyn Jones.

Large figures of St Bride and St Paul by David McFall are perched above the entrance piers.

The floor consists of black marble from Belgium and white from Italy.

Furnishings
Charity children Many pairs of charity children which used to be placed outside schools are to be seen in London (e.g. the charming pair in Coade stone outside the parish hall of St Botolph's, Bishopsgate). The St Bride's pair in the south-west corner used to stand outside the Bridewell Hospital, formerly the Bridewell Palace.

Royal Arms The Royal Arms, in the balustrading of the minstrels' gallery, are carved in a single block of Beer (Devon) stone weighing nearly two tons.

Stalls The modern, open stalls are finely carved and given emphasis by the large screens behind with massive Corinthian piers, supporting an entablature divided at regular intervals by round-headed pediments carrying shields.

*Reredos This memorial to the Pilgrim Fathers (Edward Winslow, one of the leaders, was a parishioner) has coupled Corinthian columns and carries eight flambeaux above. On the reredos is an oil painting of the Crucifixion, above which is an oval stained-glass panel of Christ in Glory.

Associations

As at St Margaret's, Westminster, the associations of St Bride's are too numerous to mention in detail. It was the first church to use the Book of Common Prayer; over 2,000 parishioners died from the Plague; Samuel Pepys, as well as his eight brothers and sisters, was christened in St Bride's; Dryden, Milton, Izaak Walton, Johnson, Boswell, Garrick, Joshua Reynolds, Goldsmith, Burke, Addison, Pope, Hogarth and Mrs Siddons all lived within 100 yards of the church. Later, Charles Lamb, Wordsworth, Keats and William Hazlitt came to this area whilst today the associations with the Press as recorded on the stalls and on many new and restored memorials are legion.

It must also be added that the parents of Edward Winslow, one of the leaders of the Pilgrim Fathers and three times Governor of Plymouth, Massachusetts, were married in St Bride's and he himself was a boy apprentice in Fleet Street. Perhaps the most significant incident, in view of what followed, was the argument between King George III and Benjamin Franklin over what form of lightning conductor to use after the spire had been struck by lightning in 1764. George III had called in Benjamin Franklin to advise him and the latter had recommended pointed ends. The King insisted on blunt ends which led to comments about 'good, blunt, honest King George' and 'those sharp-witted colonists'.

A plaque installed by the Overseas Press Club of America commemorates American journalists who have died on overseas service.

The University of Southern Illinois has a broken angel, retrieved from a former St Bride's church after it was destroyed, incorporated into one of its buildings.

John Taylor, who became vicar in 1543, named 'Cardmaker', was burned at the stake at Smithfield on 30th September 1555 for opposing the Catholic reaction under Queen Mary.

William Rich (1755–1811) came to London as apprentice to a pastry cook at 3 Ludgate Hill and married his master's daughter. Rich achieved fame in his business, not least for the wedding cakes modelled on St Bride's steeple which he could see from his window. One secret was the use of the best French brandy, 'even when it cost one guinea a bottle'.

Bridewell Sermon In 1959, an annual service was revived to receive the Bridewell Governors and children into the City. It is held on the second Tuesday of March and includes a sermon, which has come to be known as the 'Bridewell Sermon'.

General

As Prebendary Dewi Morgan, the author of the outstanding guide to St Bride's, to which I am much indebted, has written—'Nothing like' the relationship between print and the Church 'exists between the Church and any other of the business and professional groups which have such deep roots in London'. There is constant and daily contact between the institutions of our daily newspapers and St Bride's Church; gifts from prominent members such as the glass doors given by the Press Association, the wrought-iron gates erected by the Newspaper Society and the exhibition in the crypt given by Sir Max Aitken provide visual evidence of this and the many services for the Press and its members maintain the close contact. 'Today' in the exchange of news—to quote Dewi Morgan again—'St Bride's is parish pump to the whole world'.

N.B.: Further Reading: *Phoenix of Fleet Street* by Dewi Morgan.

14 St Clement's, Eastcheap

Dedication

St Clement was a 'fellow-labourer' of St Paul and was the third Bishop of Rome after Peter. Victim of Roman persecution in 100 AD and cast into the sea with an anchor round his neck, he became the patron saint of sailors.

Eastcheap, until King William Street and the approach to London Bridge was opened up, used to run further west and the church was on the street instead of being tucked round the corner in Clement Lane.

History

St Clement's appears in a charter of 1067, confirming grants of livings by William the Conqueror to Westminster Abbey. This may not be authentic, the first known rector being Stephen de Southlee (about 1308), but the abbot held the living throughout the mediaeval period. In the 13th century, the church was called 'St Clement Candlewickstrate'.

In 1349, a Lady Chapel was added.

This church, which Stow (the Elizabethan) commented was 'a very small church', was one of the first to be consumed in the Great Fire, being only a few yards from where it started in Pudding Lane, but the Wren rebuilding was a fairly late one of 1683–7.

In 1834 there was a proposal to demolish St Clement's which was defeated, but in 1872 William Butterfield ran amok in it; in Elizabeth and Wayland Young's graphic words 'he underwent a crise de nerfs'. Apart from the usual disfigurements, 'he tore apart the lovely triple altar-piece, flinging the two wings of the triptych on to side walls and leaving the centre mean and pointless where it was'. The reredos, which Sir Ninian Comper put in its place in 1933, is a doubtful asset, but some of the harm was corrected in 1936 when the organ, after reconstruction, was restored to its old position.

In 1925 the ceiling was taken down, the replacement being modelled on the previous one.

Relatively unscathed from the 1939–45 War there was further work in 1949–50 and redecoration in 1968.

Exterior
Very retiring and unassuming. The west front is stuccoed except for the upper parts of the south-west tower where the brick is exposed. The tower follows the curve of the street and is therefore on a different plane from the rest. It is unadorned except for a balustrade and stone quoins.

Interior
Lofty in proportion to the size of this small church, none of the walls are regular. As a result, the south aisle tapers inwards from west to east; it is separated from the main body by two tall Corinthian columns on high pedestals painted a rather incongruous blue. The clerestory on each side has small segmental-headed windows, those on the north with indifferent glass and the others clear. The walls are panelled to a height of $8\frac{1}{2}$ feet.

The most attractive feature structurally is the ceiling, flat with a large oblong in the centre and squares at the corners and made most ornamental with its plaster wreath of fruit and flowers in gilt panel. It has a red and gilded cornice.

Furnishings

Organ   Originally Renatus Harris, still with its front casing but enlarged. When St Clement's was shaken by bombs one night, the rector played 'Rule Britannia' on it the following morning.

Font   The octagonal marble font is 17th century and has a very pretty cover enclosing a dove holding an olive branch and capped with gilded flames (no doubt as a reminder of the Fire). It is said that the great 19th century statesman, William Gladstone, liked it so much that he brought his friends and grandchildren to see it.

Bread-shelves   On the south wall is an example of the 'dole' cupboards used for distributing bread to the poor according to specific benefactions. The Royal Arms on the cupboard are Stuart.

Doorcase   A finely-carved doorcase with broken segmental-headed pediment and decorated with cherubs' heads lies in the north-east corner.

Pulpit   An exceptionally fine and large example with a very big tester. Adorned with standing cherubs and swags, it is hexagonal, of Norwegian oak and has oval panels.

Reredos   The Comper reredos consists of three main sections each enclosed with two Corinthian fluted columns, the outer pair pedimented and the main central section segment-headed. These heads alternate with smaller pediments (two in the centre section) and segment heads below. The four panels depict the Annunciation (outer pair), St Clement, wearing the papal tiara and with anchor, and St Martin of Tours (inner pair).

Although this fine piece of craftmanship might appear well in a Mediterranean setting, it does not harmonise with the furnishings of a 17th century place of worship nor, it is safe to say, would Wren have approved of such an injection of colour.

Associations

Lovers of St Clement's claim that this is the 'Oranges and Lemons' church on the grounds that this was a rhyme for City churches only and that the mediaeval orange market was on the steps of London Bridge near the wharf where the Spanish oranges were unloaded. It seems, however, that St Clement Danes may have established the stronger claim.

General

St Clement's, the church of Candlewickward, is the smallest parish church in the City. The conflict between the colour of the reredos and of the columns with the decorous furnishings may disturb but this does not diminish the quality of the latter.

The church of St Martin Orgar was not rebuilt after the Fire and the parish was joined to St Clement's, Eastcheap. ('Orgar' may refer to Ordgarus the Dane, in which case it is interesting that two churches at the opposite ends of Old London Bridge had Danish dedications, the one on the south side being St Olave, Tooley Street.) The tower remained but was replaced by a curious brick construction in 1852–3 which can still be seen in Martin Lane (off Cannon Street) nearby, with its wooden clock dated 1853 on a bracket.

5 **St Dunstan in the East** (Ruin)

Dedication
St Dunstan was Archbishop of Canterbury in the 10th century and did much to restore monastic life after the Danish raids. Amongst his many skills, he was musician, manuscript illuminator and metal-worker.

History
The mediaeval church was one of the wealthiest in the City. In 1632, the walls were repaired in Portland stone and these stood up to the Great Fire. Wren therefore had only to rebuild the tower and spire and, in 1697 (or possibly earlier), showing his great versatility, erected one of striking originality and grace, only exceeded in height in the City by the dome of St Paul's Cathedral. Flying arches support the spire on the principle used at the pre-Fire church of St Mary-le-Bow and at Newcastle-on-Tyne and Edinburgh Cathedrals.

Small stepped buttresses are placed at the base of the spire. The tower has tracery in the upper windows and large pinnacles at the corners; broad horizontal divisions break it up into stages. The south and west doorways have crocketed hood-moulds.

In the Regency period, the walls were found to be out of true and the rest of the church was rebuilt by the architect David Laing between 1817 and 1821 in Georgian Perpendicular style, an early example of the Gothic Revival.

St Dunstan's was gutted in the 1939–45 War and has been left as a ruin to show what the City suffered. The walls, however, have been encased in cement, the mullions of the windows restored, Wren's railings made good and the whole laid out most imaginatively as a garden with trees and shrubs, flower-beds and a fountain. This won a Landscape Heritage Award in European Architectural Heritage Year (1975).

General
The tower houses a private chapel for the vicar of All Hallows by
the Tower whose residence is alongside. The bells now ring out from
a winery over the Napa Valley in California, USA.

16 **St Dunstan in the West**

Dedication
Churches dedicated to St Dunstan occur at opposite ends of the
City, although only the steeple and walls of St Dunstan in the East
near the Tower remain. It was St Dunstan who, as the powerful
Abbot of Glastonbury, did so much to restore monastic life after the
Danish raids of the 9th century and later became Archbishop of
Canterbury.

History
It is probable that a Saxon church existed here because Lanfranc,
the first Norman Archbishop of Canterbury, forbade dedications to
Saxon saints for new churches.

The mediaeval church—first mentioned in the 1180s—passed
from monastic hands to the Crown in 1237 but reverted to monastic
control in 1386 when the Rectory of St Dunstan was bestowed on
the Abbey of Alnwick in Northumberland to compensate for the
loss of property caused by Scottish raids over the border. This
continued until 1536 when, at the Dissolution of the Monasteries,
the patronage once more passed to the Crown.

The building was considerably altered in 1701 when the nave
arcades were removed and a flat roof replaced the previous arched
one, so that the interior became an open panelled rectangle, with a
large pulpit next to the altar at the east end as focal point. These
alterations appear to have weakened the structure, so that it was
found necessary to pull down the old church and build in 1829–33
the present one on a site further to the north to permit of road
widening.

During the early part of the 19th century, an additional church—
St Thomas in the Liberty of the Rolls—was erected to cater for the
growing population, which now accounted for 12,000 parishioners.
This was pulled down in 1886.

Damaged in 1944 when the lantern of the tower was set alight
with incendiaries, the church was restored in 1950.

Today, St Dunstan's no longer has parish status, but in 1952
became a Guild Church concerned with the work of the Church of

St Dunstan in the West

England Council on Foreign Relations. One of the chapels has been made over to the Rumanian Orthodox congregation who brought in from Rumania the ornate screen to the west of the chancel.

Exterior

The building, which—like St Botolph's, Aldgate and St Edmund the King, Lombard Street—is orientated north and south, is octagonal in design. The tower, with its clock on a massive and elaborate bracket and, further to the right, the statue of Queen Elizabeth, makes an arresting group when viewed from across Fleet Street. The architect, John Shaw, died twelve days after the outer walls were finished but his work was appreciated to the extent of a commemorative tablet being placed over the south door by grateful parishioners: a rare tribute.

The stone tower is on the south side—the rest of the building is constructed of brick and is modelled on the tower of All Saints Pavement at York. It has long unglazed Perpendicular windows in the upper part, forming a lantern, and a straight top with pinnacles.

The statue of Queen Elizabeth, together with the figures of King Lud and his two sons below in the vestry porch, comes from the west wall of Lud Gate which was pulled down in 1760. Dating from 1586, it is probably one of the oldest representations in stone of the great Queen.

Clock

The clock, with its gold and black bracket, was made by Thomas Harrys in 1671 for £35. When the old church was pulled down, the Marquis of Hertford moved the clock to his villa in Regent's Park, which took its name of St Dunstan's Lodge from the church. This house eventually passed into the possession of Sir Arthur Pearson, the founder of St Dunstan's Organization for the Blind. The clock was returned to the church in 1936 by Viscount Rothermere. The way in which the two giants strike out at the bells and turn their heads at the sounding of the hours and quarters is similar to the action of the figures in the clock at St Mark's Square, Venice. It was the first clock in London to have a minute hand.

Interior

The octagonal interior is a surprise in London. The building is not centrally planned with an altar or pulpit in the middle, but there are seven recesses and the chancel and altar are placed in the north bay. The recesses are vaulted.

Furnishings

Screen The richly decorated icon screen, designed and painted at the beginning of the 18th century, shuts off the Rumanian Orthodox chapel from the rest of the church; it came from the Antim monastery in Bucharest and was installed in 1966.

Stained glass The north-west window, which can be glimpsed through the screen, is by Kempe and depicts Izaak Walton, the angler, and the subjects of his 'Lives'. He held the offices of 'Scavenger, Quistman and Sidesman' in St Dunstan's from 1629 to 1644.

The north window is a reconstruction after the air-raid damage, although the upper lights containing dark reds and blues by Henry Williment survive. The main lights depict four famous church leaders of the Saxon and early Norman period—St Dunstan, Lanfranc, Anselm and Stephen Langton. St Dunstan, according to the legend associated with him, is seizing the devil by the nose with his hot tongs; the devil had come to tempt him whilst he was making a golden chalice for his church.

A window on the west side commemorates John Fisher who was burned at the stake under Henry VIII.

Altar and Reredos These are early 17th century in Flemish flamboyant style from Antwerp; they are elaborately carved in oak and have canopies. The altar-rails are made from fragments of 17th century pierced carving from old stalls.

Organ Frequently altered, it still contains some material from the Renatus Harris organ of 1677. The organists included Frederick Oakeley, who translated and wrote the music for 'Adeste fideles'.

Monuments

Many monuments from the old church remain. These include:

Henry and Elizabeth (died 1530) Dacres A brass shows them both kneeling with labels protruding from their mouths.

Gerard Legh Died 1563. The well-made tablet is flanked by standing figures and there is a long Latin inscription.

Hoare family The banking family of Hoare is remembered by a tablet of 1725 to Sir Richard and more substantially with a sarcophagus on the east wall (1754) to another Sir Richard who, while Lord Mayor of London, presented in 1745 the wrought-iron sword-rest which is placed in front of the pews. The Hoare vault is below. This family have provided churchwardens since the second Sir Richard's death.

Edward James Auriol Drowned in the river Rhone in 1847 at the age of 17. A white marble bust showing him lying on a pillow as if asleep is placed in an arched recess apart from the memorial.

Hobson Judkin A touching inscription commemorates 'The Honest Solicitor. Who departed this Life June 30 1812'. and adds 'This Tablet was erected by his clients as a token of gratitude and respect for his honest, faithful and friendly conduct to them through Life. Go reader and imitate Hobson Judkin.'

Associations

William Tyndale Translator of the Bible was curate here.

Dr John Donne Donne, whilst Dean of St Paul's Cathedral, held the living between 1624 and 1631, the year of his death.

Heads of Tyndale and Donne can be seen on the west and east sides of the entrance arch.

Rachel Walton Rachel, the first wife of Izaak Walton, was buried in St Dunstan's in 1640.

American pioneer ancestors A framed list on a rear pew records famous names associated with American history:

Thomas West, Baron de la Warre, was married in St Dunstan's in 1596. He was a member of the Virginia Company and became first Governor of the State of Virginia in 1610. Delaware Bay, River and State are named after him.

George Calvert, 1st Lord Baltimore, was buried here in 1632. He promoted a charter for the foundation of the state of Maryland. The colony was started by his eldest son, Cecil, who became the 2nd Lord Baltimore. The City of Baltimore is named after him.

Lawrence Washington was buried in St Dunstan's in 1617. His sister Anne and brother, also Lawrence, who was first Governor of Maryland, were baptised here in 1621 and 1622 respectively. They were ancestors of George Washington.

Charles Dickens St Dunstan's eight bells were the chimes of Dickens's 'Christmas Carol'.

'Praise God' Barebones Barebones, after whom 'Barebones' Parliament was named, was parish constable and married in the church in 1648.

Samuel Pepys Pepys records in his Diary how he made a pass at a young lady sitting near him during Divine Service, but was repulsed with a hat-pin.

General

Although just within the City boundaries, St Dunstan's is far removed in style from a typical Wren City church. Lantern tower, clock and Queen Elizabeth statue, familiar to Fleet Street journalists and Temple lawyers alike, combine with its octagonal interior to make it a highly individual building distinct from any other London church.

7 St Edmund the King, Lombard Street

Dedication
Born in Saxony about 840 AD, Edmund became King of East Anglia in 855 at the age of fifteen. He was defeated in battle by the invading Danes in 870 and, refusing to deny his Christian faith or to treat with his opponents, he was tied to a tree, used as an archery target and finally beheaded at Hoxne, Suffolk. The great mediaeval Abbey of Bury St Edmunds grew up over the burial place of his remains.

The church of St Edmund the King is the only one now dedicated to him in the City of London.

History
Most of the early history is surmise. Records show that Matilda, the wife of Henry I, bestowed the living on the Priory of Holy Trinity, Aldgate and that in 1150 'Daniel the Priest' was rector. At this time, known as St Edmund Grasschurch, it stood in the London grass market established for the sale of hay, herbs and vegetables. Other than this, nothing is known of the mediaeval church which probably had a shrine dedicated to St Edmund. The building was destroyed in the Great Fire.

There is some doubt as to whether Wren himself or his surveyor assistant, Robert Hooke, designed in whole or in part the new church; also whether the north/south orientation was due to the exigencies of the site or the desire—as Gerald Cobb suggests—to capitalise from the sale of leases on the west and east sides. The demand for space was illustrated in later years by part of the small frontage on one side of the entrance door being let for a gunsmith's shop and part on the other side being used as a shed to house the parish fire engine. Work on the post-Fire building lasted from 1670 to 1676, the spire following and being completed in 1706.

Subsequent repairs and alterations were numerous, including fairly gentle treatment by William Butterfield in 1864. St Edmund's was unlucky to be the recipient of a bomb in the 1914–18 War (one of the few churches in the City), which brought the roof down and necessitated its reconstruction. Damage from incendiaries in May 1941 caused the loss of stained glass and, more important, the Queen Anne Royal Arms. Restorations were carried out by Rodney

Tatchell in 1957, who also rebuilt the vestry and enlarged it to provide offices in 1968.

Exterior
St Edmund's narrow stone frontage is divided into three bays with arched windows and quoins, the centre pedimented tower bay slightly projecting. The windows have cherub's head keystones and are surmounted (the main entrance door also) by a horizontal lintel supported on console brackets.

The parapet of the tower, which has a prominent cornice, is embellished with urns and pineapples. Above is a lead lantern and concave spire capped by gilded ball and vane. The whole steeple is a most agreeable composition made more satisfying by the way in which the belfry stage of the tower is linked Italian-fashion by concave side pieces to the corners, which are decorated with large urns. At one time there were four more urns at the base of the spire and eight further up—a sad loss.

A handsome clock projects on a bracket.

Interior
A plain small rectangle without aisles, which with its richly-decorated and carved furnishings looks, as commented by T. Francis Bumpus, rather like the private chapel of a nobleman's house. The design is strongly Dutch in character. The ceiling is flat and makes an awkward join with the semi-dome, painted with a figure of Christ over the altar.

The walls have pilasters and are panelled up to a height of eight feet. Arched niches are only penetrated in two places for windows.

At the south end, unusual recessed side galleries with metal rails flank the organ.

Furnishings
Font A small furnishing dating from Wren's time, of good quality and with the unusual feature of having a semi-circular balustrade round it and of being placed in the south-west corner. The cover is decorated with gilded figures of four of the apostles out of the original twelve. (See plates p. 67 and 69).

Organ The organ is also unusual in having its case divided into two, one part at the south end and the other on the west wall. The south end casing came from St Dionis Backchurch (see 'General'). It was originally a Renatus Harris instrument but is much changed. The arms are Stuart Arms.

Churchwardens' Pews There are two high carved churchwardens' pews on each side of the south entrance.

St Edmund the King. Font

Hatchments On the east wall are two hatchments (coats-of-arms in lozenge-shaped frames), one of which in the chancel has the arms of Princess Charlotte, only daughter of the Prince Regent who became George IV.

Fresco On the wall of the vestry hall is an old fresco, depicting a Dominican friar, discovered on the site of St Nicholas Acons church (destroyed in the Great Fire).

Sword-rest Dates from 1753 and was ordered by the church to mark the election of one of their parishioners as Lord Mayor.

Pulpit Without tester but enriched with much fine carving.

Lectern Made up of re-used panelling.

Choir-stalls Enriched with pierced panelling and urns.

Altar-rails The altar-rails have turned balusters of unusual shape.

Communion table The Wren-period Communion table has elaborately carved legs.

Reredos A richly-decorated furnishing with six gilded panels and gilt lettering on a dark red background. The panels contain the Ten Commandments, the Lord's Prayer and the Creed together with figures of Moses and Aaron painted by William Etty in 1833. Behind is a segmental pediment with urns.

Doorcases At the sides of the reredos are two handsome door-cases with broken segmental pediments decorated with urns emitting flames.

Stained glass The strongly-coloured east window was originally intended for St Paul's Cathedral and was made in Munich but objection was taken to the angels being coloured red and it lay in the Cathedral crypt until eventually presented to St Edmund's as a memorial to the Duke of Clarence who died in 1892. (See also Royal Fusiliers in *Associations*.)

Monuments
Dr J. Milles, Dean of Exeter, who died 1784. This marble monument by the elder Bacon is on the east wall and shows the figure of Hope resting on an urn. The memorial also includes Edith, his wife, who died at the age of thirty-five. Dr Milles was rector for forty years.

Rev Studdert Kennedy On the west wall is a wooden tablet to Rev Studdert Kennedy, 'Inspired Preacher, Writer and Poet', who was an army chaplain in the 1914–18 War, nicknamed by the troops 'Woodbine Willie' and rector here from 1921–9.

Charles Melville Hays, President of the American Grand Trunk Railway, who was drowned in the Titanic disaster, is remembered by a brass tablet on the west wall.

A contemporary font of Wren type—in Willen Church, Buckinghamshire for which Robert Hooke was the architect

Associations

Joseph Addison, poet and essayist, was married here to the Dowager Countess of Warwick on 9th August 1716, his next-door neighbour.

German bomb In a glass case on the west wall are fragments of the German bomb which fell at 10.00 am on 7th July 1917 and caused so much damage.

Royal Fusiliers Stained glass 'Victory' window on the east side commemorates this Regiment. Below is a simple battlefield cross with the names of those killed in the 1914–18 War.

General

St Edmund's is a modest church but, like most of the City churches, highly individual. Its steeple makes an attractive addition to Lombard Street and its projecting clock blends well with the banking signs which are so much a feature of this thoroughfare.

After the Great Fire, the parish of St Nicholas Acons (not rebuilt) was joined to St Edmund's. Later additions were St Dionis Backchurch (demolished 1878) and All Hallows Lombard Street (demolished 1938 but tower and furnishings removed to Twickenham) bringing with it St Benet Gracechurch Street (demolished 1867) together with its own parochial attachment, St Leonard Eastcheap (not rebuilt after the Great Fire).

Over and above its parish duties, St Edmund's is engaged in specialised work concerned with Personal Relationships.

18 St Ethelburga-the-Virgin within Bishopsgate

Dedication

St Ethelburga the Virgin was almost certainly the daughter of Offa, the great King of Mercia who ruled from 757 to 796 AD.

This is believed to be the only Anglican church in the whole country with this dedication.

History

The first reference to St Ethelburga's church was in 1250 and the carved quinquefoil (five-lobed leaf) from a canopy in the north wall and the shaft buried in the south wall may have come from this building.

The present church, one of only seven mediaeval places of worship to survive in the City, was built in the first half of the 15th century, although the west window is 14th century. From 1366 until the Dissolution of the Monasteries, patronage was in the hands of the Prioress and Convent of St Helen.

In 1629, a west gallery reserved 'only for the daughters and maidservants of the parish to sit in' was installed. In 1862, presumably because of there no longer being need for such accommodation, this was removed.

Just before the 1914–18 War, a thoroughgoing restoration was carried out and many of the fittings date from that time. Apart from damage to the roof and ceiling, this building's powers of survival carried it through the 1939–45 War.

In February 1954, St Ethelburga's became a Guild Church particularly concerned with the Church's Ministry of Healing and is an independent 'island'—without union of benefices—within the parish of St Helen's nearby.

Exterior

A humble west front—the side walls cannot be seen—is sandwiched between two very large office blocks, creating one of the most striking contrasts in the City. This front is built of bare Kentish ragstone rubble except for the top, which is repaired in brick and is capped with a charming 18th century two-storey turret and weathercock dating from 1671. Until 1932, and in order to provide additional income, two shops were permitted to cling to the wall on each side of the entrance porch (as one sees today in the Netherlands), with later a connecting upper storey which almost completely hid the 14th century window. They dated from 1570 and 1614.

Interior

One is immediately carried back to mediaeval times and given a picture of what London's crowded, small churches used to look like. The interior resembles that of a modest village church and one can hardly realise that Bishopsgate is just outside. On the floor of the porch is a motto, taken from an ancient temple of Aesculapius, which has been let into the pavement and which reads, *Bonus Intra Melior Exi* ('Come in good, go out better'). The interior space consists of panelled nave, clerestory and south aisle, with lancet windows, leading to the chancel and Chapel of St George. The screens separating nave from chancel and chancel from the Chapel, together with the oak gallery at the west end, the refitting of the chancel in oak, paving it in stone, and the reflooring of the porch were all part of the 1912–14 restoration. A door at the south-east corner leads to the vestry room. Despite the fact that there are very few of the old fittings and that all the window tracery except in one place in the west window has been lost, the atmosphere of the church remains unaffected and the gilt colour adds to the pleasure that this tiny interior affords.

Furnishings

The chancel screen with tracery of almost filigree delicacy, and rood-loft above, is the work of Sir Ninian Comper and, although modern, is a great asset to the interior.

The parclose screen also dates from the 1912–14 restoration.

Organ casing Designed by Sir Ninian Comper.

Font The font dates probably from mid or late 18th century. The pillar is decorated with lilies and round the bowl are carved the emblems of the Passion. The delightful ogee-shaped font cover came from St Swithun's, London Stone. On the upper surface, a brass motto in Greek is inlaid round the bowl in the form of a palindrome which translated reads, 'cleanse (my) transgression, not only (my) outward appearances'.

Stained glass The east window, dating from 1871, is by Kempe and includes St Ethelburga but not the one to whom the church is dedicated. The one shown was the daughter of King Ethelbert and Queen Bertha of Kent, who did so much to help St Augustine's mission to England in 597 AD. Of considerable interest are the three windows by Leonard Walker referring to incidents connected with the voyage of Henry Hudson to discover a route to Japan and China via the North Pole. The first, on the south side and the gift of the Hudson Bay Company, shows him and his crew taking Holy Communion at St Ethelburga's on April 19th, 1607 four days before setting out; the second, also on the south side, and the gift of USA citizens, depicts him sailing up the Hudson River; and the third, on the north wall beside the pulpit, donated by British Empire citizens, shows him cast adrift by mutineers. Another window on the north side, also by Leonard Walker, commemorates W. F. Geikie Cobb, who was rector from 1900 to 1941 and much beloved.

The west window has three pieces of 15th century glass.

The heraldic glass in the east window of the Chapel of St George (north of the sanctuary) showing the Arms of the City of London dates from the Restoration period.

Painting The painting alongside the third Hudson window is a rare early 16th century work of the Flemish artist, Peter Coeke van Aelst, showing Christ healing the beggar.

Mural The mural on the east wall, in a rather pale tone, is by Hans Feibusch. It shows in the centre the crucified and risen Christ, on the left St Luke with a patient, and on the right St Ethelburga talking to children. It was completed in 1962.

Associations
Sir Henry Hudson See *Stained glass*.
  John Larke Amongst the incumbents was John Larke, a friend of
Sir Thomas More who, like him, went to the block for refusing to
acknowledge Henry VIII's supremacy over the Church.
  John Wesley preached here in 1785.

General
St Ethelburga's, measuring 60 × 30 × 31 feet is the smallest church
in the City and, although all about it is modest and humble, it is one
of the most evocative churches in London. It is the country in the
City (*rus in urbe*) and there must be many who have taken
advantage of the disused burial ground in the rear with loggia,
terracotta fountain and pool to enjoy a moment's relaxation from
the rush and bustle of daily work.

19 St Giles' without Cripplegate

Dedication
Tradition states that St Giles, born of royal parents in Athens, went
to France about 666 AD and became a hermit, living in a cave. In a
stone carving above the north door of the church he appears with a
hind which, according to legend, he saved from hunting dogs. St
Giles includes blacksmiths, beggars, cripples and maternity in his
patronage.
  'Cripplegate' may indicate that more cripples gathered here than
at other gates or it may refer to the Saxon word 'crepel', a burrow
or underground passage.

History
Although St Giles' was one of the very few City churches to have
survived the Great Fire, it seems to have been as combustible as
most, having been swept by fire in the middle of the 16th century, at
the end of the 19th century and during the 1939–45 War. It also
appears to have had more than the usual share of rebuildings,
restorations, alterations, etc.
  Records start with a church which may not have been much more
than a shrine built about 1090 by Alfune, first almoner to the Priory
of St Bartholomew and friend of Rahere who founded it. This was
erected on ground outside the gate which had become swampy from

St Giles' without Cripplegate

the silting up of the Walbrook where it ran under London Wall. Enlarged in 1333, it was rebuilt, after drainage, in 1357 and again in 1390 and once more between 1545 and 1550 after the first fire. The tower was heightened in 1682–4 by John Bridges. Restorations took place in 1704–5, repairs in 1764 and, in 1790–1, the pitch of the roof was raised. In the 19th century, alterations including renewal of roof and clerestory were made between 1858 and 1869 (see tablet on exterior of south wall), the south side refaced and castellated in 1885–6, chancel raised and pews lowered in 1888 and there was more restoration after a fire in 1897. In 1903–4 the north side was refaced and castellated to match the south.

Finally, in the 1939–45 War, St Giles' was hit by an early bomb in August 1940 but not made unusable. However, four months later it was completely burned out.

For some years, it remained a desolate ruin in wasteland subject to vandalism and desecration until taken in hand and restored by Godfrey Allen, and re-opened in 1960.

Exterior

St Giles' today is cut off from the busy world outside and lies open on all sides in a cloistered position surrounded by the dull plum-coloured Barbican development. Most of what is seen is Victorian refacing and castellation but the tower retains the stonework built of material obtained from an earlier church together with the brick of the 1682–4 heightening. It is crowned with a charming open cupola of wood and there is a prominent north-west stair turret.

Interior

A large, open and airy interior in the Perpendicular style with nave and aisles of seven bays, formed of slender clustered columns and moulded arches. It is typical of pre-Reformation Tudor interiors which have survived in London like St Margaret's, Westminster, St Helen's, Bishopsgate and St Dunstan's, Stepney.

The extension of the clerestory at the end of the 18th century has resulted in an abbreviated chancel with sanctuary arch built during the 1858–69 restoration. Stone arches in the sanctuary remain from an earlier period.

The sanctuary roof is panelled, with bosses, and coloured blue.

The west gallery and organ raised on a loft, costing £10,000, was installed after the War; so too was the good modern arched-brace roof of light tone. Pews and panelling are also new.

The only stained glass is at the east and west ends, and with few exceptions, the furnishings are post-war. The stone corbels are a pleasant survival from the past and the door to the rood-loft can be seen on the south wall.

Furnishings

Organ The organ came from St Luke's, Old Street and dates from the 18th century. It was made by Jordan and Bridge (Father Willis reeds) and modernised by Noel Mander in 1970. The case contains 17th century work by Renatus Harris from St Andrew's, Holborn.

Font and cover The marble font and cover also came from St Luke's. The cover is a delightful, octagonal domed structure with pilasters at the angles surmounted by an entablature, and garlands in octagonal panels below.

Sword-rest An exceptionally fine sword-rest bearing the arms of the last four Aldermen of Cripplegate to serve as Lord Mayors is placed against the pier on the south side of the nave at the entrance to the choir.

Lectern The lectern was presented to the church by the then vicar, the Revd Prebendary Albert Barff, in 1888 as a memorial to his illustrious predecessor, Bishop Lancelot Andrewes (see *Associations*). It was saved from the bombing.

Sedilia and piscina An attractive example with Roman tiles incorporated into the sedilia.

Monuments

John Speed, (like the historian John Stow, a tailor) historian and map-maker, was buried here in 1629. A memorial in the south aisle shows him clasping a book in his right and skull in his left hand. This was restored by the Merchant Taylors in 1971.

Thomas Stagg, attorney-at-law, is remembered by a tablet in the south-east corner. This records that he was 'Vestry Clerk of this Parish March 1731–19th February 1772 on which day he died in the 76th year of his age. That is all.'

Associations

St Giles' is very rich in associations.

John Milton The poet and his father were both buried in the church, John in 1674 and his father in 1647. A bronze statue (once outside) in the south aisle commemorates the poet and a stone in the floor of the chancel marks where he was buried. There is also a bust to him in the south aisle by John Bacon. It is rumoured that the grave of John Milton was opened in 1793 and that parts of his body were sold to ghoulish viewers. A lock of hair alleged to be Milton's can be seen in Milton's Cottage at Chalfont St Giles.

Milton was reunited with his first wife Mary in St Giles'.

Oliver Cromwell was married to Elizabeth Bourchier in the church on August 22nd, 1620.

Lancelot Andrewes, the great Anglican divine and one of the translators of the Authorized Version of the Bible, was vicar here from 1588 to 1605. Later, he became Dean of Westminster and held various bishoprics.

Sir Martin Frobisher, the great Elizabethan mariner and Arctic explorer, who died from wounds at Brest, was buried here in 1594. In 1888, a memorial was erected to him to commemorate the tercentenary of the defeat of the Spanish Armada. This was demolished in the bombing of the church.

Holman Hunt, painter of 'The Light of the World' (copy in St Paul's Cathedral) was baptised here in 1827.

William Shakespeare attended St Giles' for his nephew's baptism in 1607.

Plague St Giles' suffered more than most from the dreadful Plague which swept through the City in 1665. In the last week of August of that year, there were 600 deaths and, altogether, 8,000 people died in the parish; on one single day (18th August) there were 151 funerals. The very high death-rate may have been due to the parish pump being located in the churchyard. After the Fire in the following year, many refugees camped out around St Giles' in tents and this was the nucleus of the building development which followed.

General
St Giles' has a long and distinguished history. The mediaeval guilds who were the forerunners of the City Livery Companies first established chapels in the church and it has been the place of worship of many great figures of the past. From an architectural point of view, although so much Victorianised, it is an interesting survival of a Tudor church. Now today it is taking on a new lease of life with another set of residents, already numbering 4,500, and maybe increasing to 7,000, living in the Barbican flats (the Barbican was a mediaeval watch tower). It ministers both to the City working population and, unlike most City churches, to a full resident population.

St Luke's, Old Street, which was carved out of St Giles' in 1733, was reunited with the parish in 1966. The strange steeple (see plate p. 179) remains amongst the ruins.

20 St Helen's, Bishopsgate with St Martin Outwich

Dedication
A rare dedication in London to the mother of Constantine, the first Christian Roman Emperor. She is credited with having miraculously discovered in Jerusalem the true Cross upon which Christ was crucified.

History
There is no evidence to support the claim that Constantine founded a church here in memory of his mother and the first authentic mention is in 1161 in a grant of land made to the Priory at Southwark. A few years later the church is mentioned as belonging to the Dean and Chapter of St Paul's Cathedral who, in 1210, gave permission to a man named William, the son of a goldsmith, to found a Benedictine nunnery in the grounds of the church.

At that time, the parish church probably did not extend beyond the limits of the present south door but when the nuns' church was built alongside in the 13th century terminating where the west end is now, the parish nave was extended to the same point, thus producing the famous and very unusual double nave which is such a hallmark of this church. A line of arches and some kind of screen were set up between the nuns and the parish congregation, but this did not prevent sly winkings and there were reproofs from the Dean and Chapter of St Paul's for the ostentatious veils worn by the nuns and the number of small dogs kept by the Prioress. Later, they were told that dancing and revelling must cease except at Christmas and at other times of recreation, and on no account must 'seculars' be present.

A south transept was added when the parish nave was lengthened and, in 1374, two chantry chapels—the Chapels of the Holy Ghost and of Our Lady—were built to the east of the transept. About 100 years later, Sir John Crosby, alderman, business man and diplomat, left money for 'renewing and reforming' the church, which resulted in the present nave arcade being built and the roofs reconstructed.

The nunnery, suppressed in 1538, came into the ownership of the Leathersellers' Company but the conventual buildings, other than the nuns' choir which has been preserved intact, were not finally dismantled until 1799. In the meantime, certain Livery Companies paid for repairs and alterations to the church in the 1630s from which time date the sumptuous doorcases and the exterior south door.

Numerous repairs took place in the 18th and 19th centuries

St Helen's, Bishopsgate. Daughter of Sir John and Lady Spencer culminating in a major work by J. L. Pearson, the eminent Victorian architect, in 1892–3, particularly affecting the chancel and the level of the floors. Most of the glass dates from the 19th century.

St Helen's survived both the Great Fire and the 1939–45 War and the only major work after the War was in 1966 to take away the Victorian vestries and erect new vestries, offices and a rectory to the south of the church.

St Martin Outwich Church, which used to stand where Threadneedle Street and Bishopsgate meet, was a mediaeval place of worship which was burnt in a fire of 1765 and rebuilt in 1796; when the latter building was demolished in 1874, the parish was joined to that of St Helen's.

Exterior
The principal façade is on the west, approached through an arch from Bishopsgate and after traversing a little courtyard. The 17th century bell-turret and the two symmetrical halves, with five lights without tracery under a depressed arch knit together under wavy battlements and string course, make a charming composition. The door to the nuns' old nave on the left is 16th century and that on the right leading to the parish nave 14th century.

The south façade is more irregular because of the new vestries etc. and the old south transept, and any effect of intimacy is lost in the large open piazza separating it from the giant office block in Leadenhall Street. A pedimented doorway in stone with date 1633 on each side of the keystone and *LAUS DEO S. HELENA* above, together with wooden doors, are interesting examples of a style then being followed in London.

Interior
The main impression from the top of the stairs leading down into the church is one of civic opulence with a grand coloured monument on the right, and the wide open space of the double nave. And yet at the same time St Helen's is not a very large church. The effect of sumptuousness is heightened by the very rich doorcases at the entrance and leading to the vestry.

The naves are separated by a typical Perpendicular four-bay arcade of shafted columns and low arches dating from the end of the 15th century. The low-pitched roofs which are largely original and the windows without tracery are in the same style. The south nave terminates in Pearson's chancel, with screen, sedilia and reredos installed by him. The north nave continues uninterruptedly to the east end where it is separated from the chancel by two arches which were opened up in the 14th and 15th centuries.

To the right is the south transept, housing the organ, from which lead off to the east the Chapel of the Holy Ghost and the Lady Chapel. At the east end of the chapels are mediaeval floor tiles.

Apart from the west and north walls, pre-Tudor features can be seen in the lancet window in the north-west corner, blocked windows further along the north wall and the opening to the nuns' night staircase to their dormitory; to the right of the doorway is an Easter sepulchre with crested recess and, below, a blank stone arcade with nuns' squint.

At the west end, internal framing supporting the belfry is enclosed in walls of timber made to resemble stone.

Furnishings

Font A simple font of elegant design made of black and red marble with a cover to suit. Dates from 1632 but the bottom three steps are 19th century.

Poor-box (See plate p. 82) To the west of the south porch is a poor-box of about 1620 in the form of a caryatid shown as a 17th century figure of a bearded beggar, holding out his hat.

Doorcases These have open segmental pediments with angels on them. The more sophisticated south-west doorway has fluted columns whilst the south doorway bears a Charles II Royal Arms.

*Pulpit A magnificent Jacobean example richly carved and dating from 1615. The sounding board with inlaid work is about 1640.

Sword-rest In the chancel is a rare example of a pre-Fire sword-rest made of wood, consisting of two twisted columns decorated with wreaths supporting an entablature bearing the Royal Arms and the Arms of the City. These are upheld by winged angels beneath which are the Arms of Sir John Lawrence, Lord Mayor in 1665, the year of the Plague, who bravely stayed at his post.

Choir-stalls Thirteen choir-stalls originally in the nuns' choir are now in the chancel. They are 15th century and have grotesque arm-rests.

Organ Together with its case provided in 1744: repaired and enlarged since. Moved from the west gallery in 1868. Musical instruments are carved on the case.

Monuments

Whilst the title of 'Westminster Abbey of the City' is far-fetched, this church certainly holds the palm in London amongst parish churches for the number and splendour of its Elizabethan and Jacobean monuments. Taking them in a clockwise direction from

St Helen's Church. Poor-box of bearded beggar holding out his hat *c* 1620

the west end, some of the more notable are:

John Robinson, died 1599, and his wife Christian. From St Martin Outwich: a wall monument showing nine sons and seven daughters.

Hugh Pemberton, died 1500, and his wife Katherine. Also from St Martin's. A tomb-chest with canopy and wall panel. Only ten sons in brass remain, the parents and daughters having disappeared.

William Kirwin, died 1594, and wife Magdalen. Beneath the third arch of the north arcade enclosed in iron railings. He and the sons on the south side, the women on the north. A small tomb-chest without effigy. The inscription refers to the buildings he erected and comments on the narrow space he now occupies.

William Bond and Martin Bond Wall monuments to the east of the north wall. Martin was the Commander of the City Trained Bands at Tilbury in 1588 to whom Queen Elizabeth made her stirring speech before the Armada. He is shown in his tent, with sentries outside and a groom with his horse. Pevsner describes this as 'a monument with much atmosphere'.

Sir Thomas Gresham, died 1579. A fine free-standing tomb-chest of Siena marble without effigy but with large coats of arms. The black helmet on the east wall is a made-up piece. Sir Thomas founded the Royal Exchange.

Sir Julius Caesar Adelmar, died 1636. East of nuns' choir. By Nicholas Stone. A curious tomb-chest with, instead of an effigy on the black marble top, a deed with seal broken off in which he states that he has paid the debt of nature.

Sir William Pickering, died 1574. Under arches between the two nave east ends. He was Ambassador to Spain under Queen Elizabeth. This, in marble, is the grandest of the Elizabethan monuments, showing him recumbent under a six-poster with coffered arches. It is surrounded by wrought-iron rails.

Sir John Crosby, died 1475 and his first wife, Agnes, died 1460. He built Crosby Place, once situated to the south of Great St Helen's of which the Hall was removed to Chelsea in 1910. Tomb-chest with quatrefoil panels (see *History*).

John de Oteswich and wife. Also from St Martin's. Between chancel and south transept. It is in the Chapel of the Holy Ghost. This is the oldest of the monuments and may date from the 14th century. Alabaster effigies in flowing robes.

*Sir John Spencer, died 1609 and wife. To the north of the south entrance. A spectacular wall monument, showing the daughter kneeling at a prayer-desk to the left and recumbent figures of the parents, all on a tomb-chest between two black obelisks and with

two arches behind. Recoloured in 1950. On the top is a large
achievement with winged skull and hour-glass above.

The daughter (see plate p. 79) is alleged to have eloped with the
Marquess of Northampton who spirited her away in a bread basket.

Brasses There are seven brasses ranging in date from 1470 to
1535 showing priests and civilians. All are in the south transept
except for one to John Leventhorp, died 1510, in the nuns' choir.

Stained glass There are fragments of old glass in the north
windows and in the Chapel of the Holy Ghost, mainly 17th century
armorial except for the 15th century roundels in the chapel which
are pot metal. The rest is 19th century, including a window above
the Lady Chapel altar recording the sight by the Emperor
Constantine of the Cross in the sky before the battle of Milvian
Bridge. A west window shows various St Helen's worthies.

General

St Helen's is the most considerable mediaeval parish church in
London which has come down to us and, in its monuments, gives us
a clear indication of the wealth and prestige of the City merchant,
making the nuns appear as merely a frivolous, if long, interlude.
Today, St Helen's is concerned with very different people and
exercises a vigorous ministry amongst the workers of the City, many
of whom, to quote R. G. Ellen, have 'accepted the challenge of the
Christian Faith' within its walls. Attendance at Tuesday lunch-hour
services averages five hundred.

21 Church of the Holy Sepulchre without Newgate

Dedication

Originally dedicated to St Edmund, King and Martyr, the church
was variously called 'St Edmund without Newgate', 'St Edmund
Sepulchre' and 'St Edmund and the Holy Sepulchre'. Later, the
name Edmund was dropped.

The name of Holy Sepulchre was probably adopted at the time of
the Crusades. Those taking part used to set out from the church,
possibly because its position just outside the north-west gate of the
City corresponded with the site of the Sepulchre and Calvary
outside Jerusalem, and, at one time, there was a Saracen's Head Inn
next to the church. A very clear perspex model of the Church of the
Holy Sepulchre in Jerusalem is to be seen at the west end of the
north aisle.

History

First mention was in 1137 AD when Rahere, the Prior of St
Bartholomew's, granted the living to Hagno the Clerk. Whatever
then existed was rebuilt in the middle of the 15th century at the
expense of Sir John Popham, Chancellor of Normandy and
Treasurer to the Household of King Henry VI. The historian Stow
states that this munificent patron also added a handsome chapel on
the south side. There were many fraternities linked to the church
and a number of chantry chapels. Between 1624 and 1634 the tower
and battlements were rebuilt.

Although a gilt cherub high up on a wall at Pye Corner where the
adjacent Giltspur Street and Cock Lane meet is supposed to mark
the spot where the Great Fire burnt itself out, this did not save Holy
Sepulchre from being all but destroyed. It had to be rebuilt and so
impatient were the parishioners to get this done that Wren's services
were not called in until later, if at all, with consequent detriment to
the work done.

Subsequently, this place of worship has been the victim of varying
tastes. In 1790, Georgian round-headed windows and a straight
parapet were substituted for the 15th century tracery and
battlements; about a hundred years later in 1878–80 these were
brought back again with the exception of the east window; round
arches were put under the tower in 1790 and then taken away in
1878–80. In 1834–6, a new roof and ceiling were provided and in
1873–8, the tower and porch were restored. Other changes took
place in 1878–80 with the removal of the pews and galleries and the
complete refacing of the south porch. A number of mediaeval
fragments then came to light, including part of an Easter Sepulchre
in the north chapel.

As compensation for all this tampering, the church survived the
1939–45 War intact except for minor damage. It was redecorated in
1967.

The patronage passed from the Prior and Canons of St
Bartholomew at the Dissolution to the President and Fellows of St
John's College, Oxford, who still retain it.

Exterior

Holy Sepulchre presents a Perpendicular exterior in Victorian dress,
complete with battlements, tall sturdy tower of ragstone and three-
storeyed porch. The outsize crocketed pinnacles give one a jolt and
the thorough refacing is disturbing but there is at least a harmony of
style which the interior lacks.

The tower, rebuilt in 1711–14, is in four stages with angle

buttresses terminating at the third stage and windows (paired at the top) with ogee crocketed hood-moulds. There is a balustrade and the pinnacles are panelled. The aisles, faced in Portland stone, are continued alongside the tower and there is an attractive 17th century sundial on the south aisle parapet.

A watch-house used for deterring body-snatchers (destroyed in the War) was subsequently rebuilt.

Interior

The interior of the porch is the most enjoyable mediaeval feature, for its fan groined vaulting with cusps and liernes reaches right down to the floor. Seventeen carved bosses are placed at the intersection of ribs.

The main body of this largest of City parish churches, measuring 150 by 162 feet, has an air of dignified spaciousness but the mixture of styles is worrying. Tall classical round-headed arcades of seven bays supported on Tuscan columns with high plinths exposed by removal of box-pews separate the nave from the north and south aisles. These date from the Wren period but the flat nave ceiling, deeply coffered with gilt domes and flat surfaces, only from 1834–6. The aisle ceilings are groined and there is no division between nave and chancel.

The north chapel was originally dedicated to St Stephen but after the War was made over to the Musicians and is now known as the Musicians' Chapel.

At the west end of the north aisle in front of the City of London Rifles memorial are small mediaeval pavement squares which came from Christ Church, Newgate, and were part of what used to be known as 'Queen Margaret's Pavement'. On the south side is the Regimental Chapel of the Royal Fusiliers, the City of London Regiment, and just in front of this the calcined remains of a piscina with parts of a shelf for cruets and a drain. Being almost opposite the door to the rood-loft high up on the north wall, it is clear that this piscina would have been next to the rood-screen.

Furnishings

Beginning with the vestibule, the main furnishings of interest are:

Font and Font-cover At the north end of the vestibule is a finely-carved font cover of 1690 on a white pedestal which at one time was in Christ Church, Newgate but which, according to some accounts, was rescued from the burning building by an unknown postman on the night of the 30th/31st December 1940 raid. It is decorated with cherubs.

Holy Sepulchre's own font at the west end of the south aisle is an attractive marble one with baluster stem and fluted bowl adorned with cherubs' heads, which was given by a parishioner in 1670. For a time, it was replaced by a showy Victorian font but restored to its rightful place in 1932. The cover is octagonal.

Pews Some of the Wren pews are to be seen at the west end.

Royal Arms The Arms at the west end of the south aisle are of the design current between 1714 and 1801.

Pulpit/Reading Desk On the left a reading desk and on the right the pulpit proper, dating from early 18th century; both have attractive stairs.

*Organ The chief treasure is the superb Renatus Harris organ built by him in 1677 and rebuilt in 1932 by Arthur Harrison. For 200 years it lay in its proper place at the west end but was moved first in 1878 to the St Stephen Chapel and then in 1932 to its present position. The west front with central carved CR monogram (Charles II) is original but the south is Victorian. Beneath are carved backs of the former galleries. Handel and Mendelssohn are reputed and the Wesleys known to have played on it. More cherubs' heads embellish the case.

Altar-rails and Sword-rest Fine early 18th century wrought-iron examples.

Reredos   A plain example with fluted gilt pilasters and embroidered panels of Wren period. Segmental head.

Monuments

Many attractive memorials are draped around pillars and set on walls.

Edward Arris, died 1676 and wife. This monument is in the form of two frontal busts in circular niches and is on the south wall near the font.

Picture East of the rood-loft door is a copy of Raphael's 'The Marriage of the Virgin'. The original painted in 1504 is in Milan.

Stone Built into the north-east pillar is a stone presented in 1964 from the Church of the Holy Sepulchre, Jerusalem.

Associations

Mediaeval associations are for the most part grim, but subsequent ones are more agreeable.

Newgate Prison Where the Central Criminal Court of the Old Bailey now stands was once Newgate Gaol. From here, condemned prisoners were led to Tyburn and at midnight, before the day of execution, the sexton would pass through an underground passage (door-head can still be seen on south wall) and ring his handbell (in a glass case by the south-east pillar) outside the victim's cell and recite admonitory lines. At 8.00 am the tenor bell from the tower would ring out to speed him on his way. These 'services' were paid for from a sum of £50 given in 1605 by Robert Dowe for this purpose.

The great bell of the tower also used to toll the curfew.

Smithfield Martyrs John Rogers, who was rector from 1550 to 1555, was the first Protestant martyr to be burned at Smithfield in 1555.

Robert Ascham, the beloved tutor of Lady Jane Grey and Queen Elizabeth, was buried here in 1568.

Resurrection Men During the 18th century, the burial ground of Holy Sepulchre was a convenient place for the resurrection men to ply their macabre trade. It was the source for specimens for hospital anatomy lectures at St Bartholomew's; these were left at an inn opposite, labelled with the dealer's name, to be collected the following morning. The Watch House erected to defeat their ends was built in 1791.

Musicians' Chapel As a boy, Sir Henry Wood learned to play the organ in this church and became Assistant Organist at the age of 14. His ashes were brought here in 1944 and lie under the central window to Saint Cecilia, the patron saint of Music.

Kneelers and furnishings are practically all connected with musicians. The windows are in memory of St Stephen Harding (there is a St Bernard dog to remind one that he introduced St Bernard to the Cistercian Order), of John Ireland showing scenes from his life, and of Dame Nellie Melba with peaches in the bottom right-hand corner to remind us that she gave her name to her favourite dish: Peach Melba. The east Magnificat window above the altar commemorates Walter Carroll.

Sir Malcolm Sargent The blue carpeting, some kneelers and one of the altar frontals in the sanctuary were given in 1969 in memory of Sir Malcolm Sargent.

Captain John Smith The brass plate on the south wall of the choir is a copy of the one (no longer identifiable) which originally marked the spot where he was buried. It records his adventures when he was reputed to have cut off the heads of three Turkish champions in individual combat as a soldier in Hungary and his rescue from death by the Princess Pocahontas. He later became the first effective Governor of Virginia and Admiral of New England. A window on the south side is also in memory of him.

Regiments At the west end of the north aisle is a War Memorial and Book of Remembrance to the 6th City of London Fusiliers ('The Cast-Iron Sixth') and on the other side the Regimental Chapel and Book of Remembrance of the Royal Fusiliers, who are also commemorated by the Memorial Garden of Remembrance outside.

General

Although only just mediaeval, Holy Sepulchre will always attract visitors because of its musical traditions and its rich associations. The Royal School of Church Music was started here by Sir Sidney Nicholson when he was organist and, at the annual Festival of St Cecilia in November, combined choirs from St Paul's Cathedral, Westminster Abbey, and the Chapel Royal sing together.

At one time, the parish extended within the City walls but the part that was inside was taken over after the dissolution of the Greyfriars monastery in 1547 by Christ Church, Newgate (now alas a ruin except for its splendid tower). This part, however, has now been reunited with Holy Sepulchre and the parish includes St Leonard's, Foster Lane, St Martin-within-Ludgate, St Mary Magdalene Old Fish Street and St Gregory's by St Paul's.

22 St James's, Garlickhythe

Dedication

The Apostle James, sometimes called St James the Great, became the patron saint of Spain after what was presumed to be his body was discovered in a marble coffin by a Galician peasant during the year 816 AD. Around his shrine was built the famous cathedral of St James of Compostela, which during the Middle Ages became a leading centre of pilgrimage. 'Garlickhythe' recalls the sale of garlic on the bank of the Thames nearby.

History

The first mention of a place of worship on this site is 1170; whatever existed was rebuilt in 1320 and later endowed with several chantries, no doubt for the saying of prayers for the souls of some of the six Lord Mayors who were buried there. Repaired in the first half of the 17th century it fell a victim to the Great Fire in the second .

Much of the subsequent history is recorded inside the tower through which one enters: the rebuilding by Wren between 1676 and 1683, repairs to the steeple in 1854, restoration 1883–5, and finally

St James's, Garlickhythe

the post-war restoration of 1954–63. There were other repairs and alterations in 1838, 1866 and 1897 when the plaster was removed from the tower. The Churchwardens' accounts contain details of the expenditure incurred at the re-opening in 1682; they included 4s 6d for 'Wax Links to enlighten my Lord Mayor home'.

Damage was caused by a bomb from a German aeroplane which fell on 13th June 1917 and from a 500 pounder which fell in 1940 but fortunately did not explode; greater damage was caused by flames from incendiaries sweeping across the road from the other side.

Due to the sympathetic restoration after the War by Lockhart Smith and Alexander Gale when the roof (ravaged by death-watch beetle) and upper part of the walls were rebuilt, the tower refaced, and the stained glass removed, St James's has emerged as an authentic Wren church with much to enjoy both inside and out.

Exterior

Seemly and dignified with one of Wren's delightful little spires (cf. St Michael Paternoster Royal next door and St Stephen's, Walbrook). This was added in 1714–17 some time after the tower was built.

The 125 ft high steeple consists of a plain tower which projects from the west end completed with pierced parapet and vases, above which rises the charming spire. This is in three square stages, the lowest with diagonally projecting coupled colonettes and entablature, rising by means of scrolled ramps to the second stage and the whole completed by an attractive weather-vane. This design creates strong contrasts of light and shade.

Prior to the war, a handsome clock supported on a bracket and surmounted by a quaint figure of St James complete with staff, shell, wallet and hat used to project from the tower at the junction of the first and second storeys, but it was destroyed by the bombing.

The central windows in the sides are much higher than the others. The west door is arched and adorned with a cherub's head keystone and demi-columns carrying a pediment. The handsome iron railings with grape motif were the gift of the Vintners' Company.

At the east end is the unusual feature of a projecting chancel.

Interior

This tallest of Wren's interiors with lofty columns raised on high bases encased in wood has similarities with that of St Stephen's, Walbrook, in that the columns open out in the middle to create transepts. The aisles are lower than the nave, which has a deeply coved ceiling leading up to a central flat portion richly plastered and gilded to pick out the design. The coving is penetrated by the clerestory vaulting. The chancel, unusual in that it is structurally separate, has a barrel vault.

The many windows, now happily relieved of their Victorian stained glass, and the clerestory, led to St James's being called 'Wren's Lantern', but the east window has been replaced by a painting (see *Furnishings*) The centre windows in the side aisles are circular.

The walls are panelled up to a height of nine feet and the only gallery—at the west end—is carried on graceful gilded Corinthian stanchions of Sussex iron.

Furnishings
The iron (sword-rests, lion and unicorn etc) and woodwork are both notable. Some of the finest of the woodwork came from St Michael's, Queenhithe, after it was demolished in 1875.

Pulpit From St Michael's. A beautifully carved furnishing with fine tester and elegant staircase of twisted balusters and with the refinement of a peg for the wig of the preacher.

Stalls The backs of the well-carved stalls also came from St Michael's.

*Organ The pride of the church and one of the few Bernard Smith instruments that could be restored to its original condition although it incorporates alterations to the casing; all the front pipes are original. On the top are trumpeting cherubs, the shell of St James and the usual crown and two mitres.

Chandelier A recent and very attractive furnishing, the chandelier was a gift after the War from the Glass-Sellers' Company and is modelled on one in the Wren chapel at Emmanuel College, Cambridge.

Royal Arms An excellent Stuart coat of arms which came from St Michael's, Queenhithe, is placed on the west gallery.

Painting The painting above the altar-piece of the Ascension is by Andrew Geddes and was given by the curate in 1815 who later became rector.

Hatchments On the south wall are two hatchments (coat-of-arms in a lozenge-shaped frame).

Amongst other furnishings are churchwardens' pews, altar table, altar-rails with two ranges of spiral balustrades, fine doorcases (from St Michael's) in the north and south-east corners acting as screens, and a 17th century font cover. An amusing feature is the row of wig-pegs at the west end.

Associations
Seven Livery Companies hold their annual services in St James's.

General
After being out of action for nearly ten years, it is satisfying to see a church reappear, one with which Wren himself would probably not be displeased. The parish now includes St Michael Paternoster Royal next door, the transfer of which bought with it the parishes of St Martin Vintry and All Hallows the Less (not rebuilt after the Great Fire), St Michael's Queenhithe, All Hallows the Great and Holy Trinity the Less (demolished in the 19th century).

3 **St Katharine Cree**

Dedication
St Katharine (Katherine or Catherine) professed her Christian faith at a sacrificial feast at Alexandria decreed by the Roman Emperor Maximilius. For this, she was subjected to torture on a toothed wheel but, upon the wheel breaking at her touch, she was executed with a sword in 307 AD. The Catherine-wheel became her emblem and, being of royal blood, she was later the patron saint of the reigning Queen of England.

Cree was another word for Christ and recalls the link with the important Augustinian Priory of Holy Trinity within Aldgate, sometimes called Christchurch, in whose cemetery St Katharine's was built.

History
The first church called 'St Katharine de Christ Church at Alegate' was built about 1280 by the prior of the monastery in order that the canons 'be not disturbed by the presence of the laity at the services' (compare St Margaret's at Westminster.)

Rebuilt at the end of the 15th century this church, except for the lower part of the tower, was pulled down by Sir Thomas Audley after it had been given to him by Henry VIII. There was no further reconstruction until Charles I's reign at a time when Gothic forms were giving way to Classical. This third church, sometimes wrongly ascribed to Inigo Jones, was erected between 1628 and 1630 (the latter date can be seen on the keystone of an arch in the north-west corner) and consecrated in January 1631 by Archbishop Laud. The strange rituals, his 'Bowings and Cringings' at the consecration were later used at his trial as evidence against him.

An engraving of 1736 shows odd, wavy cresting round the outside of the building which has all but disappeared, and also a square turret which was replaced by the present Tuscan colonnade surmounted by a cupola in 1776. Repairs and 'beautification' were carried out in 1805 but, apart from new glass, some of which is no longer there, little more was done in the 19th century.

As St Katharine's had apparently escaped serious damage in the 1939–45 War, the Laudian church has come down to us relatively little changed. Repairs, however, to the damaged south wall revealed more serious structural trouble than anticipated; the church was classed as dangerous and in danger of demolition. Fortunately means were found of consolidating the walls and a new use found for the building as Headquarters of the Industrial Christian Fellowship. The able restoration by Marshall Sisson led to reconsecration on 6th July 1962.

The church of St James, Dukes Place, was demolished in 1874 and the parish added to that of St Katharine's.

Exterior

The mediaeval south-west tower, erected at the turn of the 14th/15th century, (although the top was rebuilt in 1776), remains, but the rest of it (apart from the later cupola) is Carolean. The windows are a curious mixture. There is a large west window but in the tower south wall, a strange reversion to Saxon-type openings is found; on the south façade facing Leadenhall Street the windows are square-headed with Gothic tracery and the centre light a little higher than the others; the large east window is square, the lower half being blocked in.

A sundial on the south wall, dating from 1706 is inscribed 'Non sine Lumine'

A quiet churchyard-cum-garden is entered through the church. It has a large plane-tree and an arch with skeleton on top enclosing a tablet recording its laying out by the firm of Fitch Lovell Ltd (see *Associations*) who also provided the fountain. The gateway used to be on Leadenhall Street and was built by William Avenon in 1631. The skeleton on top is a reminder of the graves that used to lie in the churchyard.

Interior

This most interesting hybrid provides a bright and attractive interior. The arcades of six bays have Corinthian columns supporting arches with Renaissance rosettes under the soffits, whilst the clerestory with pilasters above follows late Gothic forms. There is no division between chancel and nave which has necessarily lost much of its character by the aisles being boxed in for offices. The view eastwards, however, to the Catherine-wheel window in a square frame, remains less affected.

The plaster ceiling is an intricate Gothic pattern of ribs with tiercerons made even more ornate over the chancel. Seventeen coloured bosses represent armorial bearings of City Livery Companies.

The south-east and north-east corners have been converted into a Laud Memorial Chapel (his portrait is on the wall) and baptistery respectively. The Laud Chapel was furnished by the Society of King Charles the Martyr, the sovereign who was Laud's patron but who eventually signed his death warrant. From the baptistery a fine doorcase of 1693 leads to the vestry and beyond to the garden.

Interior walls are panelled with wood from the old pews.

Furnishings
The organ was made by Father Smith in 1686 and rebuilt by Father Willis in 1866. Some of the stops have original 'Father Smith' pipes; the finely carved case is supported on fluted columns of oak with carved capitals, attributed to Grinling Gibbons.

Royal Arms The Royal Arms in the north-west corner of the church are those of Charles II.

Font The small octagonal marble font was given by Sir John Gayer (see *Associations*) who was Lord Mayor in 1646. It has an ogee cover painted blue and gold with the City's arms.

Pulpit Of cedar wood and finely carved with the usual cherubs' heads, leaves and pods. The sounding board is hexagonal and is inlaid with seven different woods.

Reredos Came from St James's, Dukes Place, after that church was pulled down. Enclosed in fluted Corinthian columns and pilasters.

Altar-rails and table Semi-circular rails enclose the sanctuary, where there is a fine Adam-type altar table with delicately carved legs, restrained swag decoration and ovals round the top rails.

Monuments
Sir Nicholas Throckmorton, died 1577. After nearly losing his life in the Marian Persecution, he became Ambassador to France and Chief Butler. He is shown recumbent under a canopy between Tuscan columns supporting an entablature and above a skeleton. There is elaborate strapwork at the back. It is in the Laud Memorial Chapel.

Samuel Thorpe, died 1791. At the west end there is a bas-relief to Samuel Thorpe by John Bacon with a standing woman bending over an urn.

Associations
Sir John Gayer, who provided the font, encountered a lion in the Syrian desert in 1643 when on a mission to the Near East. The lion, however, in answer to prayer left him alone. Out of gratitude for his escape, he endowed the Lion Sermons, preached each year in the church on October 1.

James Fitch set up his cheesemonger's shop nearby in 1784. His descendants developed it into the well-known firm of Fitch Lovell Ltd. They restored the little garden (north-east of the church) which used to be part of the Priory churchyard.

SS Lancastria A wooden tablet on the south wall commemorates 4,000 people who lost their lives in the troopship *Lancastria* when she was sunk on 17th June 1940 and lists the names of the rescue ships.

General
St Katharine's is a rare survival of a church built at a time when few churches were constructed, between the age of Inigo Jones and that of Christopher Wren. Many commercial and industrial City concerns have contributed to the furnishings and the church is exercising a valuable ministry as Guild Church for Finance, Commerce and Industry, in promoting the study of such matters as full employment, the impact of automation and income distribution, with teach-ins, lectures, seminars, study groups etc. amongst those intimately concerned with these matters in the City.

Parish work is now looked after by St Andrew Undershaft.

24 St Lawrence Jewry

Dedication
According to tradition, St Lawrence suffered martyrdom in 258 AD under the Roman Emperor, Valerian. When told to give up the treasures of the Church he disposed of the plate secretly, assembled poor and outcast citizens and presenting them said '*these* are the treasures of the Church'. For this, he was flayed and roasted alive on a gridiron which became his symbol and is represented on the weathervane of this church.

'Jewry' refers to this part of the City where the Jews lived from the time of William I until they were expelled in 1290 by Edward I.

St Katharine Cree. Gateway

St Lawrence Jewry

St Lawrence Jewry. Wren vestry

History

The first mention of a church on this site was in 1136 but a Saxon building may have existed here before that. The mediaeval place of worship was consumed in the Great Fire of 1666; the foundation stone of Wren's rebuilding was laid in 1671 and it was re-consecrated in 1677 at a service attended by Charles II.

From 1294, patronage was in the hands of Balliol College, Oxford, but when the parish of St Mary Magdalene, Milk Street was united with that of St Lawrence after the Fire (St Mary's was not rebuilt), the living was shared jointly with the Dean and Chapter of St Paul's Cathedral; this lasted until 1957 when it became the Guild Church of the Corporation of London.

In 1892, the parish of St Michael Bassishaw was closed and joined to St Lawrence's, but the latter has now itself become temporarily part of the new parish of St Vedast-alias-Foster, although it may revert before long to being on its own again.

The church was gutted during the air-raid of 29th December 1940; restoration was carried out by Cecil Brown and it was re-opened in 1957. The Wren vestry (see plate p. 99) decorated with paintings by Sir James Thornhill and reputed to be one of the finest small rooms in Europe could not, however, be restored—a grievous loss.

Exterior

St Lawrence's is set forward in the forecourt of Guildhall with the east end facing the approach to it, and the south alongside Gresham Street. Although Wren did not normally pay a great deal of attention to the adornment of walls if they could not be seen, the importance of the east side approach led him to create a façade for it with Corinthian columns supporting a pediment. The south side is plainer with five round-headed windows flanked by two doors with circular windows above.

The building is of irregular shape. After the Fire, buildings took the external dimensions of property boundaries as a means of establishing claims. Wren consequently had to conform to the sites he was given, and he squared off interiors by varying the thickness of the walls, although here there is irregularity inside also. The tower is aligned with and projects from the west wall but the steeple—a glass-fibre copy of the old one—faces down Gresham Street; it rises to a height of 175 feet and the shaft is in the form of an incendiary bomb!

Interior

Stately, as befits the official Corporation place of worship, and handsomely restored. The interior is of the 'hall' type, designed to enable as many people to see and hear the preacher as possible. There are, however, two chapels, one on the north side called the Commonwealth Chapel in memory of the part played by the City—and which it still plays—in the development of the Commonwealth, and the other at the west end called the Tower Chapel, a replica of that used temporarily after the bombing for holding services from 1943 until St Lawrence's was re-opened.

The effect created is one of spaciousness: pilasters with Corinthian capitals, a coved ceiling, dark oak panelling round the walls, and gilded plaster work on the ceiling, which reproduced the original Wren decoration; all combine to make a dignified setting for the Corporation Church.

An interesting feature of the east windows is that, due to the irregularity of the building, the reveal on the altar side is at right angles to the wall whilst the one on the other side is splayed.

The west gallery accommodates the choir and part of the large new organ. Another to the north, which is quite small, above a doorway, is called the Trumpeters' gallery, evidence of the use of the church for the ceremonial occasion.

Furnishings

The furnishings are in keeping with the high estate of the church. There are pews for the Lord Mayor (front right), the Queen's Sheriffs, the Court of Aldermen and, in the south aisle, the Esquires. The main pews came from Holy Trinity, Marylebone. Many of the other furnishings are the gifts of City Companies with whom the church has had long associations.

Organ This was built by Noel Mander in 1956 to replace the one destroyed and has three manuals. The choir organ is detached from the rest of the instrument and is placed on the west wall of the Commonwealth Chapel to enable the case to remain in appearance like the old Renatus Harris one.

*Vestry door The doorcase with Corinthian capitals leading to the vestry is especially fine. There are cherubs' heads and swags above.

Font Dates from 1620 and comes from Holy Trinity, Minories. It lies under the organ gallery. The cover incorporates wood from the roof of Guildhall.

Screen A carved oak screen separates the Commonwealth Chapel from the nave; it incorporates in the centre a section of wrought-iron made and given by the Royal Marines to mark their affiliation in 1974 to the church. The arms, apart from the Royal Arms, are those of the Province of Canterbury and the Diocese of London.

Chandeliers A magnificent set of eight chandeliers designed by Cecil Brown adds further distinction to the interior.

Piano The Steinway Concert Grand was once the property of Sir Thomas Beecham.

Stained Glass Although a departure from Wren tradition, and one may have reservations concerning it, the stained glass, being all, except for the roundel windows in the sanctuary, by one man— Christopher Webb—imparts a harmony and illustrates much of the building's history and associations. It also provides colour without which the church might appear unduly sombre.

The east windows represent St Paul (commemorating the Dean and Chapter of St Paul's) and St Catherine (the patron saint of Balliol College, Oxford) signifying the former joint patronage. They also show the arms of the Dioceses to which the vicars of St Lawrence's later became Bishops. On the south side, the patron saints of the three united parishes appear and there are windows to Sir Thomas More, who was born in the parish and to William Grocyn, St Lawrence's most famous vicar. Sir Christopher Wren, accompanied by his Master Carver and Master Mason, are depicted in the vestibule.

Reredos The tall reredos, embellished with pediments and angels with trumpets, replaces the one lost in the bombing but the painting showing St Lawrence's martyrdom was saved and is in the vestry; the one now seen in the church is modern and depicts the incident leading up to the martyrdom.

Monument
On the north wall of the chancel, a memorial (which survived the air-raid) commemorates John Tillotson who was Archbishop of Canterbury from 1691 to 1694 and was lecturer (a kind of lay-reader) here for thirty years. He was married and buried in the church.

Associations
William Grocyn The most notable of the incumbents was William Grocyn, who was appointed in 1496. He was a great teacher of Greek and, as can be read on the window commemorating him, Erasmus wrote 'He is the patron and preceptor of us all'.

Sir Thomas More Lived in the parish and delivered discourses on St Augustine's 'City of God' in 1501.

Samuel Pepys Attended Divine Service here on 12th February 1664. He did not think much of the preacher but was pleased with the church which he considered 'very fine'.

City Companies The associations go back many years. The Girdlers' Company have held their annual service here since 1180— probably a unique length of time. The Loriners, who presented the litany desk, and the Haberdashers also hold their annual services here.

New Zealand Society St Lawrence's is the church of the New Zealand Society, who actively support it and each year commemorate their National Day here.

General

Although St Lawrence's is the official civic place of worship, there are weekday services for all, as well as music recitals and talks by prominent people, and it is used by countless City workers as a centre of quiet and spiritual refreshment during the busy daily round. Despite the irreparable loss of the Wren vestry, we must be glad that it lives again and that we can enjoy what has been described by Alec Clifton-Taylor as 'the most beautiful of the restored interiors' of London.

25 St Magnus the Martyr

Dedication

The Magnus officially regarded as the patron saint of this church was the Norwegian Earl of the Orkneys. He was killed by his cousin Haakon in 1116, buried in Kirkwall Cathedral and canonized in 1135. There was, however, a stone church on the site mentioned in 1067 dedicated to St Magnus so that this must have been an earlier saint.

History

The stone church mentioned in 1067 was granted by William the Conqueror to Westminster Abbey, although patronage during the mediaeval period appears to have been shared with Bermondsey Abbey. Information is scanty. The parish received an annual levy from a chapel on London Bridge, dedicated to St Thomas of Canterbury, as compensation for loss of alms from travellers entering London from the south. William Yevele, the master mason who worked on Westminster Hall and built the nave of Canterbury Cathedral, founded a chantry in the church and was buried there;

woodwork from Westminster Hall can be seen in the baptistery.

An early 16th century visitation exposed lax habits amongst the ministers who were accused of spending time fishing and in taverns when they should have been taking services.

The church escaped a fire on London Bridge in 1600 but being close to the source of the Great Fire in 1666 was one of the first to be destroyed; Wren used what was left of the walls to rebuild the church between 1671 and 1687, the steeple as usual following later (between 1703 and 1706).

The combination of another fire in 1760 which started in an 'oyl' shop next door and the widening of London Bridge in 1759–60 brought great changes to the structure. The fire destroyed the vestries at the west end and damaged most of the roof; the widening of the bridge led to the westernmost bays of the aisles, including the vestries, being removed to make space for a portico and footway for pedestrians under the tower. The north doorway was also taken away which spoilt the balance of this side.

These losses must have been largely compensated for by the commanding position which the alterations gave to the church at the City end of the bridge. This was to a great extent lost when London Bridge was moved further west in 1832, exposing the church to the ultimate indignity of having Adelaide House rammed up against it so that today it has ceased to have any contact with the bridge, and those crossing it approach the church at belfry level.

In 1782 the windows on the north side were reduced to small circular openings to reduce traffic noise. In 1924–5 Laurence King and the ecclesiastical decorator, Martin Travers, rearranged the interior, including the creation of the Lady Chapel and the South Chapel, giving it the strong Anglo-Catholic flavour it now has. 1939–45 War damage was slight; there was a restoration in 1951 and, in 1965, the church was redecorated.

Exterior

The obscuring of the view from London Bridge and the overpowering mass of Adelaide House has spoilt the approach from the south and west; on the north the reduction of the windows to circular openings, although decorated with swags and panels, has limited the view to a blackened wall. But the steeple, 185 ft high, closely resembling although a much plainer version of the one at St Charles Borromeo at Antwerp, remains a striking feature.

Built of Portland stone, a tall octagon capped by a lead dome and spirelet surmounts the balustraded tower; this has arched windows and is enriched with coupled Corinthian pilasters at the angles. As

St Magnus the Martyr

at St Charles Borromeo, there are vases at the corners of the balustrades.

On the west side, one of the City's handsome projecting clocks remains, dated 1709. At one time, it was decorated with gilded figures. The donor was the Lord Mayor of that year who, it is stated, wished to promote punctuality because of having missed an important appointment when an apprentice.

In the tiny churchyard is a piece of timber from a Roman wharf dated 75 AD and stones from the first arch of the original London Bridge dating from 1173.

Interior

Votive candles, statues and even an icon make one realise the wide range of Anglican churchmanship. Much of what is seen dates from the restoration in neo-Baroque style by Martin Travers in 1924–5; he reassembled the old reredos, added the side altars which are set diagonally, and placed the modern rood on the top of the reredos.

The crudely-coloured south aisle windows and statue of St Magnus also date from that time.

Wren's structure is spacious, consisting of nave separated from aisles by tall slender and fluted Ionic columns with panelled walls and barrel-vaulted ceiling penetrated by openings from the oval clerestory windows. The various restorations have left unaltered the old floors and original levels—an attractive feature.

Fine double staircases with turned balusters and Corinthian columns lead to the organ which is placed above a gallery supported on wrought-iron posts as at St Mary's Rotherhithe.

This is a fine interior and T. S. Eliot writes of St Magnus's 'inexplicable splendour of Ionian white and gold'. (plate p. 105).

Furnishings

There is much excellent iron and woodwork although some of the later additions bring a splash of colour of which Wren would hardly have approved.

Organ Another gift from Sir Charles Duncombe (see clock in *Exterior*). Made by Abraham Jordan in 1712, it was the first to operate with the swell mechanism. The 1670 case, enriched with musical instruments, comes from the Grinling Gibbons school.

Font Given by three parishioners in 1683, it is of marble with a nice oak cover looking like a house. The figure of Charity appears in a cartouche on the top.

Box-pews Two box-pews used as cupboards remain at the west end.

Bread-shelves The shelves in the vestibule were used for distributing bread to the poor.

Icon The 19th century Russian icon on the north wall depicts Our Lady of Perpetual Succour. It is said that the last Tsar used to give icons of this type to friends.

Stained glass In the westernmost window of the north side is a panel which came from the old hall of the Plumbers' Company of glass dating from 1671 with arms of the City of London and the Plumbers' Company. Other glass on this side by Alfred L. Wilkinson includes the arms of the Plumbers', Coopers' and Fishmongers' Companies. The post-war glass on the south side shows patron saints of the combined parishes, plus St Thomas of Canterbury.

Crucifix The large mother of pearl crucifix near the south altar was made in Bethlehem.

*Reredos and side altars The reredos is a splendid piece although the upper part is modern. The pelican symbolizing sacrifice can be seen above the Commandments. It is decorated with four Corinthian columns, entablature and pediment. In front are fine 17th century rails made of Sussex wrought-iron displayed to advantage.

The side altars were made up from a doorcase (from the old north doorway) and old woodwork and carvings. The south-east chapel has Wren's altar table. The altar-piece of this chapel has urns on top.

Pulpit The notable pulpit, dating from Wren's time, was originally a three-decker. It has a very large sounding-board and is supported on a slender stem designed by Wren.

Paintings Most of the paintings are copies; the picture of St John the Baptist in the baptistery is by Alfred Stevens.

Statue The 1924 statue of St Magnus on the south side shows him in winged helmet, holding an axe and a model of the church. Close by is a votive lamp in the form of a sailing ship.

Other furnishings include a sword-rest near the pulpit with royal arms dating from 1800 to 1816, Lord Mayor's seat, combined bishop's throne and stall, wrought-iron candlestick with seven branches, hatchments, a marble stoup on pillar in the vestibule, and chests dating from 1614 and 1673. There is also a statue of our Lady of Walsingham by Martin Travers in the Lady Chapel.

Associations

Miles Coverdale After publishing in 1535, in conjunction with William Tyndale, the first Bible in the English language, Miles

Coverdale became rector here between 1564 and 1566. He was buried in St Bartholomew-by-the-Exchange but after that church was demolished in 1841 his body was brought here together with the tablet dating from 1837 on the east wall.

City Companies The Coopers', Plumbers' and the Fishmongers' Companies all hold their annual services here.

General

There are probably few churches in the City which have suffered visually so much from property development. Internally, the excess of colour is hard to digest. Nevertheless, this is one of the notable City interiors with fine furnishings.

St Magnus' is still a parish church, incorporating St Margaret's, New Fish Street, which lay where the Monument now stands and where lampreys used to be sold under its walls (not rebuilt after the Fire), and St Michael's Crooked Lane (demolished in 1831 to make way for King William Street).

26 St Margaret's, Lothbury

Dedication

St Margaret, the maiden of Antioch, was martyred for refusing to give up her Christian beliefs. The origin of 'Lothbury' is unknown but it may be another name for the Walbrook stream which used to run beneath the church.

History

The history of St Margaret's follows the familiar pattern of many City churches. First mentioned in early mediaeval times (in this case in 1181 when it was recorded that a certain Reginald was priest there), rebuilt in the 15th century (about 1440 according to the historian Stow), destroyed in the Great Fire of 1666 and again rebuilt by Sir Christopher Wren. Mercifully, however, it escaped World War II bombing.

Prior to the Fire, St Margaret's was repaired by the parishioners in 1621.

Wren carried out the rebuilding between 1686 and 1690 in Portland stone. The tower, however, and spire were not built until 1698 to 1700.

At one time, small shops clung to the church wall until they were removed in 1771.

Under the City Churches Re-organisation Measure a new parish was created in 1954, the full designation of which is St Margaret's, Lothbury and St Stephen's, Coleman Street with St Christopher-le-Stocks, St Bartholomew-by-the-Exchange, St Olave Jewry, St Martin Pomeroy, St Mildred Poultry and St Mary Colechurch. St Martin Pomeroy and St Mary Colechurch were destroyed in the Great Fire; the others, with the exception of St Stephen's, Coleman Street, which perished in the 1940 air-raids, were demolished in the 18th and 19th centuries.

Exterior

Set sideways to a quiet street, St Margaret's is of irregular shape with the tower on the south-west corner. The fine jointing of the Portland stone, the elegant doorcase balanced by a vestry window at the other end and the charming lead obelisk spire raised on a bell-shaped dome all combine to give pleasure.

Interior

The interior consists of a nave and south aisle separated from the main body by two Corinthian columns; the aisle was made into a chapel in 1891 by the erection of a low screen with alternate wood and iron uprights, the lower half constructed from altar rails which were once at St Olave Jewry and the upper half designed by the Victorian architect, G. F. Bodley.

On the north wall, which is shorter than the south due to the irregular shape of the site, pilasters—taking the place of the columns on the other side—support the entablature. Panelling covers the walls up to a height of eight feet.

A small gallery on the west side contains the organ.

The ceiling is flat but coved at the sides.

Furnishings

The losses of the churches with which St Margaret's is associated were St Margaret's gain. It has been the recipient of one of the finest sets of furnishings in the City which, tastefully arranged by Bodley, are a major attraction.

*The pièce de résistance is the *Screen*. Stretching right across the interior and one of only two such Wren furnishings (the other is at St Peter's, Cornhill), this is a sumptuous piece. Presented originally by a wealthy Hanseatic merchant, Theodore Jacobsen, to All Hallows the Great, Upper Thames Street, it came to St Margaret's when All Hallows was demolished in 1894 to make way for a brewery. It has four divisions on each side of the middle entrance which is capped by a wide open segmental pediment with William &

Mary Royal Arms; below is a large eagle. The divisions are
separated by twisted balusters, winding round one another in spirals
of exquisite delicacy.

Reredos This is another splendid furnishing with Corinthian
columns carrying two segmental pediments. It has openwork foliage
volutes at the sides, and above, a bas-relief of the Ascension by
Bodley. Paintings of Moses and Aaron dating from about 1700
which came from the church of St Christopher-le-Stocks fill what
were once windows on each side. Stone medallions of the patron
saints of the associated churches are carved in the reredos.

Pulpit Yet another sumptuous furnishing with tester but not
from the same hand. The tester, enriched with fruit and flowers, came
from All Hallows, but the pulpit of which it originally formed part
was considered too large for St Margaret's and went to St Paul's,
Hammersmith. The pulpit at St Margaret's was made specially for it.

Organ Dates from 1801 and was made by G. P. England.

Candelabra The two brass candelabra in the sanctuary, dating
from the beginning and end of the 18th century came also from All
Hallows. Those in the nave are copies of the candelabrum on the
left side of the sanctuary and were installed in 1962.

Communion rail This furnishing with delicate two-strand
openwork balusters came from St Olave Jewry.

South Chapel The screening off of the south aisle to make this
chapel gives it the appearance of a separate miniature church with
its own individual furnishings. These include:

Font This small stone font has been attributed to Grinling
Gibbons and shows fine craftsmanship. Supported on a baluster
stem, the round bowl is decorated with cherubs' heads between
which are cut reliefs of Adam and Eve in Paradise, the Return of the
Dove to Noah in the Ark, the Baptism of Christ in the Jordan by
John and of the Eunuch by Philip. The wooden cover depicts the
dove of peace within a cherub-headed crown.

Reredos Less elaborate than the main reredos, it is nevertheless a
feature of interest with two pilasters, an open segmental pediment,
two inscription boards and hanging garlands. Above is the sacred
tetragrammaton (the Hebrew consonants of the Divine Name)
which indicates that it may have come originally from a synagogue
in Old Jewry.

Stained glass The central window on the south side of the chapel
contains the arms of the Scientific Instrument Makers' Company
who hold their services in St Margaret's. The window on the north
side which was presented in 1969 contains the coat of arms of the
Tin Plate Workers' Company.

Monuments

Sir Peter le Maire Dates from 1631 and may be by Hubert Le Sueur who, two years later, made the fine equestrian bronze statue to Charles I in Trafalgar Square. The metal bust came from St Christopher-le-Stocks.

Mrs Simpson The beautiful bust of Mrs Simpson on the side of the door leading to the chapel, dating from 1795, is by Joseph Nollekens.

Alderman John Boydell On the other side of the door is a tablet in memory of Alderman John Boydell, who was Lord Mayor of London in 1790. It was designed by Thomas Banks and carved by F. Smith in 1791 for St Olave Jewry.

General

This small place of worship measuring 66 by 54 feet and 36 feet high is like a casket containing great treasures. Although less than 200 people now reside in the parish, it serves some 10,000 City workers who pursue their labours within the confines of the area covered by its ministry. Music recitals are also given in the church.

27 St Margaret Pattens

Dedication

St Margaret of Antioch, according to tradition, was beheaded for her faith after many sufferings, choosing prison rather than submit to the will of a local ruler.

'Pattens', wooden soles mounted on large iron rings to raise the wearer above the mud, used to be made and sold in the lane beside the church but, although there are two pairs in a glass case on the south wall and a notice in the vestibule asking women to take off their pattens before entering, it is by no means certain that the name is derived from this footwear (see plate p. 112 of notice re pattens in Hawkesbury Church, Gloucestershire).

History

Reference is made to a small wooden building in the year 1067 and to 'St Margaret de Patins' in 1275 but nothing is known of the mediaeval place of worship. Whatever existed was taken down in 1530 and a rood or cross was set up in the churchyard (hence Rood Lane) to collect money for a new church. Reforming zeal led to the destruction of the cross a few years later but the church was completed in 1538. Repaired in the first half of the 17th century, it did not last beyond the Great Fire.

The Wren rebuilding, which started in 1684 and was completed in 1687, except for the steeple, was later than most. St Gabriel's, Fenchurch Street (not rebuilt after the Fire) was then added to the parish. The steeple followed between 1699 and 1703.

Subsequent history was relatively uneventful. 'Beautified' in 1855, re-seated in 1879–80 and restored in 1955–56 after bomb damage when the north gallery was converted into lecture rooms, St Margaret's remains a basically Wren building.

Exterior
The church lies at the corner of Eastcheap and Rood Lane set back from the pavement with attractive 18th century frontages on the right, and filling the view as one looks up St Mary at Hill. The plain exterior is dominated by the north-west tower and spire rising to 200 feet, the highest in the City after St Mary-le-Bow and St Bride's. Mediaeval in spirit, the needle-shaped and lead-sheathed spire capped with ball and vane is the only Wren example of this type, and is decorated with sunk panels.

Hawkesbury, Gloucestershire. Notice in S. porch

St Margaret Pattens. Drawing of 1881

The tower terminates in a handsome balustrade and sharply-pointed stone pinnacles at the corners, echoing the somewhat severe lines of the spire.

Two lead rainwater heads on the north wall are dated 1685.

Interior

Also plain structurally, but with enjoyable furnishings. It is rectangular with one aisle on the north side separated by piers from the nave forming a Lady Chapel. The piers support the north gallery but change to columns above. A gallery on the west side supports the organ. All the clerestory windows are circular.

The Lady Chapel has a former doorcase as reredos.

The panelled vestry dates from the Wren period.

Furnishings

Churchwardens' pews The only examples of this type in the City, with carved canopies and some crown-glass lunettes in the backs. Many feel that the inlaid 'CW' with date 1686 stands for Christopher Wren who attended service in this church but the letters could also indicate 'Churchwarden'. Initials St G. F. on the south and St M. P. on the north side stand for St Gabriel's, Fenchurch Street and St Margaret Pattens.

Beadle's pew and Punishment bench The beadle's pew on the north side of the chancel would appear well-positioned in relation to what is reputed to be a punishment bench below, where offenders against good behaviour were forced to sit for the rest of the service. The bench is suitably decorated with a carved devil's head.

Reredos An attractive furnishing. It contains a painting by the 17th century Italian artist, Carlo Maratti, of Christ attended by ministering angels in the Garden of Gethsemane. A peapod in the wood carving possibly means that it is the work of the Grinling Gibbons school.

Choir-stalls These were made out of the original high pews of the nave and the date 1709 with initials 'PH' appears on the front panel of one of them. Those nearest the nave carry a rather mettlesome lion and unicorn.

Lectern Unusual in that the eagle has a viper gripped in its talons.

Sword-rests Notable—one of pole design and a larger one of frame design which includes the arms of Sir Peter Delmé (see *Monuments*). They are made of Sussex iron.

Hour-glass stand The stand enclosing the hour-glass beside the pulpit was specially made from 18th century wrought-iron.

Cross The copper cross in the middle of the south wall weighs

¾cwt. and is a copy of the one at St Paul's Cathedral. It was taken down for safety from the top of St Margaret's spire.

Tapestry Also on the south wall are two 18th century pieces of tapestry, one depicting Pilate washing his hands and the other Joseph with his brothers.

Organ The organ in its 18th century case has been extensively rebuilt since it was installed.

Font Decorated with four cherubs' heads and dating from 17th century, it has an 18th century cover.

*Royal Arms A fine example of Stuart Royal Arms dating from the reign of James II.

Wooden pegs A reminder of past fashions is the line of wooden pegs at the west end of the Lady Chapel and on the south wall for hanging wigs during hot weather.

Monuments
Charles I Below the cross is a wooden board painted with the Arms of the King and containing the words 'Touch not mine anointed'. This was brought to the church by the Rev James Fish (see *Associations*).

James Donalson A tablet on the south floor recalls James Donalson, who died in 1685. It states that he was the City Garbler whose job was selecting the best in spices.

Sir Peter Vandaput, a merchant who was Sheriff in 1684. The monument is wrapped round a pillar on the north side.

Susannah Batson, died 1727. Attractive small memorial with cherubs' heads. By vestry door.

Sir Peter Delmé, who died in 1728—fishmonger, governor of the Bank of England, alderman and later Lord Mayor. The monument which hangs on the south wall near the chancel is by the great Flemish sculptor, Michael Rysbrack.

Associations
Thomas Wagstaffe Rector at the time William III came to the throne and deprived of the living because he refused to give his oath of allegiance to the Dutch monarch. He later became non-juring Bishop of Ipswich.

A Della Robbia plaque in the middle of the Lady Chapel reredos was given by parishioners in his memory.

Dr Thomas Birch This distinguished rector wrote a history of the Royal Society of which he was secretary. He died in 1766 as a result of falling from his horse.

James Fish, rector from 1866 to 1907, was a well-known

Tractarian and during his time the church became famous for its musical services. He instituted services in memory of Charles I on January 30th each year, the anniversary of the King's execution.

Crew of submarine K4 In the Lady Chapel is a shrine (made of teak from the ship *'Britannia'* in which they were trained) to the crew of the submarine K4 rammed by accident on 31st January 1918. It was presented by the wife of the commanding officer, Commander David de Beauvoir Stocks.

Pattenmakers' Company and Basketmakers' Company hold their annual services here. Flemish immigrants made baskets in Rood Lane.

General
Although, apart from the spire, this is not structurally one of Wren's great churches and is not helped by the stained glass, especially the yellow cross in the east window put in after the 1939–45 War, the furnishings have much to offer to the visitor. Many are unusual and some, such as the churchwardens' pews, are unique. They are made more enjoyable by the clear descriptions.

St Margaret's is now a Guild Church, serving as a Christian Study Centre and with Offices and Library for the College of Preachers.

28 St Martin-within-Ludgate

Dedication
St Martin, according to legend, was a Roman soldier who met a beggar when riding in bitter weather to Amiens. Having no ready money, he cut his cloak with his sword and gave half to the beggar. Later, in 372 AD, Martin became Bishop of Tours and spread the Christian faith in northern Gaul.

'Ludgate', named after the mythical King Lud, was one of the six gates leading into the City. Called 'Lutgata' in the early 12th century it had become 'Ludgate' by 1235; a chapel dedicated to the Virgin Mary above the east front of the gate was linked to St Martin's. Rebuilt in 1586, the gate survived the Great Fire but was pulled down in 1760. The statue of Queen Elizabeth was transferred to St Dunstan in the West. Unlike the other 'gate' churches, St Martin's was situated within and not outside the gate.

History
Tradition takes the story back to Cadwallader, King of the Britons, who—according to a 13th century chronicle—built the first church

in about 600 AD and was buried in the crypt in 677, but recorded history does not go back beyond 1174 when there existed a church hard up against the Wall. This was rebuilt in 1437 and contained a chantry to Wm. Sevenoke who some say was another 'Dick' Whittington rising to become Lord Mayor. There were also many chapels.

Although Ludgate, which the mediaeval church touched, survived the Great Fire, St Martin's did not. Moreover, the steeple had been damaged earlier on 4th June 1561 by the same flash of lightning which brought down the spire of Old St Paul's. The Wren rebuilding was a late one (1677–87). He moved the site a little further north and incorporated part of the Wall in the western part of the new church.

Since then, St Martin's has been treated fairly gently and, as it managed—thanks to a favourable wind—to escape destruction in the December 1940 air-raid, we have a largely authentic Wren place of worship to enjoy.

Exterior

St Martin's is set sideways to, and can only be approached from, Ludgate Hill. The front facing it (south) has an elegant three-bay façade of Portland stone with tower in the middle slightly projecting and segment-headed windows with horizontal mouldings and pedimented niches flanking it. Above, scrolled volutes lead the eye easily towards the belfry stage of the tower and then skilfully merge via an octagonal stage to the lead-covered upper part of the steeple, consisting of ogee dome, charming balcony, lantern and obelisk steeple. This slender Continental-looking spire was designed to provide a counterpoint to the swelling lines of the dome of St Paul's and is matched on the other side of the Cathedral by the spire of St Augustine's, Watling Street; there is a point halfway down Fleet Street from which the spire can be seen to cut the dome exactly in half.

Interior

This is one of Wren's most ingenious designs. He succeeded in converting a sloping site which was wider from north to south than from west to east into a square by inserting a lofty south aisle containing vestibule and vestry between the outer wall and the body of the church. This is screened off by a partially enclosed arcade with beautifully plastered coffered arches and embellished with pilasters. By so doing, he killed another bird by insulating the interior from the noise of the outside traffic.

In the square thus created, Wren constructed another of his cross-in-square designs (cf. St Mary at Hill and St Anne's and St Agnes') but here, the columns—elevated on unusually tall pedestals—are closer together and very lofty. The barrel vaults of the arms of the cross, the entablatures of which reach to pilasters on walls where they stop abruptly, meet in the centre to form a groined middle section. As at the other two churches, the spaces between the arms are lower and have flat ceilings.

Galleries which formerly existed on the north and south sides have been removed but the west organ gallery reached by stairs with twisted balusters remains. The walls are panelled.

Chancel and sanctuary were raised in the 1890s but this does not detract from the impressive, if rather dark, interior, although the cutting down of the pews accentuates their lack of height in relation to the pedestals of the columns.

Furnishings
The furnishings are good and largely original.

Organ Although much rebuilt, the Renatus Harris (Father Smith?) organ dates from 1684. It is smaller than most and has only two manuals. Below the gallery there is a white marble pelican.

Font The font, given by one Thomas Morley in 1673, is a small elegant example in white marble with fluted bowl. Like the font at St Ethelburga's, Bishopsgate, it is inscribed on top with a Greek palindrome which, roughly translated, reads 'Wash my sin, not my face only'.

Candelabrum The fine, large brass chandelier in the centre was once in the Cathedral of the Island of St Vincent in the West Indies. How it came here is not known.

Stained glass Of no merit and adding to the darkness of the church.

Pulpit Original of standard hexagonal type. The sounding-board which has been made into a table came from St Mary Magdalene, Old Fish Street (burnt down in 1886).

Reredos The reredos is rather flat and has pilasters only. The raised centre carries a segmental arch and there are vases at the sides.

Paintings On the north side of the altar is a painting of the Ascension by R. Browne (wrongly attributed to Benjamin West) dating from 1720. On the south side are panels of St Mary Magdalene, St Gregory and St Martin copied by a Belgian artist.

Churchwardens' Double Chair The most remarkable furnishing is the double chair for churchwardens to the south of the reredos, dating from 1690 and the only known example of its kind.

Doorcases On the south side giving access to the vestry and vestibule are three splendid doorcases, notably the one attributed to Grinling Gibbons in the south-east corner decorated with large winged cherubs' heads in the spandrels, garlands down the sides and Corinthian pilasters. Another on the north side leads to a chapel.

Monuments

Thomas Berry A brass with figure in fur gown in the vestry records a benefaction of '12 penie loves to 12 poor foulkes every Sabathe day for aye' by Thomas Berry (Beri), a fishmonger. It is dated 1586. Fine carved bread-shelves can be seen on request.

Richard Harris Barham, author under the name of Thomas Ingoldsby of 'Ingoldsby Legends' was buried in St Mary Magdalene's in 1845 and his memorial was transferred to the wall near the entrance. There is also a memorial to his three children in the vestibule.

Bell A 1693 bell is placed on a square iron chest in the north-east corner.

Cistern A lead cistern dated 1779 is kept in the vestry.

Associations

Samuel Purchas, publisher of Richard Hakluyt's *Pilgrimes* known as 'the English Ptolemy' became rector in 1614. He was a friend of the American Indian Princess Pocahontas and her husband, John Rolfe.

Captain (later Admiral) William Penn, father of the founder of Pennsylvania, was married here on 6th June 1643.

Middlesex Yeomanry St Martin's is Regimental Chapel of the Middlesex Yeomanry.

General

St Martin's is no longer a parish church and now forms part of the parish of the Church of the Holy Sepulchre in Holborn. The transfer carried with it the former parishes of St Gregory's by St Paul's (not rebuilt after the Fire) and St Mary Magdalene, Old Fish Street (now part of Knightrider Street). The latter was burnt down in 1886.

Its Guild activities relate to liaison with the Metropolitan Police. It is also the Chapel of the Honourable Society of the Knights of the Round Table.

29 St Mary Abchurch

Dedication

An earlier spelling—'Abechurch'—led the historian, Stow, to think that the prefix 'Abe' might mean 'Up', referring to the slight eminence upon which the church was built; or it may be derived from the name of a founder or benefactor such as 'Abba'.

History

Earliest mention is of 'St Mary of Abechurch' at the end of the 12th century. Little is known of the building described in mediaeval times as 'a fair church' except that it had aisles, a bell tower and was decorated with murals, and that it had chantry chapels dedicated to St George and the Holy Trinity.

Being near the seat of the 1666 Fire, it was soon consumed and the parishioners had to wait some time before Wren rebuilt it between the years 1681 and 1686. In the meantime, they used on the site a temporary tabernacle from which the altar table still remains. This was housed in St Paul's Cathedral during the 1939–45 War and upon it in 1951 was laid the the American Roll of Honour presented to the Dean by General Eisenhower.

Subsequently, St Mary's has been singularly fortunate in the sensitive treatment received at the hands of restorers. 'Beautified and repaired' in 1708 when the ceiling was probably painted, Victorian 'improvements' relatively few, and skilfully restored by Godfrey Allen after the 1939–45 War, St Mary's is little altered. Although the ceiling and the organ were seriously damaged by blast and water, the bombs led to the discovery of a mediaeval crypt, probably 14th century, under the courtyard and removed the Victorian glass and tiled floor, which was then lowered 18 inches to its former level.

The living originally belonged to the Priory of St Mary Overy, Southwark, from whom it passed in the 15th century to the Master and chaplains of a College of Corpus Christi attached to St Lawrence Pountney church nearby. Later, Queen Elizabeth was persuaded by Archbishop Matthew Parker to grant it to the College of Corpus Christi and the Blessed Virgin Mary, Cambridge, of which he had been Master, in whose patronage it still remains.

St Lawrence Pountney was not rebuilt after the Fire, its parish being added to St Mary's, but in 1954 the latter became a Guild Church and its parish added to that of St Stephen's, Walbrook.

Exterior

The church is tucked away in a quiet courtyard between King

William Street and Cannon Street, with a paved forecourt—once the churchyard—cobbled in geometrical designs. Externally, St Mary's is in much the same homely vein of hipped roofs and dark red brick with stone dressings as St Benet's, Paul's Wharf, and also has a similar if not quite so charming lead steeple, made up of an ogee-shaped dome supporting an open lantern and a simple spire, all in lead. Cherubs are carved above some of the windows.

The red brick was once covered with stucco.

Interior
The interior is larger than that of St Benet's, measuring 63 by 60 feet, and is without aisles. It has the unique features in a Wren City church of a painted domed ceiling and a genuine Grinling Gibbons reredos—the only authenticated Gibbons' work in the City other than the font cover at All Hallows by the Tower and furnishings in St Paul's Cathedral.

Although architecturally the dome falls short of that at St Stephen's, Walbrook it is nevertheless a masterly achievement, for Wren succeeded in supporting it on the four brick walls without creating any outward thrust and so dispensing with the need of buttresses. It rests on capitals used as corbels, except at the west end where a column and pilaster are used.

The painted ceiling depicts female figures representing the Christian virtues seated above the wide diameter modillion cornice (the dome is over 40 feet across) with shells between. In the centre the Hebrew name for God (tetragrammaton) is surrounded by rays of glory and a worshipping chorus of angels and cherubs. There are clouds too and garlands. This fine feature which was originally painted by William Snow—'painter-stainer'—(not Sir James Thornhill as at one time thought) was beautifully restored after the War by Walter Hoyle.

There is a fine west gallery once used by the boys of Merchant Taylors' School.

The walls are panelled.

Furnishings
Most of the original ones remain, including the superb reredos. Taking them in order as one enters, they consist of:

Doorcases Two richly carved doorcases with fluted pilasters, garlands in the segmental heads and urns on top, the north one carrying in addition a copper pelican and nest which, until it was removed in 1764 for safety reasons, used to be the weather vane.

Royal Arms The Royal Arms of James II are above the south doorcase.

Poor-boxes Original boxes to receive alms, square in form on square pedestals, remain on each side of the west vestry door—a rare feature.

Font and font-cover The marble font in a railed enclosure was made by William Kempster, one of Wren's best craftsmen (his brother Christopher carved the stonework) in 1686. The font-cover by William Emmett is a delightful piece, showing the four Evangelists in niches under shaped arches, the whole looking like a small pavilion.

Pulpit The 1685 pulpit with the uncommon feature of having its original steps was made by another of Wren's great craftsmen, William Gray. It is similar to that at St Clement's, Eastcheap, in having a very large tester, not unlike an old tricorne hat.

Pews The richly carved pews on the north, south and west sides are original and one of those on the south side once had a cupboard or kennel beneath for dogs!

Organ St Mary's had no organ before 1822 when one was built by J. C. Bishop. It was so badly damaged during the War that a new one by Noel Mander was installed. The carved oak front, however, dates from 1717 and came from All Hallows, Bread Street (demolished 1877), after a spell at All Hallows, East India Dock Road.

Candelabra The mahogany columns which support the lights come from Lockinge House, Berkshire and were given in 1957.

*Reredos The star furnishing, known to have been designed by Grinling Gibbons himself. As late as 1946, a letter signed by him addressed to the churchwardens of St Lawrence Pountney requesting their share of the cost of the 'Olter Pees' was discovered. The reredos is a magnificent furnishing and the largest to be found in a City church. Corinthian columns support an entablature with parts of a segmental pediment above. Behind these is an attic with a raised concave centre and urns emitting flames, a reminder of the Fire. Wherever space permitted Gibbons himself carved trails of flowers and fruit of great delicacy and lightness; the pelican above the central round-headed panels is also his work but joiners made the columns, urns and the main structure of the reredos.

Monuments

Sir Patience Ward, who died in 1696. To the south of the reredos is a fine monument to this former Lord Mayor (1680) and Whig politician. It is in the form of a tablet with mourning putti and above, between urns, an allegorical figure on a concave-sided pedestal.

Edward Sherwood On the south wall of the chancel is an
elaborate memorial to Edward Sherwood, who died in 1690.

Associations
St Mary's is perhaps not so rich in associations as other City
churches but, as well as Sir Patience Ward, two other Lord Mayors
were parishioners and gave sword-rests to commemorate their
mayoralty.

General
Perhaps the least altered of Wren's City churches and containing the
work of some of his best craftsmen, St Mary's is a fascinating
church to visit. Lovable and homely without, beautifully furnished
within, we must indeed be thankful that this church has been spared.

No longer a parish church, it is now a Guild Church. Whilst it has
some associations with various Livery Companies, its closest is with
the Fruiterers', whose arms are now in the great south window.

30 St Mary Aldermary

Dedication
As a church on this site was mentioned about 1080, 'Aldermary'
may mean that it was older (alder) than St Mary-le-Bow, once called
St Mary Newchurch; but St Mary-le-Bow argues that 'alder' could
also indicate 'altera' (the other) Mary, i.e. Mary Magdalene.

History
The old church was the burial place of many Lord Mayors, for one
of whom—Thomas Romeyn, Lord Mayor in 1310 (grocer)—a
chantry chapel, according to the historian Stow, was endowed. Two
hundred years later, the then Lord Mayor (Sir Henry Keble)
provided funds for a new church. Started in 1510, it was completed
after his death in 1518, except for the tower. Work on this began in
1530 and the lower part erected; the material was Caen stone (also
used for the tracery of the windows on the south side). The upper
part did not follow until nearly a hundred years later in 1629. What
may have been the crypt of Keble's church, measuring
approximately 50 by 10 feet, was discovered in 1835.

The tower survived the Great Fire but the rest of the church had
to be rebuilt. Another benefactor—Henry Rogers—left money for
the repair or building of a place of worship and his niece-executrix

directed this to St Mary Aldermary on the condition, so it is stated, that the new church should be a faithful copy of the old, although no written evidence has been produced. This is probably the reason why Wren's rebuilding in 1681–2 follows Gothic instead of the usual Classical forms.

Repaired in 1823 it later — 1876–7 — underwent one of the most drastic Victorian restorations in the City. St Mary's was stripped of most of its furnishings (reredos, altar-rails, panelling, organ screen, gallery front and pews) and dull Victorian substitutes put in their place. A screen was put up at the west end dividing the lobby from the nave and stained glass introduced.

The glass was destroyed during the 1939–45 War and a post-war restoration was carried out by Arthur George Nisbet.

Exterior

The opening up of Queen Victoria Street has given St Mary's a conspicuous position. Ashlar stone-faced throughout and with a commanding south-west tower, it stands out amongst the routine commercial buildings.

The tower has prominent polygonal buttresses shafted at angles; these are panelled to their full height and culminate in pinnacles topped with finials renewed in the 19th century. The finials are now of glass-fibre as the stone ones were considered dangerous and taken down in 1927; they lie in fragments at the foot of the tower.

Interior

Slender clustered piers, slightly pointed nave arcade arches, three-light aisle and clerestory windows combine to produce a typical Perpendicular interior, but the ceiling is another matter. Although it might have followed the pattern of contemporary work, there is no similarity to the stone fan-vaults of the 16th century. The rosettes in large saucer domes and the fan tracery are beautiful but the use of plaster instead of stone gives what Elizabeth and Wayland Young describe as 'the sweetness of confectionery'. There is more plaster decoration in the spandrels of the arcade (foliage and coats of arms).

The east wall is slanted owing to the shape of the site.

Furnishings

The furnishings left after the Victorians had gone their determined way consist of:

Font This, as the Latin inscription records, was given by someone named Dutton Seaman in 1627. It is unusual in being enclosed with twisted baluster rails probably salvaged from the old altar-rails. The material is marble and the font is scalloped underneath; the ogee font cover is plain.

Poor-box On a flat twisted barley-sugar stem.

*Doorcase A splendid piece with broken segmental pediment, now at the west end, decorated with fluted Corinthian pilasters, fruit and flowers. It came from St Antholin's (see *General*).

Sword-rest A notable example in wood with cherub's head at foot and lion's head accompanied by more cherubs and crown at top. Dating from 1682 it is fixed to the south-east pillar of the nave.

Pulpit A fine Wren-period example but minus its tester. It is hexagonal with panels and is decorated with cherubs' heads and garlands of fruit and flowers.

Of post-restoration furnishings the *lectern* is embellished with four carved figures of saints on posts and the *glass* in the north window contains the coats-of-arms of the Innholders', Vintners' and Salters' Companies. The west window by John Crawford and dating from 1952 commemorates the defence of the City during the 1939–45 War.

Monuments

John Seale who died in 1714. The monument depicts figures representing Time and Death hanging a draped curtain and is adorned with two cherubs. It is supported on the north wall by corbel brackets carved to resemble bunches of grapes.

Margaret Bearsley who died in 1802. A simple tablet with a wreathed urn by the younger Bacon. It lies on the south wall of the chancel.

Rene Baudouin who died in 1728. A cusped wall cartouche having small dark red and blue panels with shields and an oval dome. Baudouin was a Huguenot refugee. It is attached to the south wall.

Blank monument A curiosity is a completely blank monument with urn and swag on the north wall of the chancel. The story is that it was put up by a woman for her husband. But she married a second husband before she had thought what to say about the first. The sculptor was Francis Bacon.

Associations

Henry Gold Rector in Henry VIII's reign and involved in the 'Holy Maid of Kent' visions. For this he was condemned to stand in St Paul's Cathedral throughout the sermon and thence taken to the Tower, being finally executed at Tyburn.

John Milton married his third wife in the pre-Wren church in 1663.

Lord Chief Justice Jeffreys, the despicable judge, was buried here on 2nd November 1693.

Skinners' Company hold their annual services in the church.

General

It is sadly ironic, and a measure of the harm done by the Victorians, that the money for the restoration in 1875–6 from which this church has visually so much suffered came from the sale of the site and the demolition of St Antholin's Church, Budge Row. The latter was one of Wren's most original creations, being in the form of an elongated octagon with oval dome and stone spire. (St Antholin's dedication was derived from a 4th century Egyptian hermit, St Anthony, corrupted to Antholin.)

St Mary Aldermary is in the parish of St Mary-le-Bow together with St Thomas the Apostle, St John the Baptist, Walbrook (not rebuilt after the Fire) and St Antholin's; it is now an independent Guild Church to promote retreats and the devotional life.

31 St Mary at Hill

Dedication

The suffix 'at Hill', referring to the ascent from Billingsgate, helped to distinguish this church from various other St Mary dedications.

History

Earliest mention is 1177 when the Norman church, called 'Sanctee Mariae Hupenhulle', was described as adjoining the Town House of the Abbots of Waltham Abbey, Essex. It later had a chantry and four chapels.

The church was enlarged towards the end of the 15th century and aisles added on each side, the southern one being on the site of the Abbot's kitchen. It had pews (unusual at such an early date) and the number of chapels rose to nine. A piece of stone carving from the church depicting in relief the Resurrection, which probably once stood on a gateway (cf. St Giles-in-the-Fields) is placed on the wall beside the south entrance door in the vestibule. It dates from about 1600.

Not completely destroyed in the Great Fire, the tower and part of the side walls were incorporated into Wren's church, begun in 1672 and one of the first of his rebuildings to be completed (in 1677). In 1695 money was provided for a spire.

A hundred years later, the steeple had to come down and in the 1780s George Gwilt erected the present brick one. He also rebuilt the west front (moving the main doors further west), reconstructed part of the south front and renewed the vaults and ceilings.

In 1827–8 what remained of the old walls was rebuilt by the architect James Savage, at which time he repaired and refitted St Mary's. Twenty years later in 1848–9, the same architect was responsible for a thorough restoration, during which the ceiling decoration was changed to its present delicate Adam-type design and William Gibbs Rogers was engaged to provide new furnishings.

Towards the end of the 19th century, St Mary's—like St Mary Woolnoth—was under threat from railway extension but survived this and the 1939–45 War. In 1967 the architects Seely (Lord Mottistone) & Paget embarked on a two-year programme of cleaning and repairs to the plaster and wood; at the same time ugly Victorian light fittings were replaced with the present pendant ones and the church brightened by alterations to the glass, notably removing most of the Victorian glass and substituting pure white Reamy antique, a translucent glass which allows the natural light to filter through. This restoration greatly enhanced the visual pleasure of this City church.

Exterior

The west end and main approach is in Lovat Lane; the east end abuts on to St Mary at Hill street from which one can enter via the small churchyard. The red brick battlemented tower (the rest of this front is yellow brick) has a homely appearance and is set at an angle to the Lane; the east end is slightly more circumstantial with its splendid projecting clock, Venetian window, some rustication and broken if awkward pediment. There is Portland stone facing but the plinth has been covered in stucco. In the churchyard is a lead cistern dated 1788 and, beside the south door, a tablet recording that the burial ground was closed on 21st June, 1846.

Interior

Sumptuous and impressive. Although much of the decoration and many of the furnishings date from the 19th century, this is one of the most enjoyable interiors in the City. The structural design shows one more facet of Wren's versatility in planning. It is a Greek cross in an irregular rectangle, the barrel-vaulted arms of the cross leading into a central square formed by four fluted Corinthian columns from which rises, by means of pendentives, a shallow dome. The four corners between the arms of the cross have low flat ceilings. The plan was drawn by Wren from Dutch mid-17th century interiors to which it is closely akin.

A fine west gallery is supported on pillars enriched with carved fruit and flowers.

Savage's plasterwork on the coved ceiling consists of delicate rosettes and arabesques with much coffering (dome and arches) executed in a restrained manner with gold leaf and blue being used against a white background. The corner ceilings are plain except for egg and dart cornices and the use of little rosettes. The walls with pilasters are painted in two shades of white.

Adjoining the first bay of the south wall from the east end of the church is a panelled study, dating from the 17th century but rebuilt in a building and repair programme, started in 1834.

One of the joys of this church is that the Victorians left the box pews so that the seating is in harmony with the rest of the church and blends happily with the wood-enclosed bases of the columns.

Furnishings

These look 17th century but in fact much is Victorian—the work of a very talented carver in wood, William Gibbs Rogers, who closely studied Grinling Gibbons. Reredos, communion table, altar-rails, pews and font are pre-19th century but pulpit, rector's pew, reader's desk, lectern and probably organ-case are Rogers' work.

Font White, octagonal marble bowl mounted on a pedestal rising from a black base. It has a carved ogee domed wooden cover. There is an exquisite piece of ironwork nearby from a font cover of St George's, Botolph Lane, which was joined to St Mary's after the Fire.

Organ Installed in 1834, replacing a smaller instrument dating back to 1787 and made by Samuel Green, which in turn succeeded the original Father Smith organ. The splendid casing is decorated with garlands of flowers, fruit and birds; the front has bold clusters of musical trophies.

Sword-rests The finest set in the City; there are six in all, five at the west and a sixth near the chancel. The decoration is especially elaborate.

Churchwardens' pews These pews with richly carved ends are situated partly under the organ-gallery.

Box-pews The only church in the City where one can see a complete set of box-pews (72 in all). They add enormously to the character of this interior and provide a Dickensian atmosphere.

Stained glass Highly coloured (gold, blue, red) interlinked circles as a border in the north and south windows. Six circular medallions, two heraldic shields and inscription in two east windows.

Pulpit A 'tour de force' by Rogers, having a long, wooden

St Mary at Hill. Reredos

staircase with carved balusters almost suitable for a private residence. The large sounding-board has bosses of flowers which project 12 inches. There are bunches of fruit and flowers on the back.

Chandeliers Two double-tiered eighteen-branched gilt-fired chandeliers above the choir stalls were given to mark the rehabilitation of the church in 1968–9 by the Watermen's and Lightermen's Company of the River Thames, and by the Billingsgate Ward Club respectively.

Chancel stalls The openwork stalls in Renaissance style are also Rogers' work.

*Reredos This particularly fine altar piece is original, much gilded according to the custom in Wren's time and containing the usual panels with Ten Commandments, Creed and Lord's Prayer. It is surmounted by a segmental-headed open pediment decorated with cherubs' heads. (plate p. 129).

The altar table and communion rails are contemporary with the reredos.

Monuments
John Woods, died 1658, his wife and son. A tablet with Corinthian side columns and a shield of arms. On the north wall.

Daniel Wigfall, died 1698. A fine, carved tablet which came from St George's, Botolph Lane.

John Harvey, died 1700. A tablet on the south wall also with shield of arms.

Thomas Lavall and his wife. An elegant wall monument with urns and arms.

Associations
Prebendary William Carlile, founder of the Church Army, was rector here from 1892 to 1926. He filled the church, and the trombone which was used at his services is preserved in a glass case in the vestibule.

General
Victorian insensitivity to the character of the 17th and 18th century places of worship has often to be deplored but here we see work so sympathetic that it is hard to recognise which is which. Although much altered since the church was built by Wren, St Mary's is a gem amongst City churches, emerging a better place than it was before and one can only wish that those concerned had had more to do with other churches.

The parish of St Andrew Hubbard was joined to St Mary's after the Fire. St George's, Botolph Lane was demolished in 1904 and together with its attached parish, St Botolph's, Billingsgate, was also added to St Mary's, which is the parish church of Billingsgate Market. Finally, when St Margaret Pattens became a Guild Church in 1954, this, together with St Gabriel's, Fenchurch Street, was included in the parish of St Mary at Hill.

32 St Mary-le-Bow

Dedication
The most likely supposition is that 'le Bow' refers to the arches of the crypt under the church, giving rise to the name of St Mary of the Bows or Arches.

History
The Norman place of worship of which the crypt remains—the oldest parochial building in London—was called St Mary Newchurch which could mean that it replaced an earlier building or that it was not as old as St Mary Aldemary (Alde Mary) at the other end of Bow Lane.

The history of the mediaeval church is remarkably full of incident. In 1091, the roof blew off, killing several people; in 1196 a bad character called William Fitz-Osbert, who had killed an officer, barricaded himself in the tower and had to be smoked out; in 1271, the tower—no doubt weakened by the previous incident—collapsed, killing more people and in 1284, a quarrel over a woman led to a goldsmith, Lawrence Duket, being hanged inside the church; this necessitated stopping up the doors and windows with thorns until the building had been purged of this desecration. In 1331, a temporary wooden structure placed beside the church fell at a time when Queen Philippa, wife of Edward III, was viewing a tournament.

The tower took a very long time to rebuild; it was not until 1512 that the new steeple, built of Caen stone, was completed on a new site. Although perhaps not so notable as its successor, it must have been impressive for it had four lanterns at the corners and a fifth supported on flying arches, all intended to provide illumination for the street.

Much of this tower survived the Fire but it had to be taken down and, ample funds being available, Wren was given the opportunity to erect one of the greatest creations of his genius. Buildings were acquired to enable him to stand the new steeple on Cheapside and it was connected by a vestibule to the body of the church. In the rebuilding, he came across the Norman crypt and also a Roman tesselated pavement and, being impressed by the solidity of the Norman columns, he used the crypt to support the north and south sides of the new St Mary's with consequent problems when it had to be rebuilt again after the 1939–45 War. Wren's rebuilding was completed in 1673 except for the steeple which took another seven years. It was the most expensive of his City churches.

There were modifications in 1867 (galleries removed) and in 1878–9.

On 10th May, 1941 the whole building was engulfed in flames from incendiary bombs. Restoration began in 1956 under the direction of the architect Laurence King and was finished eight years later. This time, it was possible to save the steeple but it had first to be taken down and the foundations strengthened; the bells, a semitone lower after being recast, rang out again on 20th December 1961. The rest of the church, including the Norman crypt of which the walls and columns survived, was rebuilt on the structural design of the old building but with modern furnishings.

St Mary-le-Bow has close links with the Province of Canterbury and the City of London. The Court of Arches, the supreme Court of the Province of Canterbury, has continued to meet in the crypt since the 12th century and, until 1847, the whole church came under the Archbishop. The legend that, to be a Cockney or true Londoner, you must be born within the sound of Bow Bells probably derives • from the ringing of the curfew which came to define the City's limits, although the curfew was also rung at All Hallows by the Tower, St Giles', Cripplegate and St Bride's, Fleet Street.

Exterior
The exterior is dominated by the steeple. This rises majestically to the belfry stage, decorated by pairs of Ionic pilasters. Lively corner ornaments of scrolls with vases on top make an easy transition to the spire stages. These consist of a circular colonnade of 12 columns thrusting upwards by means of flying buttresses to a square stage, also with 12 columns, and completed with an obelisk spirelet of Aberdeen granite which is topped by a copper ball and the famous dragon weather-vane nearly nine feet long, all in the most harmonious proportions. The steeple is indeed a masterpiece. (Plate p. 133.)

On the north face of the tower, Wren affixed to the second storey a balcony to commemorate the Crown Sild from which royalty in

St Mary-le-Bow. Steeple

the Middle Ages viewed jousts and other shows. This Sild, or balcony, was built after the collapse of the wooden structure in 1331. On the north and west fronts of the lower storey, Wren introduced fine doorways with much decoration including oval windows and cherubs holding garlands of fruit all enclosed in a rusticated arch.

The west front shows clearly how the steeple is joined to the church by a vestibule. In front is a garden with a statue of Captain John Smith (1580–1631) first among the leaders of the Settlement at Jamestown, Virginia.

Interior

The interior follows Wren's structure, with arcades of three arches divided by piers with attached Corinthian half-columns and a broad, curved elliptical ceiling, divided into panels (mainly green in colour) and pierced by the clerestory windows. The proportions are almost square ($65\frac{1}{2} \times 63$ feet) but given direction by the wrought-iron parclose screens at the east end which enclose the vestry and sacrament house respectively. There is no division between nave and chancel.

The internal space has been arranged to suit modern needs with flexible seating, a free-standing altar and the cross raised aloft to permit uninterrupted view of the episcopal chair behind. The impression is one of openness and adaptability with a minimum of furnishings to enable the church to be used for various purposes as well as liturgical worship.

The carved corbel heads at the tops of the nave arches represent people concerned with the rebuilding (bishop, architect etc.).

Furnishings

None of the old furnishings remain. The modern ones consist of:

Organ There was no organ when Wren rebuilt the church.

Pulpits The provision of two pulpits harks back to the early days when there were separate ambos or reading desks on each side of a church. This arrangement is admirably suited to the lunch-time dialogues between the rector and well-known celebrities on topics of Christian concern which are so much a feature of St Mary-le-Bow today.

Stained glass Designed by John Hayward and dating from 1964, the east window shows Christ in majesty; to the north the window depicts St Mary cradling the church in her arms with representations of the bombed City churches around, whilst on the other side the window shows St Paul with the sword of his martyrdom and the book of his Epistles. Other windows depict the seals of the City in ruby with St Paul and St Thomas à Becket, who was born in Cheapside; below appear the arms of the twelve great Livery Companies. They provide a vivid splash of colour with the green of the lizards in one of the coats of arms particularly gay.

Monuments

The only monument of any note, though damaged, is to Bishop Newton who became rector in 1744.

Bells Although this book normally does not cover bells, Bow Bells are so famous that it should be mentioned that there are 12 of them with names like Katherine, Fabian, Cuthbert etc. and that the Great Bell of Bow which ends the nursery rhyme 'Oranges and Lemons' was recast in 1956.

Associations

SPCK The Society for Promotion of Christian Knowledge was founded in the vestry in 1698.

Trinity Church, Wall Street, New York In 1697, Bishop Compton obtained a charter from William III for Trinity Church, New York, in which it was laid down that all should be ordered there 'as it is in our church of St Mary-le-Bow in London'. This led to an association which has continued ever since.

Sir Richard Whittington The story of Dick Whittington turning again upon hearing the bell of Bow may be legendary but there is no doubt that it could have been heard on Highgate Hill.

General

St Mary-le-Bow could well claim to be the most renowned of the City parish churches. It has emerged from fires and destruction as strong as ever with a special affection in the hearts of people all over the world and with a distinctive place in the ministry of the Church in London.

The following parishes are now annexed to St Mary-le-Bow: St Pancras Soper Lane, All Hallows Honey Lane, All Hallows Bread Street, St John the Evangelist Friday Street, St Augustine's Watling Street, St Faith under St Paul's, St Mildred's Bread Street and St Margaret Moses.

33 St Mary Woolnoth with St Mary Woolchurch Haw

Dedication

The full mediaeval title was St Mary Woolnoth of the Nativity. 'Woolnoth' is obscure in origin. It could be a corruption of Wulfnoth who was possibly the first church's founder or it may derive from the wool market which stood nearby in the Middle Ages, added to the dedication to distinguish this from other churches called St Mary. A neighbouring church, St Mary Woolchurch Haw, not rebuilt after the Great Fire and which used to exist where the Mansion House now stands, was unmistakably connected with wool.

History

A timber church may have been built here in Saxon times by Wulfnoth and replaced after the Conquest by a stone one but the first sure ground is a reference to the 'Parish of Winodmariecherche' about 1198. 'St Mary Wolnoth' is mentioned in 1273. Whatever there was gave way to a rebuilding about 1440 and, according to the historian John Stow, another in 1486.

The mediaeval place of worship escaped complete destruction in the Great Fire, the steeple and part of the walls surviving. Wren rebuilt the north side facing Lombard Street, and put on a new roof but otherwise used what remained. This cosmetic treatment was not a success and the church became so insecure that the parishioners were afraid to worship in it.

They petitioned the Commissioners under the Fifty Churches Act of 1711 for a new church and, although the Act was designed to encourage the building of churches where none existed before, they were successful and obtained Nicholas Hawksmoor as architect.

As usual, he built (between 1716 and 1727) something highly original and this, although extensively altered by William Butterfield in 1875–6, has come down to us today. Many attempts have been made to do away with the church (in 1863, 1892, 1897, 1900 and in the 1920s); in particular the City and South London Tube Railway tried to acquire the site in 1897 for their station at the Bank but they had to be content with burrowing underneath, having the bones in the vault removed to Ilford (see inscription on south wall) and underpinning the church with huge girders.

In 1967–8 the exterior was cleaned and the interior redecorated using gold leaf; a new cast lead roof was installed.

Exterior

St Mary Woolnoth occupies a prominent position in the hub of the City. It presents one of the most unusual façades of any church in the area, massive, uncompromising and of almost fortress-like aspect. Hawksmoor has concentrated his ingenuity on the west side facing the open area and the north side facing Lombard Street. The south side could not be seen before King William Street was cut through in the 19th century. The west face which provides the main entrance retains the original gates in front. The lower part of the projecting centre has banded rustication running right across and curving round the Tuscan columns at the corners; above, a stage with attached Corinthian columns extending the full width supports a heavy entablature and only then does the steeple divide into two low, balustraded turrets. There are few curves and the impact made is one of mathematical solidity.

The Lombard Street façade carries three large rusticated niches enclosing Corinthian columns supported on concave pedestals set diagonally and carrying an entablature which curves inwards. Above is a heavy cornice on console brackets. A prominent feature is the projecting clock, mentioned by T. S. Eliot in *The Waste Land*.

Beside the entrances to the Tube station grimy-faced cherubs can still be seen on doorways which used to lead to the vault.

Interior

The lofty well-lit interior provides a pleasing contrast to the formidable exterior. The plan is that of a Roman atrium with a square central area set in a larger square which forms an ambulatory around it. The inner space is carried up above the roof to create a lantern with large semicircular windows acting as a clerestory and giving plenty of light. The ceiling is coloured blue with a gilt centre and star decoration. The lantern rises above an entablature which is carried on groups of three large Corinthian columns at the corners.

These columns look unduly massive for the relatively small interior, an impression accentuated by the removal of the galleries which were considered unsafe by Butterfield. Being too good to discard, the curious expedient was adopted of affixing them to the walls with their tapering supports dangling.

At the east end, an imposing black canopy with barley-sugar columns over the altar, echoing Bernini's famous baldacchine at St Peter's, Rome is a striking feature. It is squeezed into an arched recess.

Butterfield raised the chancel using polychrome tiles and took away the high pews.

Furnishings
Altar-piece This is of oak and carries the Decalogue (Ten Commandments).

Pulpit A Hawksmoor furnishing, square and rather bulgy in outline with panelled sides. Butterfield lowered it and raised the sounding-board which is elevated on square piers, thus creating an absurd relationship between the two.

Organ The organ is a Father Smith instrument and the case (later pushed back) is mainly of his time. There is now a second and larger one.

Communion rails These are of wrought-iron and a fine fitting.

Monuments
W. A. Gun, who died in 1806. The monument is situated in the gallery at the west end. It shows a woman standing by an urn.

Edward Norman Butler (1907–63). A tablet on the south wall commemorates this 'Churchwarden, Preacher, Goldsmith, Oarsman, Gardener, Antiquary'.

Associations
John Newton St Mary Woolnoth will always be remembered for the ministry of John Newton (1780–1807) who, in his own words on the tablet near the pulpit, was 'once an infidel and libertine' but was 'appointed to preach the faith he had long laboured to destroy'. It was his sermons which inspired William Wilberforce to get slavery abolished.

Some of our most popular hymns—'Amazing Grace', 'How sweet the name of Jesus sounds', 'Glorious things of Thee are spoken'—were written by John Newton.

A case contains his biography and other articles associated with him.

Lord Mayors Many Lord Mayors, going as far back as mediaeval times, have contributed generously to rebuildings, restoration and chapels. The bones of no less than five lay in the vaults until they were moved to Ilford in 1897 when the Tube line was built. One of the most famous was Sir Martin Bowes, ancestor of the Queen Mother, Lord Mayor in 1545, whose helm and gauntlets plus funeral achievements are exhibited in a case given by the Goldsmiths' Company next to the altar on the south side.

Claudius Buchanan According to an inscription near the pulpit, Claudius Buchanan, founder of many Anglican missions in India, owed his conversion to sermons preached here.

Hannah More Hannah More, the originator of cottage meetings, received 'Spiritual inspiration' here.

William Owtram This former rector was one of the eleven clergy who stayed at their posts in the City during the terrible Plague of 1665.

British Columbia St Mary Woolnoth is the official City church for the Government of British Columbia.

General

Next door to the Mansion House, the church must owe its continued existence to the patronage of the Lord Mayors. It is Nicholas Hawksmoor's only City church and, because of its compactness, is one of the most commanding ecclesiastical buildings of this forceful architect.

It is now a Guild Church in the parish of St Edmund the King, Lombard Street, concerned with the relief of stress.

The year 1977 marked the 250th anniversary of this unusual church.

34 St Michael's, Cornhill

Dedication

St Michael, the leader of the angels against the forces of evil, is sometimes portrayed with the orb and sceptre, symbols of heavenly and earthly rule. In Doom paintings it is often he who weighs souls to assess whether they go up to Heaven or down to Hell. More than 600 churches in this country are dedicated to St Michael.

'Cornhill' is one of the two hills (the other 'Ludgate') which attracted the Romans to found their British capital at London; and John Stow, the historian, refers to the corn market being held there 'time out of mind'.

History

St Michael's is one of the few Saxon foundations in the City, and it is recorded that the living was given by Alnothus the Priest to the Abbot of Evesham in 1055 AD. In 1503 it came into the hands of the Drapers' Company who have held it ever since.   During the Middle Ages the church received many bequests from distinguished residents for the saying of masses for their souls and to relieve the poor; there were as many as five chantries. Stow mentions that there was a cloister on the south side where members of the choir lived and where there was a pulpit cross similar to the one at St Paul's. His father, grandfather and great-grandfather were all buried in the cloister garth.

It was one of the first churches in the City to have pews, dating from as early as 1475.

It appears to have always had a tower and, before this was rebuilt in 1421, even a spire. The curfew was rung from it for 160 years after that date. The tower survived the Great Fire and was patched up by Wren when he rebuilt the church between 1670 and 1677. However, it became unsafe and in 1715 work started on a new one but came to a halt for lack of funds in 1717. It was only resumed with the aid of a grant from the Fifty New Churches Fund, not being finally completed until 1722, when Wren was 90. The earlier work may have been his but, after resumption, is generally ascribed to Nicholas Hawksmoor, who worked in Wren's office, although Gerald Cobb thinks it more likely that the later work was carried out by another member of his staff, William Dickenson.

The Cornhill fire of 1748 seriously threatened the steeple. Many repairs to the fabric took place in the 18th century, especially in 1790 when the windows on the south and east sides were made circular and various new furnishings including a pulpit installed. The character, however, of the church today largely stems from a drastic 'restoration' by Sir George Gilbert Scott between 1858 and 1860 and later in 1867-8.

St Michael's did not suffer in the 1939-45 War and in 1952 some of the harm done by Scott was corrected, but the church remains essentially Victorian.

Exterior

Even for the City, St Michael's is hemmed in more than most churches. From Cornhill there is only an imperfect view of the church's main feature—the fine, well proportioned 130 ft high Gothic tower—and at pavement level, buildings obscure all but Scott's over-encrusted doorway. On the south side, however, a small remnant of the churchyard remains.

The tower has large angle turrets with panelled and crocketed pinnacles terminating in foliaged finials with sharp spikes; these once had vanes. Three-quarters of the way below the top there is a string-course of carved heads, alternately old and young.

The tympanum of Scott's doorway shows St Michael trampling on devils and on the right side is a bronze statue of him by Richard R. Goulden, a memorial to those from the parish killed in the 1914-18 War.

St Michael's, Cornhill. Pelican in Piety

From the south side the round-headed Lombardic aisle and circular clerestory windows give a chapel-like effect.

Interior

The recently redecorated interior has nave and aisles of four bays in semi-classical style with groined vaulting. The plain arches are carried on Tuscan columns with low bases. Ceiling decoration is confined to transverse bands of rosettes. The chancel slightly projects. Scott's mark is left in the Lombard-type tracery of the windows, the stained glass, the choir, the pink marble reredos of mainly Italian design, the black and white tiles on the floor and the carved wooden angels with wings below the corbels. He cast out the old Communion rails, which found their way to Great Waldingfield in Suffolk. He also covered the walls with polychrome decoration, but this was corrected by painting them in gold and white after the War; the windows were then lightened. On the credit side, he engaged W. Gibbs Rogers to work on the pews, and he, as at St Mary at Hill, did excellent work.

Furnishings

The only original furnishings are the font, part of the organ and the altar-table.

Pelican On a pedestal at the west end is this magnificent bird carved in wood standing on its nest and feeding its young. (Plate p. 141). It is very large and one of the finest examples of this emblem of sacrifice, the long curved bill being particularly well executed. It was supplied through George Paterson, a painter, in 1775.

Organ Originally Renatus Harris but enlarged in 1790 and subsequently altered several times, but retaining nine of the original Harris stops. The organ was rebuilt in 1976. The church has a fine tradition of organ playing and Purcell may have used this instrument. Amongst organists known to have played on it were Dr Harold Darke, the composer William Boyce who wrote 'Hearts of Oak', and Dr Theodore Aylward.

Bench-ends These were carved by Rogers and repay detailed examination. At the west end of the south aisle can be found the Scapegoat with the mark of the High Priest on its forehead (taken from Holman Hunt's picture) and the Return from Egypt after Herod's death; in the north aisle there is a figure of Charity feeding and protecting three children, and another Pelican.

Pulpit and Lectern These are also Rogers' work. The lectern won a prize at the great exhibition of 1851.

Altar-table The original late 17th century oak table remains.

Poor-box Supported on a fluted pedestal with clawed feet. The vase for money is supported on two dolphins.

Monuments

John Newman, died 1615. The monument is a demi-figure 'elegantly gesticulating' (Pevsner).

John Vernon, who died in 1616. This monument, high up on the north wall, is also in the form of a half-length figure and replaces one destroyed in the Great Fire. It bears the cartouche of the Merchant Taylors' Company, of which he was a Master.

Cowper family Near the south-west door in the vestibule are monuments of three of the illustrious ancestors of William Cowper, the poet.

Stained glass Early Clayton and Bell work (1858) of good quality. It depicts the life of our Lord on earth from Annunciation to Crucifixion and Glory.

Associations

Thomas Gray, the author of Gray's *Elegy*, was baptised here in 1716. In a glass case in the vestibule is a walking-stick which belonged to him.

Coffee-house The first coffee-house to be opened in England was situated in St Michael's Alley and in 1657, when it was introduced, a tent was pitched in the churchyard for the sale of coffee.

City Companies The Drapers, the Merchant Taylors, the Master Mariners and the Guild of Air Pilots and Air Navigators all attend their annual Election-day services here.

General

St Michael's shares with St Mary Aldermary the distinction of having the only purely Gothic steeple in an existing Wren church, although the tower of St Alban's, Wood Street remains. It also shares with St Mary's the dubious distinction of being one of the most Victorianised churches in the City and, even allowing for the brightening of the interior since the War, the harm done by insensitive restoration cannot be undone.

The church is involved in the Ministry of Healing and special services and meetings are geared to this work. It remains a parish church and is scheduled to be the centre of a wider ministry, grouping several parishes. Two other parishes (St Benet Fink and St Peter le Poer) were incorporated some time ago, after demolition of their churches in 1844 and 1907 respectively.

35 St Michael Paternoster Royal

Dedication

The archangel Michael (the name means 'who is like God') is the leader of the forces of good against the forces of evil represented by Lucifer, the Fallen Angel of light. He is sometimes portrayed—as in the centre light of the east window—as thrusting Lucifer down with a lance.

'Paternoster' refers to Paternoster Lane, where rosaries used to be made and 'Royal' comes from the town of La Reole near Bordeaux from which merchants in the City imported wine as early as 1282. A neighbouring church, destroyed in the Great Fire and not rebuilt— St Martin Vintry—also recalled the wine trade.

History

St Michael's is first mentioned about 1219 when it was referred to as 'St Michael of Paternosterchierch' and was also included in a list of churches for taxation compiled by Pope Nicholas IV in 1291. In 1361, the church was called 'S. Michael in the Riole'.

Its mediaeval fame, however, will always rest upon its being Sir Richard Whittington's church. In 1409, this admirable four-times Lord Mayor (to whom however the legend of Dick Whittington and his cat did not attach until nearly 200 years later), who lived next door, provided funds for the building of a new church. He also founded, for the saying of prayers for his soul and the souls of his family and benefactors, a College of Priests adjacent, from which College Hill gets its name. In 1424, masters of the College became rectors of St Michael's. It was dissolved in 1540.

Sir Richard was buried in the church when he died in 1423 but his body has more than once been disturbed and now cannot be found. Efforts made in 1949 to locate his tomb only produced a mummified cat which, however, was unlikely to have been Sir Richard's, the church with his monument having gone up in flames during the Great Fire; it was rebuilt under Sir Christopher Wren between 1686 and 1694 except for the steeple, which was not completed until 1713.

The usual Victorian 'doing-over' was carried out in 1866 by the ubiquitous William Butterfield, ostensibly in memory of Whittington.

St Michael's survived the early air-raids of the 1939–45 War but unfortunately fell to a flying bomb in 1944. After some opposition from the diocese and the Royal Fine Arts Commission which was overcome by the City Corporation, it was restored by Elidir L. W. Davies, designer of the Mermaid Theatre, the Whittington Hall

St Michael Paternoster Royal

being added at the west end. Re-consecration took place in December 1968. The area south of the building has been laid out as the Whittington Garden.

No longer a parish church, nor made into a Guild church, the tower and west end have been converted for use as the headquarters of the Missions to Seamen, and the status of St Michael's is that of a chapel under the Bishop of London, the parish being joined to that of St James Garlickhythe nearby. The transfer of the parish carried with it the parishes of St Martin Vintry and All Hallows the Less (not rebuilt after the Great Fire), St Michael's, Queenhithe, All Hallows the Great and Holy Trinity the Less (demolished).

Exterior
The exterior shows a simple building of stone with tall round-headed windows and a tower in the south-west corner. The windows have the nice little touch of cherubs' heads as keystones. There is a strong cornice which carries on round the tower and binds it to the body of the church. The steeple (plate p. 145) is plain in the lower parts but as at St James's Garlickhythe next door and St Stephen's, Walbrook, Wren has exercised his ingenuity in the top stages, all three displaying varying examples of his skill. At St Michael's they form an appealing composition, consisting of a recessed octagon carried round in a circle with eight columns at the angles, each with its own entablature, above which is a small octagon with a domed top stage and weathervane. The tower has square-headed windows at belfry level and small circular windows above with a pierced parapet on top. The whole steeple is just over 128 feet high.

Interior
A simple rectangle without aisles measuring 67 × 47 feet. The walls are panelled. Some of the original furnishings remain despite war damage. There is a west gallery supporting the organ (dating from 1749) with coat of arms.

Furnishings
The woodwork is fine.
   Candelabrum The single candelabrum is an exceptionally fine piece and unusually early. It is marked 'Birmingham, 1644'. This came from All Hallows the Great.
   Sword-rests The gilded sword-rests are for the Lord Mayor's sword of state on the north side and, on the other side, for the hats of his attendants.
   Altar-piece, Pulpit, Lectern, Door-cases These are all original,

carved in wood. The pulpit has a canopy. The figure in front of the lectern, another All Hallows furnishing, represents Charity. There are altar-rails with turned balusters on three sides of the sanctuary, which is unusual.

Moses and Aaron These figures on the east wall also came from All Hallows the Great.

Stained glass The glass destroyed in the War has been replaced by interesting modern glass by John Hayward. The theme is the confrontation between good and evil.

The westernmost window on the south side depicts the young Whittington at the base, complete with cat, and above, the City with streets paved with gold and at the top in red the seal of the Mayor with heraldry on either side.

Monument

Sir Samuel Pennant died whilst Lord Mayor in 1750 from jail-fever contracted from prisoners in the dock. Such hazards led to sweet-smelling herbs being placed in docks to guard against infection.

Associations

The chief associations with Sir Richard Whittington are recorded under 'History'.

Peter Blundell, founder of the famous school near Tiverton, Devon, familiar to readers of 'Lorna Doone', was buried here in 1601.

General

The uninterrupted view from the south due to the layout of the Whittington Garden and the careful restoration of the building adds to the pleasure of visiting this church.

36 St Nicholas Cole Abbey

Dedication

The popular but little-documented St Nicholas, beloved of children as Santa Claus, was Bishop of Myra in Asia Minor during the first half of the 4th century. The patron saint of travellers and seamen, nearly four hundred churches are dedicated to him in this country, mainly round the coast.

The origin of 'Cole Abbey' is obscure. The most widely accepted theory is that it is a corruption of 'Cold Harbour', a mediaeval type of lodging house, and that such an establishment existed nearby.

History

The church is mentioned in a letter of Pope Lucius II in 1144 and in 1272–3 it is called 'Sci Nichi retro fihstrate' (St Nicholas behind Fish Street), a reminder of the pre-Billingsgate fish market which used to exist here. The historian Stow records that, in Elizabeth's reign, a lead and stone cistern fed by lead pipes from the Thames and donated by a rich fishmonger was set up against the north wall of the church 'for the care and commodity of the Fishmongers in and about Old Fish Street'. Many of them were buried at St Nicholas'.

The steeple and south aisle were rebuilt in 1377 and, at the time of the Reformation, there were three chantries served by chantry priests. A carved stone head from the mediaeval church found during the 1962 restoration lies behind panelling near the south-west door.

More than once renovated in the early part of the 17th century when new battlements were added to the steeple, it was one of the first churches to be rebuilt by Wren after the Fire, the work being started in 1671 and completed in 1677. During the 19th century, rearrangements were carried out in 1874.

In more recent times the fabric was so blackened by smoke issuing through a vent from steam trains of the underground railway which passed beneath, that the church came to be called 'St Nicholas Cole Hole Abbey'.

Gutted by fire-bombs in May 1941, restoration in the Wren style was completed by Arthur Bailey in 1962.

Patronage during the 16th century passed from St Martin-le-Grand through various hands and, in the following century, was for a time with a Puritan Colonel Hacker, one of the Charles I regicides who was beheaded at the Restoration.

Exterior

Before Queen Victoria Street was built between 1861 and 1871, St Nicholas' lay in a narrow street and entrance was from the north side, but now the church stands out prominently at the top of the road which runs beside the podium, now tidied up and planted, on the south side after the bomb devastation. There is no clerestory but a handsome balustrade encircles the top and the round-headed windows have a refinement of straight hoods supported on console brackets. Those on the south side, built of Portland stone, used to have shops hard up against them.

The north-west steeple consists of a low tower with good belfry windows but under skimpy pediments rising above the cornice, and a rather endearing inverted trumpet-shaped spire. (see plate p. 149)

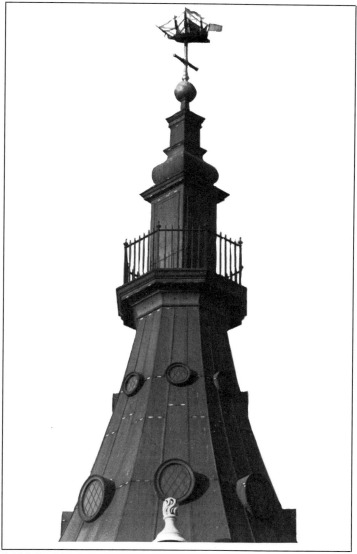

St Nicholas Cole Abbey. Trumpet-shaped spire with ship vane

This, with many round and oval lunettes, was destroyed in 1941 but has been rebuilt; the slightly concave sides are surmounted by a balcony similar to the one at St Martin's, Ludgate, and is crowned by a delightful vane in the form of a ship which was once at St Michael's Queenhithe (demolished in 1876). The spire has also been likened to a lighthouse—perhaps in deference to St Nicholas.

Interior

An open, rectangular box without divisions of any kind. The walls, apart from gilt Corinthian pilasters and panelling, are perfectly plain and without colour; but the light woodwork of the furnishings, which include some which were rescued, and the decorative treatment provide plenty of life.

A screen at the west end containing some of the original panels and richly carved with fruit and flowers shuts off the stairs to the organ gallery, vestry and base of the tower. The east end is made striking by the rather dark glass of Keith New and the elaborate gilt adornment of swags, fruit, flowers and cherubs' heads with a chalice over the altar.

Furnishings

Doorcases The three west doorways and the main entrance on the south are liberally supplied with cherubs' heads, which abound in this church. Carvings from the former reredos are to be seen above the south doorway.

Font The richly and beautifully carved font cover with ogee supports carrying a crown is original.

Royal Arms These are the Arms of Charles II.

*Chandelier A splendid example and also original.

Pulpit Another Wren furnishing, elaborately carved but without tester.

Altar-rails The finely turned rails were also rescued. They too are decorated with fruit and flowers.

Stained glass The three east windows by Keith New, dating from 1962, depict in the form of rivers the rôle of the church (shown as an Ark) in spreading the Gospel throughout the world with the help of the Seven Gifts of the Holy Spirit.

Organ The original instrument dated 1779 was disposed of and replaced by the present new one.

Associations

Plague Ninety-one out of the 125 parishioners died in the 1665 Plague—an appalling proportion.

George Whitehead, the great Methodist preacher, delivered his sermon on Profane Swearing here in 1737.

Bowyers' Company This Company holds its bi-annual commemorative service in the church. In the north-east corner, a brass plaque commemorates a famous Bowyer, James Wood, who was buried here in 1629.

Thomas Sowdley, who was vicar here during the reign of Edward VI, obtained a licence to marry. For this he was probably deprived during the reign of Queen Mary but came back again as soon as Queen Elizabeth ascended the throne, thus becoming the church's first married incumbent.

He hawked his wife round the streets during Mary's reign to try and rid himself of what had then become an embarrassment.

General

This is an interesting little church, performing important work as a Guild Church in the field of Mission and Unity throughout the world, particularly amongst the Anglican Communion.

The former parish which used to include St Mary Mounthaw, St Mary Somerset and St Peter's, Paul's Wharf (all disappeared except the tower of St Mary Somerset) has been transferred to St Andrew by the Wardrobe.

37 St Olave's, Hart Street and All Hallows Staining with St Katherine Coleman

Dedication

Olave Haraldson was a popular figure in early 11th century London because he helped the English king, Ethelred the Unrede, to throw back the Danes. At the Battle of London Bridge in 1014, he fastened cables round the supporting piles and pulled the bridge from under the invaders. Later he became king of Norway, where he was killed in battle in 1030 by nobles opposed to his forceful propagation of Christianity.

'Staining' may indicate an early use of stone instead of timber for building churches, or refer to a holding belonging to the manor of Staines. 'Coleman' was possibly the name of the builder of St Katherine's (pulled down in 1925 after being rebuilt in 1734).

History

The dedication to St Olave would argue that there was a place of worship here in Saxon times but first mention is not until 1222, when the church was called 'St Olave towards the Tower'. A ribbed- and groin-vaulted crypt of about 1250 AD with the unusual accompaniment of a well remains; it is used as a chapel.

Most, however, of what we see today is basically mid-15th century, when two fellmongers (skinners), Richard and Robert Cely, contributed generously to the rebuilding of the church, following the current plan of nave, aisles, clerestory and large east window.

Pews with their own outside staircase for the Navy Office, then in Seething Lane, were installed in 1661 on the south side and, in the following year, the present vestry was added.

Admiral Sir William Penn (father of the founder of Pennsylvania) and Samuel Pepys used their influence to save St Olave's in the Great Fire of 1666 by having houses in the path of destruction blown up so that this church was one of the few to escape destruction.

In 1731–2, a brick top was placed on the tower by John Widdows and a new east window was installed in 1822 but, apart from the attentions of Sir Gilbert Scott in 1863 and Sir Arthur Blomfield in 1873 (the Navy Office pews had been removed in 1853), St Olave's remained relatively intact until April/May 1941 when it was hit by four bombs.

Work on restoration started in 1951 when King Haakon VI of Norway laid a dedication stone, next to which is a fragment of Nidaros Cathedral, Trondheim, and the church was re-hallowed for use in April 1954. The architect was Ernest Glanfield.

Exterior

A typical, low-roofed, 15th century church of ragstone with a south-west tower. The bell-turret was enlarged after the War and a south porch added.

The clock came in 1891 from All Hallows Staining (demolished 1870). The 15th century tower of All Hallows still stands in Mark Lane.

One of the most striking features is the churchyard gate of 1658 in Seething Lane (see plate, p. 153) with its skulls, crossbones and spikes, called by Charles Dickens (see *Associations*) 'St Ghastly Grim'. It has a large segmental pediment.

The entrance to the old South Gallery and Navy Office Pew is marked with an inscription.

Interior

The walls and most of the arcades survived the bombing and the structure has been carefully restored to its original state. The wide arcade is of three bays with columns of Purbeck limestone (not the

St Olave's, Hart St. Entrance gates to former burial ground—'St Ghastly Grim'

more familiar so-called marble) separating nave from aisles. There is no division between the nave and chancel. The rebuilt low-pitched roof, unchanged by the Victorian restorers, was constructed in 1632; it is panelled and has bosses at the intersections.

Aisle windows consist of three pointed lights under depressed arches and the large unorthodox 1822 window remains at the east end with new glass.

A fortunate survival from the bombing was the 1662 vestry which has a 15th century doorcase and a delightful stucco ceiling with fine panelling (it came from St Katherine Coleman) and adorned in the centre with an angel in an oval.

Furnishings
Organ A new instrument hides behind the western screen.

Font The attractive and well-designed font of marble replaces a Victorian one. It is moveable.

Pulpit This late 17th century furnishing with Caen stone base was saved by being stored in the crypt of St Paul's Cathedral during the war. It was once in St Benet's, Gracechurch Street.

Communion rails These are contemporary with the pulpit; they have twisted balusters and are decorated with three little lions.

Stained glass With the exception of the Churchwardens' window in the north aisle, all the stained glass is post-war dating from 1953 by A. E. Buss. St Olave can be seen in the left light of the east window.

Monuments
There is much of interest; some are brightly coloured.

Sir John Radcliffe, died 1568 and wife. Fragments of him recumbent and his wife kneeling remain in the north aisle.

Peter Cappone, died 1582. A kneeling figure.

James Deane, died 1608 and wife. They are shown kneeling under an arch and between columns with gilt Corinthian capitals. Attractive designs in the corners.

Two children in chrysoms lying on a skull (indicating that they died soon after birth) and looking like small mummies are placed pathetically below. This monument is perched above the vestry door.

Andrew, died 1610 and *Paul Bayninge*, died 1616. To the left of the sanctuary and against the wall there is this interesting but somewhat comical monument to the two Bayninge brothers, both Aldermen of the City. Their hands are raised beseechingly and, being set on a circle, they look like figures on a clock.

St Katherine Coleman

Elizabeth Pepys, died 1669. Next to the brothers and in the north-east corner is a frontal bust erected by Samuel Pepys to his long-suffering wife with the inscription that says she bore no children because she could bear none worthy of herself. By John Bushnell, it was stored in St Paul's crypt during the War.

Samuel Pepys He outlived his wife by over 30 years and died in 1703. There was no memorial until Sir Arthur Blomfield designed one based on Pepys' portrait in the National Portrait Gallery. It was placed on the south wall in 1884 where the old Navy Office pew used to be. A pew end on this side has been carved with a replica of the Navy Office Verge (wand or staff of office).

Pepys was buried beside the Communion Table, alongside his wife.

Sir Andrew Riccard, died 1672. Kneeling being no longer fashionable by this date for memorials, Sir Andrew is shown in a standing posture in the north aisle.

Brasses There are several 17th century brasses.

Associations

Rev John Letts' daughter A tablet on the tower records the remarkable escape from death of the daughter of a rector, who fell from the top floor of the rectory to the basement stones below.

Charles Dickens, in his *Uncommercial Traveller* writes of the churchyard of St Ghastly Grim with affection, despite his name for it. He refers to its 'ferocious strong spiked iron gate, like a jail'.

Clothworkers' Company St Olave's has close associations with this Company which holds its annual service here and whose arms appear in a south aisle window. They transferred the old Norman crypt, now at All Hallows Staining, from Islington, where it lay under Lamb's Chapel, and also provided the present church hall.

General

This small church is a precious survival of a typical City mediaeval place of worship, one of only the very few remaining. Still an active parish church, it will long be remembered for that lovable diarist with a roving eye who told us so much about the London of his day and carried out so efficiently and honestly his important duties as Secretary to the Admiralty. Pepys referred to St Olave's as 'our own church'.

38 St Peter upon Cornhill

Cornhill

'Cornhill' was one of the two hills upon which the Romans founded London. The corn market, according to John Stow the historian, was held here 'time out of mind'.

History

A brass tablet in the vestry dating from Henry IV's reign (1399–1415) states that St Peter's was founded by King Lucius in 179 AD, and that it was 'the Metropolitan and chief church of this kingdom' for 400 years until St Augustine moved it to Canterbury. Whatever may be the truth of this—there was certainly a Bishop Restitutus of London who attended the Council of Arles in 314 AD and may have come from St Peter's—it has stood the church in good stead, for, despite rival claims, the rector of St Peter's had precedence in the mediaeval Whit-Monday procession to St Paul's Cathedral, which actually used to start at St Peter's. In more recent times St Peter's, because of its importance, was specifically excluded from the operation of the Union of Benefices Act of 1860 and therefore saved from demolition and had no other parish joined to it. The church with what William Kent calls 'holy boldness' celebrated its 1700th anniversary in 1879.

First mention goes back to pre-Conquest times, when about 1040 it was called 'St Peter binnon London'. As with its neighbour, St Michael's, there were many chantries, and St Peter's had its quota of Lord Mayors' burials; altogether seven altars existed. It was a sanctuary for fugitives from justice.

Another indication of its importance was that one of the four grammar schools in the City, founded in 1425 (refounded by Henry VI in 1447), was established at St Peter's and there was also an important library attached to the church. The school continued until the 18th century.

There was a Brotherhood and Guild of St Peter's connected with the Fishmongers' Company founded for religious observances.

In addition to a main square tower there was a battlemented turret at the south-west corner.

All but the base of the tower was destroyed in the Great Fire. Wren turned his attention to the rebuilding of St Peter's between 1677 and 1681 and it was reopened the following year. A curious vestry minute of St Michael's, April 24th, 1679, resolves: 'That leave be given to the Parson of St Peter's to walk in the churchyard'. Presumably his own was out of use at this time.

The church suffered far less than St Michael's from subsequent interference, but J. D. Wyatt in 1872 was responsible for repaving and reseating the church and for garish glass which unfortunately survived the 1939–45 War.

Exterior

St Peter's is best viewed from the south and east. On the north side, as at St Michael's, nothing can be seen except the entrance. St Peter's also has a little churchyard to the south which in this case is enhanced by two plane trees; from this side one can see that the exterior materials are yellow stucco, dark red brick and green copper.

The principal façade, which has no doors, is the eastern one facing Gracechurch Street. Wren had to give up 10 feet on this side for road-widening but, in view of its importance, made it more ornamental than usual. Five uniform arched windows on the ground floor, separated by pilasters, are surmounted by an upper floor with one arched and two circular windows, and the whole is capped by a pediment. Curved pieces join the upper to the lower floor in Italian fashion.

The 140 ft. high steeple retains its pre-Fire lower stage of brick. The upper part of the tower has three round-headed louvre windows on each side, above which rises the harmonious group of small dome, lantern and obelisk spire all covered in green copper. There are many string-courses on the tower giving horizontal emphasis.

A carved, gilded figure of St Peter with keys can be seen on the churchyard gate.

Interior

The south door gives access to the vestibule under the organ gallery, with the main body of the church, of which the east and west walls are not parallel, on the left. The atmosphere is one of homely comfort and warmth enhanced by the excellent furnishings (apart from the pews and the glass). Five bays separate the tunnel-vaulted nave from the narrow aisles, which have transverse tunnel vaults opening out into the nave, and their own arches. The panelled ceiling is attractively decorated with plaster designs. There are side chapels to the chancel.

Pillars with Corinthian capitals become pilasters further up, showing where the former galleries existed. Their high panelled bases are on a level with the wall panelling which extends to the height of the window-sills.

Furnishings

Starting from the west end, the following are the main furnishings of interest:

Doorcases Four fine doorcases in the vestibule are contemporary with Wren's rebuilding. They have Corinthian pilasters.

Table A notable 17th century long wooden table now in the vestry was once used for Holy Communion by Puritans.

Chest An ornate Hanoverian chest is used as a seat in the vestibule.

Bread-shelves Affixed to the wall above the chest are capacious bread-shelves used for storage and distribution of bread to the poor.

Organ Originally 'Father Smith' (1681) but much altered. The gallery and case date from the same time. The original keyboard upon which Mendelssohn played in 1840, leading him to pronounce the organ as the 'finest in London' and on which he has left his autograph dated 3rd September 1840, is still in the vestry.

Font Made of marble, octagonal and with leaf decoration growing up the lower part of the stem. It also dates from 1681 but the cover is said to have escaped the Great Fire and therefore to be earlier. A wrought-iron bracket to raise the cover remains in the south-east corner where the font used to stand.

Pews These have curved ends but are somewhat dull. Two high pews of the old 'Wren' seating remain at the back for churchwardens.

Pulpit A fine large furnishing with stairs and a big tester. It was as usual lowered by the Victorians.

*Chancel-screen The pièce de résistance; it is one of only two from Wren's time in the City and the only one in its original setting. (St Margaret's Lothbury has the other but this was originally in All Hallows the Great.) Wren was not in favour of screens and we owe its presence to the insistence of the rector at the time of the re-opening, William Beveridge (later Bishop of St Asaph). He emphasised the special sanctity of the chancel and the desirability of privacy for Communicants. The design is said to be by Wren and his sixteen-year-old daughter. The sections are divided by very thin shafts whilst the centre curves up and is flanked by broad, fluted pilasters. There is a Royal Arms of Charles II in front.

Reredos Also contemporary with the Wren rebuilding but less ornamental than usual. It has the uncommon decoration of the Lamb of Sacrifice with the sun or morning star shining forth from it and burning in its rays the sacred name of Jehovah.

Communion rails Date uncertain. They have balusters in the shape of Doric pillars.

Monument
On the south wall of the chancel is a poignant circular memorial with seven cherubs' heads to seven children of James Woodmanson, who all died in 1782 in a fire at their home whilst their father was at a ball in St James's Palace.

Associations
George Borrow, traveller, linguist and author was married here in 1840.

Charles Dickens The churchyard of St Peter's has been identified as the churchyard where Lizzie Hexham received the unwelcome attentions of Bradley Headstone in the novel *Our Mutual Friend*.

The Poulters' Company hold their annual service here.

British Sailors Society The church is associated with the British Sailors Society.

General
A most attractive interior with outstanding woodwork and one only wishes that one could see it better. St Peter's remains a parish church not at present linked with any other. It is the Regimental church of the Royal Tank Regiment, the Old Comrades Association, the Devonshire Regiment, and the Bedfordshire and Herts Regiment, all of whose arms can be seen in the glass in the north and south aisles. The Church is also used, in addition to its normal services, by the Players of St Peter upon Cornhill for dramatic performances from the cycles of mediaeval mystery plays.

39 St Stephen's, Walbrook

Walbrook
Walbrook refers to the small stream which, like the Fleet, used to flow through the City into the Thames.

History
There can be few parishes where, as here, the first church (earliest reference about 1096 AD) was built on the west side of a stream but where subsequent churches were erected on the other side. The second church, built 1439 and destroyed in the Great Fire, was put up on the east bank and Wren's building (1672–9) followed suit.

St Stephen's, Walbrook

This was badly damaged by incendiary bombs in May 1941; it was restored by the architect Godfrey Allen, including reconstruction of the wood and plaster dome in 1951–2, and reopened in 1954.

The parish includes the former parishes of St Swithun's, London Stone, St Benet Sherehog, St Mary Bothaw, St Laurence Pountney and St Mary Abchurch.

Exterior

Except for the steeple, which was not begun until 1713, the exterior is fairly plain. The steeple, which has been described as 'playful', consists of a square stage at the base with three projecting columns, deeply recessed behind the balustrade and with the entablature carried outwards round the columns. Above this there is a smaller square stage without columns crowned by a diminutive lantern. (See (plate p. 161) The steeple is some inches out of the perpendicular.

Interior

Entrance is by the unusual route of climbing 12 steps which follow the old line of the east bank of the Walbrook to a lobby which is the western apse of the church. One is greeted by what many call Wren's masterpiece in parish church architecture—a most ingenious and intricate design in what is virtually a plain rectangle. A forest of 16 beautifully proportioned Corinthian columns sort themselves out into a pattern which gives both a longitudinal effect with nave stretching towards the altar and that of a centrally planned church with arms radiating from the middle like a Greek cross and the whole surmounted by a most impressive dome. This unique double effect is achieved by omitting some of the columns in the middle to form a circular space but without interfering with the straight line of nave and chancel. The dome, weighing over fifty tons, is carried on eight arches. This design has been much admired over the years and is generally regarded as the prototype for St Paul's Cathedral, the dome probably being the first to be built in England.

In 1888, the box-pews were removed and a mosaic pavement was laid in the centre.

Windows are of all shapes and sizes. They were filled with stained glass dating from before the War.

Furnishings

Most of the furnishings were saved from war damage and are of interest.

West lobby with splendid organ gallery and case above All woodwork of the Wren period.

St Stephen's, Walbrook. Roof of dome

Font Of stone, with an exceptionally beautiful octagonal font-cover, each panel decorated in high relief with garlands above and small figures on top.

Pulpit The staircase has twisted balusters and the tester is decorated with putti standing on it—again Wren-period.

Panelling The panelling in front of the north chancel stalls is decorated attractively with circular openings and cherubs' heads. The stalls still bear the marks of the incendiary bombs.

Painting On the north wall is a painting by Benjamin West—the only American President of the Royal Academy—of the stoning of St Stephen. This at one time blocked the west window.

Reredos Another Wren-period furnishing.

Monuments
Sir John Vanbrugh was buried in the north aisle. His fellow architect Nicholas Hawksmoor is often attributed with the epitaph:

> 'Lie heavy on him, Earth! for he
> Laid many heavy loads on thee'.

Dr Nathaniel Hodges On the north wall is a tablet to the hero of the Great Plague in 1665 who died in a debtors' prison.

Associations
Grocers' Company The arms of the Grocers' Company are displayed in the church and on the wainscot.

Charlotte Brontë visited St Stephen's with her sister Anne in 1848.

Henry Pendleton, rector in the 16th century, was the famous 'Vicar of Bray'.

General
This is a church which perhaps fires the intellect more than the emotions and displays the scientific brain of Wren at its most brilliant, known as his masterpiece because he personally supervised the work. But St Stephen's today is far more than a building and, through the Samaritans, is bringing solace and help to some of those most in need of it.

A noticeboard outside announces that 'the most perfectly proportioned interior in the world is not only a thing of beauty to delight the eye but a house of God to refresh the soul'.

This pleasure is today somewhat marred by another notice which says that the church cannot be decorated until the floor is raised and a steel box inserted to prevent buckling of the structure!

40 Temple Church

Dedication

Dedicated to the Virgin Mary, the Temple Church takes its name from the Crusading Order of Knights Templar, founded in 1118 to protect pilgrims on their way to the Holy City of Jerusalem.

History

The Templars moved from Holborn to the Temple area in 1161. Here they built a church which was consecrated on February 10th, 1185, probably in the presence of Henry II, by Heraclius, Patriarch of the Church of the Holy Sepulchre in Jerusalem (an inscription above the inside of the entrance door records this). Like other Templar churches (Little Maplestead in Essex and Northampton), the nave was round, modelled on the Holy Sepulchre Church itself.

The original chancel was replaced in 1220 by the enlarged chancel consecrated in 1240 in the presence of Henry III.

When the Knights Templars Order was dissolved by Pope Clement IV in 1312, the property went to their rivals, the Knights Hospitaller, and it remained in their hands until they in their turn were suppressed at the Reformation. The church then passed to the Crown, but the lawyers, who had settled in the Temple as tenants of the Hospitallers, were allowed to remain, and in 1608, were granted the freehold by James I. It thus became the lawyers' private chapel, not subject to the jurisdiction of the Bishop of London.

The church escaped the Great Fire but, in 1682, it was re-furnished by Sir Christopher Wren with box pews, pulpit and screen; he also designed the reredos.

Further restoration by Robert Smirke took place in 1828 and, in 1842, the building fell into the hands of the Gothic Revivalists who, under the architect Blore, made their presence felt throughout the church. The pavement of the chancel was then lowered about 16 inches.

During the air-raid of 10th May 1941 the nave roof fell in flames on the effigies of the knights below and caused considerable destruction elsewhere.

Carefully restored by the architect Walter Hindes Godfrey and his son, Walter Emil, it was re-dedicated in 1954 and is once more in full use by the lawyers of the Middle and Inner Temple.

Exterior

On the south side, where it lies back from an open courtyard, the church now presents a smooth ashlar-faced front with the drum of the round nave on the left and the triple lancets and buttresses of the rectangular chancel on the right.

A gabled rib-vaulted west porch provides protection for the sumptuously decorated, if somewhat weathered, Norman doorway of three orders with colonettes between; the decoration consists of lozenge, bobbin and ribbed leaf motifs. The half-length statues on the north side may represent Henry II presenting their foundation charter to three Templars.

Above the west door is an unusual circular window with tracery resembling a chariot wheel.

The north is a muddled composition with walls of coursed rubble. The organ chamber, rebuilt in 1953, has a rather formidable aspect.

On the ground, a gravestone inscribed 'Here lies Oliver Goldsmith, 1728–1774', marks the poet's supposed burial-place.

Interior

The interior is of outstanding interest, being one of the earliest examples—and a very fine one—of Gothic architecture in the whole country and using Purbeck marble on a large scale.

Despite being a victim of the Blitz, the round nave—or the 'round' as it is called—probably looks much the same today as when it was built 800 years ago. It consists of a circular Transitional Norman arcade with twisted arches supported by Purbeck marble shafted piers having prominent shaft-rings; above this is a triforium of interlaced arches and a clerestory of simple round arches. Beyond the nave runs an ambulatory with blind arcading along the wall, and a continuous stone bench underneath. The central portion of the nave is roofed in wood but the ambulatory is stone-vaulted.

In the spandrels of the blind arcading is a series of grotesque heads, some restored, said to represent souls in heaven and souls in hell—Charles Lamb's heads that 'gape and grin'. Most of their owners appear to be in hell, suffering in many cases the most appalling toothache or having their ears tugged by fearsome monsters. They are worthy of detailed examination. A more serene face is the beautiful seraph's head corbel beside the entrance arch to the south aisle.

*The five-bay chancel is a superb piece of architecture, described by Pevsner as 'one of the most perfectly and classically proportioned buildings of the 13th century in England'. The aisles, entered by skilfully designed side arches, are the same height as the nave passage and the whole—vaulted throughout—is carried on slender shafted Purbeck marble piers and wall-shafts of the same material, both with moulded caps and bases. The piers have had to be renewed, and some of the shafts which were previously made from one block are now assembled in smaller sections (canisters); but the vaulting is original.

Stepped groups of three lancets have rere-arches with Purbeck marble shafts; they are slightly elaborated at the east end.

In the south aisle there is a double piscina, a type which was only used for a short time; later, by Papal decree, celebrants of Holy Communion were forbidden to throw away rinsings of the chalice but had to consume them, so that single basins then became customary.

A grim reminder of the past is the 'Penitential Cell' to which a door in the north-west corner of the choir gives access and which has slit windows looking into the church. Knights who disobeyed the Master or broke the Rule of the Temple were confined here and it is said that Walter le Bacheler, Grand Preceptor of Ireland, starved to death there.

A basement chamber, discovered and cleared of many bones and coffins in 1950, is reached by a stairway in the south porch. This is thought to have been the Treasury of the Knights Templar. One of several wall shafts has a finely carved Transitional capital. A grille on the stairway gives access to all that remains of St Anne's Chapel, which stood against the Round Church and in which the secret initiation of the Knights is said to have taken place.

Furnishings
Effigies of knights The effigies, dating from the 13th century—two may be even earlier—lying on the floor of the round part suffered much from the bombing with the exception of the one in the south aisle to de Ros; they have been repaired as far as possible. It is generally thought that they are memorials to illustrious supporters of the Order rather than Templars themselves, although 'illustrious' hardly applies to Geoffrey de Mandeville in the cylindrical helmet who was 'a ruffian of the worst order'.

The effigies have been many times moved and the burial places of the actual people are unknown.

Effigy of bishop The monument to the fully robed bishop with feet resting upon a dragon, in a recess in the south aisle wall is one of the finest 13th century monuments in the country. There is speculation whether it represents the Patriarch Heraclius, Bishop Hugh of Lincoln, who had a house nearby and whose heart is supposed to have been returned to that city, or Sylvester de Everdon, Bishop of Carlisle, who was killed by a fall from his horse in 1255 and buried in the Temple.

Other monuments

Edmund Plowden In the north aisle is the richly decorated alabaster altar tomb, 'repaired and beautified in 1687', to Edmund Plowden (died 1584), Treasurer of Middle Temple, showing him recumbent in a long, black close-fitting gown. The effigy lies below a thin coffered arch with obelisks at the sides and heads below; there is a big strapwork cartouche at the back. The monument was saved by being bricked up during the war.

Richard Martin On the other side is a monument to Richard Martin, Recorder of London, who died in 1615. He wears a flowing scarlet robe and splendid ruff, and is shown kneeling on an embroidered and tasselled cushion before a prie-dieu.

Richard Hooker, famous divine (died 1600), *John Selden*, great lawyer (died 1651) and *Oliver Goldsmith*, poet (died 1774). Their monuments all perished in the air-raid but John Selden's gravestone can be seen below a glass panel in the floor near the entrance.

Brass In front of the choirstalls is a late heraldic brass to Edward Littleton, who died in 1664. It has 29 shields and a Latin inscription on a winding scroll.

Organ The Temple Church was the scene of an undignified confrontation referred to as the 'Battle of the Organs' between the two most famous organ-builders of the 17th century—Father Smith and Renatus Harris. They had been invited in 1683 to erect instruments and competition was so fierce that 'tempers were roused and there was even a clandestine slitting of bellows'. The contest dragged on for five years and eventually was decided by the notorious Judge Jeffreys, the Lord Chancellor, finding in favour of Smith.

The Smith organ was destroyed in the air-raid and the present four-manual instrument, originally built for Lord Glentanar's ballroom at Aboyne, was presented by him to the Temple in 1953. It bears the Royal Arms of Queen Elizabeth II.

Reredos The wide and low Wren-designed reredos, which was carved by William Emmet—joiner and wood-carver—for £45, was banished by the Victorians to the Bowes Museum at Castle Barnard in County Durham but was brought back after the war. It is inscribed with the Creed, Ten Commandments and Lord's Prayer.

Stained glass The painted glass in the three eastern windows by Carl Edwards represents subjects and heraldry connected with the Templars, including in the north window the Middle Temple lamb and flag device, together with the figures of Henry I and Stephen, and in the south window, the winged horse Pegasus device of the Inner Temple with the figures of Henry II and III. They were the gift of the Company of Glaziers and Glass Painters.

The 19th century glass in the 'Round' was partially lost in the bombing.

Pews Victorian pews have been replaced with college-type pews facing inwards. A curious feature is the hat-pegs.

Pulpit The pulpit with staircase is raised on a slender foot which, like the pews, is of lighter-coloured oak than the reredos; another post-war furnishing.

Font The 1842 font is a replica of the one at Alphington Church, near Exeter.

Sanctuary Chairs The two sanctuary chairs are the gift of the South African Bar.

Associations
Sir Christopher Wren was married here to his first wife in 1669.

General
The Temple Church is the most important survivor of Knights Templar churches in Europe and a remarkable example of the transition from the round Norman arch to the upward-pointing Gothic style where pure Norman and pure Gothic can be seen side by side. It might even claim to be the most interesting church (not a cathedral) in London.

It has brought incalculable pleasure to music-lovers because of its tradition of fine music. Under a succession of notable organists, including today George Thalben-Ball, who has been playing here since 1919 and who regards the present instrument as the finest in London, the choir has achieved world-wide fame with the recording of Mendelssohn's *Hear my Prayer* in which Master Ernest Lough as treble soloist sang 'Oh for the wings of a dove'.

41 St Vedast-alias-Foster

Dedication
'St Vedast-alias-Foster' is a combination of the name of a French saint and the English equivalent (by way of Vaast, Vastes, Fastre and ultimately Foster). St Vedast baptised Clovis, Emperor of the Franks, and later became Bishop of Arras. He died in 540 AD.

Only one other English church (at Tathwell, Lincolnshire) is dedicated to him.

History

Early history is confined to isolated references. Variously designated as 'St Faster' (1315–16) and SS Vedast and Amandus (1352), a church has existed on this site since the 12th century; the list of rectors begins with John de Ruberge in 1291. In his *Survey of London*, published in 1598, John Stow refers to 'St Fauster's, a fair church lately newly built'. An eastwards extension was added in 1614.

The Great Fire of 1666 did not completely destroy this building. Efforts were made to patch it up but eventually Wren had to be called in and it was rebuilt using what remained of the walls between 1695 and 1701, rather later than most. The steeple was erected between 1709–12 with stone that was cut at Greenwich and brought up by river.

The church was a casualty during World War II bombing but, fortunately, the tower and spire survived. Sensitive restoration by Stephen Dykes-Bower was completed in 1962, St Vedast's being reconsecrated on 25th April of that year.

Exterior

The curve of the mediaeval stone and brick wall can be seen at the south-west corner and the old structure is now exposed at the east end. The south-west steeple is one of Wren's most sophisticated constructions, built entirely of stone, with the upper stages first concave and then convex, each being knit together with clusters of diagonal pilasters, and a short obelisk spire on top. This composition acts as a charming foil to the grandeur of St Paul's dome (plate p. 171) and the elaboration of St Mary-le-Bow's steeple.

On the north side, reached through a side-door in the narthex, is a small secluded garden with timber walls called Fountain Court. A portion of Roman tessera forming part of a pavement found in 1886 under the site of St Matthew's, Friday Street, is mounted on the south wall.

The 17th century west doors date from before the Great Fire.

Interior

The interior is a plain rectangle, with clerestory, divided into nave/sanctuary and south aisle by an arcade of Doric columns. Modern collegiate-type seating replaces the former pews; older furnishings from other churches take the place of those lost in the bombing.

Screening above the seating completely cuts off the south aisle from the rest of the church and makes it a separate chapel (St Mary and St Dunstan), entered from the east end.

St Vedast-alias-Foster. Steeple with St Paul's dome from roof of Saddlers' Hall

The flat plaster ceiling is richly decorated with gold and silver paint which extends to the cornices; the design consists of wreaths and rectangles in a larger rectangle.

Much of the glass is clear so that the church is well lit, artificial lighting comes from shaded lights on the seating in additon to lighting in the ceiling of the nave and sanctuary.

Furnishings

Organ Originally made in 1731 by Renatus Harris, the organ was restored by Noel Mander in 1960. The fine casing is 18th century work, once in St Bartholomew-by-the-Exchange (demolished in 1841).

Pulpit The octagonal pulpit, decorated with fruit, flowers, lions and skulls, was originally in All Hallows, Bread Street (demolished in 1875); there is an hour-glass in the vestry which came from St Alban's, Wood Street (burnt out in 1940). This has a bronze frame embossed with cherubs' heads and angels blowing trumpets.

Font and cover The carved wooden font and cover were once in St Anne's and St Agnes', at the far end of Foster Lane in Gresham Street. This is now the Lutheran church.

Altar-piece This used to be in St Christopher-le-Stocks (demolished 1781). It went to Great Burstead church in Essex before coming to St Vedast's. The altar-table was in St Matthew's, Friday Street (demolished in 1884).

East windows These modern windows depict scenes and legends associated with the life of St Vedast. One unusual incident is the smashing of beer-barrels of a German tribe, contrasting with the promotion of 'agriculturally progressive' wine-culture. The designer was Brian Thomas, who paid careful attention to the colour and style of a surviving Clayton & Bell window adjoining.

Associations

Robert Herrick, the nature poet, was baptised in the church in 1591. Both Herrick's father and uncle were goldsmiths, whose Livery Hall is situated in the parish.

Thomas Rotherham Rector in 1465–7, Thomas Rotherham became Lord Chancellor in 1471 and held the Archbishopric of York for 20 years from 1480 to 1500.

Vladimir Vassilievitch Petropavlovsky A tablet on the south wall of Fountain Court commemorates 'Petro', Major Vladimir Vassilievitch Petropavlovsky (1888–1971), 'Soldier of the Tsar, of France, of England' with the commendably short but expressive tribute—'This was a Man'.

General

It is easy to overlook St Vedast's with St Paul's Cathedral and St Mary-le-Bow so near, but its spire and the careful restoration, skilfully blending old and new, make a visit well worth while. This little church is the sole survivor in the area of no less than twelve separate parish churches, demolished or destroyed, and in one case moved. (The other eleven were St Michael le Querne, St Matthew's, Friday Street, St Peter Cheap, St Alban's, Wood Street (tower remains), St Michael's, Wood Street, St Mary Staining, St Mary Aldermanbury (now in the USA), St John Zachary, St Olave's, Silver Street, St Mary Magdalene, Milk Street and St Michael's Bassishaw.) Two more, St Anne's and St Agnes' and St Lawrence Jewry are not at present parish churches.

42 The Dutch Church of Austin Friars

History

Amongst the many mediaeval monasteries that lay within or just outside the City boundaries was the religious establishment of the Friar Hermits of the Order of St Augustine of Hippo. Their church, originally built in 1253 and much enlarged in 1354, was a beautiful building with a very fine steeple (Stow wrote 'I have not seen the like'). It contained a number of splendid monuments, including one to the Black Prince's elder son and one to Richard II's half-brother, so that the church came to be called the Westminster Abbey of the City.

For a time after the Dissolution, this place of worship was used as a warehouse for wine and later a naval store. When, however, Henry VIII was succeeded by his son—the boy king, Edward VI— Archbishop Cranmer invited to England a number of continental divines to assist in working out new forms of Protestant worship which had been greatly stimulated by the English edition of the Bible; at the same time, there were in the country some 5,000 Dutch and German refugees from religious persecution and, as a sign of gratitude for the help of the theologians and to provide a place of worship for the refugees, the disused nave and aisles of the church of the Augustian or Austin Friars were made over to them under a charter dated 24th July 1550 and signed by Edward VI.

With the accession of the Catholic Queen Mary the refugees were once more on the move and after many privations settled at Emden in Germany until they were able to come back to England when Elizabeth became Queen.

During the night of October 15/16th 1940, the building was completely destroyed by bombs and services had to be held elsewhere in London, although once a year a service took place in the ruins. The foundation stone of a new church was laid by Princess Irene, the second daughter of Queen Juliana, on 23rd July 1950, the 400th anniversary of the original foundation. This was consecrated on 11th July 1954.

Exterior
The exterior shows a massing of rectangular spaces at different levels with a small flèche crowning the highest block where the church itself is sited. The flèche has open columns surmounted by a dome on which is perched a spirelet and weather vane. On the south side there is a well-tended and grass-covered area marking the spot where the ashes of those previously buried in the church are interred.

Interior
The interior is unusual in that the various rooms are built at different levels. On the ground floor is a spacious social hall; the church, approached by a wide flight of steps, is on the first floor.

This is an open hall without aisles and has a shallow tunnel vault. The east end is taken up by what is known in Protestant churches in the Netherlands as the Liturgical Centre. The large pulpit with canopy and the sign of the Trinity above dominates the scene, emphasizing the importance placed on the Word; there is no altar but in front there is an extendable Communion table, around which those partaking of the Lord's Supper sit for the administration of the bread and wine. Instead of using a font, the sacrament of baptism is administered from a silver basin which is placed on the Communion table.

Underneath the table is the altar stone of the original church built in 1253.

These decorous fittings for Protestant worship are supplemented by much stained glass and a striking tapestry based on the theme of Man and Creation.

Furnishings
Organ The organ is placed above the entrance. It has approximately 2,000 pipes divided over 26 stops and was built in the Netherlands.

Tapestry The unusual tapestry is by Hans van Norden and shows the river of life flowing upwards from the tree of life and carrying multi-coloured fish which change further up into white birds,

symbolising the rise of humanity. Man's participation is indicated
by the representation of fire, wheel, sword, hammer and the city
built by him as a mark of his almost unlimited abilities. Nakedness
shows man's limitations and the uplifted head, dependence upon his
Creator.

Font Given by the South African community.

Stained glass The most interesting glass, especially the west
window, in which the colour green predominates, is by Max Nauta;
the other glass is by Hugh Easton.

Windows to the north and south of the Liturgical Centre depict
the young Christ in the carpenter's shop, appropriately given by the
Carpenters' Company; and, on the other side, the meeting on Easter
morning of the risen Christ with Mary Magdalene; this was given by
the Corporation of London.

The western end shows the history of the Dutch Church in
England, whilst other windows on the south and north walls contain
the coats of arms of those towns where there have in the past been
Dutch Church Communities.

The west window depicts the history of this church; at the foot
appears on the left the boy king, Edward VI, and on the right,
Princess Irene with the trowel and mallet which she used when
laying the foundation stone of the new church. The two centre lights
show St Augustine who founded the order of the Friar Hermits of
Hippo and Johannes a Lasco, the first Superintendent of the Dutch
Church Community; the latter is seen holding the original charter.

Seal At the top of the staircase is a photograph of the original
seal, still in the possession of the church, granting the building to the
refugees and carrying the king's signature.

General
This country owes a debt to the Dutch Church of Austin Friars for
the part it played in influencing our new forms of Protestant
worship and for leading us away from the more repressive dogmas
of extreme sects like the Anabaptists to the more tolerant practices
and beautiful liturgy which the Anglican Church knows today. The
Dutch Church was a bridge between pre-Reformation Mass and
post-Reformation Matins.

Sometimes alone, sometimes amidst the bomb-damaged ruins of a former church, the tower, being the most durable part of the structure, remains; or it may have been spared from earlier demolition.

City of London
Especially noteworthy are:

Christ Church, Newgate Street
This was a fine church and one of Wren's most expensive. Built between 1677 and 1691 on the site of the chancel of the Franciscan Greyfriars church, the steeple was erected between 1701 and 1704. The Friary buildings were used as a foundling school (Christ's Hospital) for the Bluecoat boys who remained there until the school was moved to Horsham in 1902. Large steep galleries were provided for them which added considerable fuel to the fire when incendiaries fell on the church in 1940. It was not rebuilt, leaving the ruined walls and the burial ground now laid out as a garden.

The steeple, however—'one of the most splendid in London' according to Pevsner—survived and was restored by Lord Mottistone in 1960. Standing forward from the west front, the three main stages are all square, the lower belfry storey being rounded off by a curved pediment and carrying a recessed middle stage encircled by an open Ionic colonnade, above which rises a tall open spire capped by a vase. Great use is made of urns, many of which were removed early in the 19th century, being replaced during the restoration.

St Mary Somerset, Upper Thames Street (see plate p. 177)
Four Portland stone plain stages of varying height with alternate circular and round-headed windows are succeeded by an exciting crown on which Wren set eight pinnacles with panelled bases and scrolls, four at the corners having vases on top and four in the middle 20 foot high obelisks, capped with balls, which overtop the vases. These pinnacles were blown off during the War but have been restored to their former state, easily visible as the tower is on a very open site. The church itself was demolished in 1871.

St Augustine's with St Faith's, Watling Street
East of St Paul's Cathedral, this is another Wren steeple built in 1695 and deliberately designed by him, with its slender proportions,

St Mary Somerset

as a foil to the swelling dome of St Paul's (cf. also St Martin-within-Ludgate). It has a pierced parapet and obelisk pinnacles, whilst the lead spire, blown off by bombs during the War, has been restored in glass-fibre to its original Wren inverted trumpet shape. The church was destroyed by bombing in 1941 and St Paul's Choir School has now been built round the tower.

Other towers have already been mentioned:
All Hallows, Staining Street in the description of St Olave's, Hart Street, St Alban's Wood Street, (a late Wren Gothic tower, with Victorian top stage, standing in the middle of the road) in the description of St Michael's, Cornhill; St Dunstan in the East has been separately covered.

There are two Victorian towers: All Hallows the Great in Upper Thames Street and St Martin Orgar in Martin Lane off Cannon Street. Another Wren tower, St Olave Jewry in Ironmonger Lane, remains from a church demolished in 1872, but this has now been incorporated into offices.

Amongst towers in other parts of London are:

Islington
St Luke's, Old Street (see plate p. 179)
St Luke's was one of the Fifty New Churches under the 1711 Act and was probably designed either by George Dance the Elder or John James. It was built of Portland stone between 1727 and 1733. The building became dangerous and in 1959 was closed, dismantled and unroofed, leaving the walls and the unusual steeple.

Much criticised because of its unorthodoxy, the architect may have been influenced by Hawksmoor; it rises straight from the ground instead of riding awkwardly on the roof. It is strongly built of finely-jointed masonry in three stages chamfered at the base and rebated further up, terminating in a very tall tapering fluted obelisk spire.

Tower Hamlets
St John at Wapping, Schandrett (see plate p. 181)
This church was built in the mid-18th century to take the place of a rather curious structure with huge dormers and a low tower.

This not particularly noteworthy building was gutted by incendiaries in 1940 and later the nave walls had to be taken down for safety reasons.

The tower, however, was not badly damaged and was considered worth restoring. Of dark brick with stone dressings, the plain lower

St Luke's, Old Street

stages are succeeded by a more attractive clock storey and then by a most original top consisting of a concave lower part carrying a charming convex cupola, both lead-covered. This top has a somewhat continental appearance.

St John at Wapping

All Hallows', North Twickenham

History

Originally in the City of London before the tower and furnishings were transferred to Twickenham, this is one of the few City churches whose recorded history is pre-Conquest; in 1053 Brightmer, a citizen of London, gave the original place of worship to the Dean and Brotherhood of Christchurch, Canterbury.

This Saxon church was succeeded by three others, the first re-building being in 1294 and the second between 1494 and 1516; the third was erected by Sir Christopher Wren after the Great Fire.

John Stow in his *Survey of London* dated 1603 believed that All Hallows, being then near the 'Grasse Market', was the Grass church which gave Gracechurch Street its name. Earlier records, however, suggest that St Benet's, Gracechurch, may have had a better claim to the title.

Although being in the middle of the blaze, the tower still stood after the Fire. It was some time before it was decided to re-build, and the new All Hallows was not completed until 1694 (one of the last of the City churches to be re-erected).

With lavish gifts from wealthy bankers, the furnishings were of the finest and, during a re-organisation of the Lombard Street parishes shortly before the 1939–45 War, a problem arose as to what should be done about them. The fabric of All Hallows was in a dangerous state owing to soil subsidence and the building was so hemmed in by office buildings that it had become known as the 'Church Invisible'. A most imaginative solution was found. It was decided to move the furnishings together with the 104 feet high campanile and the porch—which came from the dissolved Priory of St John, Clerkenwell— to Twickenham, south-west of London, where new churches were needed, a rare example of a place of worship moving to the parishioners. A simple unobtrusive brick structure was erected by Robert Atkinson to house the furnishings. The parish in the City, which embraced St Leonard's, Eastcheap, St Dionis Backchurch and St Benet's, Gracechurch, was absorbed by St Edmund the King, Lombard Street.

In 1946 the living of All Hallows which had remained a 'Peculiar', i.e. outside the jurisdiction of the Bishop of London, for nearly 900 years, was exchanged for that of Charing in Kent and came under the Dean and Chapter of St Paul's Cathedral.

Exterior

The austere, balustraded and starkly white tower of finely-jointed Portland stone stands out as a conspicuous stranger in its new surroundings in Twickenham and, although joined to the church by a long corridor, appears separate. Tower, church and linking vestibule form an L shape round a small courtyard, the other sides being filled with the rectory and the busy highway. The porch is elaborately decorated and has an open scroll pediment.

Interior
Immediately inside the tower is a gate, which used formerly to stand where one turned in to the alley leading from Lombard Street to the church. It was moved inside the building in 1865 when still in the City. This somewhat forbidding structure with bars and spikes is decorated with emblems of death (skulls, hour-glass, skeleton and Father Time).

Furnishings
Amongst the exceptionally fine furnishings are:
   Doorcases The notable doorcases under the organ are part of the original furnishings.
   Organ Although re-built more than once, it retains its original case and much of its low Renatus Harris tone. The supporting gallery is new.
   Font The white marble font is a feature of much charm with a circlet of cherubs' heads and foliage round the rim. The cover, rather large by comparison, is richly decorated and capped with an endearing group of Charity with her children.
   Pews The pews date from the 18th century and are appropriate to their surroundings.
   Chandeliers The chandelier hanging between the choir stalls, designed by Sir Ninian Comper, came from the bombed church of St John's, Red Lion Square in London; the smaller and finer example under the tower was made in 1784 by the Master of the Pewterers' Company.
   Bread-shelves Bread was dispensed to the poor from the shelves, which are now placed on the wall beside the lectern. Before the Dissolution, such charity used to be given by the monasteries.
   Pulpit This furnishing was actually copied from the Grinling Gibbons pulpit at St Mary Abchurch. Cherubs' heads and foliage decoration abound. It has a large tester and attractive curving staircase with delicate twisted balusters.
   **Reredos* A notable example of 17th century woodwork. Richly ornamented, much pedimented, bearing in the centre the symbols of sacrifice (the lamb, and the pelican drawing blood from its breast), and culminating in seven candlesticks representing the Seven

Churches of Asia, it is a harmonious and balanced composition. Although there is no proof that Grinling Gibbons carved it, the pelican motif is also found—and there are other similarities—in the reredos of All Hallows' City neighbour—St Mary Abchurch—which is known to have been carved by him.

Royal Arms A fine Charles II Royal Arms of oak—one of only 22 known examples—is kept in the ringing chamber of the tower for lack of space in the church.

Monument

The incidence of infant mortality in the 18th century is strikingly illustrated on the tablet in the vestibule to Thomas Vardon and his six children, five of whom died before they were one year old.

Associations

John Wesley John Wesley preached his first extempore sermon at All Hallows. Fifty years later in 1788, when he was in his 86th year, he recalled his dismay at finding that he had left his notes behind on the first occasion and how a kindly woman, upon hearing his trouble, put her hand on his shoulder and said, 'Is that all? Cannot you trust God for a sermon?' He never took notes with him into the pulpit again.

Peter Symondes In a will dated 1586, Peter Symondes left a sum to provide a new penny and a bag of raisins for sixty Bluecoat Hospital Boys on the morning of every Good Friday.

General

Although some feel that the new church is unworthy of the furnishings, we cannot but be thankful that these were moved out of London to safer ground shortly before so many other examples were destroyed by bombing, and that we can now enjoy them in a good light instead of their being but dimly discernible in the old 'Invisible Church'.

St Mary the Virgin, Aldermanbury

Aldermanbury

The court or bury of the Saxon 'Ealdormen' (Aldermen).

History

First mentioned in 1181, St Mary Aldermanbury was situated near London Wall. The mediaeval building—one of the few London

St Mary the Virgin, Aldermanbury, now at Fulton, Missouri

parish churches to possess a cloister—was gutted in the Great Fire
and rebuilt by Wren at dates variously stated as between 1667 and
1687. He used old materials for the walls, facing them with Portland
stone.

The church suffered a particularly harsh restoration at the hands
of Edmund Woodthorpe—'the prince of philistine restorers'—in
1864, when he inserted Venetian tracery in the windows and
installed inappropriate furnishings. It was damaged by a zeppelin
bomb in the 1914–18 War and burnt out by an incendiary bomb on
29th December 1940.

For some years it seemed that St Mary's would remain a ruin
but a totally unexpected future emerged for it when the President of
Westminster College, Fulton, Missouri, USA, together with three
colleagues, conceived the idea of removing a ruined Wren church
from London and re-erecting it on the campus to commemorate Sir
Winston Churchill's 'Sinews of Peace' or 'Iron Curtain' Speech at
Fulton on 5th March 1946. It would become 'The Winston
Churchill Memorial and Library in the United States'.

St Mary Aldermanbury was selected, approved by the British
Council for Care of Churches, and the British architect, Marshall
Sisson, appointed to co-ordinate the transfer to the USA in
conjunction with the St Louis architect, Frederick Sternberg.

Dismantling began in 1965. Twelve columns and 7,000 stones,
each separately numbered, were salvaged, and new Portland
limestone was obtained from the same quarries used by Wren to
replace missing or crushed stones. The first consignment arrived in
Fulton during the Spring of 1966, enabling the Bishop of London to
lay the foundation stone in October of the same year and the Bishop
of Dover to re-hallow St Mary's in Fulton on the 7th May 1969.

The parish in the City of London is now linked with St Vedast-
alias-Foster, whilst St Alphage's, London Wall, included with St
Mary's after it was demolished in 1923, is now with St Giles',
Cripplegate.

Exterior

The rebuilt church is raised on a platform and the cost of
restoration and redevelopment of the undercroft in which the
museum and library are housed exceeded $2 millions. The Winston
Churchill Memorial and Library form part of the Churchill
Quadrangle on the Westminster campus.

Great efforts have been made to reproduce the pre-war church
and there are many improvements. The original pineapples,
symbolising hospitality, friendship and fertility, are still on the

corners and remain linked to the tower by concave Italian side-pieces. Victorian interference and especially the Venetian tracery have been corrected; instead, plain Wren-type windows without tracery have been substituted. The pierced parapet is no longer there but the large central lunettes at the sides are retained from the old design.

Fortunately, the east wall and gable, minus windows, survived the incendiaries so that 'the grossly oversized, very proud and jolly volute scrolls' (Pevsner) (the scrolls are called lyres in the USA) at the side of the east window escaped and can still be seen, also the small pediments above the vestry doors from St Dionis Backchurch (a City of London church demolished in 1878.).

The 106 ft high belfry is much as before except that the small pinnacles and pierced parapet are no longer there (perhaps leaving the tower top now a little stark) and simple Y-tracery has replaced the Venetian tracery (an undoubted improvement). Twenty-four circular belfry steps from the mediaeval church survive. The distinctive bell-turret with clock and open balcony terminating in ogee cap and vane has been carefully copied.

Roof material is copper coated with lead.

Interior
The interior is equally satisfying. The clear glass, suitably leaded, the simple furnishings in oak instead of Victorian stone, specially designed in the Wren manner for which the identical original stain has been used, and the faithful reproduction of the plasterwork (modillions, flowers and other designs) cast from original moulds, all combine to restore the Wren atmosphere which it did not have after the 1864 alterations.

The sandstone base of the columns could not be moved and five capitals had also to be replaced, but otherwise the columns are the original ones.

Amongst the furnishings, it is of interest to note that the case for the organ was made in 1741 for Woolwich parish church.

Associations (from City church)
William Shakespeare lived near and almost certainly worshipped at St Mary's. In the churchyard in the City, which has been attractively laid out as a public garden, there is a late Victorian memorial to two personal actor friends of Shakespeare, John Hemminge and Henry Condell, who were parishioners and to whom we owe the collection of Shakespeare's works after his death for publication, thus preserving them for posterity.

John Milton married Katherine Woodcocke at St Mary's in 1656.

Lord Justice Jeffreys An association which is probably best forgotten in the church's new home is that the notorious Judge Jeffreys, after spending four years in the Tower of London, was stated to have been buried in the family vault at St Mary Aldermanbury on 2nd November 1693. A post-war inspection, however, revealed no trace of his body.

General

St Mary Aldermanbury is now ecumenical and is the College Chapel. Services are held each Sunday during the school-year and there are many concerts. The Museum in the undercroft contains Churchilliana (letters written by him to his daughter, Lady Soames, paintings relating to Sir Winston, the lectern, chair and water glass used when he delivered the 'Iron Curtain' address) and exhibits related to St Mary's when the church was in the City. The Research Library is devoted to the life and era of this great leader. To the east of the Memorial is the Isabella R. Witmarsh Memorial Garden with plants of English origin and a sundial brought from England dated 1650.

The Winston Churchill Memorial and Library is a most imaginative project and a standing tribute to the links between two of the great English-speaking nations of the Western world.

City of Westminster

1 All Saints', Margaret Street
2 All Souls', Langham Place, with
  St Peter's, Vere Street
3 St Anne's, Soho
4 St Augustine's, Kilburn
5 Christ Church, Lancaster Gate
6 St Clement Danes
7 St Cyprian's, Clarence Gate
8 St George's, Hanover Square
9 Grosvenor Chapel
10 Holy Trinity, Marylebone Road
11 Holy Trinity, Prince Consort
   Road
12 St James's, Piccadilly
13 St John's, Smith Square
14 St John's Wood Chapel

15 St Margaret's, Westminster
16 St Mark's, North Audley Street
17 St Martin-in-the-Fields
18 St Marylebone Parish Church
19 St Mary-le-Strand
20 St Mary Magdalene, Paddington
21 St Mary on Paddington Green
22 St Mary's, Bryanston Square
23 St Matthew's, Great Peter
   Street, Westminster
24 St Paul's, Covent Garden
25 St Peter's, Eaton Square
26 St Peter's, Vere Street
27 Savoy Chapel
28 St Stephen's, Rochester Row

1 **All Saints', Margaret Street**

History
The church was erected on the site of the Margaret Chapel where, in the 1830s, Frederick Oakeley began to put into practice the teaching of the Oxford Movement. Built between 1849 and 1859 by the architect William Butterfield as a model church under the auspices of the Cambridge Camden Society, it cost about £70,000.

Exterior
The building, which is flanked by houses associated with All Saints and in similar architectural style, presents a varied façade of dark red brick embellished with vitrified blackish-blue material. The dominating feature is the spire which rises over the south-west corner; it soars to 230 feet, slender and sheathed in slate, a rare form of covering in England; the steeple has a rather awkward appearance not relieved by the ring of small lunettes at the top. The tower is of the prevailing brick, a material which was not fashionable at the time and the use of which led to some criticism.

The church is approached across a little courtyard and entered by a door set asymmetrically at the opposite corner.

Interior
One is greeted by an interior of great lavishness where frescoes, marbles, carving, stained glass, mosaics and gilding all combine to enhance the effect of sumptuousness; to quote Pevsner—'The interior is indeed dazzling . . . No part of the walls is left untouched. From everywhere the praise of the Lord is drummed into you'.

The visitor may have reservations about the taste and quality of all this but there is no doubt that All Saints' imparts a sense of vitality very welcome today and, although time has not softened the hard lines of Butterfield's work, the sense of splendour is not without attraction. There is much, too to enjoy in the stained glass with its rich reds, blues, greens and browns, particularly the west window, depicting the tree of Jesse, by Alfred Gerente.

The nave of three bays is separated from the north and south aisles by richly-shafted piers of Aberdeen granite with luxuriant stiff leaf and naturalistic leaf capitals, and there are reredoses at the east end of the chancel (very large and ornate) and of the north aisle, the latter surmounted by a disproportionately large canopy. The clerestory has three small windows for each bay of the nave.

A steeply-pointed arch leads into the vaulted chancel, which is lower than the nave. Large tripartite openings with elaborate geometrical tracery and rising from black marble columns divide the chancel from the aisles. The altar is raised high.

The south aisle is completed at the west end with a baptistery under the tower.

Furnishings
Pulpit Of inlaid marble, the pulpit is heavy and ornate; it is mounted on sturdy legs with frilly capitals.

Chancel Reredos The large chancel reredos is by William Dyce. It shows the Nativity and Crucifixion with saints under pointed arches in two tiers, surmounted by Christ in Glory and the elect surrounding Him.

Screen A low inlaid marble screen with handsome gates separates chancel from the nave.

Wall-paintings A band of wall-paintings in the north aisle dating from 1873 and executed on tiles, of which the largest depicts the worship of the Shepherds and the Magi, commemorates the first vicar.

Statue Near the pulpit, a statue of the Virgin and Child is covered with a triangular canopy capped with a curious blunted spire.

South-east chapel doors These attractive coloured doors have panels showing representations of Edward Pusey (one of the initiators of the Oxford Movement) who laid the foundation stone, W. Upton Richards (the first vicar), Harriet Byre, Richard Benson and Edward King.

South-east chapel stained glass The glass is of similar richness to the west window with reds, greens and blues predominating; the designer was O'Connor. Two of the lights depict St Edward and St Augustine.

General
High Victorian Gothic at its most assured, most ornate and most powerful. This period piece, where all is colour, provides the highest in churchmanship that one is likely to find in the Church of England, making All Saints' a major centre fo Anglo-Catholicism in this country and giving it the name of 'Cathedral of Oxford Circus.'

2 All Souls', Langham Place with St Peter's, Vere Street

History
All Souls' was one of four churches built at the beginning of the
19th century in the borough of St Marylebone to meet the needs of a
growing population. They were all Commissioners' places of
worship. In the case of All Souls', the Commissioners contributed a
little under two-thirds of the total cost of £18,323. The architect was
John Nash and the church was designed to fit in with his grand piece
of West End town planning embracing a through-way from
Piccadilly Circus to the Regent's Park terraces. This had had to take
a side-step at Langham Place, but Nash ingeniously overcame the
problem by placing his church where it could be seen both from
Portland Place and Regent Street and orientating the building
north-eastwards diagonal to the bend in the road.

His contemporaries were not so impressed and cried out at the
lack of architectural orthodoxy in mixing a classical portico with a
Gothic spire; a cartoon shows him impaled upon the sharp point.

The construction of the church took just over two years between
November 1822 and November 1824, when it was consecrated. The
site was swampy and it is to this we owe the depth and strength of
the foundations, which have proved such an asset in the recent
extensions.

Low mahogany pews, of which one third were free (i.e. not
rented), were substituted for the previous high-backed ones in 1876
but the doors and dividers which separated them were not entirely
discarded until some years later. H. S. Goodhart-Rendel, the
architect, carried out repairs in 1928 and again after the 1939–45
War: on 8th December 1940 a landmine had caused considerable
damage to the roof and necessitated taking down half the steeple.

During recent years, the need for a hall for social activities
developed into one of the most imaginative schemes for post-war
alterations which have been undertaken in a London church. At a
cost of £655,000, the entire sum met before completion, the floor of
the church was removed, a new hall dug below, exposing in the
process Nash's inverted foundation brick arches (plate p. 195 and 196)
and the floor reinstated 18 inches higher. Reconsecration took place
appropriately on All Souls' Day (2nd November) 1976.

St Peter's, Vere Street (see separate description) is now a daughter
church.

Exterior
Admirably sited at the bend of Langham Place, the main feature is

All Souls', Langham Place. Nash cartoon

the circular portico of giant Ionic columns with the unusual decoration of Coade stone winged angels between the capitals. Before Broadcasting House was erected, the famous and beloved candle-snuffer steeple was more conspicuous than now, but even so the portico and steeple still effectively close the view to the north of Regent Street.

A ring of free-standing Corinthian columns rises above the solid circular clock base from which the exceedingly sharp fluted spire juts upwards to end in the three foot bronze cone.

The rectangular body of the church is plain with two tiers of windows.

Interior

All is new and pristine with the circular vestibule and its information desk slightly resembling a hotel foyer. Inside opens a Corinthian hall with galleries on all four sides except where they open at the east end for the sanctuary. The raising of the floor has brought the shallow but deep galleries, the rake of which has been remodelled, more into the body of the church. They are supported

All Souls', Langham Place. Floor removed Aug 1975

on chamfered piers which at gallery level change to marbled Corinthian columns supporting the coved flat ceiling, divided into large rectangular gilt panels. The general colour tone is gold and grey and all is resplendently fresh and bright.

At the east end the Westall painting (see *Furnishings*) with sunburst above under a shallow arch is a valuable focal point in a sanctuary which is completely open.

Furnishings

With the exception of the organ, which was safely stored during the War, all the furnishings are modern and all, including the new organ console which can be brought forward into the centre of the chancel area, are movable. This gives great functional flexibility.

Organ Built in 1913 and rebuilt by Willis in 1951 after the War. It is now in process of further rebuilding by Harrison & Harrison of Durham using the old casing—Spanish mahogany designed by John Nash.

Pulpit On a hydraulic jacking system because of its weight. Of bronzed aluminium.

All Souls', Langham Place. Inverted arches

Lectern and Font Also of bronzed aluminium. This is a single unit, which like the pulpit is on castors. The reading desk is removable to reveal a font beneath.

Altar table Of the same material as the pulpit and lectern/font.

Painting The painting by Westall depicting Christ being mocked was given by George IV, Nash's friend and patron.

General

This is the only Nash church left in the country other than East Cowes (Isle of Wight), although the tower of West Cowes is also by him.

The openness of the architecture is reminiscent of the post-war rebuilding at Islington, the source of the evangelical tradition which plays such a big part in the life of All Souls' today. It is a stimulating thought that in an age when the Church is faced with many financial problems it has been possible to find more than half a million pounds for this live centre of Christian evangelism, where students and overseas visitors flock to participate in the church's activities, and where congregations of over a thousand are normal.

3 St Anne's, Soho

Dedication

Probably named after Anne, then Princess of Denmark, who later became Queen. Soho may be derived from 'so-ho'—a hunting cry used to draw off hounds when the area was in open country.

History

Nothing remains of the church consecrated on 21st March 1685.

It was bombed in 1940, the body of the church pulled down in 1953, and the area once occupied by the church turned into a shady green garden in a part of London near theatreland not well endowed with open spaces.

The very odd steeple which took the place of one erected in 1714 was the work of Samuel Pepys Cockerell and went up in 1803. It has a creeper-clad stone bell stage with chamfered corners, louvres and Doric columns squeezed into the angles. Above is the strange lead-covered stage terminating in two intersecting beer-barrels with a clock face on each side. The bell-stage has a pronounced batter (inward slope from the perpendicular).

St Anne's, Soho

Associations

Theodore, King of Corsica After accepting the crown of Corsica in
1736, he was driven out within a month and later settled in England
in 1749. Arrested and imprisoned for debt, he mortgaged his claims
to Corsica and died shortly after being released from prison. An
inscription on the tower records this and concludes with the
following aphorism by Horace Walpole:

> 'The Grave, Great Teacher, to a level brings
> Heroes and Beggars, Galley-slaves and Kings
> But Theodore this Moral learn'd ere Death
> Fate poured its Lessons on his living head
> Bestow'd a Kingdom and denied him Bread.'

William Hazlitt, printer, critic, essayist was buried here. He was
born in Maidstone, April 1778, and died in Soho 18th September
1830. The tablet was restored by his grandson in 1901.

Dorothy Sayers, The ashes of this well known novelist and
christian theologian, who was churchwarden here until her death in
1957, are buried beneath the tower and a plaque to commemorate
her was unveiled in June 1978.

General

There have been plans for rebuilding St Anne's but, so far,
activities—mainly concerned with social work in this seamy area of
London—have to continue from a little chapel in 57 Dean Street
(Little Chapel of the Upper Room).

4 St Augustine's with St John's, Kilburn

Dedication

St Augustine was sent to England by Pope Gregory the Great to
envangelize the Saxons. Landing in Kent in 597 AD, his task proved
to be easier than expected as, according to Bede, Bertha, the Queen
of Kent, was already a Christian and the way was thus prepared for
the conversion of her husband, King Ethelbert.

History

Built originally to serve a deprived area of north-west London, St
Augustine's, Kilburn, stands out boldly from its surroundings. It
took ten years to build from 1871 to 1880 and the tower and spire
were not completed until 1898. The elaborate decoration took
several more years.

The architect chosen was John Loughborough Pearson, one of the
most famous of Victorian church builders, who has to his credit St

Michael's, Croydon, St John's, Upper Norwood and the Cathedrals of Truro, Cornwall, and Brisbane, Australia. His work is uneven in quality but St Augustine's is generally regarded as amongst his best churches. French influence is apparent in the spire and conical-capped turrets which come direct from Normandy (St Etienne, Caen), and in the internal buttresses with their pierced openings, which recall Albi in the Tarn country of Southern France.
St John's church was pulled down in 1972.

Exterior
The exterior is dominated by the spire, which rises to a height of over 250 feet and is one of the highest in London. The openness of the site enables one to appreciate the building as a whole with its long narrow and lofty lines, its acute angles and its soaring spire. Middle Pointed or Decorated style was no longer *de rigueur*, as it had been earlier in the century, and narrow lancets predominate. There are two tiers at the east end but at the west five smaller ones are surmounted by a notable rose window, in each case conical-capped turrets providing a frame. The building material is a dark and rather sombre red brick.

A lead-sheathed flèche with bell adorns the middle of the nave roof; the south-east chapel ends in an apse.

Interior
Entrance is through a porch on the north-west side under the tower, the stone vaulting being supported on a central pillar. The effect of the interior is dramatic. The triforium on first floor level has wide, cavernous openings and arches even taller than those of the nave, thus producing the unusual feature of twin arcades. Pearson has succeeded in accentuating the effect of height in a relatively modest-sized building by concealing the comparatively low vaulting of the aisles and by making the nave arcade appear to be that of the upper gallery. He has made the church look wider by the recession created by the double aisles and has increased the effect of length by the transept bridges, which make the chancel arcades look like extensions of the five bays of the nave.

St Michael's and All Angels Chapel on the south-east side, and the Lady Chapel on the north-east side open out from the transepts. Fine wrought-iron screens separate nave from chancel and sanctuary from ambulatory.

The chancel floor is paved with inlaid marble.

This original design affords constantly changing vistas across the nave and there is a fine view eastwards on gallery level from the west end.

St Augustine's, Kilburn

Furnishings and decoration

Both furnishings and decoration are in High Victorian style, reflecting the views of the Catholic Revival in the Church of England, with much ornate carving, inlaid marble and wall-painting, all combining to illustrate the major themes of the Christian faith— Creation, Fall, Miracles, Redemption, Crucifixion and Resurrection. The decorations, starting at the west end with attractive subtly-shaded glass made by Clayton and Bell in the great rose window and lancets, continue to the east end. The murals and carved reliefs all provide colour, varying in merit, but telling a consecutive story.

Pulpit and Font Lavishly carved amber alabaster and typical of the period. The marble has a pleasing, moist-looking plastic quality.

Rood screen This is surmounted by an impressive dark figure of the Crucifixion flanked by six statues of Passion personalities.

Bishop's Chair The bishop's chair in the sanctuary has French 16th century carving.

Altar in Lady Chapel This stone altar with carved wooden reredos was designed by Sir Giles Gilbert Scott, who also provided the wooden statue of the Virgin Mary in the nave and the Stations of the Cross.

Icon The icon of St Nicholas near the font comes from Russia.

Treasures The Victorian exuberance extends to the textiles of vestments and altar hangings, silver-ware and plate, all still in use and of outstanding quality.

General

St Augustine's is a church which perhaps inspires respect rather than joy but it is one of which the Victorians can be proud and might claim to be the finest and largest 19th century place of worship in London. The acoustics are superlative and, with its fine organ and choir, nave and ambulatories so admirably suited for processional purposes, worship in this church must be an inspiration.

5 Christ Church, Lancaster Gate

History

As London reached out westwards beyond Tyburn, where the last execution had taken place in 1783, St Mary on Paddington Green proved quite unable to provide for the large new congregations. First St James's, Sussex Gardens was built and then the architects F. & H. Francis designed Christ Church, Lancaster Gate, which was erected in 1854/5 on a site formerly a market-garden.

During the incumbency from 1879 to 1884 of William Boyd-Carpenter—later Bishop of Ripon—his preaching drew huge crowds to the church and Christ Church continued to be the favoured parish church of the large number of well-to-do Victorians who lived in this part of Bayswater. They deserved great credit for the feeding, clothing and general social welfare work performed for their less fortunate neighbours in Shepherd's Bush and Paddington. For many years over £1,000 was collected at Matins alone on Hospital Sunday so that Christ Church came to be known as 'the thousand pound church'. New places of worship, too, were built— for example, St Saviour's, Cobbold Road, Shepherds Bush—out of funds contributed by the parish. All this, perhaps, is an answer to those who consider the Victorians were insensitive to the needs of others.

After the 1939–45 War, the character of the area had completely changed but the post-war ministry in the parish has adapted itself to the new circumstances, attracting the many students and overseas visitors who live in the district.

Exterior
A typical large Victorian church faced with Kentish ragstone and with Bath stone dressings. The north-west steeple has a fine tall spire with buttresses linking it to the pinnacles.

Interior
The interior is on a grandiose scale with very tall arcade, large north transept and deep chancel. The aisle galleries were removed in 1881 but the stone west gallery, raised on a transverse arcade, remains.

Furnishings
Stained glass The west window dating from 1856 is by Wailes; the east by Powells dates from 1892.
   Pulpit The alabaster pulpit was installed in 1885.
   Reredos The reredos is made of Caen stone with columns of polished serpentine.

General
This is an interesting example of how the church-builders of the 19th century responded to the needs of a pious and increasingly affluent population. To our tastes today it may appear showy internally and lacking in grace but nevertheless externally it still forms an attractive feature of the Lancaster Gate scene.

N.B.: The roof structure has been seriously affected by dry-rot. Sections have had to be removed and the church contents have been placed in store. The building is now scheduled for demolition.

6 St Clement Danes

Dedication
The most likely supposition is that Danes who had married English wives were allowed by Alfred the Great to settle in 886 AD in the no-man's land between Ludgate and Westminster. It would be natural for this seafaring people to adopt St Clement for their dedication; this saint was thrown into the sea weighted with an anchor during a Roman persecution in 100 AD and became the patron saint of sailors. The weathervane is an anchor.

History
An old timber-framed church was replaced about the year 1022 AD by a stone building, remains of which are still to be seen in the base of the tower. The living was in the hands of the Order of Knights Templar from 1189 until the order was dissolved, shortly after which (about 1324) it passed together with some land in the parish into the hands of the Bishop of Exeter; the Bishop was soon afterwards murdered in his palace across the road.

Although partly rebuilt in 1640 and a survivor of the Great Fire, Sir Christopher Wren felt it necessary to pull down the church and have it completely re-erected to his designs by Edward Pierce—one of his best masons—thus becoming the only place of worship outside the City to be reconstructed by Wren. (St James's, Piccadilly, was a new church built on a site where none had existed before.)

In 1719, James Gibbs—the architect of St Mary-le-Strand next door—added the beautiful upper stage to Wren's tower which survived the German bombs in the Second World War.

Gutted in 1941 by German Air Force incendiary bombs, the main building was left a ruin until 1955 when the RAF had it raised again to become their church. The parish was then joined to St Mary-le-Strand.

Exterior
The island site which so greatly enhances the exterior view has only existed since 1810 when a number of houses on the north side were

removed. St Clement's is unique amongst Wren churches in being designed with an apse. Unlike St Mary-le-Strand, there are two tiers of windows. The heavy porch probably dates from an earlier church.

Interior
The rebuilding, so ably executed by the architect W. A. S. Lloyd, has provided the church with an interior of great richness, lighter and more spacious than before and with a striking contrast of dark oak up to the height of the gallery and white columns with richly decorated arches supporting a panelled ceiling in white, grey and gold above. The spaciousness is enhanced by the wide floor, into which have been let over 700 badges of RAF squadrons and units cut from Welsh slate, and made possible by the pews having telescopic extensions, which can be pushed back when not required.

The eye is led to the apse of double columns at the east end with encircling ambulatory. To the west, the dominating feature is the organ.

The ancient crypt—once a burial place—has been converted into a beautiful chapel. Plates from the old coffins are fixed to the wall. The Belgians, Dutch and Norwegians have given respectively the paschal candelabrum, the stone altar and the black granite font.

Furnishings
Organ This splendid instrument, designed by Ralph Downes and made by Harrison and Harrison of Durham, replaces the 'Father Smith' one which was destroyed. It was the gift of the United States Air Force and families.

Stalls Behind the pews at the west end are finely carved stalls for members of the RAF Governing Board.

Pulpit The wooden hexagonal pulpit was mercifully saved from destruction by being stored in the crypt of St Paul's Cathedral. Even there, bombs badly damaged it but restoration has removed all traces of this. Carving, which includes undercut festoons of hanging flowers, is attributed to Grinling Gibbons (circa 1685).

Lectern Of wrought-iron and brass, donated by the Royal Australian Air Force.

Bishop's chairs and tapestries In the sanctuary are two bishop's chairs set off by antique Florentine tapestry which was given by Viscount Trenchard, the 'Father' of the Royal Air Force, and Lady Trenchard.

Processional Cross Made of Cornish white tin, it was carried in procession at the service of reconsecration by the young Air Training Corps cadet who designed it.

Reredos The wooden reredos is by Ruskin Spear and depicts the Annunciation. Painted in gold, it is a highly-praised work.

East windows The three windows are by Carl Edwards and depict Christ in Glory (centre), Madonna and Child (north) and Pieta (south).

Associations

Mrs Donne The tomb to Ann—wife of Dr John Donne, poet and Dean of St Paul's—who died bearing her 12th child and was buried on 16th August, 1617, was destroyed in an air-raid.

Cecil baptisms Two sons of Lord Burleigh, Queen Elizabeth's famous statesman, were baptised here in 1561. One died young but the other rose to occupy his father's place as Lord High Treasurer and to become the first Earl of Salisbury.

Dr Samuel Johnson Although St Dunstan in the West and St Bride's were his nearest churches, the celebrated lexicographer was persuaded by a lady friend to come and hear her nephew preach at St Clement's. He seems to have continued to worship here, as commemorated by the brass plate in the north gallery and, more strikingly, by the statue outside showing Dr Johnson in characteristic pose and describing him as 'Critic, Essayist, Philologist, Biographer, Wit, Poet, Moralist, Dramatist, Political Writer, Talker'.

Oranges and Lemons There is a tradition that oranges and lemons were unloaded at a nearby wharf (there was no embankment) and carried through the churchyard to Clare Market against payment of a toll to the churchwardens. The ancient rhyme is rung daily on the bells at 9.00 am, 12 noon, 3.00 and 6.00 pm. There was also a custom whereby—on New Year's Day—the head porter at Clement's Inn opposite presented an orange and a lemon to each tenant, who was expected to pay half-a-crown for the privilege.

It may be, however, that the association merely arose from the fact that Clement rhymed with lemons and this is supported by the fact that St Clement, Eastcheap, is also associated with the rhyme.

William Webb-Ellis The Rugby schoolboy who made himself famous by picking up the ball in a game of football and so initiating the game of rugby was rector here.

General

This church is now firmly enshrined in the hearts of countless flying men and women, bearing the memory of more than 125,000 who died in defence of their country. Beneath the north gallery is the American Shrine which commemorates the names of 19,000

members of the United States Air Force, who laid down their lives
in the Second World War while serving in this country. One must
marvel at the way in which this place of worship, destroyed by
an enemy Air Force, has risen again and been made even more
beautiful by the Royal Air Force, Commonwealth and Allied Air
Forces.

7 St Cyprian's, Clarence Gate

Dedication
St Cyprian was a Carthaginian lawyer who, in his middle years, was
converted to Christianity and, much against his will, appointed
Bishop of Carthage. He was martyred in 258 AD, accepting his fate
with forbearance and even bequeathing fifty gold pieces to his
executioner. The dedication was chosen by the founder, who had to
overcome the objections of the Bishop of London, because he was
especially struck by St Cyprian's tender loving care for people and
the consideration with which he treated them.

History
If ever a church was the creation of one man, St Cyprian's was.
Charles Gutch was the son of a clergyman and had held various
curacies, including three in London from one of which he was
dismissed for preaching against the sins which he considered were
sapping the life of young men. Although Gutch had no special
connections with the district, he felt the call to exercise a ministry in
the north-east part of the borough of St Marylebone which, at the
time, although middle-class, was poor. Many London parishes were
then being divided in order to make them easier to work and he was
able to obtain the agreement of the rector of Christ Church to hive
St Cyprian's off from his parish.
    The granting of parish status was officially confirmed in May, 1866
but it was to be a long time before a church could be built. Without
any assurance of residence or stipend, Gutch had to conduct his
various missions and to operate generally from a temporary place of
worship, consisting of two houses with a coal-shed between, which
G. E. Street, the architect and one of the trustees of St Cyprian's,
had converted. Eventually, not long after Gutch's death in 1896, a
site for a permanent building was obtained and St Cyprian's,
although at the time consisting of little more than walls and pillars,
was dedicated on 30th June 1903.
    The architects were Bucknall and Comper, the latter being Sir

Ninian Comper, and no church in London reflects to a greater degree his love of the mediaeval. Damage was caused by bombs during the 1939–45 War and that suffered on the south aisle floor has been left as a memorial.

Exterior
The exterior is completely plain and unpretentious without tower or steeple of any sort and consisting of a simple roofed rectangle of wall, bottle-glass windows and buttresses.

Interior
Gutch, in his earlier years, had been much influenced by the Oxford Movement and was anxious to bring back Catholic traditions to Protestant worship. Comper was, therefore, free to exercise his highly individual mediaeval style to the full. Screen, altar, frontal and dorsal, font cover, stained glass are all his and the furnishings are the most complete expression of his tastes in London.

The interior, assisted by the absence of pews, is open and spacious. The nave is separated from the aisles by seven bays with tall and slender columns; above is a low clerestory with segmental-headed windows. There are chapels on each side, a Lady Chapel on the south and the Chapel of the Holy Name, not completed until 1938, on the north. The latter contains the original altar used by Gutch in his temporary church.

The roof is a form of queen-post truss with tracery in the spandrels of the braces and fibrous plaster panels.

Furnishings
The furnishings are the main feature. Everywhere, Comper's hand is apparent, giving light and gaiety to this 20th century mediaeval interior.

Organ The fine organ is housed in the west gallery above the narthex.

Font This was given in 1930 and has a most intricate and imposing tall, gilded, spire-like cover. Apart from the Spanish-style posts in the Chapel of the Holy Name, this is the only item in the church which is not entirely Gothic, the lowest stage being of classical design.

Pulpit The pulpit was given anonymously in 1914 and is made of oak.

Rood-screen A reversion to the old rood-screen, stretching right across nave and aisles, with rood and loft above, elaborately carved and with painted figures representing saints on the panels. The tracery is of lace-like delicacy, providing a rare example of an open loft. It was completed in 1924.

Lady Chapel screen The figures depicted on the screen are, most appropriately, all of women saints.

Altar The stone altar in the sanctuary is one of the largest in the country. The elaborate canopy was completed in 1948.

Stained glass The symbolism of the glass is explained in detail in the excellent guide. Suffice it here to draw attention to the two quatrefoils at the top of the Lady Chapel window, showing the coat of arms of the Borough of St Marylebone; on the left the Virgin Mary and Child stand on the river 'le Bone' and on the right the river is shown with her lily and rose.

General

St Cyprian's is a highly-praised work of the Catholic Revival and has been described by Comper himself as 'the last development of a purely English parish church with lofty aisles and clerestory'. It is a period piece and unique amongst London churches as showing what Anglo-Catholic liturgy of the beginning of the century demanded. Aesthetically, it can give much pleasure, but one is inclined to over-praise because of the exuberance and colour of the furnishings.

8 St George's, Hanover Square

Dedication

St George, the patron saint of England was born of Christian parents in Cappadocia. He was martyred during the Diocletian persecution in 303 AD.

History

The memory of the 1715 uprising is underlined by the desire in the dedication to consign the Jacobites to oblivion. The spirit and, to some extent, the style of this building is Hanoverian. At one time, it was even intended to mount a statue of George I on the pediment of the portico—but this did not materialise.

The church was erected as one of the Fifty Churches under the 1711 Act to provide a suitable place of worship for the new estate that was being developed north of Piccadilly and south of Oxford Street, an area where it was still possible at the time of building to shoot woodcock and snipe. The parish was carved out of the much larger one of St Martin-in-the-Fields.

John James, the chosen architect, had been Assistant Surveyor to Wren at St Paul's Cathedral and had succeeded James Gibbs as Surveyor to the Commissioners of the Fifty. The first stone was laid on June 20th, 1721 and the new place of worship was consecrated on March 23rd, 1725.

Fairly extensive alterations were made at the end of the 19th century, which included the provision of the chancel to accommodate a choir.

Exterior

The most striking feature is the handsome portico which projects on to the pavement in front of the church proper. It was by way of being a trend-setter to be followed almost immediately in the rebuilding of St Martin-in-the-Fields and, a little later, at St George's, Bloomsbury. However, the placing of the tower over the west end of the church proper and behind the portico resulted in an awkward composition which was not satisfactorily resolved until Thomas Archer built St Paul's, Deptford where he made the tower circular and enclosed the western projection with an embracing semicircular portico, thus integrating the two. The 'happily incongruous' (Pevsner) cast-iron hounds within the portico at St George's came from a bombed-out shop nearby.

The tower, with diagonally projecting coupled colonettes carrying a prominent entablature, is modelled on St James's, Garlickhythe, a Wren motif, emanating from the Netherlands, also found in the form of single colonettes at Chelsea Royal Hospital. The small dome above is rather an anticlimax.

At the east end, a broad flight of steps gives independent access to the vestry.

Interior

The architect had to operate on a cramped site but nevertheless John James has succeeded in providing space for a substantial congregation in a building not noticeably large. The general effect of the rather square proportions is perhaps not particularly inspiring but the ceiling of square panels is nicely gilded. Galleries on the north and south sides are supported by the square pillars of the nave, from which spring Corinthian columns. At the west end, the galleries are canted round to enclose the organ. At one time, there was an upper circle gallery on each side of the organ for charity children.

The Venetian window at the east end has a segmental head and is enclosed with coupled columns. The shallow chancel is enhanced with attractive columns gilded in the flutings.

Furnishings

Reredos This still retains the original painting of the Last Supper, attributed to William Kent, who designed the two fine sanctuary chairs. The colours are dark and, in consequence, the painting does not draw the eye.

Pulpit Lowered during the Victorian restoration and placed on the present six columns. Rather squat with rich but shallow decoration and a wrought-iron staircase.

*Font A beautiful furnishing, oblong in shape with a fluted bowl and made of an attractive veined marble. It is decorated beneath the rim with a pleasing pattern of sheaves, oak-apples and leaves.

*Organ A splendid feature. Originally built by Gerard Smith, the nephew of the famous Father Smith, it has suffered many vicissitudes including a serious fire in 1896. Fortunately some of the old work survived and it has now been rebuilt once more by Harrison and Harrison.

Stained glass Although a muddled composition, the bright colours provide the focal interest at the east end which the reredos lacks. The glass is Flemish, dating from about 1525, and was originally made for a convent at Antwerp. It was brought to St George's in 1840. The theme is the tree of Jesse; Christ seated on an elaborate throne is shown in the centre light, at the top of which appear set in medallions the somewhat incongruous trio of St George, Victory and Minerva. Part of the original window featuring God the Father could not be fitted into the space available and is at Wilton, near Salisbury.

Candelabra A nice feature.

Associations

George Frederick Handel, the great composer, was closely associated with St George's from the time he came to live in Brook Street nearby in 1724 until his death in 1759—a span of 34 years. It was at Brook Street that he wrote some of his greatest works—'Saul', 'Israel in Egypt', 'The Messiah' and many other oratorios. He had his own pew and worshipped regularly in the church.

General

St George's is a dignified church, well suited to its setting in a smart area of London.

9 Grosvenor Chapel

History
Like St Peter's, Vere Street, but built a few years later, the
Grosvenor Chapel was an estate chapel to serve a residential
development on privately-owned land. It was completed about 1730
as part of the Grosvenor Square scheme. The builder, Benjamin
Timbell, may also have been the designer.

In 1831 it became a chapel of ease to St George's, Hanover
Square.

At the turn of the century Sir Ninian Comper made considerable
alterations to the east end which changed the chapel's character.

Exterior
A plain and somewhat Colonial-looking structure, the chapel, built
of yellow brick, has round-headed windows in front and also at the
sides. The portico with four Tuscan columns is surmounted by a
slightly projecting bell-turret with a short copper spire.

Interior
Sir Ninian's alterations have complicated the simple chapel interior;
he installed a screen with large Ionic columns between the chancel
and Lady Chapel. The east end has blue and gold decoration.

The original galleries on three sides with square pillars below and
short Ionic columns above remain.

The nave ceiling is coved and the aisles groin-vaulted.

Furnishings
Pulpit The pulpit, which has an attractive carved staircase, is
contemporary with the building of the chapel.

Communion rails Also contemporary. Of wrought-iron.

Reredos Divided into three parts by pilasters, a Comper fitting.

General.
This is an appealing survival of an estate chapel, the only one in
Mayfair and still playing a useful part by providing a centre for the
pastoral care of young Anglican graduates and professional people.

It is also actively associated with the William Temple Association
which has its London Branch at the chapel and holds weekly
services in it.

The chapel is under the care of a priest-in-charge, who lives in one
of the contemporary houses adjoining, assisted by a committee
which includes the rector of St George's.

Grosvenor Chapel

10 Holy Trinity, Marylebone Road

History

Although St Marylebone Parish Church had been rebuilt only a few years before, the development of fashionable residential suburbs northwards from Oxford Street during the late 18th and early 19th centuries when the Nash terraces were growing up around Regent's Park, had, by the 1820s, already made it too small for the greatly increased population. The Commissioners, therefore, entrusted Sir John Soane with the building of a new church at the east end of Marylebone Road. Begun in 1824 and consecrated on 31st May 1828 it was one of the most expensive of all the so-called 'Waterloo' churches built after the Napoleonic Wars with the £1 million thanksgiving fund voted by Parliament in 1821. The parishioners, however, paid for the extra cost of the columns and urns on the lower stage of the tower.

In 1878, G. Somers Clarke substituted a round apse for the previously flat east end.

After the 1939–45 War the shifting of the population and the change in character of the area from studios and drawing rooms to large embassies and medical consulting rooms made the church redundant and, in 1955–6, it was adapted to become the headquarters of the Society for Promoting Christian Knowledge (SPCK).

Exterior

As at St Marylebone Parish Church, although on the opposite side of the road, the orientation is north and south. The materials used were Bath stone and brick. The west end has a handsome if shallow portico of four Ionic columns below a balcony; the tower above consists of a square main stage with free-standing Corinthian columns, each with its own entablature projecting at the angles, and urns of typical 'Soane' design. The top stage is circular with columns and the summit is a round stone cupola. The outside pulpit forms part of a memorial to Canon William Cadman, rector from 1859 to 1891, a gifted preacher who attracted large crowds.

The long sides are straight but with Ionic demi-columns half sunk into the walls.

Interior

The western half of the nave, including side aisles and galleries, has been converted for SPCK needs, the seating going to St Lawrence Jewry in the City. Small vestry chambers have been installed in the

Holy Trinity, Marylebone Road

north-west and south-west corners of the shortened eastern part. The apse remains as remodelled by Somers Clarke, with mosaic decoration, but panels of the Evangelists, the Nativity, the Last Supper and a group of angels were added at the end of the century. Seating is restored in the remaining part of the nave for occasions such as the SPCK Founders' Day, and the chancel is still fitted for worship, including a weekly celebration.

Below is a vast crypt now in full use as the Society's book warehouse.

Furnishing
Font Preserved under a cover in the south-west vestry chamber.
Monument The charming 'Smith' monument by Sievior, dating from 1834, is now in the north-west vestry chamber.

Associations
Many famous people lived in the district and amongst those who attended Holy Trinity were *Lord Roberts* of Afghan War fame and *Florence Nightingale*.

General
Although there may be regrets that this 'Soane' church has been so much changed there is cause for thanks that such a good use has been found for it to ensure its continued existence.

11 Holy Trinity, Prince Consort Road

History
A successor to earlier places of worship in the neighbourhood, Holy Trinity was one of the last works of the eminent Victorian architect, G. F. Bodley, being built in 1902–3. There was restoration in the 1950s.

Exterior
The church, faced with Bath stone, lies endwise to the street and displays an elegant west window with beautiful 14th century tracery. There are two aisle windows in the same style and a projection to the left for the extra aisle on the north; decorative niches are placed either side of the central window. A small and rather rustic gable houses the bells. The orientation is north and south.

Interior
The five-bay nave with lean-to aisles is lofty, spacious and
admirably proportioned, uncluttered by pews and well lit. Clustered
tall and slender shafted columns give an air of lightness and grace.
The wooden roof is of the wagon type.

A screen and rood separate nave from choir with sanctuary
beyond. The Lady Chapel, dating from 1906, lies on the north side
and there is an organ loft to the south.

Furnishings
Font Plain with attractive ogee cover.
  Pulpit Painted in 1964.
  Altar-piece Gilded and carved altar piece dates from 1912.

Associations
Dr Hannay (George Birmingham the author) was rector here.

General
The excellent proportions, the beautiful window tracery and the
discreet colouring add sparkle to this unexpectedly attractive
church.

12 St James's, Piccadilly

Dedication
The Apostle James was beheaded by order of Herod Agrippa I in
42 AD. Tradition later relates that disciples took his body to Spain
and that it was discovered in a marble coffin by a Galician peasant
during the year 816. St James became the patron saint of Spain and
his shrine at Santiago de Compostela was a leading centre of
mediaeval pilgrimage.

History
The church was erected to serve the estate being developed by Henry
Jermyn, Earl of St Albans, on land originally leased and then
purchased by him. Sir Christopher Wren, the chosen architect,
started building in 1676 and the new place of worship was
consecrated on 13th July 1684; a spire was added in 1699. St James's
was the only church built by him on a completely new site. This was
before Piccadilly was constructed and entrance was from Jermyn
Street.

Over the years alterations and additions were made but a major

renovation carried out in 1937 was erased during a German air-raid
on 14th October 1940 when St James's was severely damaged by
high explosives and incendiaries. For thirteen years services were
conducted in the south aisle until the church was rededicated on
19th June 1954 after restoration by Sir Albert Richardson.

Exterior
A plain brick building with Portland stone dressings. On the north
and south sides are two tiers of windows, round-headed above and
segmental below; at the east end, a tall Venetian window is placed
above a tripartite rectangular window. Projecting from the west end
is a balustraded tower, now once more completed with a steeple—
built in glass-fibre.

   An unusual feature is the outside pulpit with sounding-board on
the north wall; installed in 1902 it was used for conducting open-air
services before the advent of mechanised transport in Piccadilly.

   The approach from Piccadilly is made agreeable by the Garden of
Remembrance which, due to the generosity of Lord Southwood,
newspaper proprietor, was created out of the damaged churchyard.
Lord Southwood's memorial adorned with putti is a pleasing
addition.

Interior
Wren wrote in 1708 that churches should be large but not too
large—'The Romanists, indeed may build larger Churches, it is
enough if they hear the Murmur of the Mass, and see the Elevation
of the Host, but ours are to be fitted for Auditories. I can hardly
think it practicable to make a single Room so capacious, with Pews
and Galleries, as to hold above 2,000 Persons, and all to hear the
Service, and both to hear distinctly, and see the Preacher. I
endeavoured to effect this, in building the Parish Church of St
James's, Westminster, which, I presume, is the most capacious, with
these Qualifications, that hath yet been built. . . .'

   The interior with north and south aisles is indeed wide and
spacious. Galleries on three sides which curve round the west end as
in a theatre are supported by square piers encased in oak, above
which rise Corinthian columns with entablatures to carry the tunnel
vault of the nave into which the transverse tunnel vaults of the aisles
open; the galleries are ornamented with egg and dart and other
decoration.

   The elegance of the proportions and the refinement of the
decoration impart an air of much distinction. The rising ceiling is
divided by transverse ribs enclosing large panels; plaster-cast

St James's, Piccadilly. East end

mouldings from surviving fragments, supplemented with drawings and photographs, enabled the restorers to reproduce the original plaster-work.

Furnishings
St James's is fortunate in having three furnishings—the font, the organ-casing and the reredos—containing work known to have come from the hands of Grinling Gibbons, saved from destruction by being stored at Hardwick Hall in Derbyshire during the 1939–45 War.

Royal Coat of Arms A fine William and Mary coat of arms is placed above the new staircase in the north vestibule.

*Organ An exceptionally fine instrument, originally built in 1684 by Renatus Harris for King James II to be used in his Roman Catholic chapel at Whitehall Palace; after he fled to France it was given by Queen Mary to St James's where it was installed by Father Smith. Bomb damage necessitated its reconstruction but the Gibbons case with its six figures on top was brought back.

*Font This Grinling Gibbons feature is sculptured in white marble. The shaft represents the Tree of Life with a serpent coiled round it. Figures of Adam and Eve stand on either side. Round the bowl are three bas-reliefs—the Ark of Noah with the dove bearing an olive-branch, the Baptism of Christ and St Philip's Baptism of the Eunuch.

Pulpit The hexagonal pulpit dates from 1862.

Communion rails Bronze and white marble. Very lavish.

*Reredos The Gibbons work on the altar caused John Evelyn to write in his diary that: 'There was no altar anywhere in England, nor has there been any abroad, more handsomely adorned'. The reredos, carved in limewood, is crowned by a large segmental arch.

East Window Dating from 1954 and by Christopher Webb, it contains scenes from our Lord's life and Passion, also the coming of the Holy Ghost at Pentecost. In the upper light, Christ appears in Glory, surrounded by Angels and seated on a rainbow. The symbolism of the Pelican feeding its young with its own blood is depicted in the head of the light.

Monuments
Earl of Romney, died 1704. The memorial by W. Woodman in the north gallery has putti between twisted columns and inscription with trophies.

Lord Huntingdon, also died 1704. This, stated to be by Francis Bird, is nevertheless similar in style but the putti are outside the

St James's, Piccadilly. Grinling Gibbons font

columns, which are only twisted in the lower parts. The memorial is in the south gallery.

James Dodsley, died 1797. In the north-west vestibule and by the famous sculptor, John Flaxman, it is in the form of an open book.

Associations
Van der Velde Amongst the celebrities commemorated are father and son Van der Velde, the famous Dutch marine painters, who continued to work in this country even when England was at war with the Netherlands.

Baptisms These include *William Pitt, Earl of Chatham*, the great Prime Minister; and *William Blake*, poet, artist and mystic.

Incumbents The holding of this living seems in the past to have been a passport to preferment. Four rectors, namely the great William Temple who was here during the 1914–18 War, Dr Thomas Tenison who was the first rector (1685–92). Dr William Wake (rector 1695–1706) and Thomas Secker (rector 1733 to 1750) all became Archbishops of Canterbury. Many others were later deans or bishops and the present rector, Rev William Baddeley, was previously Dean of Brisbane.

General
The homely brick exterior set in its peaceful garden and the stately interior make a striking contrast to the bustle outside and there is much cause for gratitude that this outstanding Wren church, the parish church of the Royal Academy, has come back to life.

13 St John's, Smith Square

History
St John's church was built under the 1711 Act to meet the needs of new residential areas in Westminster, the parish—like St Martin-in-the-Fields—being carved out of the older one of St Margaret's.

The story of Queen Anne, when asked by Thomas Archer the architect what design she would like, kicking over a footstool and telling him to build a church like that, is certainly fictitious but the name of 'Queen Anne's footstool' has stuck, the four towers being supposed to represent the upturned legs.

In fact, the positioning of massive towers at the corners was due to a tendency for the building to sink during construction and the towers were conceived by the architect to ensure that the sinking would be uniform. Alterations, however, to the pinnacles and the steps were made at the same time without his knowledge or consent.

The site in the middle of a square was purchased in 1713 but building took a long time; St John's was not consecrated until June and not opened until November 1728. Costing over £40,000, it was the most expensive of the churches built under the 1711 Act.

In 1742, not long after completion, it was gutted by fire and, in the subsequent reconstruction, 12 Corinthian columns supporting the ceiling were omitted.

Further alterations were made in 1824.

In 1941, during the air-raids, the church was once again gutted by fire and remained a burnt-out shell until it was sold for £50,000 to a Trust who have carried out a restoration enabling St John's to be used for various cultural activities, mainly concerts; the parish was united with that of St Stephen's, Rochester Row. The new church was re-consecrated in 1968.

Exterior
The outsize towers and the huge pediments give one a jolt from whichever of the four streets leading into Smith Square one first sees the church. The north and south sides, where the main entrances are situated, have large porticoes with giant Tuscan columns and pilasters supporting the pediments which are broken to allow for the introduction of deeply-recessed smaller pediments. Grand flights of steps lead up to the entrance doors.

On the other two sides are very big Venetian windows divided by pilasters. The pediments are also broken, in this case to provide space for niches.

The tall towers are decorated with pediments and enclosed with free standing columns at the corners. Both columns and pediments have Corinthian capitals. The towers are rounded off with curved entablatures with modillion cornices and crowned with lead cupolas and pineapples.

Interior
The entrance doors lead into lobbies which break up the cruciform shape of the church. These give access into what is now the concert hall, which is oblong with curved corners and projections at east and west ends. The huge Corinthian columns remain and follow the curve of what used to be the nave.

General
One of London's most controversial church designs. According to

whether Baroque was in fashion or not, opinion has varied from calling it outstandingly ugly to considering it rather fine.

Thomas Archer was a man of independent means who held the not very exacting but well-paid and curiously-named post of Groom Porter; he was the most Baroque of all our architects and St John's, which is generally regarded as his best-known work, has been described as 'the finest example of Baroque architecture in the country'.

Whether or not one likes this intrusion into a quiet Queen Anne square, it would have been a great pity if this twice-gutted and therefore rather unlucky church had been allowed to moulder and we can be thankful that new use has been found for it and that it still remains to enliven the London skyline.

14 St John's Wood Chapel

St John's Wood
This was once the property of the Knights Hospitaller of St John of Jerusalem attached to their Priory at Clerkenwell. In this wood, the conspirators under Anthony Babington against Queen Elizabeth were arrested.

History
The Chapel was built as a chapel of ease to St Marylebone Parish Church to serve a new suburb, the architect of both being Thomas Hardwick. Started in 1813, it was consecrated on 9th April 1814. It suffered under the Victorians, the pews being reduced in 1867, but was restored after war damage to its former Georgian state, being redecorated in white and gold.

Exterior
Well set on an eminence at the end of Park Road and lying in a pleasant churchyard, this church offers its most attractive face to the road with pedimented Ionic portico and turret above, all faced in stone. The sides are of brick.

Interior
The interior echoes the charm of the exterior. Tuscan columns support galleries which have their own columns bearing the slightly curved ceiling. The chancel is narrower and projects. The nave galleries have been glazed and are used as rooms. Box-pews painted white complete the picture.

Monuments
There are a number of memorials of which the following are of main
interest:

Sarah Capel, who died in 1825, commemorated by a Greek seated
figure by Sir Francis Chantrey.

Gillespie children, who died in 1832–3. An appealing group by S.
Nixon.

John Farquhar, who died in 1826. Farquhar who made a fortune
from munitions bought Fonthill Abbey with its enormous tower
from the eccentric William Beckford. Three years later, the tower
fell down. The monument is an attractive profile medallion by Peter
Rouw, the younger.

Associations
Elizabeth West, the wife of Benjamin West, the American-born
president of the Royal Academy, is buried in a vault below the
church.

Joanna Southcott, the religious fanatic, was buried here in 1814.

General
St John's Chapel is an appealing early 19th century church, 'the
ensemble remarkably reminiscent of New England' (Pevsner). It
must be familiar to thousands of cricket-lovers wending their way to
and from Lord's Cricket Ground.

15 St Margaret's, Westminster

Dedication
St Margaret, of royal descent, became a Christian at Antioch. She
was pursued by a vicious local ruler and endured many sufferings in
prison rather than submit. Amongst these, tradition relates that she
was swallowed by a repulsive dragon; with the aid of prayer and the
sign of the Cross, she emerged unscathed, but she was eventually
beheaded.

History
Three churches are known to have been built upon the site but there
is no record of the original foundation. It seems reasonable to guess
that the first place of worship was built not long after 1065, the year
of the consecration of Westminster Abbey, as a church for the
tradesmen, craftsmen and peasants who gathered in the village
around the new Abbey.

The earliest written record dates from the first half of the 12th century when the Papal judges confirmed that the parish was exempt from any jurisdiction claimed by the Bishop of London. In fact, the Abbey exercised control right up until 1840 when it, at last, came under the episcopal hierarchy.

Although the parish was thinly populated, it stretched from Lambeth Bridge to the far end of Hyde Park, covering all that we now call the City of Westminster (except parts of the Strand), an area of 44 square miles.

By Edward III's reign (1327–77), the original church was found to be too small. The headquarters or 'staple' of the wool industry had been set up beside the site where Big Ben now stands and, the church having also become dilapidated, the parishioners and merchants decided on something better. This was the building in which Geoffry Chaucer and William Caxton worshipped.

At the end of the 15th century, it gave way to what basically is the present church, built by Westminster Abbey masons. So devoted was one of them that he regularly returned his wages, and even ordinary workmen made gifts. Started in 1486, it took 35 years to build and was not consecrated until 9th April, 1523.

Seventeen years later, the parishioners had to put up armed resistance to save it from being dismantled by Protector Somerset to provide building materials for his new Thames-side palace.

In 1614, the long connection with the House of Commons began. As the Puritan movement gathered momentum, members wished to dissociate themselves from any High Church practices and 'for feare of copes and wafer-cakes' decided to worship separately at St Margaret's rather than in the Abbey. On Palm Sunday, 17th April that year, the whole House assembled in the church for corporate Communion, no doubt to test the churchmanship of each member, but all turned up. Ever since, it has been the parish church of the House of Commons. The House adjourned here to give thanks for victory and peace in 1918 and again in 1945.

St Margaret's has been frequently in the hands of restorers. Galleries and box-pews have been installed and taken out again; it has been re-roofed twice, an elaborate apse introduced at the east end and later removed, the tower heightened and otherwise altered, porches attached, exterior refaced in Portland stone, internal walls stripped, all window tracery renewed, and, finally, the east end extended by one bay.

Much changed as it is, however, St Margaret's survives as a mediaeval church of the Perpendicular period, similar to St Andrew Undershaft, St Giles', Cripplegate and St Dunstan's, Stepney.

In 1973 the church was placed by a special Act of Parliament under the control and care of the Dean and Chapter of the Abbey. One of the canons of the Abbey serves as rector.

Exterior
St Margaret's is overshadowed by its powerful neighbours but, as such, gives them scale. It lies well back from the west front of the Abbey and the level lawn, once full of puddles, provides a charming frame. The low roof-line is typical of the 15th century but the positioning of the tower to the north-west of the building gives width when viewed from the west. In the middle of the 18th century the tower was raised 20 feet but, unless misrepresented, the tower when Canaletto painted the procession of the Knights of the Garter in 1749 looked very different even then from its appearance today with its large rectangular belfry window. Clasping polygonal buttresses extend its full length and it is capped by a small wooden octagonal cupola with ogee open top.

The renewed window tracery is in the Tudor style and gives a uniform appearance. At the east end, there are stone turrets at the angles.

The exterior is much blackened on the south side.

Interior
The internal proportions are surprisingly large and there is seating for 1,000.

The spacious and graceful arcades and the tower arch are the only genuine old parts; angels with shields are placed at the springing points of the arches. The view to the large east window is uninterrupted by any chancel arch and the arcades with standard slender shafted columns stretch for eight bays. Aisles on both sides house a number of interesting monuments; the roofs are of low pitch but the interior is lightened by a tall clerestory. The 19th century chancel roof has gilded and elaborate bosses.

The south-east vestry was added in 1778.

Furnishings
Font The font, by Nicholas Stone, dates from 1641. It has a supporting stem of square section and a circular bowl of granite. The octagonal base is of red granite.

Organ A fine Walker instrument installed in 1897.

Pulpit This is a heavily encrusted and crudely coloured Victorian piece. It is decorated with crocketed finials, many cusps and abounds with barber pole shafts.

Reredos The centre-piece of the triptych is the original carving in limewood of 1753, by Siffrin Alken, based on Titian's 'Supper at Emmaus'.

*Stained glass The central feature is the huge east window which contains some of the finest glass in London. It was made in the Netherlands at the beginning of the 16th century upon the occasion of the marriage of Henry VII's eldest son, Arthur, to Catherine of Aragon, both of whom are shown kneeling at the foot. Five months later, Arthur died and, with the Reformation troubles, his brother, Henry VIII, did not want to have the glass around. Owing to this fortunate circumstance it was saved, for it passed into private hands, where during Cromwellian times it was protected by General Monk. It was brought back in 1758.

The scene of the Crucifixion is dealt with pictorially in the Renaissance manner with a strikingly blue sky.

The west window, which contains full-length figures of Elizabeth I, Henry Prince of Wales, Sir Walter Raleigh (spreading his cloak) and his half-brother, Sir Humphrey Gilbert, is by Clayton & Bell, who also made the window alongside, commemorating John Milton. It shows him dictating after his blindness. The window includes lines from the American poet, John Greenleaf Whittier: 'The New World honours him whose lofty plan for England's freedom made her own more sure . . .'

The south aisle windows, by John Piper (their theme is said to be 'Spring in London') are disappointing and out of keeping. They show geometrical forms in green, yellow, orange and grey against clear glass.

Monuments

The memorials are too numerous to list. Of particular interest are those to *Cornelius Vandun* (died 1577—north aisle), *Mary Lady Dudley* (died 1600—south aisle), *Sir Francis Egioke* (died 1622—north aisle), *Mrs Brocas* (died 1654—west aisle), *Sir Peter Parker* (died 1814—west wall). A memorial to *James Palmer*, who died in 1660, which was badly damaged by an oil bomb during World War II, has the comment that 'once a week' he 'gave a comfortable sermon in chapel of Fayer Alms Houses, which he built'.

Richard Montpasson, a contemporary of Shakespeare, kneels by the altar steps. The brass to *Thomas Cole* (died 1597) and family in the east wall of the north aisle has interesting wording.

Associations

St Margaret's is too historical a building to recount all its many associations. Amongst these may be mentioned:

Sir Walter Raleigh His decapitated body lies buried before the altar. His head is interred some distance away at West Horsley. Surrey.

James Rumsey In the middle of the south aisle, it is recorded that the epitaph by Robert Herrick 'in memory of the late deceased Virgin Mistris Elizabeth Hereicke formerly on a mural tablet in the middle of the north aisle was restored in memory of James Rumsey whom the State of West Virginia honours as the inventor of the Steamboat, which he demonstrated privately to George Washington in 1784 and publicly in the Potomac River at Shepherdstown West Virginia 3rd December, 1787'. He was buried in the churchyard on 24th December, 1792.

Cromwell Association A tablet on the exterior of the west wall was erected by the Cromwell Association in memory of those whose remains were disinterred from Westminster Abbey at the time of the restoration of Charles II and were in September 1661 summarily thrown into the churchyard. The 21 names included Oliver Cromwell's mother, John Pym, and Admiral Robert Blake.

Samuel Pepys In May 1667, Pepys entertained himself 'with my perspective glass up and down the church, by which I had the pleasure of seeing and gazing at a great many fine women, and what with that, and sleeping, I passed away the time till sermon was done'.

General

In many ways one of the best known of London's churches, it is perhaps chiefly remembered for its associations, which range from the wedding of Samuel Pepys to that of Winston Churchill, rather than its architecture. As the parish church of the House of Commons, it must always occupy an honoured place in the ecclesiastical heritage of the capital and there must be many whose memories are stirred each year by the Garden of Remembrance in the churchyard. Starting life closely linked to the Abbey, St Margaret's is now once more intimately associated with its great neighbour. It is regularly used for recitals of music and lectures as well as for services transferred from the Abbey during the months when tourism is heaviest. But it retains its own congregation on Sunday mornings, and it is one of the few churches in central London to keep a boys' choir, the choristers being drawn from Westminster City School.

16 St Mark's, North Audley Street

History
St Mark's was built as a chapel of ease to St George's, Hanover
Square between September 1825 (laying of foundation stone) and
April 1828 (consecration) by J. P. Gandy-Deering, a little-known
architect who had worked for Sir John Soane as draughtsman and
in other capacities. The Church Commissioners contributed £5,500
towards the total cost of £13,300.

The church suffered drastic disfigurement at the hands of Sir
Arthur Blomfield in 1878 when, as he had done a few years earlier at
St Peter's, Eaton Square, he introduced a Byzantine remodelling
totally unsuited to the original style of the building. He kept the
three galleries, although Jacobean-type fronts were added later. New
choir stalls were fitted in 1914.

In recent years, St Mark's—being near Grosvenor Square—was
used by the American community in London, but they have now
gone elsewhere.

Exterior
A striking and original neo-Greek façade with sturdy corner piers
and tow tall Ionic columns carrying a heavy entablature without
pediment. Behind is a square lantern pierced with Somerset-type
tracery (small circular apertures). This front is completely hemmed
in by adjoining buildings and the body of the church lies well back.

Interior
The interior is reached through a dark and gloomy three-bay
passage with classical Ionic pillars. From this opens out quite a large
church with its architecture confused by the Blomfield alterations
which included round-headed windows in the straight east wall of
the chancel.

In the north-east corner is an attractive chapel with interesting
fittings.

Furnishings
Font Plain white marble with brown fluted bowl.
   Pulpit A fine furnishing.
   Stained glass The east window designed by N. H. J. Eastlake
was made by Lavers and Barraud. They also painted the reredos.

General
There must be serious doubts as to the future of this church, which

St Mark's, North Audley Street

is now classed as redundant, but it is to be hoped that, whatever happens, the façade which makes such an attractive accent in the architecture of North Audley Street can be preserved.

N.B. Interior cannot at present be visited.

17 St Martin-in-the-Fields

Dedication

At one time known as St Martin-near-the-Cross (Charing Cross), the saint chosen could hardly be more appropriate today in view of the church's particular concern with the less fortunate members of society. St Martin, according to the legend, met a beggar when, as a soldier, he was riding in bitter weather towards Amiens. Martin had no money but instead cut his cloak into two with his sword and gave half to the beggar. The emblem of St Martin showing him dividing his cloak appears on lamp-posts and door-handles in the parish.

Open country surrounded the mediaeval church on this site so it became known as St Martin-in-the-Fields to distinguish it from other churches dedicated to this saint.

History

The first of the three churches erected was mentioned in a document of 1222 but, apart from that, little is known about it. The only pictorial record shows it as a small cruciform building and it may have been a chapel belonging to the monks who came from Westminster Abbey to work in the Convent Garden, or possibly an annexe to the great religious house of St Martin-le-Grand.

This original place of worship was replaced by a second in 1544 towards the end of Henry VIII's reign. Because of the fear of plague, the King had been concerned with the carriage of corpses through the Westminster Palace precincts for burial in the adjacent churchyard of St Margaret's. He had, therefore, caused parish status to be granted two years earlier to St Martin's so that burials could take place further away in the new parish, which stretched from Tottenham Court Road to Chelsea.

The Tudor church lasted until 1721, by which time its capacity of 400 people was totally inadequate for a parish which now numbered 40,000 people; the building was also considered unsafe. James Gibbs, who was in competition with John James for the post of architect, took the adjudication committee along the Strand to see

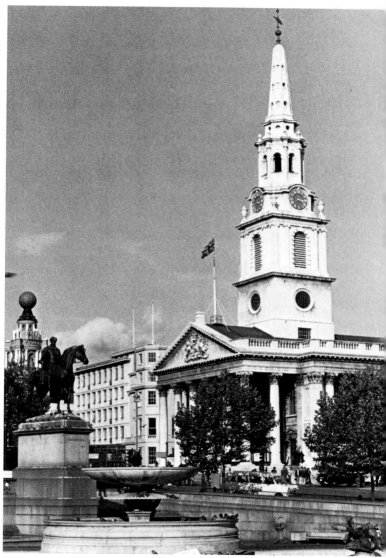

St Martin-in-the-Fields

his new church of St Mary; they were so impressed that he was duly elected by a large majority.

Exterior
The superlative siting only dates from the 1820s when Trafalgar Square was laid out; before that the church faced on to the lower end of St Martin's Lane with 'vile houses' in front of it. The improvement in the site, however, had one disadvantage in that it drew attention to the awkward placing of the steeple behind the pedimented portico on the west end of the church proper. The steeple (rebuilt in 1842) is a striking design consisting of a bell-stage with round-headed windows and coupled pilasters at the angles; above this is a recessed octagonal open lantern with attached colonettes and the whole is topped with a pierced concave-sided spire.

An imposing flight of steps leads one up to the portico, combining to make a grand entrance. The sides are impressive with giant columns and pilasters; at the east end there is a large Venetian window.

Interior
There is an almost theatrical gaiety about the interior, due in the main to the graceful plasterwork executed by the renowned Artari and Bagutti which provides sparkle and much visual pleasure. The effect is heightened by the way the nave curves round to embrace the small, narrow chancel and by the royal 'boxes' at the east end, two of which look out both into the chancel and into the nave. One old account, in fact, describes the interior as 'a little too gay and theatrical for Protestant worship'.

The lack of clerestory tends to emphasise width at the expense of height; the aisles have shallow dome vaults and there are high metal balconies at the east end.

The crypt, famed for the hospitality it gives to social outcasts, has groined vaults resting on short sturdy pillars.

Furnishings.
Painting A fine painting of St Martin and the beggar by Francesco Solimena can be seen at the west end.

Font Oval in shape and notable for its cover. Dates from 1689. Attractive rails.

Prie-dieu The prie-dieu in the nave originally belonged to King Edward VII and Queen Alexandra.

Pews The box-pews in the aisles dated from 1799 but were lowered in 1858. Initially James Gibbs' plans only provided for pews in the galleries and permanent seating was not introduced into the body of the church until 1799.

Pulpit Although replacing an earlier one the pulpit seems in keeping with the styles prevailing at the time St Martin's was built. It has a charming staircase with twisted balusters and is decorated with inlay work.

Coat of arms A fine coat of arms is placed above the chancel step.

Communion rails Of cast-iron and they may be the earliest communion rails made of this material anywhere in England.

Chest and whipping-post A chest of 1597 and a whipping-post of 1751 can be seen in the crypt.

Monuments

Far East prisoners of war Sleepers from the Burma-Siam railway are included in a memorial to Far East prisoners of war in the crypt.

James Gibbs There is a bust of James Gibbs—the architect of St Martin's—in the vestry hall.

Associations

Royalty Buckingham Palace lies in the parish of St Martin's and the links with Royalty are very close. The 'boxes' at the chancel end are witness to this. Even before the Palace became a royal home, Charles II (born June 1630) was baptised here and George I was the first churchwarden of the present church—the only monarch ever to occupy this post.

Nell Gwynne, who died in November 1687 aged 38, was interred in the burying ground of the parish.

John Constable was married here on 2nd October 1816.

Dr Thomas Tenison, who was appointed Vicar of St Martin's and King's Chaplain by Charles II in 1680 later became Archbishop of Canterbury. He is associated with the establishment of St Martin's Public Library which, according to John Evelyn, was the first Public Library in London.

Registers Early registers include:

Births Francis Bacon (January 1560)

Marriages Daughter of Oliver Cromwell (November 1657)

Deaths Sir Winston Churchill, father of the great Duke of Marlborough (1688):Richard Baxter, the Puritan divine (1691): Lord Fairfax, the Commander of the Parliamentary army (1709): John Sheppard, the highwayman (1742) and Louis-François Roubiliac, the sculptor (1762).

Link with Connecticut, USA The original design for a round

church which James Gibbs had submitted was later adopted for a
church in Connecticut, USA, owing to the close association of St
Martin's with the early history of the American Episcopal Church.

General
This church will always be remembered for the ministry of H. R. L.
(Dick) Sheppard who came here at the beginning of the 1914–18
War after horrifying experiences as chaplain on the Western front.
He kept the church open for young soldiers as they arrived at
Charing Cross Station from France and ever since it has become
known as 'the Church of the ever-open Door', offering welcome to
the homeless and stranded. It is a beacon for those who need help or
consolation, providing what Ian Nairn describes as 'charity without
strings'.

Vera Brittain, who wrote the admirable *Story of St Martin's*, has
described Dick Sheppard as 'that unusual phenomenon, a saint with
a sense of humour' and his successors, who included the great Pat
McCormick, have continued to draw huge crowds to St Martin's, so
that it has been well called 'the parish church of London'.

18 St Marylebone Parish Church

Dedication
The original dedication of St John was changed to St Mary when
the second church was built and Tyburn, the name of the brook that
ran through the area altered to Bourne. The latter was no doubt due
to the association of Tyburn with the place of execution at Marble
Arch. So the church became known at St Mary at Bourne or St
Mary-le-Bone.

History
No less than four churches have been built on or near the site which
has been edged further north as the area developed. They have
ranged from small village churches to the stately church one sees
today. The first church built in 1200, probably near the site of
Marshal & Snelgrove's store in Oxford Street, gave way in 1400 to
a place of worship built a quarter of a mile north in the High Street.
The third church, on the same site, was erected in 1740; this very
soon became inadequate but it was many years before a vacillating
vestry commissioned Thomas Hardwick to build the present church
a little further north on the Marylebone High Road, the earlier
church being demoted to become known as the Parish Chapel and

finally demolished in 1949. The foundation stone was laid on 5th July 1813 and consecration took place on 4th February 1817. It cost over £70,000.

In 1883, a churchwarden, Thomas Harris, carried out a thorough Victorianisation; the choir was remodelled in Italian Renaissance style, stalls put in and an apse built. Bomb damage in the 1939–45 War was limited to the windows.

Exterior

When John Nash was laying out Regent's Park, he made the York gate entrance axial with the portico of the church. This is a magnificent hexastyle Corinthian example with a broad staircase, flanked by additional Corinthian columns. Above rises the imposing circular tower, which has free-standing columns round the main stage, a circle of caryatids round the smaller upper stage with entablature above their heads and is completed with a beehive stone cupola. A balcony runs along the top of the sides.

Flanking the window at the east end, diagonal projecting porches were built to provide a broad staircase entrance from the High Street.

The alignment of the church is north and south.

Interior

Stately but heavily Victorianised. Double galleries used to go right round the church, with the organ, split into two sections, framing a transparency in the east window by Benjamin West and in the strange position of being over the altar. When the apse was built, the north and south galleries were curved round to embrace the choir and the upper galleries removed. Only the west end now has both upper and lower ones. Thin columns are used for support. Above the projecting porches there were private pews, set one above the other, complete with curtains and fireplaces and looking like theatre boxes; these have been removed. The former coved ceiling is now flat and rather dull. There are alcoves with ironwork screens at the east end, which has a coffered apse decorated with Corinthian pilasters. Large free-standing Corinthian marble columns frame the approach to the choir.

A Browning Chapel was arranged at the west end of the church in 1946 to mark the centenary of Robert Browning's marriage to Elizabeth Barrett, now converted to the Browning Room.

Furnishings

The main furnishings of interest are:

Choir-stalls adorned with angels, harp and trumpets.

Font, circular and made of marble.

Altar and rails The Aisle Chapel contains altar and rails etc. of the Browning Chapel and a painting of the Holy Family by Benjamin West, American President of the Royal Academy, which was originally the reredos of the high altar.

Organ The organ includes a Schulze swell organ formerly in Charterhouse School.

Stained glass Fragments of stained glass from the bomb-blasted windows have been used as borders for the present windows.

Browning Room The contents consist of a window given by the Browning Study Groups of Winnipeg, a table, a chair and carved angels from their home in Florence, and a medallion portrait of Robert.

Monuments
The monuments are minor.

Associations
One or other of the three St Mary's churches has been the scene of many famous marriages, including the fictitious one of the Rake in Hogarth's well-known cycle of paintings (in the Sir John Soane's Museum, Lincoln's Inn Fields). The pew inscription in the painting can still be seen on the wall of the west aisle. This scene was set in the second church, where also Francis Bacon married Alice Barnham in 1606. In the third church, Richard Brinsley Sheridan married Elizabeth Linley in 1773. The most famous, however, was the secret marriage of Robert Browning to Elizabeth Barrett in the present church in 1846.

Amongst those baptised were Lord Byron (1788), Lord Nelson's daughter Horatia (1803) and Charles Dickens' son (date not available). The church is described in *Dombey and Son* and was probably the setting for Mr Dombey's second marriage to Edith Granger.

The site of the earlier church and its churchyard is now marked by the Garden of Rest in Marylebone High Street. A tablet commemorates some of the notable people buried there, including James Gibbs, the famous 18th century architect of many of London's best churches (1754) and John Michael Rysbrack, the great Flemish sculptor (1770). Charles, the brother of John Wesley and writer of many famous hymns, was also buried there and an obelisk has been erected to his memory.

General
This church is a fine accent point in the Marylebone Road and has a long and interesting history.

19 St Mary-le-Strand

Dedication
With such a concentration of churches, it was often necessary to distinguish one London church from another similarly dedicated— in this case by adding the location.

History
The earliest mention of a church on this site is 1147 and Thomas a Becket, who was murdered in 1170, was at one time rector. Thereafter it existed, variously named as Church of Innocents or Church of Nativity of our Lady and the Innocents of the Strand, until 1549 when in a high-handed manner the king's uncle, the Duke of Somerset, had it demolished to make way for his new mansion between the river and the Strand. The dispossessed congregation had to go to the Savoy Chapel nearby.

This continued until the reign of Queen Anne (1702–14) when the first of the Fifty Churches was erected to take the place of the Church of Innocents. The architect chosen was James Gibbs, a young Scot and a Roman Catholic, who later was to build St Martin-in-the-Fields. Work proceeded between 1714 and 1717 but the new place of worship was not consecrated until 1st January 1723.

Exterior
Splendid use has been made by Gibbs of the island site, which is a little to the north of where the earlier building was located, to provide London with one of its most beautiful churches. Originally the intention was to complete it with a campanile for a bell at the west end and, 80 feet in front of this, a 250 foot high column to be crowned with a statue of Queen Anne. But the last of the Stuart monarchs died in 1714 and presumably with the Hanoverian accession this was no longer considered appropriate. The idea was happily abandoned, therefore, in favour of a steeple and rounded west porch, a most felicitous combination which adds greatly to the visual enjoyment of this building. The steeple consists of a rectangular stage with detached columns at the angles and pairs of

coupled pilasters on the west and east faces, carrying a narrower stage with similar embellishment but with single pilasters, the whole being surmounted with a concave-sided top stage capped with a little lantern.

The flanking façades on the north and south are adorned on the upper floor with alternating round arches and pediments which effectively break the line of the balustrade whilst the apsed east end is decorated with delicate vine trails between the windows. The absence of windows on the ground floor served to prevent the worshippers from being distracted by passing traffic.

St Mary's is built of Portland stone.

Interior
A rather narrow interior of which the most arresting features as one enters are the coved ceiling, coffered with alternate lines of lozenges and squares, and—less agreeably—by the windows of madonna blue in the apse. The walls are panelled and inlaid wood is placed round the altar. There are no aisles but the apse is framed by coupled columns and is charmingly decorated with cherubs' heads, clouds, etc.

During a visit to Rome between 1703 and 1708, Gibbs came under the influence of Carlo Fontana, Surveyor to Pope Clement XI, and St Mary's is the most Italian in feeling of Gibbs' churches— so much so that it has been called an 'expatriate Roman'. The ceiling is similar to two of Fontana's churches in Rome.

Furnishings
Font The font is of alabaster on a baluster stem.
   *Pulpit The ample double-curved pulpit was at one time affixed to the wall and therefore hanging; the short squat foot was added later when it was placed on the ground. The adornment of cherubs' heads and vine trails has been ascribed to Grinling Gibbons because his signature of open pea-pods appears, but this may well be the work of one of his pupils. A fine furnishing.
   Doorcases Attractive pedimented doorcases lead to vestries.
   Altar-rails The fluted rails have turned balusters of slender proportions typical of the early 18th century.

Monument
A brass plate on the south wall of the chancel commemorates a former rector, Alfred Bowen Evans DD, 'who with quaint sallies of native genius adorned the graver studies of the divine and the fervid eloquence of a thoughtful preacher. . .'

Associations
Charles Edward Stuart It seems likely that St Mary-le-Strand was the church where Charles Edward Stuart, the Young Pretender, who was on a secret visit to London (there is a plaque on the house in Essex Street nearby where he stayed), was received in 1750 into the Church of England—no doubt with a view to furthering the Jacobite cause.

Charles Dickens' father, who was clerk in the Navy Pay Office of Somerset House, was married in St Mary-le-Strand on 13th June 1809.

Hackney Cabs The first rank was established in 1634 in front of St Mary-le-Strand.

General
St Mary's commandingly closes the vista east of the Strand. With St Clement Danes behind, the churches look like two great ships sailing down the highway. The diminutive island site, attractively planted with magnolia trees, is all that is left of the churchyard which, as a plaque shows, at one time extended to the forecourt of the Waldorf Hotel.

St Mary-le-Strand has been partially cleaned and is being adapted for presentation of music recitals and as an exhibition gallery. A £400,000 restoration fund to make urgent structural repairs, extend cleaning and provide new glass was launched in September, 1977.

20 St Mary Magdalene, Paddington

History
The church of St Mary Magdalene is an offshoot of All Saints', Margaret Street. The moving spirit behind its building was R. T. West who was curate at All Saints'; the architect was G. E. Street who was a member of the congregation and the church was erected to accommodate those people wanting a similar High Church form of service who lived in Paddington.

Built in stages between 1868 and 1878, during which period the roof caught fire and had to be re-erected, St Mary Magdalene was consecrated in 1878.

Exterior
The lay-out of St Mary's was largely determined by the difficult site upon which it was built. It had been a dumping ground of the spoil dug out of the Regent's Canal which runs alongside and the plot of

ground was neither level nor were any of the sides parallel. There was room for a south but not a north transept and the polygonal apsed east end (actually south) followed the boundary line of the land, the thin tower with its banded horizontal belfry stage and tall spire being fitted in between the transept and the apse. The tower and spire, as at All Saints', look German in their proportions.

Interior

The same site limitations made themselves felt inside for there was no room for more than a small passage aisle on the north side and this provides a disturbing contrast with the broader south aisle. The sexes in High Churches of this type were separated at the time it was built and, as it was thought that there would be more women than men attending services, they were given the benefit of the south aisle; in fact, men outnumbered women and they must have been pushed for room in the north aisle.

The lack of balance between the two sides is further accentuated by different arcades, the south consisting of clustered columns with 13th century foliage decoration, the north, adorned with statues and medallions, of plain octagonal pillars with the bays divided by two sub-arches; the clerestories, however, which are similar, help to pull the design together.

The painted roof is of the ceiled wagon type.

Again because of the difficulties of the site, the architect put the vestries below, where there is also a charming chapel—the Chapel of St Sepulchre—with gay and colourful fittings by Sir Ninian Comper completed in 1895. These include screens, altar with tester, wall-painting, glass and a small organ with an attractively painted case.

General

The open site and low-rise surrounding buildings make this church a prominent feature in a largely residential area.

N.B. Not normally open except during services.

21 St Mary on Paddington Green

History

The history of worship on this site goes back to a small chapel which existed prior to the founding of the parish by Westminster Abbey in the early part of the 13th century. The Abbey administered

St Mary Magdalene, Paddington. View from south-east

and maintained the church they built until the Reformation, after which it continued to serve the parish until it was demolished in 1678.

The second church, which had a much shorter life, had a bell-turret at the west end surmounted by a small spire. From this steeple bread used to be thrown—according to a strange annual custom—to be scrambled for by the people below.

The present place of worship was built between the years 1788 and 1791, being consecrated on the 27th April of the latter year. The architect was John Plaw and St Mary's is the only ecclesiastical building put up by him. It remained the parish church until 1845 when this status passed to St James's, Sussex Gardens.

Alterations in the 19th century considerably changed the character of the building but a quite outstanding restoration begun in June 1972 by the architect Raymond Erith has brought back the original 18th century atmosphere and made St Mary's into a place of exceptional charm and one admirably suited to its present needs.

Exterior

The yellow brick church is situated on slightly raised ground on a Green now hemmed in by the motorway which runs alongside. The building is in the form of a Greek cross, the centre square with a white cupola above—and the arms lower and narrower. There are porticoes on the south and west sides, the former being the main entrance.

Interior

The work so splendidly conceived by Raymond Erith was completed in 1973. Box-pews have been brought back, the floor has been re-paved with Portland and York stone slabs, with marble in the central aisle and sanctuary, and new lighting, including an attractive chandelier designed by Erith, has been provided. The original font, pulpit, altar and altar-rails of very thin iron have been made good whilst a new organ has been installed in his memory.

Galleries on three sides recede into the arms of the cross, making with the angles five sides of an octagon. The galleries are supported by columns, those at the angles being especially robust to carry the four upper columns, on which the shallow dome rests. Considerable play is made with segmental vaults and arches, helping to give this enchanting interior its special appeal.

Furnishings (see Interior)

Monuments Amongst many fine monuments there are two by Peter

St Mary on Paddington Green. From south-east

Scheemakers and one by John Bacon.

The two Scheemakers memorials are in the south-east corner of the gallery commemorating:

Eleanor Boucher, 'of respectable family of the Addisons in Maryland' USA, born 1740 died 1784. She was the wife of Rev Jonathan Boucher.

John James The inscription states that 'in a monument in this churchyard belonging to Rev Jona^n Boucher are laid the remains of Rev John James sometime curate and afterwards rector of Arthuret and Kirkandrews upon Esk, County of Cumberland'. He died in 1786 in the 27th year of his life.

Frances E. Aust Only the lower part with a relief medallion remains but it is a fine example of John Bacon's work, dating from 1796.

Charlotte Cumberbatch, who died in 1818. Two ornate figures.

Thomas Combe A tablet on the south side below the gallery commemorates Thomas Combe, Prebendary of Canterbury Cathedral, born in Philadelphia, Pennsylvania, who died in 1822.

Joseph Nollekens, the sculptor, by W. Behnes on the south wall of the chancel, dating from 1823.

Sarah Siddons, the famous actress who died in 1831 is commemorated by a tablet, but outside on the Green there is a statue to her and her tomb is in the churchyard.

Burials include Mary Cadogan, Emma Hamilton's mother and William, the father of Wilkie Collins, the author of *The Woman in White*.

Associations
John Donne, the famous Dean of St Paul's Cathedral, preached his first sermon in the original parish church.

William Hogarth was married to Jane Thornhill in the old church in 1730.

General
This is one of London's most delightful church surprises. Motorists hurtling along the Westway probably have little idea that just below them is an exquisite little 18th century church, beautifully restored and with a vigorous life. Its excellent acoustics make it particularly suited for the concerts which take place at St Mary's in addition to the regular worship.

The recent restoration has removed 19th century excrescences, brought back the 18th century beauty and adapted the church to 20th century needs.

22 St Mary's, Bryanston Square

History

St Mary's was one of four Commissioner churches built to serve the needs of the St Marylebone area, in this case the Portman estate west of Baker Street. The Commissioners contributed just under two-thirds of the cost. The architect, Sir Robert Smirke, who was one of three official members of the profession attached to the Board of Works, was about to begin work on one of his famous London creations, the British Museum. His churches, however, show an extraordinary lack of versatility and the characteristic, not very well-proportioned elongated pepper-box was to appear at churches going up simultaneously at Wandsworth, West Hackney and Bristol, whilst his St Philip's Church, Salford, near Manchester (built 1825) is almost a carbon copy of St Mary's, upon which work began in 1821, consecration taking place on 7th January 1824.

In 1875 Sir Arthur Blomfield made various alterations, including provision of space for a choir, and we owe to him the separation of the font, pulpit and altar which previously lay one in front of the other—a 'low' Church arangement not uncommon at the beginning of the 19th century.

An expert redecoration was carried out by Sir Albert Richardson after the 1939–45 War.

Exterior

The tower is finely sited in Wyndham Place and it is hoped that one day the forecourt may be turned into a precinct, but the opportunity of a through vista from Marble Arch was lost when Bryanston Square was laid out.

Differences in detail of the tower from that at St Anne's, Wandsworth are that the lower stage has attached fluted half columns instead of pilasters and the openings in the top stage are longer, whilst it retains its original clock made in 1823 by John Moore & Son of Clerkenwell (which has recently been repaired); and the siting on a semicircular portico of unfluted Ionic columns is in the middle of the south wall and not at the west end. The portico is impressive but the Bath and Portland stone of which it is built does not contrast well with the stock brick of the rest of the church.

Interior

Galleries carry tall Doric columns of wood with iron filling supporting a gently curved elliptical ceiling which has been recently restored after storm damage with epoxy resin. The sanctuary is

St Mary's, Bryanston Square

flanked by vestries. A 1914–18 Memorial Chapel lies at the east end
of the north aisle.

Furnishings
Organ A fine Harrison organ which is also used for recitals and
concerts.
  Font An octagonal font in the south-west corner.
  Pulpit The large pulpit is supported on eight grey upward-
tapering Corinthian columns embellished with ironwork.
  Stained glass A pleasant grey-gold window in the north aisle,
together with a window from the demolished St Paul's, Great
Portland Street but not much else.

General
This is a dignified place of worship, suffering like many other
London parishes from diminishing congregations due to residents
moving out, and with increasing financial needs for necessary repair
work.

23 St Matthew's, Great Peter Street, Westminster

History
Built by Sir George Gilbert Scott between the years 1849–51.

Exterior
Distinctive features are the sturdy short tower on the south side and
the large porch. The tower, built of Kentish ragstone, is completed
with a low cap.

Interior
The 5-bay arcade has arches dying into the columns which are
without capitals. There are two aisles on the south side of which the
outer has been converted into a chapel dedicated to Frank Weston,
Bishop of Zanzibar, a great Anglo-Catholic figure.
  A rare peculiarity is the placing of the Lady Chapel (by Sir Ninian
Comper) at the top of a flight of stairs on a level with the former
rood loft. The west window has odd geometrical tracery.

Furnishings
Sculpture A fine sculpture by Allan Howes dating from 1951 of the
Crucifixion is placed at the west end of the inner south aisle.
  Lectern This is a notable Spanish lectern of the 15th century in
wood and traceried.

Altars The Weston Chapel altar dates from 1928 and is by Martin Travers. The Lady Chapel is one of the first two of the English type in which the altar is enclosed on three sides with riddel curtains like the sides of a four-poster bed. The posts are surmounted with angels holding torches.

General
In May 1977, St Matthew's was severely damaged by fire which destroyed the organ loft, gallery, roof and the notable metal rood screen with wooden loft designed by George Bodley and dating from 1893. The form which the restoration will take is still under discussion.

24 St Paul's, Covent Garden

Covent Garden
This was the garden of Westminster Abbey or Convent.

History
The garden was made over at the Dissolution to the Russell family. Francis Russell, the fourth Earl of Bedford, obtained permission from Charles I to develop his estate, one of the earliest property developments in London outside the City and Westminster*. He engaged Inigo Jones as architect for a splendid piazza with a church building as 'the focal climax of the whole design'. All three being men of taste, this must have been a notable sight. Inigo Jones, however, was kept on a shoe-string as regards the church and the Earl told him that he would not have it much better than a barn. The architect's reply 'Well then, you shall have the handsomest barn in England' has passed into the annals of architectural history.

Following Tudor extravagance in domestic design, Inigo Jones determined to work to strict classical proportions and St Paul's was to become the first classical church—and the last for a good many years—in England. It was also, apart from St Katharine Cree in the City, the first place of worship to be built in London after the Reformation, a period of almost 100 years. Work was begun on 5th July 1631 and completed in 1633, consecration, however, not taking place until 27th September 1638. At first a chapel of ease to St Martin-in-the-Fields, St Paul's became a parish church in 1645.

The great portico on the east front was destined never to serve as principal entrance, for Bishop Laud insisted on the altar being placed against the east wall.

*As it then was.

In 1788 the architect, Thomas Hardwick, carried out a major renovation and re-fronted the church in Portland stone but only seven years later it was destroyed by fire except for the walls, portico and south-east chapel. A faithful reconstruction was carried out by Hardwick, and St Paul's was reconsecrated on 1st August 1798.

In 1871 William Butterfield, the Victorian architect, raised the chancel, also making changes in the position of the pulpit to suit current taste.

The original piazza in which the market-gardeners sold their own fruit and vegetables developed into the huge wholesale fruit market with massive buildings we knew as Covent Garden until it recently moved to Nine Elms, Battersea.

Exterior
This has been likened to a box with a big lid on it, not unlike a large version of a Swiss chalet. Originally, the effect would not have been so strong, as there were two cupolas on the roof and the eastern portico had wings. The proportions of the building were stated to be those of Solomon's temple in Jerusalem. The portico and the very wide eaves are the dominating features; it is supported by pillars at the corners with two Tuscan columns between.

The western end is the main entrance. Here, too, is a massive pediment with deep eaves. The side walls have simple arched windows each with its own frame. An attractive small garden makes a pleasant frontispiece.

Interior
A 'perfectly plain parallelogram' (Pevsner), there are no aisles. The dimensions, 100×50 feet, make it a double square. The altar is enclosed with columns from the north and south galleries which were dismantled by Butterfield. The west gallery is borne on Roman Doric columns. The ceiling, originally painted by Matthew Goodrich, is an attractive feature although now plain, and may be in the form planned by Inigo Jones himself.

Furnishings
Pulpit A two-decker pulpit and lectern in oak of the early 19th century with good carving.

Organ Built by Henry Bevington in 1861, incorporating part of the case designed by Hardwick in 1795. Restored by Noel Mander in 1967.

Stained glass East windows, dating from 1968–9, by Brian Thomas.

Monuments
There are two by the notable sculptor, Flaxman:

John Bellamy (died 1794) known as the 'Father of the Whig Club'.
Edward Hall (died 1798) in a Grecian style.

Associations
St Paul's is rich in associations with the stage and will long be remembered as the opening scene of Shaw's *Pygmalion*, afterwards made into the musical *My Fair Lady*. Here also Samuel Pepys watched a Punch and Judy show on 9th May 1662.

Ellen Terry The ashes of Ellen Terry are kept in a casket on the south wall in an ornamental niche.

Charles Macklin On the same wall is a tablet commemorating the actor, Charles Macklin, reputed to have lived to the age of 107 although his coffin plate says only 97; this gruesome monument recalls his stabbing a fellow actor in the eye.

20th century stage personalities Panels on the screen at the west of the church commemorate more recent stage personalities, including Charles B. Cochran, Ivor Novello, Leslie Henson and Bransby Williams.

J. M. W. Turner The great painter's parents were married here on 29th August 1773 and he himself was baptised in the church on 14th May 1775.

W. S. Gilbert, of Gilbert and Sullivan fame, was baptised here on 11th January 1837.

Burials Many actors were buried in the vaults and precincts. Amongst other people are Sir Peter Lely—court painter (1680), Samuel Butler—author (1680), William Wycherley—dramatist (1715), Grinling Gibbons—the great carver in wood (1721), Thomas Rowlandson—caricaturist (1827).

Royal Naval Division The colours of this Division, created by Winston Churchill during the 1914–18 War, are laid up in the north-east chapel. Celebrated members were Rupert Brooke, A. P. Herbert and Lord Freyberg, VC.

Hustings The portico was used in the past for election hustings, including a poll in the 18th century between Charles James Fox and Sir Cecil Wray which was the scene of a bitter struggle and lasted for forty days.

General
The removal of the Market to Nine Elms means that the area is in process of redevelopment, with results that cannot at present be foreseen. In the meantime, St Paul's is linked with St Anne's, Soho

and it is hoped that it can remain as a place of worship for a local community. This unique Inigo Jones church continues to be the headquarters and spiritual centre of the Actors' Church Union.

25 St Peter's, Eaton Square

History
St Peter's was built early in the last century to serve the developing district of Belgravia. A Grecian plan submitted by Henry Hakewill was adopted, building started in September 1824 and consecration took place on 20th July 1827.

A serious fire in December 1836 was made good by the architect's son, J. H. Hakewill, who kept to his father's 'chaste and simple design.'

In the 1870s, Sir Arthur Blomfield interfered with this design by adding a chancel and later altering the nave.

In September 1904 a faculty was granted to erect a screen and pulpit, and to form a south chapel.

Exterior
A fine portico of six Ionic columns raised on steps provides a dignified entrance but for some reason the church is not aligned with the square.

The tower rises above a large attic storey over the west bay of the nave and the yellow brick walls have tall round-headed windows.

Interior
Blomfield inserted a recessed arcade in a type of Byzantine Romanesque with clerestory under the original pitched roof in 1873 but retained the three galleries. This combination gives a very odd appearance. The ceiling is domed and the chancel is richly decorated.

The unusual wrought-iron screen contains a lectern which Pevsner likens to a birdcage.

The east window is by Clayton & Bell.

General
St Peter's is remembered for the ministry in the 1870s of H. Wilkinson, who later became Bishop of Truro. The large church, seating 1650 people, was crowded with the élite of Belgravia when he was rector and this was probably the reason for retaining the galleries.

26 St Peter's, Vere Street

History
Originally known as the Marybone and later the Oxford Chapel, St
Peter's was commissioned by Edward Harley, Earl of Oxford, built
between 1721 and 1724 and opened on Easter Day, 1724, as a
proprietary chapel to serve the residents of the new estate which he
and his wife, Lady Henrietta Cavendish-Holles, were developing
around Cavendish Square. The Earl chose as his architect James
Gibbs, who already had St Mary-le-Strand to his credit and was at
the time working on St Martin-in-the-Fields. Gibbs was thus able
to use the same carpenters and builders for the Chapel, which was to
be a 'St Martin's' in miniature.

In 1832, there was extensive restoration and the Chapel was then
dedicated to St Peter. Fairly gently treated by J. K. Colling in 1881,
it has come down to us relatively unspoilt and is now a chapel of
ease to All Souls', Langham Place.

Exterior
A plain rectangle of brick is set off by large pediments at each end,
stone doorcases and quoins, and completed with a charming little
cupola at the west end, the whole knit together with modillion
cornices. The cupola is set upon a square brick base with original
clock and consists of two octagonal open lanterns one above the
other capped by a little dome. Below the cupola is a Tuscan portico
with metope frieze and smaller pediment; it is flanked by stone
doorcases and round-headed windows.

At the sides are two tiers of windows with red surrounds, round-
headed above and segmental below, and at the east end the
pediment rises above a stone Venetian window.

Interior
The appeal of this little church increases as one enters. The open
construction (see plate p. 256) enables the visitor to appreciate the
curved ceiling and the lively, delicate work of the famous plasterers,
Artari and Bagutti. Galleries run round three sides supported on the
north and south by large columns. As so often in London churches,
the replacement of box-pews by ordinary pews has left the pedestals
high and dry; the columns are extended above the capitals to
support the ceiling.

The open chancel is small but given emphasis by the generous
arch, decorated with rosettes in the soffit. The east window depicting
Christ with the woman at the well was designed by Sir Edward

St Peter's, Vere Street. Drawing of 1908

Burne-Jones and executed by William Morris.

Above the sanctuary are four theatre-like boxes formerly used by the Harley family and other favoured people, with fine wrought-iron work.

Furnishings
Organ A modern rebuilding in 1965 with angel trumpet stops, after which it was moved back to the west gallery from the north side of the chancel where the previous organ had been sited after the 1881 restoration. The original organ was a Shrider instrument and the first organist was Joseph Centlivre, at one time principal cook to Queen Anne. In 1773, the year in which he was elected a Fellow of the Royal Society, Dr Charles Burney, a friend of Samuel Johnson, David Garrick, Joshua Reynolds and Edmund Burke, was appointed organist.

Altar-rails Attractive examples of the spiral type, contemporary with the time of building.

Stained glass With the exception of a window in the north-west of the church by Powell, all the stained glass is by Burne-Jones and William Morris.

General
St Peter's is a charming survival of an estate chapel and a pleasant surprise amongst the shop-windows of the big stores.

St Peter's, Vere Street. Interior looking west

27 **Savoy Chapel**
(full name The Queen's Chapel of the Savoy)

Savoy
The land covered by what came to be known as the Precinct of the
Savoy was given in 1246 by Henry III to his wife's uncle, Peter of
Savoy, after whom the locality was named.

History
Since that time, the area has had a chequered history. The Manor
passed through various royal hands until it came to John of Gaunt;
during his tenure it was plundered and burnt in Wat Tyler's
rebellion of 1381.
   At the beginning of the 16th century, Henry VII founded the
Hospital of the Savoy, completed after his death in 1515 when the
original of the present chapel was built. The Hospital provided a
night's lodging, food and clothing for 100 poor men but was
suppressed in Edward VI's reign. Revived under Mary Tudor, it
drifted on for another 150 years with its original aims forgotten,
being used successively as a military hospital, barracks and prison.
In William III's time, the district, being outside normal jurisdictions,
became a disreputable quarter and the Hospital was finally dissolved
in 1702.
   Many foreign communities, French Protestants, German
Calvinists, and Lutherans, had chapels in the Savoy.
   In 1772, the Duchy of Lancaster took over the property and have
since appointed the chaplains, but the old Hospital buildings were
not cleared away until the early 19th century.
   A chapel is known to have existed at the end of the 14th century
but the present building is all that is left of three chapels built for
the Hospital and probably consecrated in 1515. It not only served
the Hospital and those living within the Precinct but also
worshippers from St Mary-le-Strand, who had been
unceremoniously deprived of their church by Protector Somerset
when he built his house in the Strand in 1548. This lasted for over
150 years until their new church was consecrated in 1723.
   The chapel had its usual share of 19th century repairs and
alterations, aggravated by a fire in 1843 and culminating in a
rebuilding after being almost completely burnt out in 1864. The
architects involved were Robert and his brother Sydney Smirke
(Robert was the architect of the British Museum).
   Just before the 1939–45 War, in 1937, King George VI put this
chapel at the disposal of the Royal Victorian Order, founded by

Queen Victoria in 1896 to provide recognition for those who had rendered signal service to the Sovereign. Further alterations by Malcolm Matts were made to fit it for this purpose.

Happily, the fires of the mid-19th century were not repeated during the War and, although the chapel was damaged six times, the ill-effects were limited to the windows.

In 1957–8, the dignified and spacious Antechapel was built along the east side including a new Royal Robing Room and Chaplain's Room. The architect was A. B. Knapp-Fisher.

Exterior
The simple rectangle of grey stone with belfry at the west end lies in the south-west corner of a comparatively large churchyard but dwarfed by the massive hotels and offices surrounding it. The chapel is without buttresses and runs north and south.

Interior
The rather sad exterior is soon forgotten when one sees the opulent interior. The Antechapel, which is reached by steps in the left-hand corner, makes an imposing and gracious introduction to the chapel itself. What is seen is the reconstruction by Sydney Smirke in 1864–6 which followed the pattern of the old Tudor Perpendicular building. The aisleless nave is of five bays and the eye is immediately drawn to the roof which, although only a 19th century copy, recalls the spectacular Tudor roof with its 88 quatrefoils interspersed with 14 shields of kings and queens, dukes and earls connected with the chapel.

There is panelling around the walls and the 16 stalls at the south end were placed there for the Royal Victorian Order.

Furnishings
The furnishings are unusual in that there is no pulpit (removed in 1939), although there is an old hour-glass. The chaplain's preaching desk takes its place.

Reredos Designed by Sydney Smirke and erected in 1864, it has twelve double panels with cusped and crocketed pinnacles and finials. At the sides are figures of SS Peter and Paul in decorated tabernacles. The centre painting of the Madonna and Child is 14th century work.

Lectern The rather grand lectern by Gilbert Bayes in the Antechapel is in memory of Laurence, son of Henry Irving the famous actor, and his wife who were drowned when the *Empress of Ireland* foundered in 1919. It is of bronze and enamel.

Piscina The piscina, a relic from the Tudor chapel, was discovered behind a monument after the 1864 fire. The head of Christ is Florentine work of about 1520, formerly in the master's lodging.

Needlework panel The panel dating from 1600 on the south side of the chancel was given by Sir Harold Wernher of Luton Hoo as a contribution to the furnishings of the Victorian Order. It shows the Garden of Eden complete with camel, elephant and unicorn and the background includes a castle, windmill and other buildings.

Stained glass All the windows except the last four towards the south end were destroyed by the bombing. The survivors include one on the east side to Richard D'Oyly Carte, who staged the Gilbert and Sullivan operas, showing a procession of angelic musicians. The last window but one on the west side looking north commemorates the safe-keeping of the altar plate during the 1939–45 War in the Cathedral of St John the Divine, New York. The arms of the Cathedral and also those of Washington Cathedral are included.

In the vestry is a patchwork of 13th and 14th century glass collected by Dr F. J. Grayling and given to the Chapel by his stepson's children in accordance with their father's desire.

Monuments

Alicia Stewart and Nicola Murray. There are no monuments of note but in the chancel on corbels are two figures from earlier monuments in the shape of kneeling figures, one to Alicia Stewart who died in 1573 and the other to Nicola Murray who died in 1612.

Brass

Thomas Halsey and Gavin Douglas The oldest memorial is the brass in the chancel commemorating two bishops, Thomas Halsey and Gavin Douglas, both of whom died of the plague. It dates from 1522.

Thomas Britton Facing the churchyard on the east wall is a stone commemorating Thomas Britton, who died in 1839 at the age of 101.

Associations

From April to July 1661 the Prayer Book Conference—held in the Hospital master's lodgings— tried unsuccessfully to reconcile Dissenters and Low Churchmen to the doctrine and liturgy of the Church of England as expressed in the Book of Common Prayer. Although abortive, it led indirectly to the Revised Prayer Book of 1662 still used today.

The window on the east side, which is blank, was by Sir Edward Burne-Jones, and formerly commemorated Dr Archibald Cameron of Lochiel who was executed at Tyburn on 7th May 1753 for his part in the 1745 Jacobite Rebellion.

John Wilkinson, who was minister from 1728 to 1756, celebrated illegal marriages in the Chapel and was sentenced to transportation. In 1755, he married 1190 couples. He died at Plymouth two years later before he was due to be transported.

Geoffrey Chaucer and John Wycliffe were followers of John of Gaunt and must have known the Savoy well.

General
This little chapel is packed with associations and is of especial interest because of its links with Royalty.

28 St Stephen's, Rochester Row

History
Concern at the lack of churches, as voiced in Parliament in 1839 by the Whig statesman, Lord John Russell, led to more places of worship being built in the Metropolis during the following ten years than at any time since the reign of Queen Anne.

Amongst these and built to serve a slum area of Westminster, was St Stephen's, Rochester Row. It was financed entirely by the Baroness Burdett Coutts as a memorial to her father, from whom she had inherited a fortune, and erected on a site chosen for her by Charles Dickens, the houses on which were so verminous that the start of building was held up for two years.

The Baroness laid the foundation stone in 1847 and St Stephen's was consecrated in 1850. The architect was Benjamin Ferrey.

Exterior
The combination of Bargate stone from Godalming, Surrey for the main fabric and Morpeth, Northumberland sandstone for the dressings gives this church a distinctive appearance but led to structural problems which caused the spire to lean dangerously out of true so that it had to be truncated.

Interior
The church was built at a time when the views of the newly-formed Camden Society on worship and its setting, as publicised in the *Ecclesiologist*, held sway. St Stephen's was, therefore, built in the prescribed Middle Pointed or Decorated style considered at the time

as the highest form of Gothic architecture.

The tall nave arcades with clerestory above, built of Caen stone, provide a spacious and well-lit interior. The finely carved capitals are by G. P. White, who later worked at Rochester, Salisbury and Wells Cathedrals. The capital nearest to the pulpit is interesting in that it contains portraits of twelve noteworthy people connected with the church at the time of its construction, including Queen Victoria and the then Bishop of London.

Furnishings

Pulpit Also of Caen stone with fine tracery in front.

Stained glass Of the original windows by W. Wailes, only one remains; this is in the south aisle. In the same aisle is a Burne-Jones window with his usual strong reds, blues and greens.

Monument

The large monument to William Brown, died 1855, by G. G. Adams records in the epitaph that he was buried in the chancel; this was despite the fact that, by Order in Council, no one was to be buried in the church except Baroness Coutts and Mrs Brown 'who were to be embedded in a layer of powdered charcoal, and entombed in brickwork well cemented' (Basil Clarke). The Baroness was, in fact, buried in Westminster Abbey.

General

The high level of the interior stonework gives St Stephen's an air of quality and the unusual mixture of building stones a distinctive external appearance.

Camden

1 St George's, Bloomsbury
2 St Giles-in-the-Fields
3 St Pancras, Old Church
4 St Pancras
5 *All Saints', Camden Street*
6 *St Alban the Martyr, Holborn*
7 *St George the Martyr, Queen Square, Bloomsbury with
   Holy Trinity and St Bartholomew's, Gray's Inn Road*
8 *St John's, Church Row, Hampstead*
9 *St John's, Downshire Hill*
10 *St Mary Magdalene, Munster Square*
11 *St Michael's, Camden Road*

1 **St George's, Bloomsbury**

Dedication
St George, the patron saint of England, was born of Christian parents in Cappadocia. He was martyred during the Diocletian persecution in 303 AD.

History
Before New Oxford Street was cut through the area in 1847, parishioners attending St Giles-in-the-Fields from the northern part of the parish had to pass through one of the most squalid districts of London, known locally as the 'Rookery' and the scene of Hogarth's 'Gin Lane'. They petitioned the Commissioners of the 1711 Act for a new church and, although the proposed site was only a short distance from St Giles', were successful in their application.

Nicholas Hawksmoor, the architect, was commissioned, work was completed in 1730, and St George's was consecrated in January of the following year.

Except for interior rearrangements in 1781, the church has come down to us largely as built and, like Hawksmoor's other London ecclesiastical edifices, is unusual and conceived on a grand scale.

Exterior
A magnificent hexastyle portico of six Corinthian columns, two deep with coffered ceiling and modelled on the Pantheon portico in Rome, leads into the church from the south side. Plain pediment and a flight of steps complete this entrance piece.

An extraordinary steeple rises from the ground to the west and, in this position, avoids any conflict with the portico. A tall, square base with large belfry openings rising to a short stage with many columns then proceeds to a stepped pyramid modelled on a free rendering of Pliny's description of the Mausoleum of Halicarnassus. At the top, George I attired in Roman dress, representing the saint and standing on a Roman altar with arm raised, surveys the scene. This statue, donated by a local brewer, gave rise to the epigram:

'When Henry the Eighth left the Pope in the lurch
The protestants made him the head of the church;
But George's good subjects, the Bloomsbury people,
Instead of the Church, made him head of the steeple.'

Sir Robert Walpole, the great Whig Prime Minister, considered it 'a masterpiece of absurdity' as no doubt many would have agreed when a couple of lions contended with two unicorns on the angles of

the pyramid for possession of the Crown. The beasts were removed
in 1871.

However one may feel about it, this façade is perhaps the most
grandiose of any amongst London's 18th century churches.

The north façade (ritual east) facing Little Russell Street is also
worth inspection. A large pediment rises above five bays of two
storeys with pilastered blank arches on the ground and columned
arched windows on the first floor. There is a delicate cornice.

Interior
Almost a cube, with a small clerestory but given direction by the
differing treatment of each of the four sides. Hawksmoor's design
provided for the altar being in the small eastern apse so that the
church was aligned west/east along the short axis with an entrance
on the western side under the tower. The parishioners found this
inconvenient and, in 1781, the interior was rearranged with the altar
on the north; the gallery on this side was removed and the altar
niche appears to have been transferred to the new position. This
materially changed the original effect but had the advantage of no
longer directing those entering by the main portico to the side of the
church but to the long axis from south to north. The ceiling
mouldings have been arranged to form rectangles in line with both
axes. The alteration occurred before the altar piece from the chapel
of the demolished Montague House had to be accommodated so
that this did not affect the issue.

One might ask why the coupled Corinthian columns and
segmental arch are impressively repeated at the north end if it was
not the altar end from the beginning; this was probably done either
for architectural balance or mere decoration.

Similar coupled columns are to be seen below a gallery at the
southern or entrance end.

This is one of the gayest of Hawksmoor's interiors and a
refreshing contrast to the state of Christ Church, Spitalfields and St
Anne's, Limehouse. It has been tastefully redecorated with much
attention to correct colour tones.

Furnishings
Some of the furnishings came from St John's Church, Red Lion
Square, nearby, which was demolished after bomb damage in the
Second World War.

Monument
Charles Grant In the west chapel, the monument to Charles Grant

shows him 'obviously exhausted) (Pevsner) with a figure of Faith
bending over him.

General
St George's is a handsome stranger in the Bloomsbury scene and its
magnificent entrance front is a fine architectural addition to this part
of London. Situated as the church is near London University and
the British Museum, its ministry is largely amongst students and
young professional people. Until recently it served the Anglican
Chaplaincy of the University.

2 St Giles-in-the-Fields

Dedication
According to tradition, St Giles lived as a hermit in a cave in
France. He became the patron saint of various unfortunates with
whom this church has had particularly close associations (see later).

In the Middle Ages, the parish lay in open country and even when
the present church was built in the 18th century, it was situated on
the edge of built-up London and, although itself in a seamy quarter,
the northern part of the parish was a favoured residential area.

History
St Giles' started as the chapel of a leper hospital founded in 1101 by
the Scottish-born Queen Matilda, wife of Henry I. It probably
became the church of a village with the lepers screened off, but it
did not rank as a parish church until 1547 after the hospital had
been dissolved by Henry VIII. The almshouses were founded in
1656 by the son of Shakespeare's patron, the Earl of Southampton.

The earliest illustration shows a building with a round tower
capped by a dome; this was replaced by a larger steeple in 1617 but
shortly afterwards the church was considered ruinous and a Gothic
brick building took its place between 1623 and 1630. This was
largely paid for by Dame Alicia Dudley, daughter-in-law of
Elizabeth's favourite, the Earl of Leicester; it was consecrated by
Bishop Laud.

Less than 100 years later, the new church was itself in a bad state
from damp, probably caused by the large number of Plague victim
burials, and the parishioners petitioned the Commissioners of the
1711 Act for another place of worship. At first they refused because
it was not a new foundation, but eventually allocated £8,000
towards it. Although the well-known Nicholas Hawksmoor drew a

St Giles-in-the-Fields. From south

design, the comparatively unknown Henry Flitcroft, son of William III's gardener, was preferred as architect and he erected between 1730 and 1734 a building in the Wren/Gibbs tradition which possesses one of London's 'best-loved' steeples. His model for the church is to be seen in the rotunda at the west end.

The ever-busy Blomfield and Butterfield made alterations in 1875 and 1896 but there was not too much interference with the fittings. St Giles' mercifully escaped the worst of the bombing, which merely removed most of its Victorian glass and, after a beautiful restoration and redecoration in 1952–3 by architects Gordon Jackson and Norman Haines, and the rector himself, we are able to enjoy this interesting and attractive place of worship very much as Flitcroft left it.

Exterior

An unusually dominant position for Central London; even the egregious eyesore of Centre Point does not smother it (see plate p. 266). the main façade is the north side, which has rusticated base and two tiers of windows, round-headed above and small rectangular below. At the east end, a Venetian window flanked by pilasters projects, as also do vestries at the north-east and south-east corners. The churchyard to the east and south is now a public garden leased to Camden Council.

In front of the west end where the architect's name appears prominently on the main frieze is the interesting feature of a stone 'lych-gate' dating from 1804, which incorporates a crowded wooden bas-relief of the Resurrection dating from 1687 and said to be based on Michelangelo's *Last Judgement* in the Sistine Chapel at Rome.

The relatively plain body with a green copper roof is offset by the striking 160 foot high steeple, very similar to that of St Martin-in-the-Fields but which, instead of riding awkwardly on the portico, rises straight out of the façade. The bell storey with coupled pilasters is succeeded by a pretty clock stage, followed by a tall octagonal lantern with attached columns and balustrade above, and finally an obelisk with raised bands which is surmounted by a gilded ball and vane.

Interior

The interior is a well-proportioned Georgian design with square piers supporting galleries from which rise circular stone Ionic columns, now painted Etruscan red, carrying the elliptical barrel ceiling with a design of transverse arches and panels picked out with rich gilded plaster decoration. There is no clerestory. The east end is in two stages with Ionic pilasters and a pediment above the window.

The groined aisle vaults spring from elegant gilded corbels on the walls which are partially panelled. The only stained glass is in the east window depicting the Transfiguration.

Furnishings

Font This is a furnishing put back in 1952 after being taken to West Street Chapel near Cambridge Circus in 1875. It is attributed to Sir John Soane, who was a vestryman and parishioner. Circular on a tapering octagonal shaft, it has honeysuckle and Greek key decoration. It dates from 1810. The attractive wooden cover was made in 1952.

Organ This was orginally installed by Father Smith in 1671 and retains all his original work but has been much restored since. The Royal Arms on the gallery are those of George III.

Pulpit This was once a three-decker. What remains is a beautiful inlaid mahogany furnishing. It was given by a former rector, John Sharp, who became Archbishop of York and dates from 1676. Flitcroft insisted on it being retained.

Another pulpit, very plain by comparison, at the east end of the north aisle, was also once in West Street Chapel and, when there, the brothers Wesley preached regularly from it between 1743 and 1791. It has a green base, is cream above and was formerly also a three-decker.

Chandeliers The four brass chandeliers are mainly 18th century but the largest probably dates from 1680.

Mayoral Chair On the north side of the sanctuary is a mayoral chair (formerly in Holborn Town Hall) with the arms of the Duke of Bedford on top, presented by the Camden Borough Council.

Altar-piece This pleasant furnishing comprises a central framed panel, with Ten Commandments and a scrolled pediment framing surmounted by a pelican, and two side panels of Moses and Aaron, painted by Francisco Vieria, court painter to the King of Portugal.

Altar-rails The wrought-iron rails and gates were replaced in 1952; they had been moved forward by Butterfield.

Monuments

George Chapman At the west end of the north aisle is a monument to George Chapman, Elizabethan dramatist (died 1634) in the form of a Roman altar said to be by his friend Inigo Jones. It is not well preserved, having formerly stood outdoors in the churchyard.

Lady Frances Kniveton Next to the Chapman memorial is a monument to Lady Frances Kniveton, daughter of Alicia, Duchess of Dudley, who was a great benefactor to this church. It is in the form of an effigy in a shroud.

John Barnfather, who died in 1793. At the east end of the north aisle, this monument is oval in shape with a feminine figure beside an urn.

John Flaxman A memorial was placed in the vestibule in 1930 by the Royal Academy to John Flaxman, the sculptor, who died in 1826. It is a bronze cast of one of his own works at Micheldever Church, Hampshire, depicting a figure battling with devils and helped by angels ('Deliver us from Evil').

Andrew Marvell, the poet, and *Luke Hansard*, printer of the House of Commons journals, are commemorated by tablets.

In the south porch, not always open to the public, are:

Iron Chest, of 1630 and probably foreign with camels' feet.

Mosaic, by G. F. Watts, formerly on St Giles' School and erected here in 1974.

Tombstone of Richard Pendrell (Penderel) who died in 1671. One of the most courageous acts in the escape of Charles II after the Battle of Worcester in 1651 was the hiding of the King in the Boscobel oak-tree and the concealment of him by the Pendrell brothers in their house where they dressed him as a woodcutter. In January 1922 the slab was removed from the churchyard where the table tomb can still be seen.

Associations

The church of St Giles seems to have had more experience of human misery than most. The frightful horror of the Great Plague started here and, as with its namesake at Cripplegate, many victims were buried in the churchyard.

In addition, condemned prisoners passed St Giles' on their way from Newgate to Tyburn for execution and scores of these unfortunates were also buried here. They received the last refreshment of a bowl of ale ('St Giles' bowl') and the sexton tolled the great bell when they were passing. Claude Duval, the highwayman, and a hangman, Edward Dennis, were also buried in the churchyard.

Amongst other victims was Oliver Plunkett, Archbishop of Armagh, condemned for high treason in 1681 and canonised in 1975 who, together with five now beatified Jesuit fathers who had also been executed, was buried under the north wall. A further eight beatified Roman Catholic martyrs are also buried in the churchyard.

Sir John Oldcastle, the Lollard, was hanged in chains over a slow fire in 1417 near the church.

Amongst less untimely deaths associated with St Giles' were the following:

Cecil, Lord Baltimore, initial Proprietory of Maryland, who fitted out the ships which took the first Maryland colonists in 1633, died in St Giles' parish in 1675 and was buried in the churchyard, although he was a Roman Catholic. Four Calverts related to him were buried in the churchyard before 1711, and thus St Giles' is Maryland's chief London connection.

Dr William Balmain, co-founder of New South Wales, after whom a suburb of Sydney is named, was buried in the churchyard in 1803. He was a surgeon with the First Fleet.

Arthur William Devis, painter of large historical canvases (such as 'The Death of Nelson') was buried here, and has a tablet in the north aisle.

The baptisms include:

John Milton's daughter Mary, baptised here in 1647.

Admiral Lord Rodney in 1719.

William and Clara Shelley (3rd and 4th children of the poet) and Clara Allegra Claremont (Byron's illegitimate daughter) baptised here in joint ceremony 1818.

J. C. Patteson, murdered bishop, baptised here in 1827 (tablet in south aisle).

General

St Giles', one of Camden's three borough churches, proudly calls itself 'A Civic Church of Camden' and can justifiably claim to be a most interesting London church, both architecturally and historically.

3 **St Pancras Old Church**

Dedication

St Pancras, the boy of 14 who was martyred in 304 AD, not only gave his name to a well-known railway station and to two churches nearby but to a whole Borough. He is the patron of youth and the avenger of false oaths.

History

St Pancras Old Church has had a long history and a travel-writer in 1700 stated that the first building even took precedence in age and seniority over St John Lateran of Rome which carries us back to 314

AD, only ten years after St Pancras was put to death. The site—a small hillock above where the River Fleet used to run—is still older and, according to one expert, was a pre-Christian rural shrine.

First reliable mention, however, of St Pancras-in-the-Fyldes, as it was once called, is in the second half of the 12th century and the present place of worship was probably rebuilt about 1350 to serve a parish which extended from Ken Wood in Highgate to the boundary mark still to be seen on the shop-front of Heal's in Tottenham Court Road.

In Elizabeth's reign, although the Marian incumbent was apparently allowed to stay on, the church fell on bad times and John Norden writing in 1593 records that it 'standeth all alone as utterly forsaken, old and wether-beaten'. By 1642 it was deserted and Parliament ordered that it 'bee disposed of unto lodgings for fifty Troupers'. Services were resumed later but between 1675 and 1689 the vicar was arrested for debt and imprisoned.

By the early part of the 19th century, the vicar at that time was distinguished enough to become first Bishop of Calcutta and Primate of all India. In 1847–8, the church suffered a drastic restoration under A. D. Gough. It was given an almost complete neo-Norman casing, the old tower with its quaint bell-shaped cap was taken down to allow the nave to be lengthened by 30 feet and a new tower erected on the south side (at one time higher than it is now) with a top resembling a dovecote. Galleries were added round the interior.

With the completion of the new St Pancras church nearby in the Euston Road in 1822, the old church became a chapel of ease to it but was reinstated as a parish church in 1863.

Restorations took place in 1871 and again in 1888, the latter by Sir A. W. Blomfield. In 1925 the roof timbers were exposed and the side galleries taken down; after the War during which it had been badly damaged, the church was repaired and restored.

In 1956, the benefice was combined with that of St Matthew's, Oakley Square.

Exterior
Despite the almost completely early Victorian exterior, St Pancras' still retains, owing to its setting in what is now a public garden, a rustic appearance (see plate p. 273).
The entrance is through attractive gates. The west door and the wheel window above were part of the 1847–8 alterations. Part of the Norman wall with Roman tiles remains on the north side and the north and south doors are recognizable as being of that period.

The churchyard, to which an extension of St Giles-in-the-Fields churchyard had been added earlier was made into a public garden in 1877.

Interior

The interior has even more of the village atmosphere and is larger than one might expect. Access is under a large western gallery still retaining early 18th century scroll work on the panelling. The nave, long and narrow, is closed by a light iron screen installed by Blomfield, beyond which is a flat-roofed chancel without stalls but with many monuments. Part of a 13th century lancet window suggests that it was altered at that time.

Furnishings

Font The attractive font cover dates from about 1700.

Piscina and sedile The piscina is 13th and the sedile 15th century but both are much restored.

Reredos A 'Blomfield' furnishing. The high altar table contains panels from the old pulpit.

*Altar-stone The most exciting item. The altar-stone was found buried under the old tower during the 1847–8 alterations. It is incised with five consecration crosses, the form of which gives reason to believe that it dates from the 6th century.

Monuments

Amongst many monuments are:

Mary Beresford A brass of 1588 in the chancel is to Mary, wife of John Beresford.

Robert and Lawrentia Eve On the north wall is the upper part of an early 16th century table tomb from the north side of the altar with a canopy and the matrices of kneeling brass figures. There is no inscription.

Philadelphia Woolaston, who died in 1616, is commemorated by a monument in the form of a semi-reclining effigy with figures standing on each side.

John and Elizabeth Offley and family. South-east of the chancel is a tablet to the Offley family with an ornamental epitaph of the 1670s.

William and Mary Platt Next door to the Offley tablet is a large monument to William Platt who died in 1637 and his wife who died 50 years later in 1687. They are shown as frontal busts in two oval recesses. The monument was removed from Highgate Chapel in 1833 and restored by St John's College, Cambridge.

Samuel and Christina Cowper Samuel Cowper, the miniature

St Pancras Old Church   St Pancras Old Church and Soane monument in churchyard painter, who died in 1672, and his wife in 1693, are commemorated by a small cartouche in the chancel with palette and pencil.

Richard Draper, who died in 1756, is remembered by a monument in the shape of a tall column with an urn on top.

Churchyard
Blackmailers, murderers, pimps, duellers, a highwayman, a forger and a spy, together with suicides, all found their last resting-place in Old St Pancras churchyard. But there had been notable people too—distinguished emigrés from the French Revolution and the Corsican patriot, Pasquale de Paoli, whose bones were returned to their native land when the Midland Railway encroached upon the churchyard. Thomas Hardy, the author, worked as an architect's apprentice in supervising the reburial of other remains in a pit and it may have been this experience which gave him his preoccupation with churchyards in his novels. The burial ground was the scene of the mock funeral and attempted body-snatching in Charles Dickens' *Tale of Two Cities*.

Many of the old headstones are arranged radially round a tree.

Amongst those buried in Old St Pancras churchyard are:

Johann Christian Bach ('the English Bach') in January 1782.

Chevalier d'Eon in May 1810. The Chevalier dressed as a woman when engaged on some of Louis XV of France's missions and continued to dress in this way so that his sex was debated until his death.

The last survivor of the Black Hole of Calcutta, aged 90.

Members of the Rhodes family The family graves were restored by Cecil Rhodes in 1890.

Former St Giles-in-the-Fields churchyard
Although the St Giles-in-the-Fields extension (see *Exterior*) was quite separate from, but contiguous to, Old St Pancras' churchyard when they were used as burial grounds, the main interest of what is now one public garden is the:

*Soane Monument (see plate p. 273).

This monument north-east of the church was erected by the architect Sir John Soane to his wife who died in 1815. It is enclosed in a canopy carried on pillars with pierced pediments on each side and a little knob on the top. The tomb is surrounded by stone railings decorated with typical Soane carved blocks (acroteria).

Soane himself was buried here in 1837.

Also buried in the St Giles cemetery was *John Flaxman*, the sculptor, in December 1826.

Associations
Joseph Grimaldi, the famous clown, married his second wife at St Pancras Old Church in 1801.

P. B. Shelley, who lodged nearby, first saw and fell in love with Mary Godwin when she was visiting her mother's grave in the churchyard. The mother's remains were moved to Bournemouth in 1851.

General
At times neglected, deserted, its ministers even held in contempt, but also the recipient of loving care, St Pancras Old Church—looking perhaps a little wistful today—survives, despite severe restoration, as an extraordinarily countrified, almost village church, sandwiched between the bustle and noise of the main railway line behind and one of London's busy roads in front.

N.B. Not normally open.

4 St Pancras

Dedication
Pancratius (Pancras in English), the boy martyr, was born in Phrygia, Asia Minor, of noble and wealthy parents who died when he was young. Entrusted to the care of his uncle, they went to Rome where they were converted to Christianity. During the Diocletian persecution, Pancratius refused to give up his beliefs and was beheaded on the Aurelian Way on 12th May 304 at the age of 14.

History
The spread of London made the village church of St Pancras, holding about 150 people, inadequate and, despite opposition from the parish on economic grounds, a new church was authorised by Act of Parliament on 31st May 1816. In 1818, a site was acquired alongside the New (later Euston) Road and a design, submitted by a local surveyor William Inwood and his son Henry William was accepted; in the following year Henry William travelled to Greece for the purpose of making drawings to complete the design.

The first stone was laid by the Prince Regent's brother on 1st July 1819 and the new St Pancras church consecrated three years later on 7th May 1822. Built of brick faced with Portland stone in neo-Grecian style, it was the most expensive church erected in London since St Paul's Cathedral, costing about £90,000.

In 1880, the interior was redecorated in dark colours but the restoration in 1952–3 partially corrected this. The chancel was reconstructed in 1889.

Exterior

The Greek influence is apparent wherever one looks. The 156 foot high tower is a highly successful adaptation of the Temple of the Winds at Athens and the fine hexastyle portico of six fluted Ionic columns is based on the Acropolis Erectheum on which the building is largely modelled.

The tower rises in receding octagonal stages, the two lower ones enclosed with eight columns, and terminates in a simple finial and cross. The portico leads up to three entrance doors which, in the same way as the windows of the sides, all taper upwards in Egyptian fashion. The inner façade is decorated with much elegant detail, egg and dart, acanthus, rosettes and bobbins, whilst the centre door has a projecting lintel.

The north and south sides are plain except for more egg and dart adornment and a lively motif of acanthus leaves along the top of the wall. The windows are in two tiers, in the upper storey twice as large.

At the east end, the designer has placed two projecting wings copied from the Hall of Caryatides, containing almost detached vestries, and entrances to the burial vaults. The terracotta caryatides, demurely draped and modelled around cast-iron stanchions, were designed by Charles Rossi; he made them too tall and a slice had to be taken out of their middles in order to fit. The east end wall is curved into an apse and enclosed in Ionic columns.

Interior

Behind the portico is a vestibule with chambers at the sides containing staircases. This leads into the open and undivided hall interior which has galleries at the sides and west end supported on slender columns with lotus leaf capitals copied from the Elgin marbles. The west gallery supports the organ.

Until 1889 there was no chancel and the pews went right up to the Communion rail at one level; it was then that the floor was raised, choir stalls inserted, gilded screen provided and a marble wall built, separating the chancel from the nave. Behind the chancel, the sanctuary rises dramatically to create a splendid focal point. The screen of unfluted Ionic columns stands clear of the walls and is made of scagliola (composition of marble chippings, paste and glue); the bases and capitals are copied from the Temple of Minerva.

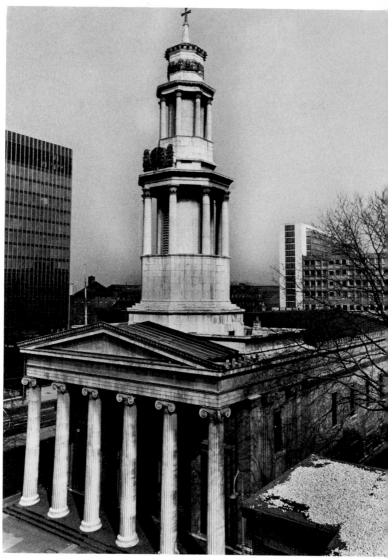

St Pancras

A flat, coffered unsupported ceiling covers the interior in one large span of 60 feet.

In the south-east corner, a Lady Chapel—dedicated in 1914—houses the original altar and marble railing from the chancel. The chapel apse is decorated with gold acanthus leaf on a blue background and the walls with plaster frieze are panelled in brown marble.

There is another chapel on the other side, dedicated by the Bishop of Edmonton in September 1970. This is a memorial to a former assistant curate, provided by his sister. Its screen was designed by Cecil Brown.

Furnishings
Royal Arms The Royal Arms displayed on the front of the west gallery are those in use at the time the church was built.

Organ casing This is a noteworthy feature.

Font The alabaster font is octagonal. Decorated with the Star of

St Pancras. Projecting wing with caryatides

Bethlehem, it is mounted on a plain base.

Stained glass All the glass is by Clayton & Bell, one of the better Victorian glass-makers. The east windows date from 1860–6, the 26 north and south windows from 1881–2. The latter are divided into 14 large windows above gallery level, illustrating the Te Deum by depicting Apostles, Prophets and Martyrs, and 12 smaller ones below, based on sentences of the Litany referring to the Life and Passion of Jesus Christ. Deep reds, greens and gold together with white predominate whilst the large borders are brown.

*Pulpit The wooden octagonal pulpit raised on four Ionic columns with a delicately curving staircase was made from the famous Fairlop Oak of Hainault Forest. It is a fine feature.

General
This notable neo-Grecian building with its elegant detail was naturally hateful to the Gothic Revivalists but perhaps they felt that there was not much they could do about it. Apart from the stained glass and the raising of the chancel which have not detracted from the general character, and the darkening of the interior (later corrected), they left it largely alone.

Other Churches in Camden
The Borough of Camden which includes Hampstead has many other churches of interest.

All Saints', Camden Street (5)—built in 1822–4 by the Inwood brothers (designers of St Pancras) and now made over to the Cypriot Community—has a splendid, broad, semicircular Ionic portico parts of which came from an Ionion temple and which carries a slender, circular steeple.

Two saints dear to the English—St Alban, the first English martyr and St George, whose white banner with its red cross became the basis of the Union Jack—are commemorated at churches in Holborn and Bloomsbury. Despite its cramped site, **St Alban the Martyr, Holborn** (6) is an impressive Butterfield building but altered by Adrian Scott after war damage. **St George the Martyr**, Queen Square (7) dates back to 1706, when it started as a chapel to serve a 'genteel neighboourhood'. It was drastically recast by Teulon in the 19th century.

St John's, Hampstead (8) is an 18th-century building with the unusual arrangement of the tower at the east and the chancel at the west end. It has many artistic associations—John Constable is buried with his family in the south-east corner of the old churchyard

All Saints', Camden Street

and there is a fine bust to John Keats on the west wall of the north aisle. Towards Belsize Park, **St John's, Downshire Hill** (9) is a rare survival of a proprietary chapel with a charming and well-restored interior of box-pews and galleries.

St Mary Magdalene in Munster Square (10), designed by the promising architect Richard Carpenter who died young, was a pioneer church of the Gothic Revival and, in its unspoilt and uncluttered state, is of great interest both architecturally and liturgically.

Bodley and Garner, two other Victorian architects, are represented at **St Michael's, Camden Road** (11) in a church with an elegant and well-proportioned interior.

St Alban the Martyr, Holborn. Bodley and Garner reredos (destroyed in war)

St John's, Downshire Hill, Hampstead

St Michael's, Camden Road. Interior looking east

Greenwich

284

1 St Alfege with St Peter, Greenwich
2 St Luke's, Charlton Village
3 St Nicholas', Deptford
4 *St Mary Magdalene, Woolwich*
5 *St Nicholas', Plumstead*
6 *St Saviour's, Eltham*

1 **St Alfege with St Peter, Greenwich**

Dedication
St Alfege was Archbishop of Canterbury and met a violent death.
Appointed in 1006, he courageously refused to allow a ransom to be
paid to the invading Danes for his release from capture and was
martyred on 19th April, 1012 on ground where the church now
stands. St Peter's, which used to be situated nearby, was destroyed
during the 1939–45 War and the parish was then united with that of
St Alfege.

History
There was a church in Greenwich in 964 AD but the first one on this
site, in the area originally known as East Greenwich (Deptford being
West), may have been erected soon after the martyrdom; the second
church was probably a rebuilding in the 13th century. Little is
known of it but John Morton, who later became Henry VII's
Chancellor and a Cardinal, was vicar here from 1444 to 1454 and,
owing to the proximity of the royal palace, the church in Tudor
times was the scene of many great occasions. Henry VIII was
baptised here and his sister, Mary, was married in St Alfege's to
Thomas Brandon, Duke of Suffolk, in 1514. The tower was rebuilt in
1617 and a painting by Vosterman of about 1680 shows this to have
been tall and plain with a cupola on top rising above a low roofed
fabric.

In 1710, a severe storm led to the collapse of the roof, due, it was
thought, to one of the supporting piers having been undermined by
numerous burial excavations. The building was considered beyond
repair and the parish successfully applied for funds to reconstruct it.
The application probably led to the 1711 Act, although this applied
mainly to new places of worship. Nicholas Hawksmoor was the
chosen architect and, in the short time of two years (1712–14) the
third St Alfege's was built, being the first of the churches to be
completed under the Act. Consecration was, however, delayed
because the parishioners objected to the stipulation that a Royal
Pew should be provided. Eventually this was installed in the west
gallery and the ceremony took place on 29th September, 1718.

Hawksmoor had included a tower in his design but, owing to
shortage of funds, it was never erected. Instead, the old tower was
re-cased by a local architect, John James, this being completed in
1730.

Victorian restoration was gentle and no attempt was made to
Gothicise the building but in 1941 incendiaries caused extensive

St Alfege with St Peter, Greenwich

damage. A most careful restoration by Professor Richardson, who retrieved as much as he could of the old material, brought back the church as closely as possible to its former state.

Exterior

As at St Botolph's, Bishopsgate, the main façade, which faces the street, is the eastern one. The portico here has a deep, heavy pediment, supported by giant Tuscan columns, with a frieze broken in the centre to allow an arch to rise up into the pediment.

The frieze is carried round the sides which are decorated with large pilasters. Projecting vestibules approached by open staircases are centrally positioned in each wall.

The tower rises unconvincingly from the pedimented west end. John James provided a square base above which is the clock stage leading to a circular section surrounded by columns and capped by a small dome with diminutive spirelet.

Interior

Diagonally projecting pairs of giant columns flank the reredos and east window which lie in a shallow apse with depressed vault and trompe l'oeil coffering. The oval ceiling rises from corbels and is suspended from tie-beams. Light-toned galleries on three sides are replacements of the original ones, which had carving attributed to Grinling Gibbons. They are supported on thin legs but have fine ironwork.

At the east end of the north aisle is a Lady Chapel dedicated to the Virgin Mary. The murals behind the altar are by August Lunn.

A spacious vestibule with vestries leading off completes the west end.

Furnishings

The 1941 bombing destroyed all the fine furnishings except the reredos, one window and the wrought-iron-work.

Pulpit A copy of the original but without the Grinling Gibbons carving.

Iron-work The wrought-iron-work of the altar and gallery rails in Jean Tijou style is original (Jean Tijou was the most famous smith of the Wren period and worked at St Paul's Cathedral and Hampton Court).

Royal Pew The Royal Pew, which caused so much trouble during building, has been removed to the south side from the west gallery where it interfered with the siting of the organ. The Stuart Royal Arms in front were copied after the bombing.

Stained glass The only window to survive is a small 19th century one in the south-east corner of the vestibule; this represents Cardinal Morton. All the other windows are post-war work by Francis Spear, representing various scenes from the history of the church (e.g. baptism of Henry VIII) and, at the east end, Christ in Glory with the emblems of the Passion below.

Painting The original painting at the east end was by Sir James Thornhill, famous for the painted Dining Hall in Greenwich Hospital. With the aid of parts that remained, it has been most expertly restored by Glyn Jones who did, however, have to improvise for the sanctuary ceiling.

*Organ One of the most precious possessions is the organ console which was probably used by Thomas Tallis, Gentleman of the Royal Chapel from 1530 to 1585. He was the composer of Tallis's Canon which is the setting for the Hymn 'Glory to Thee, my God, this night'. Experts consider that some of the octaves of the middle keyboard are of Tudor origin.

Tallis was buried in the old church. A reproduction of the original brass is near the south aisle east window and, at the west end of the same aisle, there is a window in memory of him.

Monuments/Associations

There are no memorials of note, but St Alfege's has close associations with *General James Wolfe*, the victor of the Heights of Abraham battle in Canada against the French, who is buried in the family vault and commemorated by a tablet and the replica of his coffin plate let into the floor.

General Gordon of Khartoum fame was baptised in the church in 1833.

General

St Alfege's does not reach the heights of other Hawksmoor churches, partly because he was not allowed to build his tower, but the royal and other associations make this skilfully restored church of much interest.

2 St Luke's, Charlton Village

'Charlton'
Settlement of free husbandmen or churls (churl-ton).

History
The Manor of Charlton is mentioned in the Domesday Book and
reference is made to a church even earlier in 1077. Little is known of
the latter apart from its being made of chalk and flint, that it
acquired several altars and shrines and that it came under the Abbey
of Bermondsey. At the Dissolution, the Manor passed into secular
ownership and was purchased by Sir Adam Newton in 1607. It is to
him that we largely owe the present church erected about 1630 with
money left by him and incorporating some of the old walls. The
north aisle was added in 1639 with contributions from various
families and it may have been then or later in the century that the
tower top was added (very similar to the one at St Nicholas'
Plumstead erected 1662–4).

Nineteenth-century alterations consisted of an extension to the
chancel in 1840, and rearrangements in 1874. The tower was
repaired in 1934.

St Luke's suffered considerably from blast damage in the 1939–45
War, involving extensive work on the roof; modern vestries were
added in the north-east corner.

Two daughter churches, St Mary's and St Richard's, were built in
St Luke's parish with the aid of a War Damage Commission grant
in 1956 to cater for the growth of population to some 15,000 people.

The latest improvement has been the clearance of the churchyard
in 1972.

Exterior
The area near the church which was only developed recently is still
called 'The Village' and the homely brick exterior lying close to the
handsome Jacobean Charlton House (now taken over by the
Greenwich Borough Council) gives some substance to the illusion.
St Luke's presents a charming rural appearance with its Dutch
gabled south porch and simple tower in which the clasping
buttresses are carried up to form turrets, the whole crown being
crenellated. The simple Y-tracery belfry windows are also of brick
and above is a strong modillion cornice encircling the tower and
following the line of the turrets.

The sundial was placed on the south wall in 1934 and is an exact
replica of one that had been there for 300 years.

St Luke's, Charlton. Tower and south porch

Interior

A curious mixture of styles with a nave of two bays separated from the north aisle by round-headed arches and by a square pier. The arches presumably reflected Renaissance influences but in fact look early Norman, and the pier has slim attached diagonal shafts. The old chancel is also of two bays. The windows have Gothic tracery and the south chancel window could be 15th century. All is whitewashed under a wagon roof (the nave roof reconstructed in the 17th century and the one in the chancel 20th century). Three unequally spaced tie-beams are exposed at the west end.

The chapel in the north aisle was installed in 1927.

The various internal alterations have left the interior rather inconvenient for modern needs because of the difficulty of seeing and hearing clearly from all parts but it is nevertheless full of interest to the visitor.

Furnishings

Font Dated by Pevsner as 'later 17th century', it is of wineglass shape on a baluster stem with four scallops on a shallow round bowl, three turned inwards and one outwards. There is also drapery carving. The cover is of oak, carved with fruit and flowers and is probably contemporary with the font.

Hatchment On the west wall of the north aisle is a hatchment with quartering of various families.

Royal Arms On the same wall in a gilt frame are the Royal Arms of Queen Anne.

Pulpit The pulpit dates from mid-17th century with restrained carving of cherubs' heads and scroll decoration and bearing the arms of Sir David Cunningham. Under the tower is a pulpit sounding-board.

North chapel altar Originally made for the Chapel of St James in Charlton House and consecrated in 1616, it was given to St Luke's when the house was taken over by the Council.

Stained glass The north window with 17th century heraldic glass was removed for safety during the war and replaced afterwards.

Choir-stalls and communion rails Recent additions.

Monuments

Amongst the many monuments the following, proceeding from the south door, are of particular note:

Sir Adam, died 1630, and *Lady Newton* Near the entrance door is this fine monument by Nicholas Stone who was influenced by Inigo Jones. It is in black and white marble with broken segmental pediment and coat-of-arms. The inscription was composed by Sir Adam himself.

Lady Grace, Viscountess of Ardmagh, died 1700. Similar but with broken pediment curved. At the side are winged angels and there is attractive carving on the front panel. It is in the baptistery.

Edward Wilkinson, died 1567. On the south wall is a square sandstone memorial to Edward Wilkinson, Master Cook to Queen Elizabeth and 'Yeoman of the Mouth' to King Henry VIII, Anne Boleyn and King Edward VI. It is Dutch in style, an early example, decorated with a helm, strapwork, shields and rather agitated foliage.

Rt Hon Spencer Perceval, assassinated in the House of Commons on 11th May 1812. On the west wall of the north aisle is a tablet commemorating this distinguished and much respected statesman, and above, a beautifully modelled portrait bust by Sir Francis Chantrey.

Brigadier Michael Richards, died 1721. Surveyor general of the Ordnance to George I. The monument on the wall near the chancel shows him free-standing in armour.

Elizabeth Thompson, died 1759. Frontal bust.

General Morrison, died 1799. Female figure bent over an urn by Charles Regnart.

Brasses Brasses on the wall near the Edward Wilkinson monument are 16th century. A later one dated 1669 commemorates D. Katherine Pickering.

Associations

Charles Edward Drummond Another victim of assassination; he was killed by a madman in mistake for Sir Robert Peel at a time when his brother was rector of Charlton, and is buried in the rector's vault.

General Gordon The brass candlestick on a triangular stand in the north chapel was at one time in the English church at Khartoum where General Gordon must have worshipped before being murdered. It was rescued from the Mahdi's tomb at Omdurman in September 1898.

Flagpole Because St Luke's was a landmark from the River Thames and used as a navigational aid by naval cadets and for Admiralty chartings as from the early part of the 18th century, the church was thereafter authorised to fly from the tower on St George's and St Luke's days the British Ensign, the naval flag of the time. This is still done from the front of the church.

General

This is one of the most rural churches in the area covered by this book, erected in Charles I's reign when very few places of worship were being built.

N.B. Not normally open except during services.

3 St Nicholas', Deptford

Dedication
St Nicholas was Bishop of Myra in the early 4th century AD. Little is known of him historically but there are many legends, including his saving of three small boys from being pickled in a barrel and the rescue from the threat of slavery of three daughters of a nobleman unable to pay their dowries by casting three bags of gold through a window, the origin of the golden balls of the pawnbroker. Saint Nicholas is beloved by children as Santa Claus and is the patron saint of travellers and sailors.

History
Except for its tower, the mediaeval church was rebuilt by Charley Stanton (cf St Mary Magdalene, Bermondsey) to accommodate the growing population of shipwrights and chandlers engaged in the shipbuilding activities started by Henry VIII when he made Deptford a naval dockyard. In less than twenty years however, on the plea that the tower was in a dangerous state, a petition was submitted to the Commissioners of the Fifty New Churches for money to help finance another place of worship. Not unnaturally this was turned down and instead the building 'was Oblig'd to be supported by a thorough repair and strap'd with Iron. The Charge being near £400 AD 1716'. It lasted with this first-aid treament until the 1939–45 War.

Towards the end of the 18th century it was decided to whitewash the church and organ, and that it should be 'decently ornamented' (Basil Clarke). The building was largely left alone in the 19th century but in 1901 the upper part of the tower was destroyed in a gale. This was restored in 1903–4. Gutted in the 1939–45 War, an admirable restoration was carried out by Thomas Ford and Partners enabling St Nicholas' to be reopened for worship on 14th February 1958; structural changes were made by cutting off the eastern bay and sanctuary to provide a hall and other amenities.

Exterior
Approach is through an iron gate, the pillars of which are crowned

with gruesome and much worn death's-head skulls, but these are
encircled with wreaths symbolising victory over death. The former
charnel house (now used for oil storage) lies to the south in the
churchyard, which is enclosed in brick walls.

Except for the top, the tower of Kentish ragstone is mediaeval
and dates from about 1500. The rest of the church is brick with
stone quoins and dressings. The Dutch high-pointed gables on the
north and south sides are rather old-fashioned in style for their date.

The church is dominated by a vast power station on the north
side which has been built hard up against the walls.

Interior
The post-war alterations have left an almost square interior with the
centre bays made into short transepts. Tuscan columns support the
entablature. Scrolled metal ties appear more decorative than
structural. The large areas of clear glass make a bright and cheerful
interior.

At the west end open steps lead down into the base of the tower.

Furnishings
The main furnishings, including the reredos and pulpit which were
moved to safety during the War, add considerably to the attraction
of the church.

Royal Arms On the west wall is a nicely coloured Royal Arms.

Pulpit A lavishly decorated furnishing with staircase of twisted
balusters. The six sides have small rectangular panels at the base and
elaborate centre sections consisting of fluted tapering pilasters at the
corners with console brackets above and below, and in the middle
trompe l'oeil arches capped with turrets. The richly ornamented top
projects.

Painting The painting of Queen Anne on the east wall, restored in
1957, is by Kneller.

Reredos Like the pulpit, a fine furnishing. The curved pediment
is surmounted by a royal arms and delicate finial-type adornment.
Fluted Corinthian columns enclose panels of the Decalogue and
figures of Moses and Aaron. The reredos is distinguished by the
carvings above the side-pieces of Ezekiel (see plate p. 298) and the
Valley of Bones (the latter once being over the door of the charnel
house) and is attributed to Grinling Gibbons.

Altar-rails Of twisted baluster type and curving round the
sanctuary on three sides.

Organ The organ is now in the hall but a charming organ case
with trumpeting angel above and gilt cherubs' heads below has been

St Nicholas', Deptford. Gateway with death's-head skulls

opened out into the church on the east wall.

Doorcase A handsome doorcase with a small segmental pediment leads to the hall.

Monuments

A number of monuments, mainly 18th century, have survived.

Roger Boyle An earlier one, dating from 1615, of golden-brown alabaster, commemorates Roger Boyle who is shown praying in a tent with curtain drawn back by a cherub. A skull and dog are also included. The memorial is on the east wall below the Queen Anne painting.

Sir Edward Fenton Below the Boyle monument, a tablet flanked by coats-of-arms commemorates Sir Edward Fenton, one of Raleigh's captains, who died in 1603.

Associations

Christopher Marlowe, the Elizabethan dramatist, was buried in the churchyard on 30th May 1593 after being killed nearby (as recorded on the west wall) in a tavern brawl.

Deptford Power Station A tablet on the south-east pew commemorates the men of Deptford Power Station who lost their lives as a result of enemy action in the 1939–45 War.

St Nicholas', Deptford

St Nicholas' Deptford. Roger Boyle monument and tablet to Sir Edward Fenton

General

This interesting church situated in a relatively quiet residential part of busy Deptford affords a complete contrast to the Baroque St Paul's. It has been fortunate in its post-war restoration and is well worth visiting.

N.B. Not normally open except during services.

Other Churches in Greenwich

Woolwich's parish church is **St Mary Magdalene** (4), dating back to the 18th century. Built of stock brick, it is a bit of a 'plain Jane' outside, but the late 19th century chancel and raised sanctuary are delicately coloured. To the right is the Lady Chapel containing the old altar-piece with fine carving.

The parish church **St Nicholas'** (5) of Plumstead, which may be derived from plums or plumes of feathers, is, like St Mary Magdalene at Woolwich, set slightly apart from the main town centre. In its long chequered history it has suffered many vicissitudes

St Nicholas', Deptford. Ezekiel carving

and it was much enlarged in 1907–8. Externally, the most noticeable feature is the plum-coloured brick tower of 1662–4 with buttresses rising up into tall battlemented turrets; pleasing details within are the wellcarved kneeling angels (plate p. 300) on the choir stalls at the west end.

Although not much old work remains, this church retains a mediaeval atmosphere; it is not difficult to recall its former isolation on the edge of the marshes (plate below) and even capture something of an East Anglian atmosphere with its stone floors, long oblique vistas and comparative absence of seating.

St Saviour's, Eltham (6), although rather chunky and graceless outside, is a good example of 20th century architecture, built in 1932–3. Brick and concrete are used to advantage inside (plate p. 301), both in the structure and in the furnishings, which include a striking reredos in concrete.

St Nicholas', Plumstead. Lithograph by W. J. Estherby

St Nicholas', Plumstead. Kneeling angel on stall

St Saviour's, Eltham

Hackney

1 St Leonard's, Shoreditch
2 St Mary's, Stoke Newington
3 *St Faith's with St Matthias', Wordsworth Road*
4 *St John-at-Hackney*
5 *St Mary of Eton, Hackney Wick*

1 St Leonard's, Shoreditch

Dedication
St Leonard was a companion of Clovis, first King of the Franks, but left his service to become a monk, then a hermit and itinerant preacher. He gained fame as a healer, and for his work on behalf of prisoners and captives, ultimately becoming Bishop of Limoges. He died in 570 AD.

'Shoreditch' has many suggested derivations; 'shore' might come from 'sor' or 'scoer', meaning sewer.

History
There is a tradition of a Saxon church but the first historical evidence does not go further back than a document dated between 1141 and 1149 granting St Leonard's to the Priory of Holy Trinity, Aldgate. For a time, it came under royal control but was allocated by King John to the Precentorship of St Paul's Cathedral, from which the living passed to the Archdeacon of London where it still rests.

The old church had four aisles of which the north one was a Chantry Chapel added by Sir John Elrington in 1782 for himself and his family. By the number of monuments to eminent people, it would seem that Shoreditch, despite its name, was a fashionable quarter.

Like many of the City churches that survived the Fire (St Leonard's is, of course, outside the City), it lapsed into decay—so much so that bits would fall from the fabric during Divine Service; on 23rd December 1716 part of the tower fell with a great crack causing panic amongst the congregation. Also, being below the level of the pavement, it was unhealthy. Unsuccessful attempts were made to get money from the Commissioners of the Fifty New Churches and it was not until 1736 that it was possible to make a start on a new building. George Dance the Elder was chosen as architect and the first service was held on 23rd August 1740.

Repaired, altered and restored many times, including an intervention by Butterfield in 1870, St Leonard's lost its north and south galleries in 1857 (T. E. Knightley). In 1944, a flying bomb removed most of the roof and damaged the organ and windows; the repairs took from 1946 until 1955. There was a thorough redecoration in 1968.

The church was the first to be lit by gaslight in London (1817).

Exterior
The building is prominently placed at cross-roads in an area where the 192 foot high steeple is still dominant. The main façade is approached by four steps (there used to be ten) to a portico with four giant Tuscan columns. Above, awkwardly placed in relation to the portico as at many London churches, the tower rises with attached piers at the angles, carrying an elongated cupola, small lantern and square section obelisk spire. All of this fine frontispiece to Shoreditch High Street is in Portland stone.

The steeple bears a family likeness to that of St Mary-le-Bow and inevitably suffers by comparison, but taken by itself it is a notable and original composition.

The rest of the fabric is built of red brick with stone dressings, the sides having two tiers of round-headed windows. A frieze and balcony encircle the top.

Interior
The interior is spacious and lofty, made to appear larger by the removal of the galleries. Large Tuscan columns, each with its own entablature and frieze, support arches high up, on which rests the clerestory of small segment-headed windows.

The west gallery housing the organ has arches at the sides and circular blocked windows above. A similar pattern is followed at the east end except that the arches are also blocked, giving horizontal emphasis to a mainly longitudinal design. The chancel projects slightly and the ceiling is flat and panelled.

Furnishings
Royal Arms The Royal Arms above the west door are those of George II.

Organ Built by Richard Bridge in 1756 and still retaining the original console with ebony naturals and ivory sharps. The fine case is of mahogany. The instrument was rebuilt in 1913, and repaired and restored including regilding of the front pipes by Noel Mander in 1950 after serious war damage.

Clock Surround The finest of the furnishings, it has an exquisitely carved gilt case attributed to Chippendale (see plate p. 306).

Font The stone font, made from a single block of marble, with massive but elegantly-shaped stem and nicely carved cover, admirably following the lines of the fluted bowl, dates from 1740.

Bread Cupboards On the side walls are exceptionally interesting bread cupboards with pediments, metope friezes and unusual lozenge openings in the doors. Fifty loaves used to be distributed

St Leonard's, Shoreditch. Interior looking west

every Sunday but this practice was discontinued about 100 years ago.

Pulpit Contemporary with the building of the church, it has a sounding board on two fine fluted Ionic columns. In 1857, it went through the usual Victorian process of being lowered. It is enriched with delicate and intricate pierced carving at the base. John Wesley preached from it.

Lectern The oak lectern commemorates Henry Wilton, for nearly sixty years Deputy Clerk and Sexton of the parish.

Rood Beam The blue rood over the chancel step was set up as a War Memorial in 1923.

Stained Glass A grievous loss from the bombing was an early 17th century Flemish window at the east end depicting the Last Supper. It was replaced in 1955 by a window by A. K. Nicholson Studios representing the 'Te Deum', a memorial to those from the parish who suffered and died during the 1939–45 War.

Benefactions Boards On the east wall are interesting boards recording benefactions by former parishioners, including the gift of loaves, presumably those distributed from the bread cupboards.

St Leonard's, Shoreditch. Carved clock case

Monuments

The Austens This came from the old church and still retains its colour. Thomas Austen and his sons, Thomas and John (both members of Lincoln's Inn) were buried by the old Communion Table.

Dr James Parkinson (1755–1824) The doctor (who first described the shaking palsy disease named after him) lived all his life in Shoreditch and was a member of St Leonard's congregation. He was baptised and married in the church, and buried in the churchyard. His memorial on the north wall was erected by the nursing staff of St Leonard's Hospital.

Francis and Sarah Clerke By the west door is another memorial from the old church, to Francis and Sarah Clerke. He was a former vicar.

*Elizabeth Benson The most outstanding memorial—also from the old church—is by Francis Bird to Elizabeth Benson on the south-east wall. Two skeletons are pulling hard on the branches of an uprooted oak-tree—the Tree of Life—over which is hooked a shroud upon which the inscription is written. It is frighteningly realistic. The inscription states that she was 'sprung paternally from the ancestral Kings of Pannonia (Hungary)' and that 'in her 90th year the threads of her life were not spun to the full but snapped 17th December 1710' (see plate p. 308).

Bells Although not normally noted in this book, the bells of Shoreditch which, according to the old nursery rhyme, said 'When I grow rich', were twelve in number until 1963 when a thirteenth donated by the Haberdashers' Company was added.

Associations

Keats The three brothers of John Keats were baptised here in 1801.

Shoreditch Battalion Beside the south wall is the 1914–18 War Memorial of the 20th (Shoreditch) Battalion of the Middlesex Regiment and below, in a large case, are the drums of the Battalion.

Actors' Memorial In 1913 the London Shakespeare League erected a memorial to 'the players, musicians, and other men of this Church'. These included William Somers, Court Jester to Henry VIII, and members of the Burbage family, of whom Cuthbert built the Globe Playhouse in Southwark.

Before the Globe was built, there were two playhouses in Shoreditch, the Court and the Theatre, thus making this the first parish to have a theatre in London. This was the reason for actors living in the area so that St Leonard's became known as the Actors' Church in Elizabethan times.

Thomas Cam   In the burial register is a record that Thomas Cam died in 1588, aged 207 (sic!).

Stocks and Whipping Post   Under a thatched roof, north-west of the church, are the parish stocks and whipping post.

General

St Leonard's is a landmark for some distance in an area not over-blessed with fine buildings. The splendid steeple is in need of much money to cope with crumbling stone, but the interior has been beautifully redecorated and the blue carpeting presented by Kenneth White the architect during the 1968 restoration gives a warm and fresh atmosphere to this interesting place of worship.

N.B. Not normally open except during services.

St Leonard's, Shoreditch. Elizabeth Benson memorial

2 St Mary's, Stoke Newington

Stoke Newington
Probably means the new town in the wood ('stoc' is Anglo-Saxon for 'wood').

(a) Old Church

History
According to tradition, the Manor of Stoke Newington was one of many in and around London granted by King Athelstan to the Canons of St Paul's Cathedral and in the Domesday Book (1086) the Canons appear as Lords of the Manor. Little is known of the mediaeval church but it was probably a typical village place of worship lying under the shadow of the Manor. Thomas de London (1313) is the earliest rector to be recorded.

By the middle of the 16th century, the condition of the building was 'ruinous' and, in Elizabeth's reign—a rare time for the erection of churches (this is the only example in London)—William Patten who was leasing the Manor had it rebuilt.

Although little has come down to us today, the building being frequently altered and restored in both the 18th and 19th centuries, its village character has not been lost and, in fact, has been increased by some of the changes and especially by the contrast with the large Victorian church on the opposite side of the road. The old church is still surrounded by trees and lies in a park-like setting.

A major restoration was carried out by Sir Charles Barry, architect with Augustus Pugin of the House of Commons, between 1826 and 1829. A report at the time stated that 'the building is generally leaning towards the north, the beams are rotten . . . and the coffins floating'. Sir Charles added another north aisle to the one constructed in 1716, provided galleries on the north and west sides, plastered and painted the interior, built a clerestory and erected the timber spire which so much enhances the rural effect.

Old St Mary's was in danger of disappearing when the new place of worship (described later) was built across the road in the 1850s but the parishioners rallied to its rescue, although it ceased to be the parish church in 1858. By this time, the village was starting to be swallowed up by London.

The spire was rebuilt in the 1920s, and plaster was removed from the south aisle to reveal the old brickwork. Both churches were damaged in the 1939–45 War and, while it lasted, services were only held in the less badly damaged old church. After the War, both were restored. In the case of Old St Mary's, Barry's north aisle which had received the impact of the bomb was scrapped and the north side rebuilt.

Today, after further repairs, the old place of worship stands out fresh and bright, and acts as a splendid foil to its imposing Victorian neighbour.

Exterior
The main impression is of the extraordinary village character of this church. With its shingled spire, although this was only added in 1829 and rebuilt 100 years later, it might be a country church in the Cotswolds.

The later brickwork of the clerestory blends well with the original brick of the Tudor south aisle. Over one doorway is William Patten's motto and date of rebuilding ('1563 Ab alto') and over the adjacent entrance his initials and the family arms plus the word 'Prospice' (Look forward).

The replacement cement rendering does not so far spoil the effect and gives St Mary's a well-laundered look.

The windows are in late Perpendicular style.

Interior
The interior is of a piece with the exterior, having box-pews, double galleries at the west end, blue panelled roof, and low polygonal brick piers and arches. Curious features are the transverse walls and niches in the south aisle, known as Queen Elizabeth's chapel.

The north arcade has slender piers without capitals.

Furnishings
These are generally also in keeping.
Font A small font mounted on a pedestal dating from 1953 is placed under the west galleries.
Pulpit By Sir Charles Barry and dating from 1829. It has a spiral canopy.
Altar-piece The altar-piece is panelled and is in light gold and brown tones. A vine-trail is carried along the top.
Stained glass Fragments of 16th century glass have been pieced together in the east window.

Monuments
These are a noteworthy feature.
John and Elizabeth Dudley and 6-year-old daughter This typical Jacobean alabaster and marble monument with two kneeling figures

facing one another is on the south wall of the chancel.

Elizabeth married as her second husband Thomas Sutton, founder of Charterhouse School, and the tomb was repaired in 1808 at the expense of 'several prelates and other persons educated at Charterhouse School'.

Jane Anne Chalmers A rather charming marble tablet at the west end depicts Jane Anne Chalmers (died 1913) seated on the ground and caressing a child; there is an urn with grapes at the bottom left-hand corner.

Joseph Hurlock On the east wall, a monument commemorates Joseph Hurlock, died 1793, and wife. It is in the form of a woman bent over a large urn.

Associations

St Mary's is mentioned by Edgar Allen Poe in 'William Wilson', one of his *Tales of Imagination and Fancy*. He spent five years at school in Church Street.

(b) New Church

History

In the middle 1850s, the preaching of the rector, the Rev Thomas Jackson, drew huge crowds from all over London and these were more than the old church could accommodate. It was, therefore, decided to build a new church in the garden of the old Rectory on the other side of Church Street. Started in 1854, it was consecrated on 25th June 1858, the architect being Sir George Gilbert Scott.

There was only enough money to build the lower part of the steeple and this was not completed until 1890 by the architect's son, John Oldrid Scott.

The war damage was made good by yet another member of the family, Charles Marriott Scott, and the church rededicated on 2nd May 1957.

Exterior

The exterior is dominated by the steeple, the upper parts built of Doulting (Somerset) stone and the lower of Kentish ragstone. It is one of the highest in London of a parish church and is understood to be a reduced facsimile of Salisbury Cathedral spire. There, however, the comparison ends for it is not a particularly notable construction and inferior to the rest of the church.

St Mary's, Stoke Newington. Old church

St Mary's, Stoke Newington. New church

Interior
The new St Mary's is a grandiose building with wide spacious nave and aisles, and lofty arcades with circular marble pillars. These continue past the transepts. The capitals are profusely carved with leaves.

The chancel has the unusual embellishment for a parish church of having its own aisles. Marble steps and brass rails were added in 1890 leading to the sanctuary, which was, until damaged in the War, decorated with mosaics and enclosed in a polygonal apse.

Furnishings
The furnishings generally are showy. They include a massive pulpit with grey-green marble columns outside and shorter pink ones within, and a font with four short columns at the corners supporting winged angels and a larger central column. There have been no less than four organs: the first by Gray and Davidson cost £1,200: the next by Wm. Hill & Co. £1,550 (installed 1907): the third by Rushworth & Draper £2,500 (installed in the 1930s): and the present one after the War by Noel Mander & Co. £4,500.

The stained glass window in the north transept, with predominantly blue, green and gold colours, was installed in 1960. Amongst many items depicted can be seen radio isotopes, Greenwich Observatory and Jodrell Bank.

General
Although this is a rather insensitive church, can there be anywhere else in London with the contrast of a basically Tudor village church and a high Victorian town church standing so close together and both still ministering to the needs of a single parish?

Other Churches in Hackney
St Faith's with St Matthias', Wordsworth Road (3) a Butterfield church of the mid-1850s, is distinctive externally for its tall saddleback tower and internally for its feeling of spaciousness. St Faith's was pulled down after the 1939–45 War.

St John-at-Hackney (4) is a vast building of the last decade of the 18th century set in an ample leafy churchyard and conspicuous by its strange steeple erected some years later. The mediaeval tower from an earlier church remains.

Inside, there are many monuments from the old church, notably the reconstructed tomb-chest with recumbent alabaster effigy of Lady Latimer (d. 1583). After a serious fire in 1955, the interior, plain but made interesting by a large horseshoe gallery supported on blue fluted Doric columns, was reduced in size.

St Mary of Eton (5) in Hackney Wick was built in the early 1890s with funds provided by Eton College, who used to run a mission in the area; they are still the patrons. The church is a notable work of the eminent Victorian architect, G. F. Bodley, but the unusual gate-tower which helps to give such an interesting skyline to the elevation facing Eastway was built later in 1911–2 by Cecil Hare (plate below).

The open nave is lofty and wide with plain arches supported on massive square piers; there is a Lady Chapel in the south-east corner. This dignified interior is enhanced by the ceilings and the attractive furnishings and fittings.

St Mary of Eton, Hackney Wick. East side

Hammersmith

WESTWAY

WOOD LANE

UXBRIDGE ROAD

GOLDHAWK ROAD

Hammersmith

KING STREET

WEST ROAD

HAMMERSMITH RD

West Kensington

FULHAM PALACE ROAD

Fulham

River Thames

Walham Green

NEW KINGS ROAD

WANDSWORTH BRI. RD

Parsons Green

1 All Saints', Fulham
2 *St Dionis', Parson's Green*
3 *St Paul's, Hammersmith*
4 *St Peter's, Hammersmith*

0   1 mile
1 km

1 All Saints', Fulham

Fulham

'Fulham' may be derived from a personal name such as Fulla (akin to Old German 'vullo'). 'Ham' is almost certainly 'hamm', describing an angle of land in the bend of a river. The dedication of All Saints was first referred to in 1445.

History

History goes back to a charter of 704–9 AD granting the tenure of land to Waldhere, Bishop of London. This land later became the Manor of Fulham and was the start of the long connection between Fulham and the Bishops of London.

First mention of a church is in 1154 in connection with a dispute over tithes but there is little reliable evidence about the fabric until the 15th century when work was in progress on the tower. The church that existed then was added to here and there but by the 19th century it had become inadequate for the continuously growing population and, although at first it was decided not to rebuild, this later proved necessary because of the fabric becoming unsafe. The old church was therefore pulled down and a completely new place of worship (except for the tower) erected by Sir Arthur Blomfield, son of a former Bishop of London, in 1880–1, just before the present bridge across the River Thames on an alignment much closer to the church replaced the old wooden bridge dating from 1729.

By this time the parish, which at one time covered the whole of the Borough of Hammersmith, was no longer the quiet riverside area it had been. In 1834 Hammersmith had been made a separate parish and later as many as twenty-five parishes were carved out of the ancient Fulham area.

Damage was caused to the north transept and the vestry by a fire in 1923 but All Saints' was fortunate to escape all but minor damage in the 1939–45 War.

Exterior

The church makes a fine picture as one crosses Putney Bridge, acting as counterpoise to St Mary's, Putney (gutted by fire, alas, at the time of writing).

The Blomfield rebuilding in the Perpendicular style blends well with the old tower and is battlemented, including the large north porch added in 1880–1. There are tall clerestories and the roofs are of slate. The building material of the main fabric is Kentish ragstone with Bath stone dressings; a document of 1440 specifically exempts from requisition stone from Maidstone required for the tower. It was signed by the Secretary of Henry VI who at that time was building Eton College Chapel. The four-stage tower with stair-turret at the south-west angle was given new battlements in 1797 and was re-faced in 1845, at which time the thin wooden spire was removed. There was further extensive re-facing after the 1939–45 War.

Interior
There are typical Perpendicular arcades with slender columns of alternate shafts and hollows, aisles, tall clerestory, transepts and chancel. Most of the clerestory glass was blown out in the War. All is of 1880–1 but seemly and dignified.

The south transept is arranged as a Lady Chapel.

Furnishings
The only old furnishings are the fonts, the organ and the altar-rails, but All Saints' has a collection of monuments only rivalled in the outer parts of London by those of Chelsea Old Church.

Painting In the ringing chamber of the tower is a painting of John Hudnott, beadle and sexton, in red coat with quart pot and churchwarden's pipe, dated 1690.

All Saints', Fulham

Fonts The main font is octagonal and panelled. The moulded bowl of black marble bears the inscription—'this font was erected at the charge of Tho. Hyll churchwarden 1622'. The stem is of painted freestone, whilst the upper panels are carved with roses and the lower have cusped heads.

In the tower chapel is an older font, which was found buried close to the other when the old church was demolished. It is of early mediaeval type.

Organ Orginally built by Benjamin Jordan of Fulham in 1732 but rebuilt more than once since, the last time in 1930 to the designs of the then organist, Livingstone Hurst. It retains its original case with carved scroll work, cherubs' heads and moulded cornices, but wings have been added. The screen of the organist's seat is formed from carved upper panels taken from the three-decker pulpit that used to be in the old church.

Stained glass The greater part was made in 1880 by Heaton, Butler and Bayne and presented by members of the congregation. The window next to the north door shows Christ blessing the children, one of whom is a likeness of a child of the vicar at that time. The west window below the tower has representations of heraldic shields and in the upper tracery are fragments of German or Swiss glass of the 16th or 17th century, mostly heraldic. There is also some old glass of this type in the north porch.

Altar-rails A shortened form of the old Jacobean rails made of oak with round balusters, moulded rail and sill, and panelled standards. The carving is in high relief.

Reredos screen   Made by Heaton, Butler and Bayne in 1885 but restored in 1967. The figures, painted on zinc, are those of Moses, David, Isaiah and Aaron.

Bells The bells are worthy of special mention in that—as at St George the Martyr, Southwark—they are a complete peal of ten from the foundry of Abraham Rudhall of Gloucester.

Monuments

Amongst the wealth of mainly 17th century monuments, and taking them in order of walking clockwise round the church starting from the west end, are the following:

Sir William Butts, died 1545. He was Chief Physician to Henry VIII. This is in the north aisle.

Katharine Hart, who died in 1605. She is shown kneeling with her two sons and two daughters. In the north transept.

Sir Thomas Smith, died 1608. This is an elaborate wall monument of various kinds of marbles. In the chancel.

All Saints', Fulham. Margaret Legh monument

Lady Margaret Legh The outstanding memorial. She is depicted in stiff Elizabethan costume and holds an infant in a chrysom. On a pedestal to the right is another child similarly attired and on the left an hour-glass, which at one time was on top of the monument. She died in 1603. Also in the chancel.

Margaret Svanders, died 1529. A lozenge-shaped Flemish brass on the east wall of the south aisle shows the head and shoulders of a woman in a shroud with angels on either side engraved above an inscription and a coat-of-arms.

Viscount Mordaunt   This is a Baroque monument by John Bushnell showing the Viscount in a toga and holding a baton. He died in 1675. The monument is in the Tower Chapel.

Lady Dorothy Clarke, died 1695 and *Dr Samuel Barrow*, died 1682. This white-veined marble wall monument is by Grinling Gibbons. Dr Barrow was Lady Clarke's second husband, whom she married after her first husband had been killed in a naval engagement against the Dutch.

Associations
The main associations are with Bishops of London, eight of whom were buried in the churchyard at the east end of the church and two more, including Sir Arthur Blomfield's father, in the north-eastern part. Bishop Henchman was buried in the church itself.

General
Although very little is left from mediaeval times, Sir Arthur Blomfield has provided a church worthy of its fine river situation and its episcopal links.

Other Churches in Hammersmith
St Dionis', Parsons Green (2) is named after a City church demolished in 1878 and was built and endowed with the proceeds from the sale of the site and materials of that church. The new St Dionis', constructed of red brick, was erected in 1884–5 (tower 1895–6). It contains the 17th century pulpit and font of the City place of worship, the former approached by a staircase with delicately twisted balusters and the latter completed with a delightful cover representing the old tower.

St Paul's (3), near the Broadway and enclosed in through-roads, took the place of an old chapel of ease which had been consecrated by Laud in 1631 and which had become a parish church in 1834. It was built of pink Mansfield stone in the 1880s and is distinctive externally for the outsize pinnacles on the tall north-east tower and the narrow lancet windows.

*The well-proportioned and lofty interior has columns of Belgian marble. The church is especially noteworthy for its two excellent late-17th century monuments, to James and Sarah Smith (north wall of chancel—(plate p. 325) and to Sir Nicholas Crispe (west wall of north aisle). The latter carries a splendid bronze bust of King Charles I (plate p. 324), probably by Le Sueur, the sculptor of the outstanding equestrian statue of this monarch near Trafalgar Square. The pleasing Wren-period pulpit came from All Hallows the Great, Thames Street.

St Peter's (4), beside the Great West Road, became a parish church in 1836. It was a Commissioners' building, constructed in 1827–9 of Suffolk brick with details in Bath stone. This unassuming and rather appealing little Greek-style church, set in a pleasant square, has a somewhat original tower, octagonal at the base rising to a tall circular stage (plate p. 326). The low plain galleried interior is brightened by the use of Pompeian red on the pews.

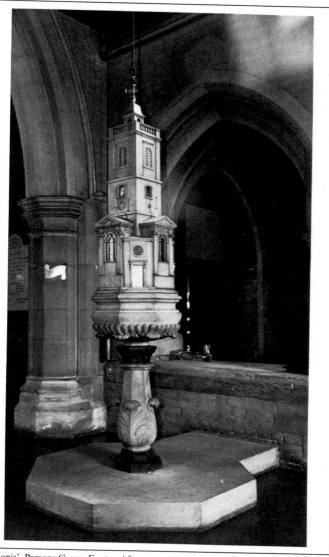

St Dionis', Parsons Green. Font and font-cover

St Paul's, Hammersmith. Sir Nicholas Crispe monument—bust of Charles I

St Paul's, Hammersmith. James and Sarah Smith monument

St Peter's, Hammersmith

Islington

T Tower

0   1 mile

1 km

Highbury

SEVEN SISTERS ROAD

JUNCTION ROAD

HOLLOWAY ROAD

CAMDEN ROAD

CALEDONIAN ROAD

HIGHBURY GR.

ST. PAUL'S RD

ESSEX ROAD

UPPER STREET

Islington

5

3

4

PENTONVILLE ROAD

CITY ROAD

GOSWELL RD

Finsbury

Clerkenwell

T

OLD STREET

1

2

WELL RD

1 St James's, Clerkenwell
2 St John's, Clerkenwell
3 St Mary's, Islington
4 *St James's, Pentonville Road*
5 *St Mary Magdalene with St James's, Holloway*

1 St James's, Clerkenwell, and St John's with St Peter's

Dedication

The Apostle James became the patron saint of Spain after what was presumed to be his body was found in a marble coffin by a Galician peasant during the year 816 AD; his shrine at Santiago de Compostela became a leading centre of mediaeval pilgrimage.

'Clerkenwell' refers to the springs of pure water near the place where, in the early Middle Ages, the parish clerks used to perform mystery plays, 'en' being an Anglo-Saxon plural.

History

Although William Kent maintains that a Papal Bull of 1486 shows that St James's was a separate and at that time new church, others aver that it formed part of the convent of St Mary (possibly only a small chapel for residents). Whatever still existed passed into private hands at the Dissolution, where it remained until taken over by the parish in 1656. Partially rebuilt earlier in 1625, it subsequently lapsed into increasing decay until the building became positively unsafe. Eventually after attempts had been made in 1718 to get money from the Commissioners of the Fifty New Churches, it was rebuilt by a notable Palladian architect, James Carr, and reconsecrated on 10th July 1792.

The tower and spire were reconstructed to the old design in 1849 and the church as a whole gently treated by Blomfield in 1882, when the central pulpit and box-pews were removed and choir stalls introduced.

St James's escaped bomb damage during the War but was redecorated in 1967.

A strange circumstance of this church was that, unlike most livings, the parish retained control of it at the 1660 Restoration until the beginning of the present century. This gave rise to unseemly electoral rivalry and a strong Evangelical tradition. One of the most famous vicars, chosen in the 1850s after a particularly stormy and exciting election, was the Rev Robert Maguire, a prolific writer of Protestant pamphlets, who carried out much work on the fabric and furnishings of the church. The patrons of the living are now the Parish Church Council and the Church Patronage Society jointly.

Exterior

Raised on an undercroft, St James's is well sited on what was at one time a pleasant green. Apart from the steeple, the exterior is severely plain stock brick, relieved with classical doorways in the first and last bays (which have stone quoins) on the south side, a balustrade, and a Venetian window at the east end. The steeple has a large square stone base, terminating in a balustrade with urns, above which is an open polygonal stage and a spire on a concave base. It is strongly reminiscent of St Martin's and St Giles-in-the-Fields and, therefore, a bit old-fashioned for the end of the 18th century.

Interior

A well-mannered interior with ceiling decoration, organ case, reredos, Communion table and rails all contemporary with the building of the church. Although basically a 'preaching box', it is made interesting by the curves introduced at the west end, noticeably in the galleries which come round to embrace the north and south sides.

Winding round the staircases leading to the galleries on the north and south sides are so-called 'modesty' boards. This interesting feature consists of metal sheets reaching down almost to the floor and designed to prevent any view of ladies' ankles as they mounted the stairs.

There is a theatrical resemblance in that, right up under the ceiling, a gallery with iron railings was introduced in 1822 by the Clerkenwell Parochial School to provide accommodation for school children, for which this church still pays £1 a year rent; charity children were pushed back to the rear of the Upper Circle into what were called 'glove boxes'. Below, on the other hand, are imposing boxes for the 'Church Officers' and the 'Corporation Officers'. Otherwise, the building is rectangular with a charming flat plaster ceiling painted in Wedgwood blue and white. The west galleries, which are still double, are reached by two graceful circular staircases situated in rooms north and south of the tower.

Furnishings

Royal Arms The Arms over the west door dating from 1792 are those of George III and are of Coade stone, an artificial material made according to a secret patent—now lost—in Lambeth.

Font Dates from 1850.

Organ Built in 1792, rebuilt in 1877 and enlarged in 1926. The decoration of the Spanish mahogany case with carved drapery over the pipes is notable.

Wooden figure of St James A wooden figure of St James which used to stand over the poor-box in the former church is now placed above the main doorway to the nave.

Communion table and wrought-iron rails are part of the original furnishings and both are curved towards the west. The altar table is of mahogany, inlaid with box-wood, and is decorated with carved plumes of feathers and a dove.

Reredos This Doric altar-piece is also contemporary with the building of the church.

Stained glass The rather garish glass with large figures in the east window depicts the Ascension of Christ and dates from 1863; it is by Heaton, Butler and Bayne.

Vestry In the vestry a chairman's tall chair and another of the 18th century are to be found. There is also a large-scale wooden model of the steeple containing a clock which still works.

Monuments

Elizabeth, Dowager Countess of Exeter A large wall tablet with armorials at the east end of the south aisle commemorates this granddaughter by marriage of Elizabeth I's great minister, William Cecil, Lord Burleigh.

Mico Wagstaff By way of showing that all are equal before God in death, next to the Countess lies Mico Wagstaff, Ironmonger.

John Bell, Bishop of Worcester 1539–43, who lived in retirement in Clerkenwell, is remembered by a brass. This was stolen and brought back in 1884. He was buried in the old church in 1556.

Gilbert Burnet, Bishop of Salisbury, died 1714. This well-known preacher and writer has a floor slab under the Communion table commemorating him and a large monument in the vestibule with a long Latin verse.

Henry Penton, who had developed the area known as Pentonville, has a memorial in the porch. He died in 1714 and there is an epitaph with gracefully ornamented obelisk.

Thomas Crosse, who died in 1729, is honoured by a Roubiliac memorial in the form of a wall monument with two busts but it is not a particularly good example of this sculptor's work.

Associations

Smithfield Martyrs On the south wall is a well-carved wooden tablet commemorating those who suffered in the fires at Smithfield. These include not only the Marian Martyrs but earlier victims (probably in one case a Lollard) ranging in date from 1400–1558.

'Sir' William Wood Adjacent is a memorial to 'Sir' William Wood, author of *Bowman's Glory*, with appropriate lines to this famous archer, erected at the expense of the Toxophilite Society. Three flights of arrows were discharged over his grave at the funeral.

Izaak Walton Two of his children were buried in the old churchyard.

Victims of Fenian outrage In the porch is a tablet to the victims of a Fenian bombing outrage on Friday 13th December 1867. The deaths occurred in houses in the immediate neighbourhood of the Clerkenwell House of Detention.

General
Thanks to sensitive restoration, St James's has kept its 18th century atmosphere. The parish now includes St John's, Clerkenwell, carved out of it in 1721 and reunited in 1931, whose church has become the chapel of the Hospital of St John of Jerusalem. It also includes the Smithfield Martyrs Memorial Church of St Peter's in Clerkenwell, established in 1869, which was pulled down in 1955 after being bombed in the War.

N.B. Not normally open except during services.

2 St John's, Clerkenwell

Order of St John
The Order had its origins in a band of soldier-monks who staffed a Hospital in Jerusalem, becoming known as Knights Hospitaller, and who, with the members of other Orders, helped to defend Jerusalem together with the other Latin principalities and territories in the Holy Land against Saracen attacks. Gradually forced back, first to Acre in Israel, then to Cyprus and Rhodes, they came to Malta, where after withstanding a savage siege in 1565, they settled peaceably until surrendering to Napoleon in 1798. The capital of Malta, Valletta, is named after the Grand Master of the Order, Jean de la Vallette.

The English Langue (as the national divisions were called) was revived in 1831, St John's Ambulance being formed in 1877.

History
Land was granted to the Order in Clerkenwell around the year 1145 and the first church, circular as customary with churches of this Order after the pattern of the Holy Sepulchre Church in Jerusalem, with a rectangular choir, and crypt underneath, was consecrated in the year 1185 by Heraclius, the Patriarch of Jerusalem, who had come over to try and persuade King Henry II to embark upon a Crusade. (He consecrated the Temple Church in the same year.)

St John's, Clerkenwell. Etching dated 1818

This building was burned to the ground by the peasants in the 1381 revolt and the prior murdered. Reconstructed in rectangular form, it was enlarged and the tower rebuilt by Prior Docwra in the early 16th century. He added the gatehouse in 1504.

At the Dissolution, the church fell on evil times. The nave was blown up during the reign of Edward VI to provide stone for Protector Somerset's new Palace in the Strand, and the Great Hall may have been used as the office of the Master of the Revels. It was rescued by Lady Burleigh, wife of the grandson of William Cecil, Lord Burleigh—Elizabeth's great Lord High Treasurer—to whom ownership had passed, and it was reopened for worship in 1623 as a private chapel, coming later into the possession of the Earl of Aylesbury, who used the crypt as a wine-cellar.

In 1706, the church became a Presbyterian meeting-house and was unfortunate enough to become the butt for a second time of an angry mob who, during the Sacheverell Riots, gutted it and burnt the contents in St John's Square.

Rescued on this occasion by two local people, Simon and Charity Michel in 1721, they sold it two years later to the Commissioners of the Fifty New Churches, who made it into a parish church which it continued to be for 200 years.

With a reduction in the number of residents, the parish was absorbed by St James's, Clerkenwell, and St John's Church given to the Order; so that despite all its vicissitudes the wheel had come full circle and it is once more the Grand Priory Church of the Order of St John.

But its misfortunes were not over because it was burnt out by enemy bombs in 1941 and it remained a shell until it was rebuilt by Lord Mottistone, using the surviving outer walls, and rededicated in 1958.

Exterior

This presents a plain red-brick elevation of no particular architectural interest but alongside there is a war memorial garden on the site of the cloister of the old Priory Church. The Crucifixion sculpture is by Cecil Thomas.

The outline of the original round church is marked in cobbles on the pavement outside.

Interior

By contrast, the interior is a blaze of scarlet from the seat coverings, further enhanced by the bright new banners of the senior officers of the Order and of the Priories and Commanderies. It is used for the main services and for investitures.

The chief magnet, however, for any outside visitor must be the rib-vaulted crypt which has come through all the burnings and desecration unscathed. It is a rare London example of 12th century work, the three western bays being Norman (1140) and the two eastern ones, together with the flanking chapels, Transitional work (1185), in which the ribs of the vault rise to a point, springing from low clustered shafts. The earlier work is plain with only simple chamfers but the later construction is more elegant with many mouldings.

Smaller services are held in the crypt, the Almoner Chapel on the south being used for memorial purposes and the chapels on the north as the vestry.

Furnishings
The church contains part of a 15th century triptych and the crypt a monument (to Ruyz de Vergara) described by Pevsner as being 'of a quality unsurpassed in London or England'.

Triptych Two wings of a triptych, the central panel having disappeared, hang behind the altar of the church. Known as the 'Weston Triptych', it was painted by the school of Roger van der Weyden and is thought to have been ordered especially for the Priory Church and to have been presented by Prior John Weston in 1480, to commemorate the successful defence by the Order against the Turks in the Siege of Rhodes in that year.

Monuments
Juan Ruyz de Vergara, Proctor of the Langue of Castile. This superb monument was purchased from Valladolid Cathedral in Spain during rebuilding in the 19th century. Of alabaster and dating from 1575, it is in the form of a recumbent effigy with a sleeping boy alongside. The Proctor wears the eight-pointed cross of the Order of St John over his breast plate.

Sir William Weston, the last Prior of the Order who, it is said, died of a broken heart in 1540 after hearing of the Dissolution of the Order. The canopy and upper part are lost. He is shown as an emaciated corpse wrapped in a shroud and placed on a rush mat.

Associations
John Wilkes, the 'scandalous' champion of popular rights against the royal rule of George III, was married in the church in 1747.

Duke of Cambridge Against the wishes of Queen Victoria, her cousin the second Duke of Cambridge, who was grandson of

St John's, Clerkenwell. Ruyz de Vergara monument
St John's, Clerkenwell. Sir William Weston monument

George III, was married here on 8th January 1847 to Sarah Fairbrother, an actress.

General
The crypt, which together with the gateway on the other side of the road, is the last remaining part of a Priory, providing in its heyday accommodation and entertainment for royalty, should be better known than it is and a visit is strongly recommended.

The gateway is the only gateway of any age in London under which a thoroughfare still passes.

N.B. Application to visit should be made to the Curator of the nearby Library and Museum at St John's Gate.

3 St Mary's, Islington

Islington
Referred to in the Domesday Book as 'Isendone' and also 'Iseldone', the name of the borough may come from words meaning lower town or fortress, as opposed to a higher one at Highbury; or it may be derived from 'Giseldine'—used about 1000 AD—meaning 'Gisla's Hill'.

History
Recorded history starts with a dispute between 1125 and 1141 between the Dean of St Paul's Cathedral and the nuns of Bromley-by-Bow as to the patronage of St Mary's. The nuns won and they retained the patronage until the dissolution of their convent in 1545.

Nothing reliable is known about the building until the middle of the 15th century when it was replaced with a new church made of a rough kind of masonry called 'boulder' with three aisles and a robust, battlemented north-west tower with a little bell cupola on top.

In 1710, a school—one of the first Church of England schools—was set up in a room over the west porch but a few years later, the building being considered inadequate for the parish's needs, a petition was made to the Commissioners of the Fifty New Churches for a new church but, as so often happened, it was turned down. Eventually in 1750, an enabling bill was passed through Parliament and a local master joiner, Launcelot Dowbiggin, chosen as architect.

Work started in 1751 and was completed in 1754.

Fears of lightning led to an extraordinary wickerwork scaffolding being erected around the spire by a local basketmaker in 1787; he was able to make money by charging an entrance fee of 6d. to see the enclosed spire.

In 1902 health hazards caused by the coffins in the crypt led to the church being closed. The following year the chancel was opened out and the three-decker pulpit which stood right in front of the altar removed. At the same time the round portico on four Tuscan columns provided by Dowbiggin was replaced with the present broad porch supported on a line of Ionic columns. The church was reopened in 1904.

All but the reinforced steeple of Dowbiggin's church was destroyed by a bomb which landed on the east end on 9th September 1940. Reconstruction to a very different design, but incorporating the old steeple, was carried out by Lord Mottistone and Paul Paget, and St Mary's was re-hallowed on 17th December 1956.

The spiritual history is even more interesting than the architectural record because, after the Reformation, Islington became a centre of extreme Protestants, many of whom suffered grievously under the Marian Persecution, from which has stemmed the Evangelical tradition which is so strong today. John and Charles Wesley started their preaching in the church and George Whitefield, not being licensed, in the churchyard outside, whilst in January 1827 Dr Daniel Wilson, who became Bishop of Calcutta and Metropolitan of India, gathered twelve clergy friends at his vicarage to discuss prayer. This was the first of the Islington Clerical Meetings and was the seed of the Islington Conference now held annually at Church House, Westminster. On the lay side, the Church Pastoral Aid Society was formed by laymen in 1836 to encourage the recruitment of extra clergy and also of lay-helpers.

Exterior

It was stated in the *Gentleman's Magazine* of February 1825 that Dowbiggin had attempted to combine the virtues of the steeples of St Bride's, St Mary-le-Bow, and St Leonard's, Shoreditch, in the one he built at Islington; but, whilst there is no question of this eclectic approach producing an architectural masterpiece, one cannot help admiring the vigour and rustic originality of his steeple. Starting from a three-stage square brick tower with broad stone quoins, topped with an octagonal balustrade and four corner urns, there is an open stage with rusticated colonettes on an octagonal base, followed by a conical bulging dome with large openings and completed with a 'weird' (Pevsner) rusticated obelisk spire. Portland stone is used for the upper stages.

The broad porch of 1903 remains but the rest is post-war reconstruction in red brick by Mottistone and Paget, with tall rectangular windows and short transepts at the east end.

Interior

A design of striking originality with large glass doors dividing the vestibule with a chapel for private prayer from the main body of the church. The interior is completely open, with a spacious sanctuary rising impressively at the east end, separated by slender black fluted pillars with lotus-leaf capitals and abacus-like rails from the transepts.

A group of eight murals with a cross as the central feature depicting Christ in His various roles as Saviour, Healer, The Son of God, etc. over the Communion words beneath—'This do in Remembrance of Me'—close the view eastwards.

In the west wall are some of the oak Tuscan pillars which supported the old gallery.

Organ and choir are kept at the west end so that the congregation have an uninterrupted view of pulpit and lectern, well suited to the church's evangelical traditions.

Furnishings

Font The original and very elegant font of veined marble was fortunately preserved by being replaced and stored away during the 1902–4 restorations. It is in a somewhat unusual position in the south aisle.

Pews Contributed by various lovers of the church, including two from passers-by.

Pulpit and Lectern These stately modern furnishings are of like design and on either side of the sanctuary under large canopies. The eagle lectern was brought in during the modernisation at the beginning of the century.

Royal Arms Beside the pulpit are the Royal Arms of George II, unveiled by the Archbishop of Sydney (see *Incumbents*) in March 1959.

Murals (see *Interior*) There is another mural by Brian Thomas at the west end showing Christ as the Judge.

Brasses Two brasses salvaged from the old church to Robert and Alice Fowler (1540) and Henry and Margaret Savill (1546) are in the Prayer Chapel on the floor of the sanctuary.

Associations

Duel Sir George Wharton and Sir James Steward (a godson of James I) fought a duel at Islington with sword and dagger in James's reign. Both were killed and, at the King's request, were buried in one grave.

Sir Richard Cloudesley, a great benefactor of Islington, was buried in the church and his tomb is in the churchyard.

Sir Edward Elgar's parents (his father was a piano-tuner) were married at St Mary's in 1848.

Incumbents Apart from Dr Daniel Wilson, who started the great Evangelical tradition which has made the Islington Conference of world-wide significance, St Mary's has had many other famous vicars and curates. Dr George Strahan (vicar from 1772 to 1824) was a friend of and frequently visited by Samuel Johnson. Dr William Barlow (vicar from 1887 to 1901) helped to set up several Evangelical theological colleges and was involved with the work of St John's Hall, Highbury, later to be the London College of Divinity and now St John's College, Nottingham. The Rev Hugh Gough (curate 1928–31 and vicar 1946–8) became Archbishop of Sydney, and the Archbishop of Canterbury, Dr Donald Coggan, was curate at St Mary's from 1934 to 1937. Another curate, the Rev David Sheppard, is now Bishop of Liverpool. The Rev Maurice Wood (vicar from 1952 to 1961) is the present Bishop of Norwich.

General

This is a church which has played and continues to play a big part in the life of the Anglican Church and the blend of Dowbiggin's steeple and Mottistone and Paget's new building symbolises how its present ministry in a heavily-populated built-up area is linked with its significant past when Islington was a quiet country village.

Other Churches in Islington

St James's, Pentonville Road (4), built in 1787 and consecrated in 1791, started as a chapel of ease to St James's, Clerkenwell. In a deprived area and looking rather shabby and neglected, the church nevertheless still makes an attractive picture with its slightly Adam-like façade and pretty cupola capped by a copper dome.

For many years, circus clowns used to hold their annual service at St James's and the most famous of them—Joseph Grimaldi—, whose grave with rose tree growing out of it beside the south wall is still carefully tended (plate p. 341)—was buried here. Richard Bonington, the talented landscape and historical painter who died at the age of 26, was also buried at St. James's.

St Mary Magdalene with St James's, Holloway (5) was built in 1812–4. Set in a large open space, the exterior has a rugged solidity relieved by a short sturdy tower which is not without appeal. The tower, which is in the east end position, is capped with a stone balustrade enlivened by gay little urns at the corners. Although a 19th century church, St Mary Magdalene has a typical and agreeably unspoilt 18th century interior with galleries and a coved gently-curving ceiling.

St James's, Chillingworth Road was built in 1837–8 and later enlarged. After being bombed in 1944, the church was converted into a church hall for St Mary Magdalane.

St James's, Pentonville Road. Grave of Joseph Grimaldi

Kensington and Chelsea

1 All Saints', Chelsea
2 St Luke's, Chelsea
3 *All Saints', Notting Hill*
4 *St Augustine's, Queen's Gate*
5 *St Cuthbert's, Philbeach Gardens*
6 *Holy Trinity, Sloane Street*
7 *St Mary Abbots, High Street Kensington*
8 *St Stephen's, Gloucester Road*

1 **All Saints', Chelsea**
Known as Chelsea Old Church
'Chelsea' is probably derived from Caelchythe, chalk wharf.

History
Until the late 18th century, Chelsea was a river village quite separate
from London. It was at one time called 'the village of Palaces' as
many notable people had fine mansions there standing in their own
grounds. Chelsea's most famous citizen was Sir Thomas More, who
lived with his family at Beaufort House.

It is likely that a place of worship existed on the site of All Saints'
Church from the earliest days. The chancel is thought to date from
the 13th century and the north and south chapels, which existed as
proprietary chapels until the 1870s, were built in 1325. The tower,
which bore a cupola until 1815, and the nave were erected between
1667 and 1670.

Towards the end of the 18th century as Chelsea expanded,
London spread towards it, until by the Victorian period they were
fused together into one urban concentration.

On the night of 16th/17th April 1941, two land mines released
from a German bomber floated down on to All Saints' and the
resultant explosion left a scene of devastation from which it seemed
that little could be salvaged. Closer inspection, however, showed
that by great good fortune the important More Chapel was less
seriously damaged than the rest of the church. After long and
sometimes difficult negotiations, it was finally decided to rebuild All
Saints' as a parish church and today, after a superlative restoration
by W. H. Godfrey, Chelsea Old Church (as it is more familiarly
known) is once more in full use with its numerous grand
monuments, although bearing the scars of war, restored to their
former magnificence.

Exterior
The church presents a homely brick exterior with its south side
facing the river. The simple, rectangular nave has been rebuilt to the
old design, also the massive tower with its strong clasping buttresses
and these, with the older parts which survived, are set in a pretty
little garden. In the south-east corner is the memorial to Sir Hans
Sloane with the charming inscription 'President of the Royal Society
and of the College of Physicians who, in the year of our Lord 1753
the 92nd year of his age, without the least pain of body, and with a
conscious serenity of mind, ended a virtuous and beneficent life'.

Interior

Attention is immediately drawn towards the east end and the wealth of impressive monuments. The nave, wider than it is long, is an unassuming and faithful copy of that which was destroyed, although the light tone of the oak contrasts too strongly with the darker tone of the pulpit and the furnishings of the chancel. A screen of three arches separates the new from the old and the monuments are grouped round the walls of the chancel and chapels, except for two in the nave.

The Lawrence Chapel to the north-east originally belonged to the Lords of the Manor—who apart from the Lawrence family included Lord Bray and Sir Hans Sloane. The bombing exposed a window in the chapel which previously had been hidden.

*The More Chapel, entered from the aisle through a depressed arch, is to the south-east. It was rebuilt by Sir Thomas More himself in 1528—the date can be seen on one of the capitals of the pillars leading to the chancel—and is undoubtedly the most interesting part structurally of the church. The capitals—by some attributed to Holbein, a friend of More, although Basil Clarke thinks that they were probably the work of French masons—are of national importance, being early and very fine examples of the new Renaissance style coming in at that time; the decoration symbolises the offices in Church and State held by Sir Thomas and includes Tudor head-dress, holy-water stoup and brush, bunch of tapers and acolyte's candles. It is interesting, in view of the derivation of the name Chelsea, to see the use of chalkstone in this chapel. An extraordinary survivor of the bombs is the original wooden roof of the chapel; the timber framing at the west end, which had been plastered over, was revealed by the bombing and has been left uncovered.

Furnishings

Royal Arms They are the Royal Arms of Elizabeth II.

Font Made of marble, the top part is original and dates from 1673. The cover is a reproduction of the one destroyed.

Chained books The chained books in the south aisle, the gift of Sir Hans Sloane, are the only chained books in any London church. They consist of the *Vinegar Bible* (1717), two volumes of Foxe's *Book of Martyrs* (1684), a *Prayer Book* (1723) and *Homilies* (1683).

Stained glass Pieces of German or Flemish 16th/17th century glass are dotted around the interior.

Pulpit Originally a three-decker, dating from the 17th century.

All Saints', Chelsea

The present one is a copy, incorporating original carving, door and one panel from the old pulpit. It is in dark wood, elevated on a pedestal with a graceful staircase containing twisted balusters.

Altar and altar rails These date from the 17th century and the rails comply with the regulations of the Bishop of Norwich that they should be 'neer one yarde in height, so thick with pillars that dogges may not gett in'. The curtain behind the altar was part of the hangings used at Westminster Abbey for the Coronation of Queen Elizabeth II.

Monuments
Chelsea Old Church possesses one of the finest sets of Tudor monuments outside the central area of London. These were scattered by the bombing and for the rest of the War were stored in the crypt of St Luke's, Chelsea. They were most skilfully replaced and reassembled by the architect Walter H. Godfrey who restored the church, and are now once more an ornament to it and one of its chief features of interest. Seven of the ten major ones are 16th century. Viewing them in an anti-clockwise direction starting from the south side, we come first to the grandest of them:

Nave
Gregory Fiennes, Lord Dacre of the South, died 1594, his wife Ann Sackville who died a year later and one child.

*Ascribed to Nicholas Johnson, it shows the main figures recumbent with hands upraised in prayer under an arch flanked by Corinthian columns with an inscription and strapwork decoration on the back. Above is a superstructure supporting a large coat of arms, two achievements and two obelisks capped with balls.

This is a sumptuous memorial and a fine example of Elizabethan sculpture.

More Chapel
Jane Guildford, Duchess of Northumberland, died 1555. She was mother-in-law of Lady Jane Grey, mother of Queen Elizabeth's favourite the Earl of Leicester and grandmother of Sir Philip Sidney. It is recessed with diapered shafts supporting a canopy enriched with fan-tracery, but was badly damaged. There is a brass against the back wall.

Chancel
On the south wall is the memorial to *Sir Thomas More*, beheaded 1535, and his first wife. Recessed, it was erected in 1532 for his wife,

for whom Sir Thomas composed the inscription.

Sir Reginald Bray, died 1539. Also recessed. A tomb-chest with lozenge-shaped panels and shields.

Thomas Hungerford, died 1581 and wife. They are shown in the typical kneeling posture of the time with small figures facing one another.

Lawrence Chapel
Sir Thomas Lawrence, died 1593. Similar to the Hungerford memorial.

Sir Robert Stanley, died 1632. He was the son-in-law of Sir Arthur Gorges whose brass is on the north wall of the More Chapel. This is a large standing wall memorial with a bust of himself and the figures of his children placed before the pedestals with large urns on top of a sarcophagus. The absence of an enclosing arch gives the memorial an unfinished look.

Sir John Lawrence, died 1638. A memorial to another member of the Lawrence family on the north wall of the chapel.

*Sara Colvile, died 1631. Daughter of Sir Thomas Lawrence. A most interesting and notable memorial artistically, erected at a time when there was beginning to be strong emphasis on the resurrection of the body and showing her rising from the tomb in her shroud with eyes and hands directed upwards; it follows the style of one of the same date by Nicholas Stone to Dr John Donne in St Paul's Cathedral and is strongly reminiscent of a later memorial at Egham (1638) to Sir John Denham.

Richard Jervoise, died 1563. Under the western arch of the Lawrence Chapel is a free-standing memorial to Richard Jervoise, son-in-law of Sir Thomas More, in the form of a Roman triumphal arch. The altar-tomb that used to be there was removed years later in order to provide room for pews. The underside of the arch is decorated with rough strapwork.

Nave
Lady Jane Cheyne, who was daughter of the Duke of Newcastle and a great benefactress to the village and the church (she provided the interior roofing). Situated on the north wall, it is a standing monument designed in 1672 with a curved front. Lady Jane is shown semi-reclining on a sarcophagus with hand on heart in a niche framed by large columns and under a segmental pediment. Pietro Bernini, who was the sculptor, was son of the great Bernini.

There is also a wealth of wall cartouches and tablets which are too many to enumerate.

Associations
Ashburnham Bell A bell, presented in 1679 by the Hon William
Ashburnham as a thank-offering for being saved from drowning,
hangs in the porch.

   Robert Henry Davies, who lived from 1821 to 1908, was
incumbent here for over fifty years. It was he who purchased the
More and Lawrence Chapels with his own money for the general use
of the church.

General
Despite being engulfed by London, the area around Chelsea Old
Church still retains some of its old riverside atmosphere. The red
brick building, with memories of its great figures of the past, tells us
much of what Chelsea was like in their lifetime when All Saints' was
their parish church. Today we are reminded even more forcibly
of its most heroic figure by the bronze statue outside, to Sir Thomas
More, unveiled in 1969.

2 St Luke's, Chelsea

History
As Chelsea developed north of the King's Road towards Kensington
a need was felt for a larger church than Chelsea Old Church and,
under the powerful impetus of the Hon and Rev Gerald Valerian
Wellesley, DD, Rector of Chelsea and brother of the Duke of
Wellington, a new place of worship was authorised by Act of
Parliament in 1819.

   The design submitted to the Board of Works by the chosen
architect, James Savage, provided for a building vaulted throughout
with panelled stone west wall and, externally, flying buttresses,
something which had not been attempted since the Reformation.
Despite the misgivings of the Board's architects, which included
Nash and Soane, Savage went ahead with his design and succeeded
in producing, in expensive Bath stone, the first thoroughgoing
Gothic Revival church in England.

   The new building was consecrated on 18th October 1824
—St Luke's Day—by Dr Howley, Bishop of London who later, as
Archbishop of Canterbury, was to crown Queen Victoria.

   Substantial alterations, which included the raising of the chancel
and sanctuary floors and the provision of many of the furnishings,
were made towards the end of the 19th century but, since then, the
only major change had been the provision of a new east window for
the one damaged during the 1939–45 War.

St Luke's, Chelsea. View from original architect's drawing

Exterior (See plate p. 349)

Surrounded by open spaces, including a wide playground, St Luke's can be viewed easily from all angles. The most arresting feature is the 142 foot high tower. Battlemented, it has octagonal turrets capped with tapering open pinnacles and is divided by nine string-courses placed at equal intervals. This handsome tower rises from a five-bay porch extending the full width of the building.

The stress of the roof is carried via flying buttresses to the wall buttresses with set-offs half-way down giving the building a rather taut appearance and accentuating the long and narrow lines. Small domed turrets surmount the east end.

Interior

The interior space follows the pattern used in the Commissioners' churches of the time in that it sets out to provide plenty of accommodation. Each element of the design was aimed to serve a functional purpose. The stone-vaulted nave is 60 feet high—the loftiest of any parish church in London—and has a triforium as well as a clerestory integrated into one composition both of which extend into the chancel. Wooden galleries are fitted in between the piers.

Eastwards the view is dominated by the raised chancel/sanctuary and the high seven-light east window. The altar and reredos are flanked by elaborate empty niches.

The original box pews were removed in the late 19th century, leaving the plinths of the nave columns exposed.

Blind panelling decorates the west end wall, above which is placed the organ casing; the console is at the east end.

In the south-east angle a chapel has been attractively fitted out as a memorial to the Punjab Frontier Force Association. A framed description tells how the link with St Luke's arose and a book records the names of those members whose memorial brasses are kept in the crypt. The Garter banner of Lord Ismay, former President of the Association, hangs on the south wall.

There is a labyrinth of vaults below the church transformed into a Youth Club in 1971.

Furnishings

*Organ One of the finest in London. It was rebuilt in 1932 by John Compton but much of the casework and some of the pipework comes from the 1824 Nicholls organ. Amongst famous organists were John Goss, who later became organist at St Paul's Cathedral, and from 1904 to 1926 the composer John Ireland. Goss wrote

many well-known hymn tunes including 'Praise my soul, the King of Heaven'.

Royal Arms The organ-case bears the Royal Arms of George IV.

Watts cartoon On the west wall of the north gallery hangs a cartoon by G. F. Watts entitled 'Time, Death and Judgement'.

Stalls At the west end under the organ are two sets of six stalls, with canopies, for wardens and guardians, dating from 1824.

Font This is a dignified and chaste octagonal example of marble. It is placed in the usual position near the main entrance but was originally at the east end. It dates from 1826.

Pulpit A massive and rather showy Victorian furnishing dating from 1893. It is elevated and adorned with marble panels. Round the tall stem and under the base are cherubs' heads.

Lectern A remarkable modern piece on a base resembling large coiled springs.

Stained glass The east window is by Hugh Easton and depicts the Trinity and saints of the church. A key to the symbols is on the pillar nearest the font.

Reredos painting Behind a curtain above the altar is a painting by James Northcote of the Descent from the Cross.

Monuments

Lt Col Henry Cadogan A memorial to Lt Col Henry Cadogan, killed in 1813 at the battle of Vitoria in the Peninsular War against Napoleon, shows two mourning soldiers contemplating a coffin. It is on the east wall of the north gallery.

Luke Thomas Flood, died 1860. A relief on the commemorative tablet shows an angel calling him to heaven.

Associations

Charles Dickens Charles Dickens was married to Christine Hogarth at St Luke's in 1826.

Charles Kingsley, author of *The Water Babies* and *Westward Ho* was a curate here for a time during the period from 1836 to 1860 when his father was rector.

General

Despite the large sum of money (£40,000), all raised by subscription, spent on the church and the great technical competence displayed by the architect, St Luke's has a somewhat cold and machine-made look about it and is not artistically a success. Nevertheless, this church will always be notable for its important place in the 19th century Gothic Revival and for the care and architectural skill which has gone into it.

Other Churches in Kensington and Chelsea

As the population of this favoured residential area grew in the 19th century, in part as a result of the Great Exhibition, the building of the museums and the founding of the Imperial Institute, many churches of note were erected. Others were built in less well-off parts of the Borough. The following are of especial interest:

All Saints', Notting Hill (3) was built in 1852–5, with young William White (nephew of Gilbert White, who wrote *The Natural History of Selborne*) as architect. The main external feature (plate p. 353) is the unusually tall, slender west tower of four stages, with an octagonal top built of coloured stones. The interior was restored after bombing in the 1939–45 War, and All Saints' has been fortunate in its post-war craftsmen. Much of the glass, including the large east window and the north transept rose window, is by Gerald Smith of A. K. Studios; other glass and furnishings, including the Lady Chapel with its striking reredos which depicts the Mysteries of the Rosary, are by Sir Ninian Comper.

St Augustine's, Queen's Gate (4). Built in 1871–6, this is one of Butterfield's characteristic London churches, designed in his highly individual manner without regard to adjacent buildings and presenting a west front of typical bands of stone and red brick (his 'streaky bacon' effect) and an aggressive bellcote. The well-proportioned interior is a good example of his skilled use of contrasts of colour and materials, including the unusual decorative treatment of black slate inlay in the chancel. Much of the effect was nullified by subsequent distempering and by new furnishings, especially the huge Baroque reredos introduced by Martin Travers but as far as possible the original colour contrasts have been restored.

St Cuthbert's, Philbeach Gardens (5) The dedication is due to the church having relics of St Cuthbert; the foundation stone came from Holy Island. It was built in 1884–7 of red brick with copper flèche and roof. St Cuthbert's is noted for its furnishings by W. Bainbridge Reynolds in the Arts and Crafts tradition. The vast reredos was the work of the Rev E. Geldart and was made in 1914.

Holy Trinity, Sloane Street (6). The present building of 1888–90, designed by John Dando Sedding who did not live to see it completed, took the place of a Commissioners' church of 1828–31 by James Savage, architect of St Luke's, Chelsea. Many artists, including Sir Edward Burne-Jones, planned the furnishing and decoration and made Holy Trinity into the finest exposition of Arts and Crafts work in a London church.

St Mary Abbots, Kensington (7). As its name implies, this church

All Saints', Notting Hill. Tower

has a long history; in mediaeval times, it was linked with the important Abbey of Abingdon. The predecessor of the present place of worship, erected in 1697, was reported in 1866 to be in a bad state and Sir George Gilbert Scott was engaged to build a new church which, to be worthy of the Lord, was to be 'truly magnifical'. The main fabric was erected in 1869–72, the 278 foot high tower and spire (the tallest in London) in 1879 and the south porch with vaulted cloister in 1889–93.

The interior does not match up to the proud exterior and the furnishings, apart from the Wren-period pulpit from the old church which some say was given to the church by William III who spent much time at nearby Kensington Palace, are of minor interest.

St Stephen's, Gloucester Road (once called Hogmire Lane) (8). The main interest of this church, built in 1866–7, is the east end of the interior which was largely the work of G. F. Bodley, carried out in 1903–4, with its massive reredos neatly set against a circular window filled with glass of rich, glowing blues.

T. S. Eliot, poet and dramatist, was churchwarden at St Stephen's for 25 years, as is recorded on a tablet on the south wall.

Lambeth

1 Holy Trinity, Clapham
2 St Peter's, Kennington Lane, Vauxhall
3 *St Mark's, Kennington*
4 *St Matthew's, Brixton*
5 *Christ Church, Streatham*
6 *St Leonard's, Streatham*
7 *St Mary's, Lambeth*
8 *St Paul's, Clapham*
9 *St John the Divine, Kennington*
10 *All Saints, West Dulwich*
11 *St John the Evangelist, Upper Norwood*

1 **Holy Trinity, Clapham**

History
In the middle of the 18th century the old church of St Mary's at
Clapham had become ruinous and it was decided not to spend more
on it but it was some years later, in 1774, that Parliament passed a
Bill for a church to be built on a new site on the north side of the
Common which was then being developed. Kenneth Couse, a pupil
of Henry Flitcroft who designed St Giles-in-the-Fields near
Tottenham Court Road, was entrusted with the work. Difficulties
were encountered with the foundations because of the wet state of
the ground but the new church was consecrated on 9th June 1776.

In 1812 a porch designed by Francis Hurlbatt was added and in
1902 A. Beresford Pite substituted a chancel for the apse. In the
meantime the Victorians cut down the pews in 1865 and lowered the
pulpit in 1875.

Holy Trinity was a late casualty from a rocket in 1945 and was
restored under Thomas Ford, who had already carried out
repairs in the 1920s.

Exterior
The church is extremely fortunate in its setting on the Common,
being one of the most open in London. It is a plain brick rectangle
with stone quoins and a stone turret surmounted by a large
octagonal domed cupola at the west end. The cupola has been
described as 'awkward' but the exterior would be rather featureless
without it.

Interior
The interior is plain, still retaining its galleries, and has been
described as a large, harmonious brick box.

Furnishing
Pulpit This is contemporary with the building of the church and
originally stood in the middle, which no doubt suited the
Evangelicals who gathered there. Until 1875 it was a tall three-
decker with a canopy supported on two pillars.

General
Holy Trinity is chiefly remembered for its associations with the
Evangelical Clapham Sect, men of importance in the City and in
Parliament who worshipped there and who secured the living for
their nominee. They included such names as the great family of

Holy Trinity, Clapham

historians (Macaulay and Trevelyan), Granville Sharp and William Wilberforce, famed for the abolition of slavery. A plaque on the south side of the exterior commemorates the group.

2 St Peter's, Kennington Lane, Vauxhall

'Vauxhall' (Fauxhall) is derived from Falkes de Breauté, second husband of Margaret, widow of Baldwin de Redvers.

History
In 1761 when Vauxhall Gardens were at the height of their popularity as a place of lively entertainment, Vauxhall or South Lambeth was a village; by 1861 Lambeth had a population of 162,000, mostly poorly housed, and St Peter's Church was built in 1863–4 to help cater for their spiritual needs.

The new church was consecrated on 28th June 1864 and is a notable example of J. L. Pearson's work, despite the fact that it was not completed as originally designed. In particular, and as so often occurred with places of worship erected in the second half of the 19th century, the planned tower and spire did not materialise; in addition only one of the four turrets was built and the decoration of the west front was never executed.

On the other hand, St Peter's escaped subsequent interference and survived the 1939–45 War. Today, like so many in the Inner London area, the parish suffers from a dwindling number of residents.

Exterior
The absence of the vertical accents which the steeple and the extra turrets would have provided detracts from the over-all impact but the church rises commandingly above the surrounding buildings including some which were constructed by Pearson and show touches of his style, as for instance the 'tourelle' of the adjoining school.

Opinions on the west front vary from 'insignificant' (Pevsner) to 'most impressive' (Clarke) but it can at least be said that it is powerful with its three-arched porch abutting right on to the pavement of Kennington Lane and its three massive buttresses. The latter enclose large plate-traceried windows, whilst above in the gable there is a circular window with similar type of tracery.

Interior
Entering through the narthex the visitor sees a fine example of 19th century architecture. Vaulted throughout and with an apsidal

chancel the interior is dignified, spacious and refreshingly free of
obtrusive detail.

It consists of a five-bay nave and one-bay chancel, aisles and Lady
Chapel, with nave and chancel of equal height without an
intervening arch. The cylindrical columns are shafted on the
aisle sides only and have large elaborate capitals each differently
carved, including one on the south side (next to the chancel) with
small figures under arches.

At triforium level the blank walling is divided into panels by
vaulting shafts and string-courses above and below; from this level
the wall slopes steeply back to the plate-traceried windows of the
clerestory. Round the apse the triforium consists of open arcades
with small windows behind, the clerestory windows become
lancets.

London grime has cast a sombre tone over the brickwork but the
Lady Chapel, which extends along the chancel and part of the nave
has been cleaned revealing the colour contrast between the yellow
stock and red brick of which the church is built. The capitals in the
chancel are also separately carved, one being of the Byzantine
basket type but with figures of Fortitude, Justice, Prudence and
Temperance added.

Furnishings

The furnishings are appropriate to the architecture.

Font Distinguished by its large pyramidal cover painted gold and
pink with a decorative window on each side; it is believed to be by
Pearson. The baptistery is in the south-west corner.

Pulpit A run-of-the-mill Victorian furnishing supported on round
columns and decorated with biblical scenes, containing large mosaic
pieces.

Screens Attractive arched parclose screens of iron separate the
chancel from the organ on the south side and from the Lady Chapel
on the north side. There is further iron work above the low marble
chancel wall.

Sedilia The most richly decorated of the furnishings with much
dog-tooth carved on the four arches and elaborate capitals. The
fourth opening is used as a credence table. Curved attractively
round the apse.

Altars The main altar is on the site of the Neptune Fountain
which used to be in Vauxhall Gardens. There are two other altars,
one in front of the chancel steps is gilded like the main altar and
has the same type of filigree decoration so that it may be
original although it came only recently from a Hertfordshire

nunnery which used to be in Vauxhall; the other altar—in the Lady
Chapel—is decorated in front with panels of beaten pewter.

Sanctuary lamps The seven lamps in the sanctuary represent the
seven early churches of Asia.

Reredos The pedimented reredos is adorned with circular motifs
and a mosaic centre-piece. This is another agreeable furnishing and
suited to its focal position.

Stained glass The triforium glass round the apse with its rich reds
is by Clayton & Bell.

Association
Edward Denny, the second vicar, was a Labour county councillor
for London. One of his sons, Sir Michael Denny, was 3rd Sea Lord.

General
St Peter's is a church of distinction by one of the best Victorian
architects, where everything—to quote Basil Clarke—is 'simple,
solid and, as the ecclesiologists would have said, real'.

It is interesting to note that the area between the church and the
railway lines which used to be occupied by Vauxhall Gardens is
again being developed as an open space, although hardly likely to
have the attractions which were such a draw to 18th century society.

N.B. Normally locked except during services.

Other Churches in Lambeth
The Borough of Lambeth has much to offer to the lover of churches
besides the two described in detail.

In the 1820s, four Commissioners' buildings were erected to cater
for the needs of an increasing population. Dedicated to the four
Evangelists (St John, St Luke, St Mark and St Matthew), two (St
John's, Waterloo Road and St Mark's, Kennington) were severely
damaged in the 1939–45 War but have been restored, **St Mark's**
near the Oval Cricket ground (3) almost entirely due to the efforts of
Wallace Bird, who persuaded the Bishop to appoint him to the
living in 1947. The Wren-period pulpit came from St Michael's,
Wood Street in the City.

Of these four churches, the outstanding one architecturally is **St
Matthew's, Brixton** (4) where the perennial problem of the steeple
riding on the roof when placed above a west end portico has been
overcome by siting the steeple at the east end, leaving the handsome
portico to answer for itself. The interior has been cleared to provide
space for a community centre but an adequate area for worship will

be provided. St Luke's, the fourth church, is situated in Norwood.

Other places of worship of particular interest are:

Christ Church, Streatham (5) beside the South Circular Road (plate below). Built in 1840–1 this was the work of a highly talented architect of only 29, John Wild, who erected a building of refreshingly crisp design in Italian basilican style. A campanile rises sheer to a height of 113 feet in the south-east corner and the excellent brickwork has many refinements of cut and colour. The interior, apart from the apse which is decorated with three mosaic

Christ Church, Streatham

murals, has been stripped of most of its decoration by war damage and is drained of colour, but there is some good modern glass.

St Leonard's, Streatham (6), with a long history, is effectively a Victorian church of the mid-19th century which has recently been restored after a disastrous fire in May 1975. It nevertheless retains its links with the days when Streatham was a sought-after village and a centre of polite society, including the circle of distinguished people, such as Burke, Garrick, Goldsmith, Reynolds, Dr Johnson and Boswell, who gathered at the home of the Thrales. Even a certain mediaeval atmosphere lingers on. At the end of the north aisle are three memorials to the Thrale family on two of which Dr Johnson composed the Latin inscriptions.

St Mary's, Lambeth (7), next door to Lambeth Palace, was completely rebuilt in 1851–2 except for the lower parts of the tower, some say as a replica of the old church. It is redundant but the Tradescant Trust plans a museum of garden history at the church. It is notable for possessing the only font in London for baptism by total immersion (installed in the south-west corner in 1904) and, outside, for its two sarcophagi to John Tradescant (d. 1638) and members of his family—he was Charles I's gardener—and to William Bligh (d. 1817) of the *Bounty* and his wife.

St Paul's, Clapham (8) was erected in 1815 as a chapel of ease to Holy Trinity. Although it would not draw the visitor for any architectural virtues, it contains one feature of great interest. This *is the monument to Sir Richard Atkins (d. 1689), his wife Lady Rebecca (d. 1711) and their three children, all of whom died before the parents; this monument, which now lies in the Lady Chapel, was once in the mediaeval church dedicated to Holy Trinity situated where St Paul's now stands. The craftmanship is of a high order; particularly charming is the standing figure of Rebecca, the youngest child who died in 1661 at the age of 8; she holds a skull in her hand.

St John the Divine, Vassall Road, Kennington (9) was built in 1871–4 to the designs of G. E. Street. It is fortunate in that there were enough funds to add in 1888–9 the fine tower and spire, unlike many others (e.g. St Peter's, Kennington Lane) with steeples planned for them which were never built. Despite extensive war damage, St John the Divine has been fully restored at a cost of £140,000 by H. S. Goodhart-Rendel. This is a large and notable Victorian church. The last bay of the nave is canted inwards to the narrower chancel.

All Saints, West Dulwich (10) is an impressive church of brick set up high on a sloping site and dominating Rosendale Road, built between 1888 and 1891 by G. H. Fellowes Prynne. The nave is in 13th and the eastern apsed end in 14th century style. It is mainly

St Mary's, Lambeth. Bligh tomb

distinctive by its canted bays at the end of the nave and the screen, characteristic of the architect, filling the whole of the chancel arch. There are ambulatories round the apse and the Lady Chapel—also with apse to the north.

The west end is incomplete and the projected tower was never built; a flèche erected over the junction between nave and chancel had to be taken down.

St John the Evangelist, Upper Norwood (11). Just beyond the boundaries of the Borough of Lambeth is this outstanding J. L. Pearson church, built over the years 1881–7. Tall clerestory lancets and a high-pitched roof impart a strong vertical emphasis despite the fact that the spire planned above the tower never materialised. The interior (plate below) is a fine work in Pearson's mature Early English style, full of subtleties and exciting oblique vistas, beautifully proportioned with clean lines, vaulted throughout and restrained in decoration. The plain yellow stock brick provides a neutral-toned background for the stone detail.

St John the Evangelist, Upper Norwood

Lewisham

1 St Paul's, Deptford
2 *All Saints', Sydenham*
3 *Church of the Ascension, Blackheath*
4 *St Lawrence, Catford*
5 *St Mary's, Lewisham*

1 St Paul's, Deptford

Deptford
Probably derived from 'deep ford'.

History
One of four major churches erected in the east and south-east of
London under the 1711 Act to meet the needs of a growing district,
St Paul's was created out of the older St Nicholas' parish in what
used to be known as West Greenwich.

The architect was Thomas Archer, our most Baroque architect.

Building began in 1712 but, as with the other three churches,
proceeded slowly and consecration did not take place until 30th
June, 1730.

The area later lost its wealth, which may have saved St Paul's
from intensive Victorianisation, for the repairs carried out in 1856
and a rearrangement in 1883 left it little altered. It was also
fortunate in a careful restoration carried out during the 1930s.

Today, as a result of substantial contributions from local
authorities and a great self-effort within the parish, much excellent
restoration at a cost of over £100,000 has been completed. More
remains to be done but the church—bright and fresh—is a joy to
visit.

Exterior
This is one of the major architectural thrills of London. Set well
back at an angle to the beautifully kept and spacious churchyard
which fans out as the church is approached, and open on the east
side, this dazzling white building of great distinction makes a
powerful impact. Thomas Archer succeeded in overcoming the
problem of the awkward relationship between portico and steeple
'riding on the roof' by making the tower circular and letting it
project into a semicircular portico around which he wrapped a wide
radial staircase.

The portico has large Tuscan columns and is crowned by a
balustrade; the steeple derived from St Mary-le-Bow recedes in
diminishing circular stages with pilasters, urns below and spiral
scrolls above, culminating in a rather attenuated spire.

On the north and south sides there are also projecting porticos
but the staircases, instead of being semicircular, emerge at right
angles to the wall and then turn to run parallel with it.

At the east end, a curved apse echoes the semicircular west front.
A Venetian window and the pediment above follow the curve.

The whole of this grand exterior is set on a raised platform which adds further stateliness.

Interior
The basically square interior is canted at the angles, behind which are vestries and staircases leading up to small galleries projecting far in front and looking like outsize theatre boxes. Above these are large windows. Giant Corinthian columns with capitals picked out in gold and a pastel shade of blue knit the composition together into one harmonious whole. The ceiling has deep panelled recesses.

The chancel, which is enclosed within a frame of pilasters flanked by Doric columns, lies in a shallow apse and is the least interesting feature.

Furnishings
Many fittings are of Dutch oak and their brown tone accords well with this bright interior. The pews are plain.

Font The Victorian font in Norman style came from Rochester Cathedral, the original having been sent to a mission church overseas. It is out of keeping.

Chandelier A fine chandelier which is a focal point adds further dignity to the interior.

Pulpit The pulpit, S in shape, has an iron staircase.

Communion rails The same material is used for the rails.

Reredos This extends on all three sides of the apse.

Stained glass The north-west window contains good 18th century glass, depicting a saint. The east windows are in Pre-Raphaelite style.

Monuments
John Harrison A tablet commemorates John Harrison, died 1753, who was founder of and first surgeon at the London Hospital. This is in the body of the church on the right-hand side near the statue of St Joseph.

Dr Charles Burney The profile of Dr Burney, brother of the novelist and letter-writer Fanny Burney, is shown against an obelisk which is in relief. There is also a bust to him. A rector of St Paul's, he died in 1817.

Matthew and Maria Finch Two separate monuments to Matthew and Maria Finch, who both died in 1745, are in the form of a standing wall monument with sarcophagus and an urn against an obelisk respectively. They are to the right of the sanctuary.

Admiral John Sayer The monument by Nollekens to the left of

St Paul's, Deptford. View from west

the sanctuary is an epitaph with large trophy. The Admiral died in
1776.

Margaret Hawtrees, a midwife, is recorded by an inscription on a
monument which reads:

'She was an indulgent mother, and the best of wives.

She brought into this world more than three thousand lives.'
The monument is to the left of the High Altar.

Obelisk in churchyard The obelisk dating from 1807 in the
churchyard commemorates the Stone family.

General

However controversial Thomas Archer's other London church—St
John's, Smith Square—may be and despite the Victorians'
description of St Paul's as 'pagan and pompous', there can be no
doubt today about its merits. Many would rate it as the finest 18th
century parish church in London and some, going even further, as,
externally, the most outstanding in the Metropolis of any period.

With its parish life transformed during recent years and the
church a focal point of the community, St Paul's—beautified and
restored in a way which the Hawksmoor East End places of worship
so sadly need—is an inspiration to all who have the future of the
Church at heart.

Other Churches in Lewisham

In addition to the thrill of St Paul's, Deptford, the Borough of
Lewisham has other more modest architectural pleasures to enjoy in
its churches.

The unpromising exterior of **All Saints', Trewsbury Road,
Sydenham** (2), an Edwardian church of 1901–3, hides an attractive
but incomplete interior. Three bays of tall, octagonal piers have
arches which die into them without capitals, all of brick banded with
stone, and a large, traceried stone screen which fills the whole of the
chancel arch. This is a feature characteristic of the architect, G. H.
Fellowes Prynne, also seen in his churches at All Saints, West
Dulwich (see Borough of Lambeth) and Holy Trinity, Roehampton
in the Borough of Wandsworth.

The Church of the Ascension, Dartmouth Row, Blackheath (3) was
founded as a proprietary chapel in the 1690s and retains from that
time a charming coffered apse framed in coupled columns/piers with
gilded capitals. Most of the rest was rebuilt in 1824. After the
1939–45 War, the galleries were removed except for the western one
which was cut back; this is supported on slender columns of iron

encased in plaster and carries a modern Baroque organ; the apse was re-decorated at this time. The exterior is enhanced with an attractive cupola. The chapel became a parish church in 1883.

A most original design is that of **St Laurence, Bromley Road, Catford** (4), built as recently as 1967–8 by Ralph Covell. The church is circular with clerestory of modern, thick glass set in concrete and has appropriate furnishings following the shape of the structure. The starkly simple Lady Chapel, predominantly blue, which has been likened to a Crusader's tent, contains a most graphic carving in jacaranda wood of the martyrdom of St Laurence by Samuel Wanjau, a noted artist of Kenya, which expresses the human face in great pain but with the body in an attitude of prayer. The exterior of the church which is less pleasing has an open-work spire set above the Lady Chapel and is surmounted by a crown with balls on the points reminiscent of the crown of Christ but looking rather like a ducal coronet.

St Mary's, Lewisham (5) is set effectively at an angle to the main thoroughfare. The tower dates back to 1471 but the church, built of an attractive greenish-golden stone, was mainly constructed in the 1770s by George Gibson who added the elegant crown to the tower capped by four balls at the corners. An unusual feature is the broad south porch with four columns and pediment.

The interior suffered a particularly insensitive Victorian restoration and the main points of interest are four monuments, which are of considerable merit, to Anne and Margaret Petrie, Mary Lushington and John Thackeray.

Southwark

1 St George the Martyr, Southwark
2 St Mary Magdalene with St
   Olave's, St John's and St Luke's
3 St Mary's, Rotherhithe
4 *St Augustine of Hippo, Lynton*
   Road, South Bermondsey
5 *St Giles', Camberwell*
6 *St James's, Thurland Road,*
   Bermondsey
7 *St Peter's, Walworth*

1 St George the Martyr, Southwark

Dedication
This was the only church in pre-18th century London to bear this
dedication. St George was born of Christian parents in Cappadocia
(southern central Turkey). His father was martyred and, after being
tortured during the Diocletian persecution, St George suffered a
similar fate in 303 AD.

He became the patron saint of England and his white banner with
red cross forms the basis of the Union Jack. The saint is usually
shown as trampling upon a fiery dragon but, in the east window of
this church, the edict of the Roman Emperor Diocletian against
Christianity takes the dragon's place.

'Southwark' refers to the southern bastion of the City of
London's defences.

History
There have been at least three churches on this site. In 1122, the
living was given to Bermondsey Priory. There was a rebuilding in
the 14th century and, prior to the Reformation, the Brotherhood of
St George and the Company of Leathersellers maintained chantries
in the church.

'Repaired and beautified' in 1629 and the south 'Ile' enlarged,
there were further repairs in 1682 and 1705 (to the steeple) but a few
years later the church was in such a poor state that a petition was
put in to the Commissioners of the Fifty New Churches requesting a
grant for repairs. No progress, however, could be made until a Bill
was passed through Parliament in 1732 authorising a rebuilding,
against the cost of which the Commissioners were prepared to
allocate £6,000.

The work by John Price—started in 1734 and completed in
1736—appears to have been badly done as frequent repairs were
needed and in 1807–8 a major restoration. At the end of the 19th
century, the architect Basil Champneys, who had reported very
unfavourably on the fabric, carried out various alterations
including the new ceiling.

Work on the south wall in 1939 helped to protect the church
during the War and the damage was made good by T. F. Ford in
1951.

Exterior
St George's is splendidly placed on an island site visible from all
sides. Built of brick with Portland stone dressings and possessing a

St George the Martyr, Southwark. From north-east

City-like steeple, it bears a family resemblance to St James's, Clerkenwell and St Mary's, Rotherhithe. The steeple—also of Portland stone—is a sturdy structure with diminishing octagonal upper stages and an almost solid spire. The clock—illuminated on three sides only—lies under elegant curved moulds. A balustrade and urns complete the tower.

The main entrance at the west end is placed between engaged Ionic columns supporting a segmental pediment. Side windows are in two tiers and, at the east end, there is a Venetian window decorated with a cartouche and garlands above.

Interior

A typical 18th century interior with galleries and low box-pews, and an open chancel and sanctuary. The galleries, which are on slender iron pillars enclosed in oak panelling, were lowered in 1742; the side ones have modern boxes for illumination which are obtrusive.

The dominant feature is the flat Basil Champneys ceiling, badly damaged during the War but skilfully restored by T. F. Ford in 1951. The design consists of cherubs amongst clouds carrying scrolls upon which are written words from the Te Deum and Benedicite, the oval plaster decoration now being delicately tinged with pink, blue and gold.

Furnishings

Organ This was transferred from the old building but was given a new case. It still contains Father Smith and Renatus Harris pipes.

Font The present font is modelled on an earlier one dating from the time of Henry VIII which was used in the local workhouse for beating oakum. It was rescued and is now in the chapel of the Old Palace School at Croydon.

Lead cistern It is rare to find one of these 18th century receptacles for water inside a church. This one, dating from 1738, is now used hopefully for alms.

Royal Arms This finely carved Stuart example once formed part of the reredos of St Michael's, Wood Street. The rest of the reredos has gone to St Mark's, Kensington.

Pulpit A delightful free-standing example, one of the tallest in London. It is supported on four Ionic columns.

Communion rails These graceful rails are of iron.

Bells Worthy of mention in that they are one of the very few existing complete peals in the country from the foundry of Abraham Rudhal of Gloucester. They were recast in 1718.

Stained glass The east window is a post-war replacement by

D. Marion Grant of the one lost in the War but the treatment of the Ascended Christ is different. Pilgrims with scallop shells are to be seen in the centre light whilst Dickens' 'Little Dorrit' is a small figure with poke bonnet in the left panel. Elsewhere St George and other saints appear. There is an interesting detailed description in the guide.

Stained glass on the south side also depicts St George and came from a nearby school after it was closed down in 1930.

Monuments
There are two small brasses on either side of the chancel arch.

Associations
Nahum Tate, the author of the carol 'While Shepherds watched their Flocks by night' was buried here in 1715.

Bonner, Bishop of London in Queen Mary's reign, was consigned to the Marshalsea prison when her sister Elizabeth succeeded to the throne and was probably buried here secretly in 1569.

General Monk, instrumental in restoring Charles II to the throne, was married here in 1653.

Anne Digwid According to the registers, Anne Digwid died at the age of 101 in 1654, having had seven husbands.

Charles Dickens lived as a boy of 12 in nearby Lant Street whilst his father was in the Marshalsea prison for debt. His experience led to his casting the area as the scene of events in his novels. Little Dorrit was born in the Marshalsea, found shelter as a waif in St George's vestry and was married in it, so that it has come to be known as 'Little Dorrit Vestry'.

The workhouse in *Oliver Twist* was inspired by the parish workhouse in Mint Street.

General
In mediaeval times, Southwark was the exit from London to the Continent and there were many, like Henry V on 26th April 1417, who stopped at St George's to offer up a prayer and make an offering before embarking upon some enterprise. Nearby at the Tabard Inn, Chaucer set the scene for the start of his pilgrims' journey to Canterbury whilst opposite lay Brandon Palace where Philip of Spain and Mary stopped after their marriage at Winchester.

Later, never having reached full civic status, Southwark lapsed into becoming the centre of activities such as bear-baiting, and of places like play-houses, prisons and even thieves' kitchens not

St George the Martyr, Southwark. Pulpit

wanted in the City. In the 18th century, St George's Fields was the scene of the Gordon Riots and in 1856 the then rector drew a grim picture of life in the Borough.

Now, things are better but through all these changes a church has existed on the present site providing help and comfort to the unfortunates around and still exercising an active ministry amongst the more fortunate of today.

2 St Mary Magdalene with St Olave's, St John's and St Luke's

Bermondsey
Probably 'Beormund's Eye', the islet (Eye is Saxon for islet) of Beormund, a personal name. There was at one time a low eminence above the riverside marshy ground.

History
The mediaeval history of the area is dominated by the great Cluniac Priory of St Saviour, founded before before the Conquest, which considerable influence until it was dissolved in 1537. It became an abbey in 1399, after severance of its connection with the parent abbey of Cluny 25 years earlier. Here at Bermondsey two Queens of England died: Margaret de Valois, widow of Henry V and later wife of Owen Tudor, and Elizabeth Woodville, the upstart widow of Edward IV.

St Mary Magdalene Church was built beside the Priory for their 'servants and tenants' (compare St Margaret's, Westminster and St Katharine Cree Church in the City) and is first recorded in 1296 as belonging to the monastery. No trace of the first church remains and, apart from the lower part of the tower, a window concealed behind the organ and some dressed stonework, the same applies to its successor.

After the dissolution of the Abbey, the church became parochial. Enlarged in 1610 by the widening of the south aisle and altered in 1621, it nevertheless became unsafe by the latter part of the century and was pulled down. The influx of rich merchants and others from the City after the Plague and the Fire may have affected the decision to build a new church.

This was constructed between 1675 and 1677 by Charley Stanton e designs of an architect who is not known, retaining the old and perhaps part of the north aisle. In 1793 galleries were d and the tower may have been heightened about this time. If was probably the cause of the trouble it gave in 1830 when the top stage was removed and the present gabled structure substituted; the west front was then re-done in 'Gothick style', all this work being carried out by George Porter, a Bermondsey architect.

Repairs in 1852 were followed by a lengthening of the chancel for choir stalls in 1883 and the provision of new furnishings and the north-east vestry.

Since then the church has been left alone, apart from necessary repairs after 1939–45 war damage and a fire in 1971.

St Olave's, the oldest church in Bermondsey, was founded before 1066. The last church on the site was erected soon after 1734 but closed, due to fall in population, in 1918 and pulled down in 1926. St John's, Horslydown was one of the places of worship built under the 1711 Act for Fifty New Churches but was not rebuilt after war damage. St Luke's was built in 1884 and demolished in 1965.

Exterior

The west front of St Mary Magdalene is practically all the rather amateur 1830 effort of George Porter in what Pevsner describes as 'playful Gothic' with stucco and the projecting aisles ending at the west end in castellated lean-to roofs. The tower has pinnacles, and the gabled top stage is capped with a diminutive lantern. Stucco was also applied to the other walls.

On the south side, there is a large window under a semicircular gable.

Interior

By contrast, the interior is basically late 17th century plus the galleries and the extended chancel.

Tuscan columns support an entablature which turns outwards at the west end of the nave to form a rudimentary crossing. The later galleries are not integrated with this, being supported on separate spindly columns and set close to those on the north side but further back on the south; they also cut across the transepts formed at the crossing and, on the south side, do not go beyond the aisle, which is wider than the north aisle.

The elliptical ceiling of the nave is irregularly groin-vaulted to conform with this pattern whilst the aisle and chancel vaults are depressed, the latter being of the coffered barrel type.

In the north-west corner is a blocked-up doorway leading at one time to and from a school which until the 1830 alterations was above the porch.

Furnishings

Organ Originally a Christopher Schrider instrument but replaced by Joseph Walker in 1853 and restored after war damage and the 1971 fire. The case was made in 1750.

Font Marble bowl wit cherubs' heads of Wren period on stem of 1808. In the south aisle.

Churchwardens pew A large rectangular furnishing with seating all round and a four-sided reading desk enabling the pew to be used as an office as well as for worship.

Hatchments The hatchments on the south wall are of the Gaitskell family.

Candelabra The two fine candelabra of Dutch type date from 1698 and 1703 respectively.

Altar at end of south aisle This was rescued from St John's, Horsleydown, after the bombing, to which church it came in 1926 from St Olave's after the latter was demolished. This is a fine example of the celebrated smith Tijou's work but, although restored, it lost its marble top in the bombing.

Reredos This was reconstructed in 1907 using the old panels of the Ten Commandments, Creed and Lord's Prayer and the paintings of Moses and Aaron from the original reredos.

Stained glass The east window dates from 1883 and depicts the washing of Christ's feet, apparently set in the house of Lazarus, Mary and Martha.

Monuments

There are interesting memorials to *William Casteil*, died 1681, who is commemorated with an elegant and fairly large epitaph and to *William Steavans*, died 1712–13.

Associations

Maypole A Puritan rector cut down, chopped up and burnt the church maypole in 1611, rather on the pattern of what the parishioners at St Andrew Undershaft had done about 60 years earlier in the City.

Sermon Another Puritan rector preached a sermon of 69 pages, ending 'one hundred and twenty-seventhly'.

James Harriott is recorded in the register as having 40 children.

General

It is strange that, apart from a stone bearing a consecration mark in a local garage, a pair of hinge pins from the south gate at No. 8 Grange Walk and possibly a couple of capitals in the church, the Abbey of Bermondsey has completely disappeared. St Mary

Magdalene maintains the link with this great monastic institution
which was the centre of life in Bermondsey in mediaeval times and
where Queens of England ended their days.

3 St Mary's, Rotherhithe

Rotherhithe
'Rotherhithe' may be derived from 'Aetheredes Hyth' (mentioned in
a charter of 898) or 'rethra' (mariner) 'hythe' (haven).

History
Whatever the derivation, St Mary's has the closest links with ships,
and the sea, and is only separated from the River Thames by empty
warehouses opposite. The mediaeval church was even closer and the
foundations were frequently flooded.

St Mary's has a long history, going back at least to the 13th
century and possibly earlier. In mediaeval times, the church came
under the Abbey of Bermondsey. It must have kept itself out of the
limelight for one incumbent, John Fayrwall, who was rector from
1537 to 1562 managed to survive the Reformation and another,
Thomas Gataker (who was rector from 1611 to 1654) the Civil War.

The old church was repaired in 1687 but, not long afterwards, the
flooding had so weakened it and the accommodation was so limited
that the parishioners petitioned the Commissioners of the 1711 Act
for a new one. The petition can still be seen at the foot of the stairs
leading to the west gallery; the parishoners refer to themselves as
'being chiefly seamen and Watermen who venture their lives in
fetching those coals from Newcastle which pay for the Rebuilding of
the Churches in London, and Parts adjacent' (there was a tax on
coal for this purpose); they asked to be allowed to 'Use duty laid on
Coals' after it was no longer required for St Paul's Cathedral.

The petition was turned down and the parishioners were thrown
back on their own resources. As a result, although work started in
1714 and the new church was open in 1715, they ran into constant
difficulties in paying for what had been done and finding the money
to carry on. The steeple and the sanctuary were not started until the
late 1730s nor completed in the former case until ten years later.
Launcelot Dowbiggin was probably the builder of the steeple; he
also built the very odd one at St Mary's, Islington.

The spire portion was rebuilt in 1861. Later, the architect William
Butterfield went through the usual processes of removing galleries,
lowering the pulpit and making a space for a choir, but without too
much harm to the simple Georgian interior.

Exterior

St Mary's lies in a quiet, leafy corner, forming a pleasant group with the old Charity school (stone children outside) and the rectory opposite without being so overshadowed by warehouses as churches on the other bank of the river so often are.

This homely and 'friendly' building is of brick (yellow with red dressings). Stone is used for the quoins and as trim for the windows, which at the sides are in two tiers, five round-headed above and three segmental-headed below. At the east end which projects there is one large window under a pediment. The whole is completed with the steeple and a neat parapet with modillion cornice.

The steeple consists of a plain brick tower with stone quoins and a stone spire, divided into a circular lower stage enclosed in Corinthian columns and an obelisk spire above. The spire looks somewhat of an afterthought.

Interior

The largely 18th century interior provides constant reminders of sailors and ships. Even the Ionic nave columns are ships' masts of oak, cased in thin plaster shells.

The columns form three unequal bays. The west gallery remains, supported on thin wrought-iron stanchions (cf St Magnus the Martyr in the City). The north and south galleries, which were taken down, have been used for the chancel stalls. There is a shallow-vaulted ceiling with panelled ribs.

At the east end, Butterfield introduced wrought-iron rails to enclose the chancel but these are no disfigurement. Otherwise, contemporary furnishings maintain the 18th century atmosphere.

Furnishings

Organ The organ is still in its original Byfield case, dating from 1764. It is adorned with musical instruments and, at the top, angels blowing trumpets.

Reredos The reredos contains fine original carving which, as the pea-pod occurs in a couple of places, has inevitably been attributed to Grinling Gibbons.

Altar-table This was made of timber from the '*Fighting Témeraire*', the famous 104-gun man of war which was at the Battle of Trafalgar. Built in 1798, it will long be remembered from Turner's painting showing it being towed to the breaker's yard at Rotherhithe.

Sanctuary chairs They were also made from 'Témeraire' timber and are a nice pair with trefoil-pierced pointed backs.

St Mary's, Rotherhithe

Pulpit Part of an old three-decker, it is hexagonal, inlaid and panelled, and has fluted angles.

Altar-rails and Sanctuary panels These are also original fittings.

Chandelier The chandelier is another attractive furnishing.

Royal Arms There is a finely carved Royal Arms of Charles II's time.

Monuments

*John Wade On the south wall, there is an outstanding wall cartouche, commemorating John Wade—'King's Carver in his Majesty's Yards at Deptford and Woolwich', described by Pevsner as 'delicious'. He died in 1743. The monument is crowned by a playful cherub. On the sides, a cherub's head on the left is set against a skull on the right, all with most delicate carving.

Captain Anthony Wood This is a monument almost contemporary with the sailing of the *Mayflower* depicting in high relief a ship in full sail very like it. Captain Wood died in 1625. Christopher Jones, the master of the *Mayflower*, was buried in Rotherhithe and a 250th anniversary commemoration plaque to mark this is recorded below the monument.

Prince Lee Boo On the north wall, there is a poignant plaque to the memory of this Pacific Island Prince, whose father was reputed to be a cannibal. The Prince befriended shipwrecked British sailors in 1783 and, out of gratitude, was brought to England, where he promptly died of smallpox at the age of 20. 'The barbarous people showed us no little kindness.'

Painting A painting in the south aisle shows Charles I holding a crown of thorns.

General

This appealing church is an interesting survival, like St Mary's, Battersea, of a riverside village church. It contains most evocative reminders of our maritime past, and still maintains a strong community life.

Other Churches in Southwark

The Borough of Southwark which embraces the oldest parts of London south of the river and where the great Priory of Bermondsey (see St Mary Magdalene) exercised its sway, offers a wide variety in its churches. Amongst those not described in detail there are three 19th century places of worship deserving of special mention: **St Augustine of Hippo, Lynton Road,** South Bermondsey (4) has a rare dedication to the North African saint who, after a wayward youth, became one of the leading influences in the thinking of the Church. The future of this little-known building is uncertain but architecturally it is a product of merit, completed in 1882–3. The interior presents a wide spaciousness in the Early English lancet style. A striking feature is the pink-coloured Dumfries sandstone used for the arcades, and the tall white Portland stone stiff-leaf capitals which are richly carved.

St Augustine of Hippo, Lynton Road, South Bermondsey

St Giles', Camberwell (5) is the South London equivalent of St Mary's, Stoke Newington, being designed by the same architect, Sir George Gilbert Scott, although a slightly earlier building. The central tower with broach spire rises to a height of 210 feet, but is restless in outline and is not improved by the fussy dormers. The interior (plate below) benefits from a notable east window of five lights—rich in blues, reds, yellows and greens—designed on the basis of a study of 13th century glass at Chartres and Rheims. On the south wall of the chancel, the sedilia and piscina from the mediaeval church dating from 1300 have been reinstalled and there

St Giles', Camberwell

is a set of brasses, dating from 1492 to 1637, on a panel under the south transept window.

St James's, Thurland Road, Bermondsey (6), one of the finest and most expensive of the 'Waterloo' churches, was designed by James Savage, architect of St Luke's, Chelsea, and was built in 1827-9. After a long period of uncertainty following war damage, this handsome place of worship, described by H. S. Goodhart-Rendel as having 'a design of great dignity and good sense' was restored and reopened for worship in 1966. St James's is distinctive for its impressive steeple terminating in a magnificent golden dragon, and for its nobly-proportioned interior with deeply-coffered nave ceiling contrasting with the shallow-coffered arched chancel ceiling.

The ten bells were cast from cannon captured at the Battle of Waterloo; and an association which has found its way into the Guinness Book of Records is the celebration at St James's on 21st June 1883 of a marriage which turned out to be the longest in Britain (82 years).

St Peter's, Walworth (7), another Commissioners' building, is the first and architecturally the most interesting of Sir John Soane's three London churches; built in 1823-5, it has a typical Ionic portico of four giant columns above which is a stone steeple, containing a very attenuated pepper-pot drum encircled with nine columns and terminating in a beehive stone dome and vane.

The galleried interior is open and light with thin arches at each end. The font (plate p. 389) has a large round top on an elegantly-shaped stem and base, all of marble.

St James's, Thurland Road, Bermondsey

St Peter's, Walworth. Font

1 St Anne's, Limehouse
2 Christ Church with All Saints', Spitalfields
3 St Dunstan's with All Saints', Stepney
4 St George-in-the-East
5 Tower Chapels (St John the Evangelist and St Peter ad Vincula)
6 *All Saints', Poplar*
7 *St Augustine's with St Philip's, Stepney*
8 *St John on Bethnal Green*
9 *St Mary's, Cable Street*
10 *St Matthew's, Bethnal Green*
11 *St Matthias', Poplar*
12 *St Paul's, Shadwell*

1 St Anne's, Limehouse

Dedication
It is not known whether the St Anne to whom this church is
dedicated was the mother of the Virgin Mary or one of the other St
Annes but it seems probable that a saint of this name was chosen
because of Queen Anne's concern for the welfare of the Church,
and in particular for her giving the money annexed to the Crown by
Henry VIII from certain mediaeval dues to form a fund, called Queen
Anne's Bounty, for augmenting the stipends of the poorer clergy.

History
At the beginning of the 18th century, the hamlet of Limehouse was
part of the large parish of Stepney but, with increasing population, a
need was felt for a separate church and under the 1711 Act for the
creation of 'fifty new churches in and around the Cities of London
and Westminster and the suburbs thereof', work on a new place of
worship was entrusted to Nicholas Hawksmoor. This was to be the
first of three grand churches to be built in Stepney by this highly
individual architect.

Construction started in 1714 and progress was steady until
financial problems slowed it down; it was not until 1724 that the
fabric was completed, after which another five years was to elapse
before a sufficient endowment for the rector could be raised.
Because of these difficulties, Limehouse did not become a separate
parish until May 1729, and consecration could not take place until
four months later in September of that year.

In 1850, on Good Friday, St Anne's was gutted by fire and it took
another six years before money could be found to carry out the
restoration. Even then, had it not been for the foresight of a
Dissenter, who much against his will had been appointed a
churchwarden, the cost to the parish would have been a great deal
more. He had persuaded the Vestry to take out insurance cover
shortly before the fire.

In 1891, the architect, Sir Arthur Blomfield, a pupil of P. C.
Hardwick who had carried out the 1852–6 restoration, rearranged
the sanctuary and provided choir-stalls.

The church survived the 1939–45 bombing but is today in a bad
state of repair and in urgent need of attention.

Exterior
Despite the increased height of surrounding buildings, this church is
still one of the most conspicuous landmarks in the East End. From

whichever way one looks at it, St Anne's is an impressive sight, but particularly from the little lane leading to the west end. The tower rises up spectacularly, with its top stages set at different angles, the lower part made broader by buttresses and attic storeys rising above flanking vestibules. The outer half of a tall circular porch projects from the centre.

By comparison the north and south sides are relatively restrained.

Mystery surrounds the pyramid on the west side of the churchyard but, at the eastern end of the building, there are two square pedestals and an artist's drawing exists which shows a pyramid on each of them. The suggestion is that they were never erected because of shortage of money but that one was supplied and after remaining in the churchyard for some time was used as a tombstone. It may well have commemorated a number of sea captains.

The clock is the highest church clock in London.

Interior
The restoration by Hardwick has retained the spacious grandeur of

St Anne's, Limehouse. Watercolour of *c.* 1840

the original building and despite the need for re-decoration and repair, the interior is a forceful piece of architecture. Giant Corinthian columns break up the rectangular space and an extra nave bay provides longitudinal emphasis. The oval plastered ceiling of the nave contrasts with the segmental arch leading into the vaulted chancel. There are galleries on three sides and colour is afforded by the large east window which, framed in coupled Corinthian columns, takes the place of a reredos.

Furnishings
Font Dates from 1853 and was designed in marble by Hardwick.
Pulpit Of oak designed by A. W. Blomfield, one of the first works of this well-known Victorian architect, and carved by William Gibbs Rogers. It is contemporary with the font.
Organ Made by Gray and Davidson, it gained a prize at the Hyde Park Great Exhibition of 1851.
Stained glass The subject of the east window is the Crucifixion, which is depicted in great detail, including even the dice cast for Christ's garments. The technique, rarely used in the 19th century, is the application of coloured enamels to white glass. The designer was Clutterbuck.

Associations
St Anne's has associations with the Maoris and a Maori Ngapuhi chief, Kamariera Te Hautakiri Wharepapa, was married here in 1864 to Elizabeth Reid of Marylebone.

General
A big question mark hangs over the future of St Anne's. With a reduced number of parishioners and a large sum of money needed in a parish which was never wealthy, the problem of restoration is a formidable one. Many would regard the church as an expensive and decaying 'white elephant' but, although Hawksmoor's art is an acquired taste, there can be no doubt that this is a major architectural monument which should not be allowed to disappear. It is to be hoped that, following the example of St Paul's, Deptford, where a church of outstanding merit has been restored to its full life and beauty, a solution can be found. A major restoration appeal has been planned.

N.B. Special arrangements to visit interior necessary as normally locked except during services.

2 **Christ Church with All Saints', Spitalfields**

Spitalfields
The name comes from the Priory of St Mary, Spittle (Hospital)
which lay where Spital Square is now situated. Sermons, known as
Spital sermons, and attended by the Aldermen, Sheriffs and
occasionally the Sovereign, were preached after the Dissolution until
1642 from a cross within the hospital churchyard.

History
Christ Church is one of the three vast churches built by Nicholas
Hawksmoor under the 1711 Act to meet the needs of parts of
Stepney which, by the beginning of the 18th century, had become
populous. Protestant refugees from France had settled in Spitalfields
in large numbers and their hand-weaving of silk brought prosperity
to the area. Work on the foundations started in July, 1714 but, as at
St Anne's in Limehouse, financial problems were to hold up
construction; this came to a complete standstill in 1719 and Christ
Church was not consecrated until July 5th, 1729 by which time the
original estimate of a little over £9,000 had risen to £40,000,
including site and minister's house.
   The Industrial Revolution dealt a death-blow to the hand-
weaving and the character of Spitalfields changed to what we see
today.
   Although repairs and restorations were carried out from time to
time in the 19th century (on one occasion after the church had been
struck by lightning in 1841), the parish has not had the resources to
maintain such a grand building and the East End is saddled with a
crumbling edifice which architecturally must not be allowed to
disappear. In 1958, it was considered dangerous and closed for
worship.
   Until recently, the building, despite the expenditure of £50,000 on
the roof and ceiling, looked a forlorn sight—in a derelict churchyard
and badly in need of major restoration—but it is encouraging to
report that as a result of the formation of 'The Friends of
Christchurch Spitalfields' funds are being raised for urgent repairs
and life is returning to the church with concerts and occasional
religious services, including a Harvest Thanksgiving on behalf of the
adjacent fruit and vegetable market, and it is hoped to bring Christ
Church back into full use. The stained glass in the east window,
which was boarded up, has been cleared and the side windows re-
glazed—a great improvement.
   The crypt is used as a rehabilitation centre for alcoholics.

All Saints', consecrated in 1839, was damaged in the 1939–45 War and closed in 1951 when the parish was united to that of Christ Church. The building was demolished shortly afterwards.

Exterior
From whichever direction one approaches, but especially from the west, this is an overpowering building. The tower and spire rise dramatically to a height of 225 feet, the tower appearing as wide as the imposing portico below. The portico, raised on steps, has four Tuscan columns with a semicircular arch in the middle. Niches are inserted into the tower face, and projecting cornices give horizontal emphasis. The spire at one time was crocketed and had spire-lights but it was altered in 1822 and smoothed to the plain broach spire we see today.

Turning to the sides, which are plainer, it can be seen that the width of the tower is a deception created by the use of very deep buttresses with concave hollows between, which are pierced by windows.

At the east end, a Venetian window placed high up is flanked by round-headed and porthole windows. There is also a line of the latter below and they appear in the north and south walls.

Interior
The interior, which has been described by Sir John Betjeman as 'massive, simple and gigantic', is a rectangle divided by giant Composite columns into aisle bays with tunnel vaults. At the east end an architrave with two extra columns in the middle to support it is carried right across the nave to create a chancel. The coffered ceiling, of wide span, is flat and has been redecorated.

The north and south galleries were removed in the 1866 restoration, thus upsetting the proportions of Hawksmoor's church and, for no apparent reason, the pedestals of the columns were chamfered.

A vestibule under the tower separates the portico from the nave.

Furnishings
Apart from the organ casing at the west end and a Royal Arms perched on the architrave, there is a handsome but very low pulpit with good carving, which was the reading desk of a former three-decker.

General
Christ Church is a sombre and grandiose building which one must hope can be restored to full life. The renewal of the ceiling, made

possible by the sale of St John's, Smith Square, gives hope that full restoration will one day be undertaken. All praise must be given to those who, despite the difficulties, are carrying on the ministry in the parish and providing dedicated work of rehabilitation in the church crypt.

N.B. Closed at present.

3 St Dunstan's and All Saints', Stepney

Dedication
Originally called 'All Saints', the name of St Dunstan was added to the dedication of the parish church of Stepney (probably derived from Stebba's Hithe or landing-place) after his canonisation in 1029.

History
Dunstan, Bishop of London 959–61 AD and thereby Lord of the vast Manor of Stepney covering all that we know now as the East End, may have rebuilt or enlarged a small Saxon church. In the 13th century, a further reconstruction (at least partial) took place, of which the outer chancel walls remain, but what we see today is largely 15th century.

The church owes its mediaeval character to the fact that, unlike many others in London, it was not pulled down in the 18th century to make way for a larger place of worship. Instead, the rising population of Stepney was accommodated in new parish churches. It was, however, found necessary to increase seating at St Dunstan's by adding galleries. These were gradually removed as congregations changed and dwindled and finally, at the end of the 19th century, they were taken away altogether.

Numerous Victorian restorations have left their mark. The north and south porches and the large north-east octagonal vestry are from this period and, in 1871–2, the exterior was refaced with Kentish ragstone.

Extensive damage caused by a fire which broke out in the organ-loft in October, 1901 and by a V.1. bomb which exploded in the churchyard in January, 1945, has been made good and St Dunstan's has survived as a mediaeval church of much interest.

Exterior
The large, leafy churchyard park, where many plague and cholera victims are buried, imparts a village atmosphere and the open space

St Dunstan's, Stepney

around has been made larger by adding recreation grounds etc. to the churchyard on three sides, providing a most agreeable oasis. From the south-west all looks mediaeval and is probably similar to many London churches as they must at one time have been. It consists of a battlemented tower with angle buttresses and pinnacles, and a long, low body with small clerestory windows. The upper part of the tower had to be rebuilt after the bombing.

A staircase at one time giving access to the rood-loft projects from the south wall; it is crowned by a beacon tower.

Interior

The dominating impression is of the long, low lines of the nave and chancel. The chancel arch was removed in the 15th century and the chancel set further back so that the nave and two aisles with their two-light clerestory windows stretch for seven bays. The total length is 150 feet, considerable for a village church as it was for so many years.

The situation of the former chancel arch is indicated by the door in the south wall to the rood-loft and by the change in design of the roof (of keel type with cambered tie-beams).

Nave pillars, from which the 18th century paintwork was removed in 1871-2, are standard 15th century work with four attached shafts and concave hollows in the diagonals. The east window (see *Stained glass*) was dedicated in 1949.

A notable feature of the chancel is the triple sedilia with coupled columns in the south-east wall; this was part of the 13th century church.

In a wall of the tower there is a stone from the walls of Carthage inserted in 1663 with the words 'Time consumes all; it spares none'.

Furnishings

*Rood A precious survival from the Saxon church (one of only two Saxon features to be found in London churches) is the rood placed above the altar-table. It depicts the Crucifixion with Our Lord in an attitude of suffering, attended by the Virgin Mary and St John. It is of great sensitivity, recalling the swaying figures of contemporary manuscript paintings. A border of rosettes surrounds the figures.

Stained glass The most unfortunate east window, portraying Christ as a muscular Tarzan and with a bad sense of colour, is by Hugh Easton but it is mitigated by the charming little scenes at the base. Another window in the south aisle is also by Hugh Easton.

Panel The appealing panel of the Annunciation in the chancel dates from the 14th century.

Coffin lid A coffin lid with tapering sides and carved cross is 13th century.

Monuments

Sir Henry Colet A memorial in the chancel commemorates Sir Henry Colet, Lord Mayor of London in 1486 and 1495, who died in 1510. It is in the form of a tomb-chest in a recess, the back of which has blank panelling, the top, cusped arches and quatrefoil parapet.

Robert Clarke (died 1610) and daughter, and *Elizabeth Starture* (died 1620) are portrayed as kneeling figures in the usual style of the times.

Mary Leybourne (died 1731) A tablet records 'She wanted not spirit nor wit or a just knowledge of her selfe'.

Associations

John Colet, the son of Sir Henry (see *Monuments*) and founder of St Paul's School, was vicar here in 1485.

Thomas Spert, founder of Trinity House, is buried in the churchyard.

Stephen Segrave, a rector in the 14th century, became Archbishop of Armagh.

Richard Foxe, rector in the 15th century and founder of Corpus Christi College, Oxford, became Bishop of Winchester.

General

Mediaeval churches are rare in London. For many years, St Dunstan's was the only parish church in the vast area of Stepney, which was largely rural, but since the 14th century, 66 other parishes and churches have been created out of mediaeval Stepney in the area now known as Tower Hamlets. 'For more than 1,000 years'—as the board outside the west door reads—'the people of God have met here to offer prayer and worship to God, and have gone out from here to love and serve their neighbourhood'. Even today, despite all that has happened, the much restored church of St Dunstan's manages to hold on to its mediaeval character.

4 St George-in-the-East

History

In the 17th and 18th centuries, the vast parish of Stepney was being broken up into smaller units and the area of Upper Wapping qualified under the 1711 Act for a new church. On a site 'in pleasantly wooded fields' beside where the once notorious Ratcliff Highway now runs, gradually arose one of Nicholas Hawksmoor's strangest flights of fancy; this was to serve a riverside parish inhabited by people who owned and sailed ships. As with his two other monumental East End churches (St Anne's, Limehouse, with which it was almost contemporary, and Christ Church, Spitalfields) building, beset by financial difficulties, took a long time; work, started in 1714, was not completed until 1726. Even then, another three years was to elapse before sufficient endowment for the incumbent could be found and the church consecrated.

Between 1859 and 1860, some of the most disgraceful scenes of modern times to take place in a Christian church occurred in St George's. The rector, the Rev Bryan King, and his curate, C. F. Lowder, were High Churchmen who introduced a very moderate form of ritual, wearing surplices instead of the generally used black gown. The Bishop who had appointed King and who favoured surplices was succeeded by a man, born a Presbyterian, determined to stamp out High Church practices; he nominated a militant Low Churchman, Hugh Allen, vicar of a neighbouring parish, to be afternoon lecturer at St George's. This led to organized disruption whenever King or Lowder tried to conduct a service: pelting the altar with garbage, catcalls, jeers: men still wearing their hats and smoking their pipes; even trombones were blown and, on one occasion, dogs drugged to make them howl were brought into the church. Press reports led to hooligans coming from other parts of London to add their quota to the disorder, whilst magistrates, influenced by Low Church members of the Vestry, did little to help. The matter was only resolved by the Rector being persuaded to hand over to a locum after his health had given way.

The position was aggravated by the deterioration of this once respectable area into a terrible slum with narrow, dirty streets, unsavoury houses and much violence.

Victorian changes to the church were mild; apart from the removal of the reredos and the decoration of the apse with Venetian glass mosaics in 1880, the rather dark Georgian interior was retained until it was swept away by incendiary bombs in May 1941. The east windows were designed by Sir Joshua Reynolds.

For nineteen years St George's lay a gaunt, silent ruin on the Highway but, in 1960, Arthur Bailey, an architect, worked out an ingenious scheme for rebuilding. It consisted of repairing the walls and tower: erecting a smaller, modern place of worship in the eastern part of the old nave: transforming the space between the west end of the new church and the old into an open courtyard and

St George-in-the-East

converting the area formerly occupied by the galleries into residential flats. Below, the old vaults would be cleared and a splendid new parish hall would take their place.

This plan was carried out between 1960 and 1964, and the church reconsecrated on April 26th, 1964, thus grafting a modern element on to the old roots.

Exterior
The gleaming white exterior of Portland stone gives little hint of the changes within and we can again stare in wonder or dismay at this strange building. Each Hawksmoor church is unlike any other and St George's is no exception, the closest resemblance being to St Anne's, Limehouse.

A massive 160 foot high tower with tall rectangular openings and deeply recessed windows rises dramatically at the west end, made to look even wider by the grooved piers at the sides. The crown is an open octagonal lantern with eight rectangular buttresses topped with Roman altars, the whole looking like a little castle.

Tall turrets, also with eight buttresses, are surmounted by copper-roofed cupolas. Resembling a profusion of pepper-pots, these contained staircases to the galleries. Projections at the west and east ends mark where the transepts used to be, forming a double Greek cross.

At the east end, an apse projects from the middle of a flat wall with large pediment.

Since 1966, the houses which obscured the view from the south and which Hawksmoor failed to get moved have disappeared, giving a much finer aspect from this side.

Interior
A spacious and lofty portico leads into the courtyard beyond which glass doors give access to the new church.

No attempt, other than restoring the mosaics dating from 1880 and replacing five panels in the ceiling of the apse, has been made to reconstitute what was there before and we see today a bright, modern interior suited to contemporary needs.

Furnishings
Font The stone font in the north aisle is the only furnishing which has survived the bombing. It came from the City church of St Benet's, Gracechurch Street (pulled down in 1867 for road-widening) and was first used at St George's in 1877.

General

Although views differ as to whether over £100,000 should have been spent to build a church in a district where four exist already, there would have been even less reason for rebuilding the huge church that was destroyed by the bombs. The new Hall and Church are in constant use as a theatre and concert hall, in this way developing as an Arts Centre, and many of the young actors and musicians who come here are attracted by the modern church to take part in services of worship, thus extending its mission well beyond the confines of the parish.

5 Chapels of St John the Evangelist and St Peter ad Vincula, Tower of London

Situation
In the White Tower and the north-west corner of Inner Ward respectively.

Dedication
St Peter ad Vincula—St Peter in chains.

History
The Chapel of St John the Evangelist was built at the same time as the White Tower and is the oldest surviving example of Norman ecclesiastical architecture in London and one of the oldest in England. It was the private chapel of William the Conqueror and, after his death, continued for a time to serve as the Sovereign's personal place of worship.

In 1381, the mild Sudbury, Archbishop of Canterbury, was dragged away from the chapel whilst at his prayers by the furious mob in the Peasants' Revolt. He was later executed on Tower Hill amidst 'ferocious yells of triumph'.

The body of Henry VI, after his murder whilst he knelt in the oratory of the Wakefield Tower on 21st May, 1471, is said to have been placed in the chapel before being removed to Chertsey Abbey in Surrey for burial—secretly 'without priest, clerk, torch or taper, singing or saying'.

Elizabeth of York, wife of Henry VII, lay here in state after her death in 1503, whilst 50 years later in 1553 the unfortunate girl queen—Lady Jane Grey—used it for prayer in the nine days of her imprisonment before execution. The rightful queen, Mary, was

betrothed by proxy in the same chapel to Philip of Spain in the
following year.

From the 17th to 19th centuries, St John's Chapel was used to
store records, but worship was resumed later and it was restored in
1968.

St Peter ad Vincula was rebuilt in 1513 and is not the first chapel
on the site. The original building was demolished by Edward I in
1286 and a new one erected between 17th June of that year and 6th
April, 1287. This lasted until 1512 when it was severely damaged by
fire, thus leading to the construction of the present place of
worship.

But, although built at the end of the mediaeval period, its
associations are no less tragic. The scaffold that faced it on the
Green was the scene of the execution, amongst others, of two of
Henry VIII's wives and of Lady Jane Grey. Their bodies were
thrown hugger-mugger into the ground below the nave, only to
receive decent burial during a restoration in 1876. They now lie
under the chancel floor beneath stones which carry their coats-of-
arms. St Peter's is also the burial-place of two martyrs, Sir Thomas
More and John Fisher, who were executed for refusing to
acknowledge the king as head of the Church. Macaulay has said of
St Peter's chapel 'in truth there is no sadder spot on earth' but
today, after another restoration in 1971, with its clear glass windows
and delicate architecture, St Peter's is a place of light and the
memory of these grisly associations is dimmed.

Architecture

These two buildings, so different in style, mark the beginning and
end of the mediaeval period. St John's shows the Norman style at its
most uncompromising and seems almost hewn out of the solid rock
like an Indian rock-temple. There is little in the way of decoration
but the way in which the nave and the gallery above are carried
round in the form of an apse and the starkness itself impart a
rugged strength which makes it a compelling piece of architecture.
The nave has a tunnel vault—a rarity in England. Being completely
enclosed by the encircling rooms there is an air of impenetrability
about it which, however, did not save the unlucky Sudbury
(mentioned earlier).

St Peter's is in a much lighter style, with slender columns. Being
detached from the adjoining buildings it stands out clearly. The west
end is crowned with a small brick tower and an attractive lantern.
The church consists of nave and shorter aisle with a flat roof.

Furnishings

The furnishings of St Peter's include the following:

Font The original Tudor font was broken into four pieces during the Commonwealth period and secreted by the chaplain in the Cholmondeley tomb. Later the chaplain was caught and executed by Cromwellian soldiery and it was not until the 1876 restoration that it was rediscovered and restored to its rightful place.

Organ One of the oldest in the City of London. It was built in 1679 by Father Smith—a famous maker of organs—for the chapel of the Palace of Whitehall, and the wooden carvings of cherubs are ascribed to Grinling Gibbons. Some of the original pipes are still in place. The organ was moved to St Peter's in 1890 and restored in 1953.

Pulpit The pulpit of English oak is modern with a glass frontispiece depicting the Crown of the King of Kings and surrounding flames which symbolise the seven gifts of the Holy Spirit.

Monuments

The oldest is the memorial to *John Holland*, Duke of Exeter, moved to St Peter's from Regent's Park Royal Foundation in 1949. It lies in the north-west corner. The stone used is a very white chalkstone and the crisp, curly, cusped arch, elaborated with trumpeting angels, gives an almost sugar-icing effect, perhaps a shade too sweet. It dates from 1447.

The Cholmondeley memorial lies under the second nave arch from the west and dates from 1544. Sir Richard was at one time Lieutenant of the Tower but later moved away and was eventually buried elsewhere, thus leaving the tomb empty and providing space for the font (see earlier).

On the north of the chancel is a standing wall monument to *Sir Richard and Sir Michael Blount*, dating from 1620. These two men—father and son—were also Lieutenants of the Tower. There are groups of kneelers, a typical Jacobean feature, and the materials used are alabaster and marble. The skull in the hand of one wife and the cap string blown over the head of the other indicated widowhood.

Opposite is a curious memorial to *George Payler*, his wife and their children showing the family in four separate ovals with the one at the foot flanked by putti.

Other monuments are to Captain Valentine Pyne, dating from 1677, with cannon and a ship in relief, Sir John More (1679) and Captain William Bridges (1716).

Associations
Henry VI Each year on 21st May, the anniversary of the
assassination of King Henry VI, representatives of Eton College and
King's College, Cambridge which he founded, lay lilies and roses on
the spot where his body was discovered (see *History*).

General
These two chapels, so tranquil today, are standing monuments to
the barbarities of the mediaeval age.

They are now used by residents of the Tower; services are held
every Sunday (Church of England at St Peter's and Free Church at
St John's.)

Other Churches in Tower Hamlets
Although the East End is not well-to-do, it is one of the richest areas
in London for fine churches.

All Saints', Poplar (6). This imposing building, constructed in
1821–3 of Portland stone and set off by an impressive tower and
spire reflects the ambition of the residents to have a church which
they felt would be worthy of them, and is a landmark in the Poplar
townscape. Internally, the most striking features are the baldacchino
(plate p. 407) and the western organ-gallery.

St Augustine's with St Philip's, Stepney (7). This, the largest
church in the East End, was built in 1888–92 by Arthur Cawston
largely at the expense of the first vicar the Rev Sidney Vacher
who was determined to have something better than the dilapidated
chapel which existed before. The red brick exterior rises to a great
height and, if the western tower had been completed, would have
been striking. One need have no reservations, however, about the
pale yellow stock brick interior, for it is vaulted throughout, has
double aisles with apsed chancel and Lady Chapel, transepts,
clerestory and a richly-moulded triforium of double twin arcades
above the nave bays.

St John on Bethnal Green (8). This was a Commissioners' building
and the second of Sir John Soane's London churches, built in
1825–8, but extensively remodelled in 1871 after a fire. The excellent
siting at the end of Bethnal Green Road has been largely spoiled by
the main railway line which cuts across the western façade (plate
p. 408); this is surmounted by a tower crowned with a small stone
cupola. The best part of the interior is the vestibule which has
exciting vistas through the arches opening to the basement under the
tower.

St Mary's, Cable Street (9). This is another church which was the inspiration of one man, in this case the Rev William Quekett who gave much selfless service in the East End. Built of stone in 1849–50, it is plain externally with a south-east tower. The main feature of the interior, which is nicely uncluttered, is the lectern.

St Matthew's, Bethnal Green (10). This church was built by George Dance the Elder in 1743–6 and rebuilt after a fire in 1859. Externally with its plain brick it looks like a cousin of the two St Mary Magdalenes at Holloway and Woolwich, but internally it

All Saints', Poplar. Baldacchino

St John on Bethnal Green

owes much to the gaily coloured re-decoration after it was gutted in the 1939–45 War. Of many attractive features perhaps the most beautiful are the Stations of the Cross in varying colours by Donald Potter.

St Matthias', Poplar (11). This church started in 1654 as a private East India Company chapel but, after being rebuilt in 1776, suffered much from an insensitive restoration by Samuel S. Teulon, who recast the exterior in the second half of the 19th century. Internally, however, it has retained what might be described as a quarter-deck appearance because of its width and openness, heightened by the use of timber for all but one of its columns (reputedly made from the masts of East India merchantmen). There is a notable memorial to George Steevens by Flaxman dating from 1800.

St Matthias' was closed in 1977 and has since suffered from serious vandalism.

St Matthew's, Bethnal Green

St Paul's, Shadwell (12). This is another church which started life in the Cromwellian period, being built in 1656 as a chapel of ease to St Dunstan's, Stepney. The present church is a 'Waterloo' church consecrated in 1820. The steeple, which is set in a spacious, leafy churchyard, is similar in design to that of St Leonard's, Shoreditch (plate below). The modest, galleried interior with columns mostly of scagliola (composition of marble chippings, paste and glue) is rather dark. It contains original font and pulpit, and charming lectern.

The church is often referred to as the Church of the Sea Captains. More than 175 names of commanders and their wives appear in the register between 1730 and 1790, including Captain James Cook whose son was baptised here in 1763. The mother of Thomas Jefferson, third President of the U.S.A., was also baptised in the old St Paul's.

The future of this place of worship is uncertain.

St Paul's, Shadwell

1 All Saints', Tooting Graveney
2 St Mary's, Battersea
3 *All Saints', Wandsworth*
4 *St Anne's, Wandsworth*
5 *St Mary's, Putney*

1 **All Saints', Tooting Graveney**

Tooting Bec/Tooting Graveney
'Tooting' may indicate the settlement ('ing') of the people of Tota.
'Graveney' is the name of a local river; 'Bec' recalls the ancient
connection with the Abbey of Bec Hellouin in Normandy, from
which the great Archbishops Lanfranc and Anselm came in early
Norman times.

History
All Saints was built out of funds bequeathed by Lady Augusta
Georgiana Sophia Brudenell-Bruce in memory of her husband, the
son of the 1st Marquess of Ailesbury (Aylesbury), who died in 1897.
The architect was L. Temple Moore and the foundation stone was
laid in October 1904, consecration taking place in July 1906.

Exterior
The exterior of yellow stock brick is fairly plain and the elevations
of the sides are broken by the gables of the aisles pointing outwards
away from the main building. The south-west battlemented tower
has two belfry windows on each side and angle buttresses
terminating at the belfry stage. There is a square-ended Lady Chapel
beyond the chancel.

Interior
The exterior gives little hint of the beautifully proportioned and
distinguished seven-bay interior within, which has the luxury of
double aisles to the nave and single aisles to the chancel, providing
many and varied vistas. The aisles are roofed in white-painted
timber and the shafts between the aisles support arches which
separate the bays transversely.

The chancel opens out into the Lady Chapel through an arcade of
three bays; a similar arcade at the west end opens out into the
vestibule.

Furnishings
Many of the furnishings were collected by the first vicar, Canon
Stephens, from Italy and France, and date back to the Renaissance
period. These have been adapted by the interior designer, Walter
Tapper, who added further fittings of his own and introduced the
olive green and gold colour scheme. All this admirably blends in
with the architecture and suits the atmosphere of the church.

Memorial plaque and bust Behind the font on the west wall is a memorial plaque and bust to Lord Charles Brudenell-Bruce.

Organ and organ-case The richly gilded organ-case, designed by Tapper, houses a fine Harrison 3-manual instrument which has not been altered.

Font The marble font and wooden cover are also by Tapper.

Pulpit The disproportionately small green panelled pulpit with octagonal stone base was probably designed by Temple Moore.

Lectern This is a copy of the fine 18th century lectern brought by Canon Stephens from Italy to St Oswald's Church, Blankney, Lincolnshire, which was his living before he came to All Saints'.

Candlesticks The very large wooden candlesticks standing ten feet high came from Florence.

Iron grille Came from a church near Lake Como and is thought to be the oldest fitting in the whole building.

*Reredos The *pièce de résistance* is the Baroque reredos from Bologna with broken segmental pediment and gilt and fluted pilasters/columns. The painting above the finely carved and gilded high altar is a copy by Raoul Maria of Velazquez' 'Crucifixion' in the Prado Gallery at Madrid.

All Saints', Tooting Graveney

Choir stalls, credence table, tester canopy and preacher's chair came from Bologna. The stalls are panelled and decorated with urns and acanthus cresting.

Lady Chapel altar-piece Origin and date uncertain, but thought to be German and may be 16th century. The carved Crucifixion above the altar could be as early as 14th century.

Stained glass The stained glass in the east window is by Victor Milner and represents bishops of the diocese in which Tooting Graveney has been situated over the years i.e. Canterbury, London, Rochester and Dorchester (transferred to Winchester). The 20th century is represented by two windows installed in 1956 of Bishop Talbot of Rochester and Bishop Simpson of Southwark.

General

This is the finest and probably the largest church in South London. In addition to being a place of worship, the church is used for musical recordings by famous conductors.

2 St Mary's, Battersea

Battersea

In 693 AD Battersea was referred to as 'Batrices Ege' or 'Badrices Ege'—probably Badric's isle—but there were at least 77 variants of the place name. In Domesday it is called 'Patricesey'. The site on which the village was built was in fact a gravel island bounded on the north by the river and surrounded by misty marshland.

History

William the Conqueror granted the Manor to Westminster Abbey in 1067. The English Pope, Nicholas Breakspear (Adrian IV) confirmed the Abbey in their ownership including the church in 1157.

As a result of this connection, St Mary's enjoyed work from the shop of the great mason, Henry Yevele, who constructed the nave of the Abbey. From his workshop came the east window, the shape of which survives in the present one. There were many alterations between the 15th and 17th centuries and by the 18th century the building had a miscellany of windows in different styles, a long staircase on the south side giving entry at the first floor, various dormers and a quite imposing battlemented tower, rebuilt 1639, with clasping octagonal buttresses.

Like other mediaeval London churches which lingered on into the second half of the 18th century, the building became dilapidated and

St Mary's, Battersea. Memorial to Sir John Fleet

St Mary's, Battersea

hardly suited to the fashionable residential suburb which Battersea had become, said to have the 'second best carriage congregation in London'.

Joseph Dixon, churchwarden and local architect, therefore submitted plans for a new church which were accepted; Richard Dixon was the builder. The frame of the east window and its glass and tracery were kept but otherwise the fabric was entirely rebuilt, although following almost exactly the ground line of the old building. Work began in July 1775 and the church reopened in November 1777.

In 1876–8, extensive reconstruction and repairs were carried out by Sir Arthur Blomfield during which he made space for a choir and provided new seating.

There was some war damage but this has been made good.

All Saints', Wandsworth

Exterior
An unassuming rectangle of pleasant yellow brick with an attractive
portico of Tuscan columns plus plain pediment, and appealing
steeple with stone quoins and green copper spire. An endearing oriel
window peeps out behind the columns. The side windows are in the
usual two tiers for galleried interiors.

Interior
A simple and largely unaltered 18th century interior fitted with
seemly pews, and galleries on three sides having unusual supporting
brackets in front with benefactions written on them. The ceiling is
flat with a scalloped motif and garlands in the centre. There is no
chancel and the nave opens out into the panelled curve of the
sanctuary with its arresting east window and roundels on each side.
At the end of the south aisle is a side-chapel with interesting modern
triptych (see *Altarpiece*). The organ is sited in the north-east corner.
There is much to enjoy and there are many fine monuments.

Furnishings
Font Of white marble and coming from the earlier church. The
existing large bowl was added by Blomfield in 1878 and placed on
top of the original basin.
Pulpit Once part of a three-decker and still very high; the lower
parts now serve as sidesmen's pews in the west corners of the
church. The decoration is Victorian.
Lectern One of the lecterns came from the studio of Holman
Hunt the artist, who painted 'The Light of the World'.
Sanctuary rails Dating from 18th century, they are made of a
combination of lead and iron. They were re-erected in 1938,
replacing a Victorian rail.
Altar-piece The side chapel altar-piece, painted by John Napper,
shows Gospel scenes in 'Battersea' terms (e.g. the Annunciation in
the centre is set against a background of Battersea Park and Power
Station).
Turner's chair The chair on which the artist J. M. Turner sat to
contemplate his riverside sunsets and cloud effects is in the north-
west of the sanctuary.
Candlesticks Made in 1938 of wood from the old roof which was
rebuilt at that time.
Chandelier A nice modern example.
**Stained glass* The east window is the most striking feature of the
church, glowing with yellow and gold. Probably by Bernard van
Linge, it was installed in 1631 by Sir John St John after his

succession to the Manor. At the base are medallions of Henry VII, Margaret Beauchamp and Elizabeth I and, in the middle, heraldic shields, all advertising Sir John's royal antecedents and his connections with distinguished families by marriage.

*The delightful circular transparencies of the Dove and the Lamb at the sides, which blend so well with the window, were the work of James Pearson in 1796. The Dove roundel was shattered by a bomb in 1944 but has been skilfully restored by Miss Joan Howson.

A new stained glass window by John Hayward has been inserted in one of the lower windows on the south side as a memorial to General Benedict Arnold (see *Monuments*).

Royal Arms
Royal Arms of Elizabeth I and of George IV are on the north and south walls of the apse.

Monuments
Nicholas Stone, Roubiliac and Scheemakers are all represented in memorials to the St Johns, Battersea's most famous family. Other important ones are in the galleries. Taking them in a clockwise direction, there are:

North side gallery
Sir Oliver St John, Viscount Grandison, died 1630 and his wife *Joan Holcrofte* by Nicholas Stone, master mason to James I and Charles I. Two frontal busts under a heavy segmental pediment and between columns.

Henry St John, Viscount Bolingbroke died 1751 and his second wife *Mary Clara des Champs de Marcilly*, Marchioness of Villette, died 1750. He was Secretary of War in Queen Anne's reign and the most famous of the St Johns; the Marchioness was a niece of Madame de Maintenon, Louis XIV's wife. The epitaphs were written by Bolingbroke himself. The monument in green, white and grey marble is by Roubiliac and of excellent quality with two portrait medallions to the left and right of the apron and, above, an urn under heavy drapery.

Sir John Fleet, died 1712. He was Lord Mayor of the City in 1693 and a member of the Grocers' Company who repaired the memorial in 1881. A wall cartouche with shields, cherubs' heads at top and bottom and very rich flower and fruit carving. Drawn curtains with prominent tassels enclose the inscription. A fine monument (plate p. 416)

South side gallery
Sir Edward Wynter, died 1686. A relatively plain memorial

recording in the inscription his more improbable exploits such as crushing a tiger to death and taking on single-handed 60 mounted Moors. A relief on the apron shows two of his feats.

Holles St John, died 1738, half brother of Bolingbroke (above). An urn with foliage trails set between two smaller urns. It is of grey and white marble and is by the Antwerp sculptor, Peter Scheemakers.

John Camden, died 1780 and his daughter, *Elizabeth Nield*, died 1791. In the form of a tall nymph standing beside a pedestal with an urn and constructed of the well-known artificial Coade stone once made at Lambeth to a formula now lost. The monument is signed by Coade with date 1792.

Crypt

Benedict. Arnold, American general. A memorial records that he, his wife and daughter were buried here between 1801 and 1828 and the inscription records that he was 'Sometime General in the Army of George Washington' and that 'The two nations whom he served in turn in the years of their enmity have united in this memorial as a token of their enduring friendship'.

Associations

St Mary's is also rich in associations and many of its vicars were outstanding men.

William Blake, poet, artist and mystic, and writer of the well-known hymn 'Jerusalem', was married here in 1782 to Catherine Boucher, daughter of a Battersea market gardener. She signed the marriage certificate with an X.

Edward Hyde, later Earl of Clarendon and Charles II's great minister, who steered the Restoration on to a firm course, married Anne Ayliffe, his first wife who was a cousin of Sir Walter St John, in the church in 1631.

Edward Adrian Wilson, one of Scott's gallant companions on the ill-fated expedition to the South Pole, lived in the former vicarage and worked at a boys' club in the district. There is a plaque on his old home nearby.

General

Much as Battersea has changed and although sandwiched between Lots Road, Chelsea and Fulham power stations, the area round the church is still a riverside oasis and the atmosphere is extraordinarily peaceful.

Other Churches in Wandsworth

At the beginning of the 19th century much of Wandsworth was semi-rural.

All Saints' (3), with a long history, is a modest unassuming church of which parts of the chancel, the porch and the north aisle date back to the 18th century; the tower dates from 1630 but was raised a storey in 1841 (plate p. 418). The galleried interior has a roomy square churchwardens' pew and two good monuments including one to Henry Smyth (d. 1627), noted for his benefactions to Surrey towns.

St Anne's (4), a Commissioners' building of 1822–4, is well sited in a commanding position. It has a disproportionately tall round stone pepper-pot tower which is almost a carbon copy of that at St Mary's, Bryanston Square by the same architect. The open and spacious galleried interior is well lit by clear glass.

St Mary's, Putney (5), which makes such an effective counterpoise to All Saints', Fulham at the other end of Putney Bridge, was largely rebuilt in the 19th century. It was the victim of a devastating fire in 1977 but fortunately the West Chapel, the chief architectural feature, survived. The church is famous for the meetings of Cromwellian leaders held there in 1647.

Roehampton

The parish church of Roehampton is Holy Trinity built 1896–8 by G. H. Fellowes Prynne. It has his characteristic traceried screen filling the whole of the chancel arch. The spire is 200 feet high.

St Anne's, Wandsworth

Bibliography

ATKINSON, THOMAS D., *Local style in English Architecture* (Batsford, 1947).

BARNES, GORDON, *Stepney Churches* (The Faith Press for the Ecclesiological Society, 1967).

BETJEMAN, SIR JOHN, *The City of London Churches* (Pitkin Pictorials, 1969).

BUMPUS, T. FRANCIS, *Ancient London Churches* (T. Werner Laurie, 1908).

CLARKE, BASIL F. L., *Parish Churches of London* (Batsford, 1966).

CLIFTON-TAYLOR, ALEC, *English Parish Churches as Works of Art* (Batsford, 1974).

COBB, GERALD, *The Old Churches of London* (Batsford, 1942).
   N.B. This has now been brought up to date in a new edition called *London City Churches* published by Batsford in 1976.

COLVIN, H. M., *A Biographical Dictionary of English Architects. 1660–1840.* (John Murray, 1954).

ELLEN, R. G., *A London Steeplechase* (City Press, 1972).

GUNNIS, RUPERT, *Dictionary of British Sculptors, 1660–1851* (Odhams Press, 1953).

KENT, WILLIAM, *An Encyclopaedia of London* (J. M. Dent & Sons, 1970, *revised by Godfrey Thompson*).

NAIRN, IAN, *Nairn's London* (Penguin Books, 1967 reprint).

PEVSNER, SIR NIKOLAUS, *The Buildings of England* (Penguin Books). 1. London—except the Cities of London and Westminster (1952, hardback 1969) 2. London—The Cities of London and Westminster (1957, later editions 1962 and 1973).

STOW, JOHN, *Survey of London* (Everyman Edition) (J. M. Dent & Sons, 1970 reprint).

YOUNG, ELIZABETH AND WAYLAND, *Old London Churches* (Faber & Faber, 1956).

Glossary

Acroteria Foliage-carved stone blocks.

Ambulatory Semicircular or polygonal aisle.

Apse Semicircular or polygonal termination to chancel.

Apse, Dalmeny, Linlithgowshire, c 1150

Architrave Lowest of three main components of entablature: surrounds (e.g. jambs, lintels) of a door or window.

Ashlar Hewn or squared stone.

Atrium Entrance hall or inner court of a Roman house, sometimes open to the sky.

Aumbry A receptacle, usually a recessed cupboard, for sacred Communion vessels.

Baldacchino (baldaquin) Canopy supported on columns.

Ball-flower

Ball-flower Form of 14th century decoration—globular flower with three incurved petals.

Baluster A small pillar usually circular: a column swelling in the middle or towards the base.

Barrel-vault See **Vault.**

Boss Projecting ornament placed at intersection of ceiling ribs.

Chapter-house, Oxford Cathedral, c 1220

Cartouche Tablet with ornate frame usually enclosing an inscription.

Caryatid Human figure used as column.

Chamfer Angle pared off.

Chrysom Robe confined in long swaddling bands worn by infant after baptism until churching of mother.

Clerestory Upper storey of nave or chancel wall pierced by row of windows.

Coade stone Artificial stone made in Lambeth by Coade and

Seely to a formula now lost.

Coffering Panels sunk in ceiling for decorative purposes.

Console Bracket or corbel frequently in form of letter S used in classical architecture to support cornices etc.

Corbel Stone bracket.

Broadwater, Sussex, c 1250

St Benedict's Church, Lincoln, c 1350

Credence table Small table beside altar upon which the bread and wine are placed before being consecrated: a shelf over a piscina.

Crenellate To embattle a parapet with notches or embrasures.

Crocket Leaf-shaped projection.

Hereford Cathedral, c 1250

Kidlington, Oxfordshire, c 1350

Choir, Lincoln Cathedral, c 1200

Litcham, Norfolk, c 1450

King's College, Cambridge

Diaper Surface decoration, incised or in low relief, consisting of squares or diamonds.

Dog-tooth Early English decoration in form of raised stars, resembling row of teeth.

Easter Sepulchre Recess with tomb-chest for holding the sacrament between Good Friday and Easter Day on north side of chancel, usually in sanctuary.

English bond The method of laying bricks in alternate courses of headers (bricks laid endwise) and stretchers (bricks laid lengthwise) as opposed to Flemish bond where headers and stretchers are laid alternately in the same course.

Entablature Horizontal structure lying upon columns in classical architecture, consisting of architrave, frieze and cornice.

Finial Foliage-shaped decorative termination to spire, pinnacle, gable, etc.

Flambeau A flaming torch.

Groined-vault See **Vault**.

Hammerbeam Beam projecting at right angles, usually from top of wall, to provide support for vertical member or arched brace of a roof.

Hatchment Arms of deceased person within a black lozenge-shaped wooden frame.

Hexastyle Having six columns.

Hood-mould Projecting moulding above arch or window to throw off water.

Iconostasis Screen of icons separating sanctuary from rest of church.

Intaglio A figure cut into any substance.

Label stop Ornamental head or other shape at end of hood-mould.

Lierne See **Vault**.

Lucarne Spire-light.

Lunette An arched opening in a vault often for a window.

Metope The space, frequently decorated, between triglyphs (three vertical grooves) in a

classical frieze (see **Entablature**).
Modillion Small projecting bracket under a cornice.
Narthex Enclosed portico or vestibule at western end of church between entrance and nave.
Ogee Partly convex and partly concave shape.

Quirked Ogee, Arch of Constantine, Rome

Orders The various classical styles applying to combination of base, column, capital and entablature.
Pier Free-standing solid support, frequently square, between arches.
Pilaster Shallow pier attached to and projecting from wall.
Piscina Shallow basin with drain usually to south of altar.

Crowmarsh, c 1150

Warmington

Prie-dieu A praying-desk or chair.
Putti Small naked boys often used in Renaissance art.
Queen-post One of two vertical posts in a roof placed on a tie- or collar-beam.
Quoin Dressed stone at angle.
Rere-arch Arch supporting the inner part of wall as in front of a window.
Reredos Wall or screen behind altar usually ornamented.
Reveal Side surface of an opening in a wall for doorway or window.
Rood A cross or crucifix.
Rood-loft Means of access for cleaning, lighting and decking rood and sometimes acting as a base for it. The loft also provided accommodation for choir and instrumentalists.
Rotunda A round building especially when domed.
Rusticated Built of stone with joints greatly emphasised.

Sacrament-house An elaborate receptacle for reservation of the Sacrament.

Saddleback Shaped like a timber gable and applied to tower roof.

Sarcophagus A stone coffin or tomb elaborately carved.

Sedilia Recessed stone seats in chancel for priest and assistants.

Segmental In the form of a segment or arc of a circle.

Soffit Undersurface of an arch.

Spandrel Triangular wall surface between two arches.

St Alban's Abbey Church, c 1400

Stanchion An upright iron support.

Stock brick Term originally used for bricks made on a special board called a 'stock' but later associated with brownish-yellow colour of bricks made in London area.

Strapwork Ornamentation popular in late Tudor and Jacobean period of crossed and interlaced bands similar to those of cut leather.

String-course Projecting horizontal band or moulding on surface of wall.

Lincoln Cathedral, c 1220

Swag Festoon in the form of carved cloth suspended at both ends.

Tesselated A mosaic of small coloured pieces of brick, stone, marble etc. fitted into cement and made up into varied ornamental designs.

Tessera The small coloured piece (see **Tesselated**) used in tesselation.

Tetrastyle Having four columns.

Three-decker Pulpit with clerk's stall and reading-desk below.

Tourelle Turret with conical cap seen in French chateaux.

Tracery Decorative treatment of upper part of windows also used on walls, screens, vaults, etc. (a) *Plate* Early form of tracery in which shapes are cut out of solid stone of window head. (b) *Bar* Tracery consisting of curved and intersecting slender shafts which follow lines of mullions. (c) *Geometrical* Tracery consisting mainly of circles, often foiled. (d) *Y* Tracery in which central mullion of window divides into two forming a Y shape. (e)

Intersecting Development of Y tracery in which more than one mullion divides into two and the branches intersect. (f)

Reticulated Tracery composed of ogee shapes producing net-like pattern. (g)

Perpendicular Tracery of rectilinear form in which mullions carry up into head of window.

Transom A bar dividing a window horizontally.

Triforium Arcaded wall passage or blank arcading above nave/chancel and below clerestory.

Triptych A set of three painted panels hinged together and often used to adorn altars.

Tympanum of Doorway, Essendine, c 1130

(b) *Fan-vault* A type of vault in which the length and curvature of the ribs, which spring from the same point, are similar.

(c) *Groined-vault* The vault obtained when two barrel vaults intersect.

(d) *Lierne-vault* A vault incorporating decorative short, subsidiary ribs (liernes).

(e) *Rib-vault* A vault with diagonal ribs projecting along the groin.

Volute Spiral scroll.

Vitruvian Scroll

Triforium, St Cross, Hampshire, c 1200

Trompe l'oeil Architectural or painting effect—often to give three-dimensional appearance to a plane surface—which 'deceives the eye'.

Tympanum Space in head of doorway arch.

Vault Arched roof of stone.

(a) *Barrel-vault* A simple round vault like a tunnel.

Volute

Voussoir Wedge-shaped stone of an arch.

Wagon-roof A curved wooden roof resembling the canvas awning over a wagon.

Wind-brace Inclined curved timber placed lengthwise along roof to strengthen it.